D0870668

Churches
respond to
BEM

Churches respond to BEM

BEM

Official responses to the "Baptism, Eucharist and Ministry" text

Vol. III

Edited by Max Thurian

Faith and Order Paper 135
World Council of Churches, Geneva

The text on the Evangelical Lutheran Church of Denmark was translated by J. B. Nicholson. The WCC Language Service translated the following:
Standing Council of the Lutheran and Reformed Churches of France, Evangelical Church of the Augsburg Confession of Alsace and Lorraine, Evangelical Lutheran Church of France, Reformed Church of France, Reformed Church of Alsace and Lorraine, United Protestant Church of Belgium, Presbyterian Church of Rwanda and Church of Jesus Christ in Madagascar.

Cover design: Michael Dominguez

ISBN 2–8254–0879–4

Typeset by Macmillan India Ltd., Bangalore 25
Printed in Switzerland

IN GRATEFUL MEMORY OF
NIKOS NISSIOTIS (1925–1986)

CONTENTS

PREFACE

By November 1986, more than 150 churches had sent in their official responses to the convergence document on "Baptism, Eucharist and Ministry" (BEM), the text adopted by the Faith and Order Commission of the World Council of Churches at its meeting in Lima, Peru, in 1982. The process of discussion on this document is continuing in many churches and we expect more official responses in the coming months.

The BEM process is of great significance for the ecumenical movement as a whole, and Volume III continues the documentation of the official responses. It has again been edited by my colleague Frère Max Thurian. I am grateful for his work as well as for the collaboration of our colleagues in WCC Publications.

We dedicate this volume to the memory of Nikos Nissiotis. Prof. Nissiotis, the creative and eminent Orthodox theologian and bridge-builder between the Eastern and Western traditions, made a significant contribution to the World Council of Churches and the ecumenical movement as a whole. The Commission on Faith and Order, in particular, whose Moderator Prof. Nissiotis was between 1975 and 1983 and under whose leadership the BEM document was elaborated and adopted in 1982, will always be grateful to one of its most competent and committed friends and colleagues. His ecumenical vision and commitment clearly shines through the text which we have included as an introduction to this volume. Prof. Nissiotis died in a car accident near Athens on 17 August 1986. May he find peace in Christ's victory over death and in the assurance of the resurrection.

Geneva, November 1986   Günther Gassmann, Director
                                           WCC Faith and Order Secretariat

---

• These responses have not been edited: we publish them here in the form in which they were received.

Introduction

THE CREDIBLE RECEPTION OF THE LIMA DOCUMENT AS THE ECUMENICAL CONVERSION OF THE CHURCHES

Nikos Nissiotis

. . . For all these reasons it may be suggested that in receiving the Lima document the churches are receiving themselves in their common struggle to build a genuine fellowship of churches. In a sense, the Lima document is their own mind, voice and decision *en route* for this goal. The text proposed for their credible reception is not one imposed on them from outside, not the challenge of some alien commission, council or movement. It is their own decision at this moment, following a long period of common ecumenical endeavour, study, prayer and action. It is a matter of their remaining consistent in their own ongoing life, not of introducing something quite new. What is new is their endeavour to make this Lima document known to the Christians in their constituencies as their own document and to summon their members therefore to a difficult conversion of heart and mind by alerting them to an ecumenical era of advanced interconfessional relationships. What is now required of them is a new spirit of convergence in theology and practice, calling for a change in their way of looking at church divisions, namely, looking at them now from within a church fellowship which is becoming more and more convinced that what unites it is more than what divides it.

(a) Within the context of the Lima document on "Baptism, Eucharist and Ministry", conversion means that each separate confessional family now regards the others with a renewed determination to appreciate them as sharers in the same apostolic tradition. This new vision does not mean that conversion occurs first in the outlook of the others, as a miraculous change in their attitude towards us; it means first and foremost that we ourselves are confronted with the urgent challenge to determined change in ourselves, to accept for ourselves this new era in ecumenical relationships. For the Lima

● Reprinted by kind permission of the Conference of European Churches from "The Reception of BEM in the European Context", CEC, Geneva, 1986, *Occasional Paper No. 17*, pp. 144–150.

document asks *us* first whether *we* recognize in it our own faith and fidelity as parts of the apostolic tradition. It asks of most of the church communities which are determined to adhere to the same apostolic tradition an understanding of this common faith and tradition in a new way and with a new language shaped by their direct sharing in the same church fellowship. The Lima document contains an indirect challenge to a renewed ecumenical conversion, for it is too unexpected to be really true to itself and to the churches yet at the same time is too demanding of them since it breaches the comfortable confessional self-sufficiency in which the churches have been accustomed to live up to the present. They have been solving the problem of the self-contradictory event in which they share, i.e. the disunity of the churches, on the selfsame grounds which the Lima document now uses to try to show them their own unity on the basis of their own statements, life and consistent fidelity.

In receiving the Lima document, the confessional families must share a corporate openness which obliges them to take up new stances expressing their awareness of having adopted a radically new way of approaching the problem of church unity entailing a positive appreciation of the faith and practice of others outside their confessional family, firstly, as possible within the one apostolic tradition, secondly, as challenging their own expression of that tradition, and thirdly, as no longer dividing them but as calling them towards a consensus. In other words, conversion, as the outcome of an advanced and bold step exemplified in the Lima document which the churches themselves have ventured on, is expected to introduce a renewal embracing the reinterpretation of the faith, the reformation of the form in which it is expressed, and the reorientation of church life.

b) It must be recognized, therefore, how difficult it is for the churches to undertake an ecumenical conversion of this kind even though they have worked and prepared for it in the persons of their representatives. The chief obstacle is that in practically none of the churches has this preparation been sufficiently widespread and effective. Up to now the overwhelming majority of ordinary church members has had no decisive share in ecumenical development. In many of the churches now invited to a credible reception of the Lima document, a reception which requires their conversion into a new ecumenical era of advanced decision and action, adequate information and direct experience of ecumenism have been minimal where they existed at all.

Another major difficulty in the Lima document requires theological authorities in churches and confessions to revise their attitudes towards essential beliefs and positions on which their particular self-identities rest. To do so may seem to them a denial and betrayal of themselves. This reaction, to some extent unconscious, is becoming daily more evident not only in the vehemently negative attitudes of some theologians but also in some official responses from churches which refuse to abandon the security of traditional scholastic theological fortresses. Such reactions are certainly frustrating but they cannot be laid at the door of the Lima document itself but derive rather from the threat it represents to typical divisive principles which confessions feel obliged to assert in order to maintain their own self-identity as separate and distinct church communities or from a pathological conformity to changeless traditional patterns and modes which embody the apostolic tradition in unchanging canonized theological forms.

In this context, the Lima document, requiring as it does of church people of all confessional families a credible reception which is only possible if they revise their radical or traditional positions, should not expect anything more from those who simply repeat "We are the One Holy Catholic Church" without saying what that makes the other "churches". The more this self-assertion is intensified, the more the insolubility of the problem is emphasized, unless you end up with so exclusive an affirmation of yourself that you either become merely a voice in an isolationist desert or deny your own part in the apostolic tradition which other churches clearly share with you. In this sense, the Lima document painfully accentuates the problem of self-identity in the measure that this identity has to be expressed in the life, thought and action of your own church in relationship with other churches or church communities.

On the other hand, the reception of the Lima document no longer permits us to go on repeating typical slogans cloaking elements of disunity rather than unity, however earthshakingly progressive these slogans may sound and however much they may seem to respect the primacy of God and to serve the church in permanent change. The Lima document urges the churches humbly to accept their responsibility for disunity, but it also shows them that it is now possible for them to converge once more towards their own centre of faith in the confidence that as they do so the Spirit will lead them. To try to overcome sacramentalism by the use of such phrases as "there is no mediation other than Christ" can become a disruptive factor hindering conversion as a prerequisite for credible reception. So too, to accept discontinuity on a basis of equality alongside continuity in the apostolic tradition in the interests of permanent change as a principle of dynamic church life can turn out to be and be seen to be a hindering principle at this crucial moment when an effort is being made to converge in the direction pointed out by the Lima document. To fail to appreciate the role of the church in the advance towards consensus out of supposed respect for God's sovereign will, while this may embody a highly respected attitude of humility, can also prove a negative axiom inimical to the achievement of a future consensus on the basis of the Lima document. We cannot maintain a principle which accepts a realistic appraisal in the life of the churches by asserting that "the barrier between the anomaly of the disunity and the manifestation of unity in Christ is functioning in unexpected ways" and then conclude from this correct statement that "his ways are not necessarily those of the churches".

While we can understand the positive ecumenical spirit in which this statement is made, other similar statements can not only betray a failure to appreciate the role the churches have to play but also, if interpreted in the setting of a church tradition with a weak ecclesiological self-understanding (and, in the light of the Lima document, the statement mentioned already does so!), become a barrier to church conversion as a prerequisite for the credible reception of the Lima document as a step on the road to an authentic church consensus centred on the conviction that the church is the body of Christ and the people of God, called upon to prove itself as such by its consistency of life under the guidance of the Holy Spirit. Certainly the churches must humble themselves in repentance for their disunity, but this should not lead to such uncertainty as to discourage them from taking all the necessary steps to recover their unity. A dualism between Christ's will and ways and those of the churches must not be put forward as a positive principle of unity. To do so could even encourage some to become agnostic and uncertain as to any possibility of the churches' contributing towards reunion and lead in the end either to complete indifference to unity or to the self-justification of the inertia of the churches in a church-centred ecumenism, as the Lima document rightly envisages.

The credible reception of the Lima document may also be hindered by the fact that this sacramentally oriented document is addressed alike to non-sacramental Christian communities which participate as churches in the fellowship of churches as provided for in the Constitution of the World Council of Churches. Reception here is probably hindered right from the outset and there is no way whereby a possible exclusivity inherent in the text itself can be mitigated. On the other hand, this was only to be expected, once the churches of the WCC had decided to propose this concept of the visible and organic unity they are seeking together, i.e. as a new church-centred event based on their common apostolic tradition and their ecclesial life in practice throughout the ages.

This is not the only difficulty, of course, betrayed or produced by the text itself in its present character and shape. Points of difficulty also arise in other areas of direct interest to churches and faithful Christians or in current tendencies in church life. First and foremost, here, of course, is the silence of the Lima text on what some call "the Petrine ministry", i.e. concerning the churches' supreme pastoral authority of spiritual leadership as necessary for the maintenance of church unity. From the standpoint of the church of Rome in particular, the largest of all the churches, it is impossible to eliminate this question as we set out on the road to a consensus based on the apostolic tradition, even though the other churches massively reject the interpretation placed on this ministry by the church of Rome and the application it makes of it. The essential question remains open, however, and the lack of reference to it obviously remains a serious gap in the Lima document.

The Lima document also seems to evade another burning contemporary issue at present dividing the churches, though here in a different way and on a quite different theme, namely, the question of the ordination of women, though this is actually referred to in one particular paragraph. But this reference is extremely feeble and betrays great uncertainty and hesitation as to whether this question has any place in a converging theology of the church and the sacraments. It seems to me that this controversial topic demands careful attention and study, pursuing further the clear understanding of ministry as a broad hospitable concept embracing not only God's sacramental relationship with his church but also service and deaconship in the church and, on behalf of the church, to the world.

We must, of course, differentiate between the three difficulties just referred to (non-sacramental churches — the ministry of Peter — the ordination of women) and those stemming from a possible lack of ecumenical ethos or from an insistence on traditional radical principles which could create hindrances to the determination to proceed to a credible reception of the Lima document. The first three are either unavoidable difficulties created by Christian communities and their fundamental faith or topics which are not yet on the agenda for converging action by the churches. What has just been said makes clear the evident limitations of the Lima document. In any case, we must make it quite clear to our people that the Lima document possesses no authority other than its own wisdom and its capacity to be of real service to the churches from which it has emerged. At this present juncture, therefore, the lack of ecumenical ethos is of greater importance by far.

c) Our last observation should finally exclude triumphalism of any kind on our part. The Lima document is no miracle text or panacea for the problems of church unity. For those who have worked closely with the ecumenical developments of the last forty years the emergence of the Lima document can come as no surprise. It was only to be expected. From the perspective of Faith and Order work it may perhaps seem to have been unduly delayed, while from the standpoint of some church authorities, who are not yet sufficiently mature to handle such a strange and disturbing document, it may seem somewhat too premature. In other words, to my mind the Lima document on baptism, eucharist and ministry is important only as a significant signpost at the ecumenical crossroads. It brings one long period of study to a close and — especially important! — inaugurates a new one which will require the churches to take decisive steps, including the practical implementation of their ecumenism which up to now has been largely theoretical.

The first requirement is that the churches should commit themselves to local ecumenism by the greatest possible degree of mutual sharing in their church life, in all its confessional, liturgical, spiritual and missionary forms.

A second step would be to give priority to a charismatic, eucharistic, eschatological ecclesiology with the emphasis on a christological pneumatology capable of transcending a traditional scholastic and confessionalized sacramentology in the way clarified in the whole of the Lima document.

A third stage would embrace the primarily pastoral and ecclesial character of church authority as representative of the fulness of the church's membership, eliminating clericalism and church leadership based on juridical power. The Lima document states very clearly: "Ordained ministers must not be autocrats or impersonal functionaries, as they are bound to the faithful in interdependence and reciprocity" since "their authority is governed by love . . ." (M16, p. 23).

Fourthly, a genuine effort needs to be made to understand and affirm the sacramental life of the church as the main dynamic for an authentic self-understanding of the church and, above all, as an authentic presence of the churches within and for their secular context. The Lima document, it may be said, is too church-centred and too sacramentally oriented, yet at the same time it is also a prophetic document which seeks to judge all the churches' claims for themselves in the light of their relevance to the world as vehicles of the word of God addressed to all human beings.

If a credible reception of this kind is to be achieved, it is imperative, finally, that the churches should make abundant use of this Lima document among their hierarchs, their ministers, parish priests and people, as well as among their teachers and students of theology.

The present debate about the Lima document and the process of its reception seem to indicate that we are living at an ecumenical moment which will be decisive for the future of ecumenical relationships. Not to accept the seriousness of this moment would be a pity, indeed, it would be to assume a heavy responsibility in the sight of God. If the churches and certain leading theologians fail to see the importance of this Lima document and its reception, this would constitute a threat not only to Faith and Order and to ecumenism but also to the renewal and life of the churches themselves. It would also discourage those who are striving to promote an ecumenical approach to theology, and ecclesiology in particular. These would join the ranks of those who limit the ecumenical task exclusively to its dimension of social activity at the expense of its very heart, which is the one apostolic faith and tradition. It would undermine their conviction that it is only by progressively uniting themselves that the churches can really contribute to and share in the ongoing renewal of the world by the defeat of injustice and every form of discrimination against and exploitation of the weak and underprivileged. At the end, the Lima document reminds the churches of this fundamental verity and humbly and respectfully asks them to make their decisions in the light of contemporary ecumenical developments in church and world.

The Conference of European Churches is therefore making a signal contribution to a credible reception of the Lima document by organizing these four study consultations on the Lima document, inviting the churches of our continent to consider it seriously in the European context and by helping them to deal with it appropriately. I conclude therefore as I began, by renewing my thanks and appreciation, and my congratulations, to the Conference of European Churches for its exemplary initiative.

GREEK ORTHODOX
PATRIARCHATE OF ALEXANDRIA

As requested by the WCC, the Patriarchate of Alexandria is herewith replying with regard to the reception of the Lima text "Baptism, Eucharist and Ministry" (BEM). Each Orthodox autocephalous church will reply separately, giving its "official" opinion. But for a truly official position on the question, a pan-Orthodox council would have to be summoned, to decide on the attitude of the Orthodox church as a whole. However, the time for such a council is not yet ripe, nor does the text call for such treatment.

The Greek Orthodox Patriarchate of Alexandria (as represented, in this reply, by Metropolitan Parthenios of Carthage) believes that the Orthodox churches will accept but not "receive" the document, because it does not express the full theological view of the Orthodox Church. Nevertheless it contains elements in accordance with Orthodox teaching. We feel that it is, as the WCC itself says, not a final text on the subjects treated, and not representative of the doctrine of any one member church.

Nevertheless, it is very much to the WCC's credit that such a convergence document has been produced on these three sacraments — though many member churches do not consider them to be sacraments. It is the first time in the WCC's history that delegates of all the Christian denominations have been able to produce together a joint statement of common doctrine, and this proves the value of dialogue within the WCC. A dialogue that will continue to be fruitful, inasmuch as it implies truth and love, courage and boldness in Christ. If the churches accept the text, it will already be a great step forward towards church unity. Christ's prayer "that all may be one" will no longer be a utopia. Without the WCC, it is possible that today's bilateral and multilateral dialogues might not have come as far as they have, that is, as far as the Lima text, which certainly deserves consideration.

As regards this consideration, the guidelines laid down by the Vancouver Assembly are being followed by the Patriarchate of Alexandria and All

---

• 350,000 members, 176 churches, 23 bishops, 147 priests.

Africa. The Patriarchate is also in agreement with the WCC's summoning of an inter-Orthodox symposium at the Holy Cross Theological School in Boston, to study BEM and to give what might be considered as a pan-Orthodox opinion. (This symposium shows the interest the WCC — notably the Commission on Faith and Order and, in particular, the general secretary of the WCC — has in the testimony of the Orthodox Church within the ecumenical movement.) The Patriarchate of Alexandria is in agreement with the findings of the symposium as being in accordance with Orthodox Tradition, and hopes that it will be followed by other such meetings, in which concordance of the member churches over BEM may, with the help of the Holy Spirit, be brought about.

The notes and observations of the pan-Orthodox symposium at Boston appear to be constructive for the progress of BEM. We therefore quote from them as follows:

1. Section on baptism
The following points call for clarification:
a) the relationship between the unity of the church and baptismal unity (§6);
b) the role of exorcism and renunciation of the Evil One in the baptismal rite (§20);
c) the role of the Holy Spirit in baptism (§§5,14).

2. Section on eucharist
a) the relationship of the eucharist to the church (§1);
b) the eucharist and unity of faith;
c) the role of the Holy Spirit, with special reference to *anamnesis* in its relation to *epiklesis* (§12);
d) the meaning of sacrifice (§8), real presence (§13);
e) the participation of baptized children in the eucharist.

3. Section on ministry
a) ordained ministry and the gifts (charismata) of the Holy Spirit (§17);
b) the link between ordained ministry and the ministry of the apostles and apostolic succession (§§10,35);
c) the ordination of women to the priesthood (§18);
d) the relationship between bishop, *episkopé*, eucharist, as well as the relationship between bishop, presbyter, deacon (relative §).

As was said, work on BEM must continue, alongside the programmes on the apostolic faith, the unity of the church and the renewal of human community, for all three are basically linked together, theologically and liturgically.

The Patriarchate of Alexandria thanks the WCC and, with God's help, will continue its humble struggle within the WCC to carry out the WCC's aim as set out in its Basis.

The struggle for union must not stop. The WCC is the battlefield of union, and its fruitfulness is continually available to all its member churches with, as its supreme gift, the Lima text, BEM.

God be with us.

> By command of His Holiness
> Parthenios of Carthage

ROMANIAN ORTHODOX CHURCH

The Romanian Orthodox Church appreciated and appreciates all initiatives and efforts aimed at finding the best ways towards mutual knowledge and rapprochement between the Christian churches, confessions and denominations with a view to achieving full consensus and Christian unity. The Romanian Orthodox Church has therefore shown interest in the BEM document — Lima 1982.

The BEM document as a whole is a text of theological convergence, but it does comprise certain statements which the Romanian Orthodox Church cannot accept as they do not meet the Orthodox teaching.

Theological convergence, as one knows, is not identical with *theological consensus*. And it is only the latter that could result in the full unity in one faith which the churches seek.

The document, however, is an important step forward towards convergence on three out of the seven sacraments of the church. By baptism, chrismation and the eucharist, which are celebrated by the bishop and the priests of the church, our incorporation into the body of Christ and our growth in Christ as members of the church, his body, are achieved through the work of the Holy Spirit. The seven sacraments of the church — baptism, chrismation, eucharist, priesthood, repentance (confession), marriage, and extreme unction — are constitutive of the church as sacred body of Christ and fullness of life of the Holy Spirit (Eph. 1:23).

We have analyzed the BEM document in our theological institutes and in interconfessional theological conferences several times, and the findings have been included in our response which complies with the indications in the preface to the Lima document on "Baptism, Eucharist and Ministry" (1982), namely:

1) the extent to which we can recognize in the BEM document the faith of our church;

- 17,000,000 members, 15 dioceses, 24 bishops, 8,165 parishes, 8,545 priests, 2,702 monks and nuns.

2) the extent to which the BEM document favours the ongoing ecumenical discussion;
3) the extent to which the document provides guidance for mission, worship and spiritual education;
4) the suggestions our church can make for the ongoing work of the Faith and Order Commission.

Baptism

1.a) Elements of convergence

In its general treatment of the faith of the church — which is based on the holy scripture and the holy Tradition — the document describes baptism as:
— incorporation into Christ and into his ecclesial body (B1);
— participation of the baptized in Christ's death and resurrection Rom. 6:4 (B3);
— gift of God and the human response to that gift (B8);
— life-long growth into Christ (B9);
— baptism administered with water in the name of the Father, the Son and the Holy Spirit (B17).

b) Critical remarks

Although this general treatment of baptism is based on the holy scripture, the terms used in the document for baptism are "*sign* of new life through Jesus Christ" (B2) and "*sign* of the Kingdom of God and of the life of the world to come" (B7) not sacrament. The terms "sign" and "symbol", used in the document as technical terms for the three sacraments, do not express the real partaking of the charisma of the Holy Spirit which is characteristic of baptism, by which the original sin and personal sins are forgiven. The holy sacraments, as a means by which the faithful partakes of the grace of the Holy Spirit, have their origin in the very incarnation of the Saviour. Semantic consideration of the term "sign" shows that it indicates a sense, a message, a direction towards a reality that it has to explain but does not carry in itself the reality it signifies. The sign is only a symbol.

The text comprises the statement that baptism "cleanses the heart of all sin" (B4) but there is no specification that it is the original sin that is forgiven and thus the baptized is freed from the bondage of sin. It is further stated in the document that "those baptized are given a new ethical orientation" (B4). If baptism is reduced to this, it no longer appears as a beginning of the ontological restoration of man as a new being in Christ.

The document dissociates infant baptism from adult baptism and only acknowledges the possibility of infant baptism in the apostolic age (B11), although that was *current practice* in the church (Acts 2:39; 16:15, 33; 1 Cor. 1:16; 110 Carthage).

Christian unity is regarded as founded on baptism alone, as a "baptismal unity", and thus the view is unilateral, the document also asking the churches to recognize one another's baptism (B6). Whereas, Christian initiation and full membership of the church are only received by baptism, chrismation and the eucharist.

2. *Baptism and ecumenism*

The BEM document is an instrument and a theological basis for further and thorough discussions on the matters already approached, to the extent to which it expresses the apostolic tradition regarding baptism.

3. *Baptism and the pastoral mission of the church*

Our church maintains apostolic tradition, according to which the administering of baptism is an opportunity for catechism, for going deeply into the truths of this important act and for providing religious-moral teachings to the family and the faithful present.

4. *Suggestions on baptism*

Our critical remarks point to some aspects regarding baptism, which must be reconsidered and analyzed thoroughly, so that the document should:
a) state clearly the sacramental character of baptism and chrismation;
b) state clearly the relation between baptism, chrismation and the eucharist, which are constitutive of the Christian initiation;
c) state clearly the relation between church unity and the so-called "baptismal unity", as the Orthodox teaching understands unity in the fullness of the faith and of the seven holy sacraments;
d) emphasize the work of Christ in the Holy Spirit in baptism and chrismation, which are celebrated by the sacramental priesthood of the church (bishop and priests);
e) emphasize the liberation from the bondage of sin and of the Evil One by baptism, also stating the importance and the necessity of the confession of faith in the Holy Trinity;
f) study thoroughly infant baptism as current practice of the church as early as the apostolic age.

Eucharist

1.a) Elements of convergence

The document presents several elements in which our church recognizes the apostolic faith on the eucharist in its general aspects:
— sacrament instituted by Jesus Christ at the Last Supper (E2);
— thanksgiving to the Father for everything he accomplished for us: creation, redemption and sanctification (E3);
— *anamnesis* of the crucified and risen Christ (E5);

— sacrament of Christ's real, unique and objective presence (E13);
— sacrament of Christ's body and blood (E13) by the invocation and work of the Holy Spirit;
— sacrament of the community with Christ and his ecclesial body; and thus sacrament of the communion of the church (E19);
— the document acknowledges the eschatological dimension of the eucharist as anticipation, as foretaste of the coming of the kingdom in Christ (E22);
— the document recommends the celebration of the eucharist more often (E28); the communitary and social implications of the eucharist are also emphasized: "Reconciled in the eucharist, the members of the body of Christ [the church] are called to be servants of reconciliation among men and women and witnesses of the joy of resurrection" (E24).

b) Critical remarks

The document acknowledges the sacramental character of the eucharist. But — as with baptism — this, too, is called "sign", as in: "The eucharist is the living and effective sign of his sacrifice" (E5); "under the signs of bread and wine, the deepest reality is the total being of Christ" (E1, Commentary 13); the eucharist is "a sign of the Kingdom" (E1); "the eucharist is a sacramental meal which by visible signs communicates to us God's love in Jesus Christ" (E1).

But, as we said previously, the "sign" only indicates without expressing the reality of the sacrament by which the body and the blood of Christ, which carry the grace of the Holy Spirit, are given.

Even more, none of the terms used for the eucharist, "sacramental meal", "supper of the Lord", "breaking of bread", "holy communion", "divine liturgy", "missa", etc. renders the *sacramental* character of the Last Supper, the moment when the eucharist was instituted by the Lord. Nor do the terms render the sacrificial and sacramental character of the eucharist.

The institution of the eucharist at the "Last Supper" is acknowledged but it is further stated that "the eucharist continues the meals of Jesus during his earthly life . . . always as a sign of the Kingdom" (E1). We, too, acknowledge the relation between the eucharist and the other meals, and this relation is part of the economy of the incarnation, by which the other meals prefigured the sacrament of the eucharist (Luke 14:24; John 6:11, etc.).

The real presence of Christ in the eucharist is acknowledged, but the statement "the *anamnesis* of Christ is the very content of the eucharistic meal" (E12) shifts importance from the real presence of Christ onto *anamnesis* or a memorial presence of Christ, without emphasizing the fundamental unity of *anamnesis* and *epiklesis*, that is, the link between the work of the Son and that of the Holy Spirit in the eucharist.

The statement according to which in the eucharist the faithful is empowered to live as a "justified sinner" (E9) is alien to the apostolic tradition, since the apostle Paul teaches that the faithful becomes a new being in Christ (Gal. 3:27; 6:15).

While the text concerning the invisible celebrant of the eucharist is correct, as in: "In the celebration of the Eucharist . . . it is Christ who invites to the meal and who presides at it . . . He is . . . the priest who celebrates the mystery of God" (E29), the text concerning the *visible* celebrant of the eucharist is ambiguous and equivocal. As it comes from the document the celebrant is always Christ; the priest is regarded as a sign of Christ (E29). Whereas, the holy scripture clearly shows that the celebration of the eucharist depends upon the charismatic and sacramental state of the celebrant (Luke 22:29; Rev. 20:19).

2. The eucharist and the ecumenical dialogue

The elements of theological convergence on the eucharist — leave aside the critical remarks above — are some progress and an important basis for further general and bilateral theological discussions to unity. But they do not justify the eucharistic intercommunion suggested in the document (E33).

3. The eucharist and the pastoral mission of the church

In the Orthodox Church the eucharistic communion supports and deepens the ecclesial communion and has an important role in the renewal of the spiritual Christian life. The holy eucharist should be received in purity, once the sins have been forgiven by the sacrament of confession (Acts 19:16, 1 Cor. 11:27–30).

4. Suggestions concerning the eucharist

If we are to achieve a full consensus on the eucharist, we think we should analyze again, thoroughly, and clarify the following aspects of the matter:

a) a more clear presentation of the reflection of the work of the Holy Trinity in the eucharist: in *anamnesis* and *epiklesis*;

b) a clear presentation of the sacrifice-sacrament relation in the eucharist and an argumentation of the real presence of Christ in the eucharist following the turning of the gifts of bread and wine into the body and blood of Christ through the work of the Holy Spirit;

c) the understanding of the eucharist as a permanent updating of the entire economy of salvation in the church, through Christ, in the Holy Spirit, since the statement "what it was God's will to accomplish in the incarnation, life, death, resurrection and ascension of Christ, God does not repeat. These events are unique and can neither be repeated nor prolonged" (E8) in the document separates the eucharist from the economy of salvation;

d) a thorough analysis and more variety in presenting the relation between the physical body of Christ, taken from Mary, the eucharistic body and the ecclesial body of the church of Christ, with a view to better

understanding the nature and the significance of the eucharist, as the church's permanent partaking of the life of Christ and as our participation in the death and the resurrection of Christ;
e) a thorough analysis of the relation between the participation in the eucharist and the confession of the whole faith of the church;
f) clarification that the eucharist is the final act of the full incorporation into the body of Christ, as a member of the church (in Christian initiation), through baptism, chrismation and eucharist; it should be made clear that the eucharist is the essential sacrament for the growth in Christ, when it is received after the pardoning of sins through confession;
g) clear affirmation of the administering of the eucharist to adults and infants.

Ministry

1. The text on ministry comprises ambiguous formulations and much hesitation, although effort is made for a rapprochement.

The document is a step forward in understanding the importance and the mission of sacramental priesthood in the church in a way which is closer to Tradition and to the early practice of the church. The term *ministry* is used either with the sense of service or with some tint of sacramentality, as in the statement *"ordained ministry* refers to persons who have received a charism and whom the church appoints for service by ordination through the invocation of the Spirit and the laying on of hands" (M7).

a) Elements of convergence

The document comprises the following positive elements concerning:
— Sacramental ministry: "The authority of the ordained minister is rooted in Jesus Christ, who has received it from the Father (Matt. 28:18), and who confers it by the Holy Spirit through the act of ordination" (M15); "As Christ chose and sent the apostles, Christ continues through the Holy Spirit to choose and call persons into the ordained ministry" (M11);
— The document acknowledges the importance of the priesthood instituted by Christ for the church as constitutive: "The ministry of such persons, who since very early times have been ordained, is constitutive for the life and witness of the Church" (M8);
— Consideration given to the ordination of the priest by the invocation of the Holy Spirit: "Ordination is an invocation to God that the new minister be given the power of the Holy Spirit in the new relation which is established between this minister and the local Christian community and, by intention, the Church universal" (M42), and by the laying on of hands by the bishop: "The laying on of hands is the sign of the gift of the Spirit, rendering visible the fact that the ministry was instituted in the revelation accomplished in Christ, and reminding the Church to look to him as the source of its commission" (M39).

—Consideration given to the "apostolic tradition" in and through the
ministry of the church, but the formulation is ambiguous: "This apostolic
tradition continues through history and links the Church to its origins in
Christ and in the college of the apostles. Within this apostolic tradition is
an apostolic succession of the ministry which serves the continuity of the
Church in its life in Christ and its faithfulness to the words and acts of
Jesus transmitted by the apostles. The ministers appointed by the apostles,
and then the *episkopoi* of the churches, were the first guardians of this
transmission of the apostolic tradition; they testified to the apostolic
succession of the ministry which was continued through the bishops of the
early Church in collegial communion with the presbyters and deacons
within the Christian community" (Commentary 34);
—The use of the term "priest": The document states that "ordained
ministers are related, as are all Christians, both to the priesthood of
Christ, and to the priesthood of the Church. But they may appropriately
be called priests because they fulfil a particular priestly service by
strengthening and building up the royal and prophetic priesthood of the
faithful through word and sacraments, through their prayers of intercession, and through their pastoral guidance of the community" (M17).

The elements of convergence mentioned above do not eliminate the
problems caused by ambiguity in the use of the term "ministry", which is not
clearly invested with sacrament.

We appreciate the statement: "The ordained ministry fulfils these functions in a representative way, providing the focus for the unity of the life and
witness of the community" (Commentary 13).

b) Critical remarks

The value of the elements of convergence is diminished by numerous
contradictory formulations, to say nothing about the ambiguity of the term
ministry, as follows:
—Although the laying on of hands of the bishop during ordination is
regarded as a "sacramental sign" (M41), sacramental priesthood is called
ministry, service or *office* which can give rise to confusion with universal
ministry (M6). Confusion also persists with regard to the organ which
institutes the ministers (priests), as there are some statements in the
document according to which the priests were instituted by the community
(M1, M44).
—The document emphasizes that "the threefold pattern of ministry" —
bishop, presbyter and deacon — was the pattern of ordained ministry in
the second and third centuries (M9), but immediately after this it states
that, in the New Testament, the ministry by bishop, presbyter and deacon
"was not the only pattern of ministry which might serve as a continuing
norm for all future ministry in the Church" (M19). At this point the

confusion between *ministry* as sacerdoce and *ministry* as service is obvious.

Ambiguity and confusion are even more obvious when the attempt is made to emphasize that in the New Testament the term *priest* (*hiereus*) refers only to Jesus Christ and the community of the baptized. It is a very subtle way of justifying only universal ministry (the royal and prophetic priesthood of the faithful—M17), although the document refers to *ordained ministry* quite often.

As regards the absence of the term *hiereus* from the New Testament, one knows that this is so in order to eliminate any confusion and rapprochement of the members of sacerdotal priesthood to the priests in the Old Testament and the pagan, idolatrous priests (Luke 1:5; 1 Pet. 2:9; Heb. 5:1; 7:12 and 23; Rev. 1:6). Christian priesthood (ordained ministry) is rooted in the New Testament and has its source in the priesthood of Jesus Christ through the holy apostles (John 20:21–23).

— We consider unacceptable the statement recommending the churches "to avoid attributing their particular forms of the ordained ministry directly to the will and institution of Jesus Christ" (Commentary 11). Such formulation denies directly the belief of the churches with the firm conscience that the structures of ordained ministry are wanted and instituted by Christ himself. The document avoids indicating the texts concerning the institution of ordained ministry by Christ as charismatic structure of the church, such as: John 20:21–23; Matthew 28:19–20; Mark 16:15–16; Acts 1:8; 2:1,3,4.

— We do not understand why, on the one hand, *the document affirms apostolic succession through episcopate* (Commentary 34) and on the other hand it asks for the recognition of apostolic succession of *the churches which have not retained or do not have episcopal succession* (M37), without stating precisely through what particular church structures apostolic succession could have been or could be preserved today.

— The same relativism is also present in the way the document militates for the recognition of ordained ministry (M53) without, however, indicating the apostolic succession in faith and charisma — insured by sacramental episcopate — as a prerequisite of it.

2. Ministry and ecumenism

The ecumenical value of the document lies particularly in the recommendation to the churches for joint efforts "in order to achieve mutual recognition of the ordained ministries" by taking into consideration the particular importance of apostolic succession (M53). The churches are indicated the steps asked of them in order to achieve mutual recognition of the ordained ministries (M53) and which must be taken into consideration.

Churches which have preserved the episcopal succession are asked to recognize both "the apostolic content of the ordained ministry which exists in churches which have not maintained such succession and also the existence in these churches of a ministry of *episkopé* in various forms" (M53a).

Our church considers that, in addition to again confusing ministry with service, such recommendation is proof of a rather superficial approach of the matter.

It is stated in the document that "there are obstacles to the mutual recognition of ordained ministries" raised by some churches' ordaining both men and women; but this is regarded as no substantive hindrance to recognition — which is a hint to the recognition of ordained women (M54).

It is the opinion of the Romanian Orthodox Church that this question and the one concerning the methods of achieving union could get competent answers only by joint decision of all Orthodox churches.

3. Ordained ministry and the pastoral mission of the church

The three functions of ordained ministry: to preach the word, to celebrate the sacraments with intercessions and to provide pastoral guidance to the faithful — stated in the document — are the church's traditional mission in the world and were entrusted to it by Christ. This threefold mission of ordained ministry preserves the life and unity of the church and strengthens the service of the *universal ministry* of the faithful, by which we understand all those incorporated and renewed in Christ by baptism, chrismation and the eucharist who participate in the whole work of the church (1 Pet. 2:5–9; 1 Pet. 5:1–3 and 5–6), each according to one's own vocation and to the gift received from God (1 Cor. 7:20; 1 Cor. 12:28–30). In this way the church can serve mankind and its needs.

Ordained ministry provides the church's service in support of the people's efforts to solve major problems in the world. The churches' joint service helps the theological discussions.

4. Suggestions

Efficient progress with a view to achieving full theological and ecumenical consensus requires radical reformulation of the chapter on ministry in the document.

First, the very term ministry has to be made clear, as it creates most of the difficulties and can give rise to a lot of confusion *for all Christian confessions in the dialogue*.

Therefore, we suggest the following:

a) In order to avoid equivocation and confusion in the theology of ministry, the terms concerning ordained ministry, universal ministry and the charismatic degrees of ordained ministry have to be defined clearly, in accordance with the holy scripture and the holy Tradition, and employed with strict reference to each of these realities in a reformulated document.

b) Ordained ministry, with its three grades of authority, is constitutive for the charismatic structure of the church. It has preserved in history the visible unity of the church. Therefore, the document should comprise after reformulation theological, historical and, particularly, canonical approaches of the relation between sacramental ministry instituted by Christ, the service of the apostles and apostolic succession in faith and in grace through episcopate in the church.

c) It should be defined clearly the difference between the grace of sacramental ministry, received through ordination, and other charisms and what we have to understand from these charisms of the early church and from those which may exist even today in the life of the church.

d) An approach of the relation between ordained ministry, eucharist and the unity of the church is both necessary and important.

e) As the document also approaches *women's ministry*, a matter which in our church was made clear long ago, we deem it necessary that the document in its new edition comprise clear statements — in the light of the holy scripture and the holy Tradition — on women's role and service in the life of the church, considering women's natural vocation and avoiding any ontological confusion, which states precisely a variety of services in the church, so that the churches may reach a consensus.

* * *

In conclusion, the Romanian Orthodox Church appreciates the document on "Baptism, Eucharist and Ministry" in its present form as the fruit of a deserving, long-time ecumenical cooperation, a theological document comprising more numerous and more varied statements as compared with any previous documents, which facilitates and stimulates theological dialogue at all levels.

We consider it a working document comprising some convergences, which opens new possibilities for further discussion and advance towards consensus.

The document is a good basis for discussions on the three holy sacraments: baptism, eucharist and ordained ministry, as these and all the other holy sacraments are essential and constitutive for the teaching and the charismatic life of the church.

The renewal of the life of the church and the renewal of the world cannot be separated from the church's liturgical and sacramental life and its unity of faith or from the church's pastoral responsibility. We are particularly interested in this document which by its purpose — to achieve the unity of faith and the unity of the churches — complies with the commandment of the Saviour to work "that they all may be one" (John 17:21).

The BEM document is a good start for the churches to make important steps in this stage of the ecumenical movement towards a visible ecclesial unity which we all wish so ardently.

The convergences in the BEM document do not authorize the eucharistic communion it suggests, since this requires first and foremost full unity in all matters of faith.

In the light of the above, the document on "Baptism, Eucharist and Ministry", Lima 1982, is a proof of confidence and also hope and a reason for the continuation of the efforts to be made with fraternal love with the view of achieving the unity of the church.

ORTHODOX CHURCH
IN AMERICA

1. The unity of the Christian church is given by God. It is the unity of God himself, Father, Son, and Holy Spirit, given to human beings for their salvation. It is a unity in faith, life, sacramental life, and action. It is a unity which can be neither created nor destroyed by any creaturely power. It is a unity which can only be discovered, believed in, accepted, celebrated, and lived.

2. The Orthodox Church in America, one of the self-governing Orthodox churches in the world, is composed of the American children of the original missionary diocese of the Russian Orthodox Church, together with Orthodox Christians of Albanian, Bulgarian, Romanian, and Mexican descent and other Americans who have entered its communion. We the bishops of this church rejoice in receiving the WCC Faith and Order Commission's statement on "Baptism, Eucharist and Ministry" adopted in Lima in 1982. We welcome this statement as a positive step towards the rediscovery of the unity of the church by Christians now sadly divided, a unity which we Orthodox believe to be essentially preserved within the Orthodox Church despite our many sins and human divisions. We thank the Commission for its outstanding work. As we offer our comments and questions we pray that the Lima statement may indeed be a significant step towards the communion of all Christians fully and visibly united in the one church of God.

One baptism for the remission of sins

3. From the very beginning of Christian history the issue of "one baptism for the remission of sins" has been discussed in the context of divisions and schisms among Christians. Today we Christians still wonder about how our common confession of "one baptism" is to be affirmed and understood, given the present existence of many divided "churches".

- 1,000,000 members, 440 parishes, 457 priests.

4. Within the World Council of Churches, and in the ecumenical movement generally, the issue of baptism has been raised almost exclusively in the narrow context of debate on mutual recognition or non-recognition, the "validity" or "invalidity" of particular instances of baptismal practice. More often than not, the debate has been limited to discussions of the legitimacy of baptismal formulae and rituals. The problems created by such an approach can be solved only in the framework of a truly orthodox, truly catholic vision of the meaning of baptism and its place in the faith and life of the church.

5. We rejoice to observe that the Faith and Order Commission's statement has adopted this broader approach to the issue of baptism. The result, we believe, is a remarkably balanced statement based on scriptural evidence and showing great respect for church Tradition. As St Basil the Great has noted, the liturgy of baptism in its basic elements is one of the church's teachings (dogmata) received through unwritten Tradition, which cannot be disregarded if we would avoid "totally mutilating the Gospel" (*On the Holy Spirit*, 66).

6. The Lima statement is a statement of theological convergences; it points to a convergence in theological thinking within and among the divided "churches" which, it is hoped, will be implemented in actual practice. For this reason it is perhaps inevitable that the Lima statement should lack the kerygmatic breath of, e.g. the commentaries on baptism of the church fathers. It represents the result of years of painstakingly difficult work by theologians coming from many traditions and backgrounds. Nonetheless, it is a remarkable achievement. We recognize its comprehensiveness and general accuracy. It rightly regards baptism "in the name of the Father and of the Son and of the Holy Spirit" as participation in Christ's death and resurrection; as conversion, pardoning, and cleansing; as gift of the Spirit; as incorporation into the body of Christ and sign of the kingdom. We do wish that the theology expressed in our sacrament of chrismation — that of pentecostal sealing with God's Spirit — had been affirmed more forthrightly; and that direct entrance into the eucharistic supper of all the fully initiated, infants included, had been upheld as apostolic and normative. We are sensitive, however, to the fears and misunderstandings of many concerning these issues; and we patiently look forward to the time when such fears and misunderstandings are overcome.

7. We are sorry to see that the relationship between baptism and faith is considered chiefly in connection with the issue of infant baptism and presented almost exclusively in terms of the dialogue between those who practise so-called "believers' baptism" and those who do not, since this debate, for the most part, avoids the central issue of the *content* of faith. For the Orthodox, the content of the credal confession of faith made at baptism is of crucial importance. We believe that the adoption of a single creed to be used throughout the universal church for baptism, as well as for other solemn

occasions of credal confession, has become an inalienable part of holy Tradition and represents today for the Orthodox Church a major criterion for recognizing or not recognizing the legitimacy of baptismal practices employed in the various Christian traditions. What faith do Christians confess at their baptism? What credal statement do they use? What interpretation is given to this statement on the part of the person as well as the church body in which the confession is made? How is this faith expressed in the baptismal rite itself? These are some of the questions which must be answered along the way to full unity in the one church of Christ. We believe that careful reflection on the Lima statement, together with further study within the WCC Faith and Order Commission of the apostolic faith, particularly as expressed in the Nicene Creed, should provide some of the needed answers in this crucial area.

8. Though unclear on the issue of the credal expression and content of the baptismal confession of faith, the Lima statement does rightly affirm "the constant requirement of a continuous growth of personal response to faith". This is an essential point. Faith leads to baptism and must be nurtured continuously in the ongoing life of the church. We therefore recognize the need to maintain appropriate catechesis in the fullest sense of that word — instruction, training, discipline — both before and after baptism, lest baptism itself come to be regarded as a mere outward formality.

9. The importance of continuous growth in faith following baptism raises another important question: that of the real significance of baptism as "incorporation into the body of Christ". The "body of Christ" into which we are initiated in baptism is the church. In it the "continuous growth in faith" after baptism is to take place. The Lima statement is quite clear in affirming this point, but it leaves the identity of this "church" otherwise undefined, without indicating much more about the nature and form of its life within the time and space of this world. Throughout our participation in the ecumenical movement, we Orthodox have affirmed that the Orthodox Church is indeed this one body of Christ; and we firmly believe that the new birth of the faithful in baptism leads to this one church. Herein, we are convinced, lies the significance of the Orthodox Church's continuing practice, authorized by the ecumenical councils, of receiving as already baptized those coming to her communion from certain groups while insisting upon baptism for those coming from other groups, whose "baptism" she is unable to recognize. While the implications of this practice for the unity of Christians in the one church of Christ have not yet been fully explored, we believe that the Lima statement has provided a useful stimulus for discussion of this important subject.

10. We eagerly await the reaction to the Lima statement in other Christian communities, particularly in regard to baptismal practices. While the Faith and Order document recognizes the possibility of differing local customs in baptismal rites, it outlines essential elements in the act of baptizing. We affirm

these essential elements and see their adoption in practice by the various churches as essential to the unity among Christians for which we all pray.

The eucharist

11. We in the Orthodox Church in America are experiencing a significant renewal in recent years in regard to the eucharist. Thanks to the work of many theologians, some of whom have influenced the WCC Faith and Order Commission's statement on "Baptism, Eucharist and Ministry", we have come to reaffirm that the church of Christ is a eucharistic community *par excellence* in her being and life.

12. It is in the eucharist above all that the church realizes herself as the body and bride of Jesus Christ within the time and space of this fallen world. It is in the eucharist that individual Christian believers together become the church of God. It is in the eucharist that the kingdom of God which Jesus brings to the world is made powerfully accessible by the Holy Spirit whom he sends from the Father to those who believe in him as Messiah and Lord. It is in the eucharist that the church's unity is actualized, her apostolic faith expressed, her catholicity manifested, her holiness given. And it is in the eucharist that the church's theological vision is lived, her evangelical mission empowered, and the spiritual life of her members nurtured and renewed.

13. We affirm with the Lima statement that the church's eucharist, or rather, the church herself in her eucharistic being and life, is indeed essentially thanksgiving to God for his mighty acts of creation, redemption, and sanctification in his Son and Spirit. We affirm as well that the eucharist is truly the memorial of all that God has accomplished in Christ, and is still accomplishing and will yet accomplish, by the Spirit's power for the life of the world. We also affirm that the eucharistic assembly must invoke the Spirit upon itself and upon its offering of bread and wine so that both the people of God and their eucharistic offering may be actualized as truly the body of Christ himself. We rejoice in affirming with the Lima statement that the eucharist is indeed a sacrifice of praise offered to God by all the faithful together with Jesus their high priest, the "one who offers and is offered", as the liturgy of St John Chrysostom declares, giving himself as a ransom for many, "on behalf of all and for all". After much confusion and division on this central issue in recent centuries, we look forward to the further clarification of the meaning of sacrifice in eucharistic worship by theologians in the days to come.

14. Finally we thank God that we may affirm with the Faith and Order statement that the eucharist is indeed the meal of the kingdom of God, not merely the sign and the foretaste, but the very presence here and now of the marriage supper of the Lamb at which those who have continued with Christ in his trials are invited to eat and drink with him, at his table in his kingdom (cf. Luke 22). For us Orthodox, and we believe for Christians from the very beginning, the eucharistic Supper has always been first and foremost the

eating and drinking already now in the kingdom of God; our entrance with Jesus into the heavenly sanctuary not made by human hands, into the presence of God himself, there to adore the thrice-holy Lord with innumerable angels in festal gathering, as the scriptures say, with the assembly of the first-born who are enrolled in heaven, with the spirits of the righteous made perfect (cf. Heb. 12). Our Orthodox divine liturgy, which we believe maintains the tradition of apostolic Christianity, testifies to this central and essential experience of Christian faith. The church's structure of worship, her rites and hymns, her vessels and vestments, her icons and incense all bear witness to the essence of Christian faith and life, namely that the kingdom of God has truly come to the world in Jesus Christ and is present with us in power by the Holy Spirit in the church. We rejoice to find that Christians today are being led through theological consensus and convergence into the knowledge and experience of this most marvellous mystery.

15. In reflecting on the Faith and Order statement on the eucharist, however, we also find ourselves compelled to admit with great sadness that we Orthodox — in America and, we are certain, throughout the world — sometimes have failed to actualize the eucharist as the communion of the faithful in a manner consistent with our own traditional teachings about this great mystery in the life and mission of the church. Although in most of our churches we have begun to participate more frequently and regularly in eucharistic communion and to understand and experience the church herself more fully as a eucharistic community, we still have not always realized the implications of the eucharist for church organization and administrative structures, for mission and for ethical behaviour. While maintaining formal dignity in worship, together with fastings, vigils, prayers, and other appropriate forms of preparation for eucharistic communion, at times we fail to apply our eucharistic vision and experience to daily life, whether as individuals or corporately. In this connection, we have in mind particularly our situation here in America, where we Orthodox find ourselves organized and administered more on the basis of ethnic and national divisions than on the basis of our apostolic faith and eucharistic practice, visibly expressing our unity in the one body and one cup of the Saviour Christ. This anomaly, altogether inconsistent with the Orthodox doctrine of the church, is urgently in need of correction.

16. With the Lima statement, we acknowledge that we are being inconsistent with our eucharistic faith and practice when we do not actively participate in "restoring and reconciling the world's situation and the human condition", when we persist in unjust relationships and maintain "manifold divisions on account of human pride, material interest and power politics". But we cannot agree with the statement, if we understand it correctly, when it speaks of "the obstinacy of unjustifiable confessional oppositions within the body of Christ". As bishops of the church of Christ we are called to ensure the unity, integrity, solidarity, and continuity of the church. We do so, as the

pastoral epistles instruct us, by guarding the truth that has been entrusted to us by the Holy Spirit, by safeguarding sound doctrine and rightly handling the word of truth (cf. 2 Tim.). That there should not be "confessional oppositions" within the church as Christ's body is clear. The church confesses one faith. Christians should be of one mind and heart. When as a matter of fact the various "churches" make confessions of faith in opposition to each other, however, there can be no eucharistic communion between them because at the eucharist the faithful confess the one Lord with one mind, one heart, and one mouth. The faith confessed is that of the church herself: the orthodox, catholic, apostolic faith. Without unity and unanimity in this faith — though not necessarily with uniformity of expression in its various aspects — there can be no eucharistic fellowship because communion in fact does not exist. To celebrate communion in such conditions, with participation in the Lord's body and blood, can only be unto condemnation and judgement. Abstention from eucharistic sharing in such conditions is an honest act which God will honour as of great service to the upbuilding of the body and to the ultimate unity of its members in spirit and in truth.

17. Looking at non-Orthodox communities in the light of the Lima statement, we find ourselves eager to see how the various bodies will react. We are especially eager to see if eucharistic celebration will become more frequent and regular in churches which now rarely serve the Lord's Supper, even becoming the normal act of worship on each Lord's day. We are also eager to see if the presiding member of the community will be recognized as called to represent Christ himself, and so will be an adequate sacramental expression of the Lord, with proper biblically-defined qualifications. We are also concerned to see if the churches will adopt eucharistic rites which conform to what the Lima statement declares as essential, and will be firm in their insistence on proper doctrinal belief, ethical behaviour, and devotional discipline — at least in principle — for those who will participate in the act of holy communion. And we are especially interested to see if all the baptized, including infants and small children, will be welcome in the various communities to eat and to drink at the table of the Lord as full members of his church and full participants of his kingdom. Finally, we are most eager to discover to what extent the churches will come to recognize themselves as eucharistic communities whose faith and order, life and mission find their source, content, and goal in eucharistic worship.

The ordained ministry

18. The Lima statement commendably situates ministry, as it does baptism and eucharist, within a broad ecclesial context. Its point of departure is the image of the church as the people of God, an image whose deep significance has been rediscovered in recent times by many Christians, including the Orthodox. In the Bible, as well as in the works of the church fathers, the image of the people of God is complemented by many others. The Lima

statement echoes some of these when it speaks of the church being "built up" like an edifice, with those who follow Christ being united by the Holy Spirit "into one body". This rich and vivid imagery reminds us that the "people", the "new community" in Christ is not just a human society or movement, not an earthly organization, but precisely the people of *God*. This reminder is pertinent to us Orthodox, as well as to other Christians. We pray that we heed it well: "Belonging to the Church means living in communion with God through Jesus Christ in the Holy Spirit."

19. The church receives her very being and life from God, through the saving work of his Son, made accessible in the Holy Spirit. Her structures, including her ordained ministry, reflect this fundamental dependence. The Lima statement calls attention to this at several points:

20. (a) As the commentary to the statement notes: "The basic reality of an ordained ministry was present from the beginning", as a permanent and constitutive element in the church's life, even though "the actual forms of ordination and the ordained ministry . . . have evolved in complex historical developments". The ordained ministry is necessary to the church's very existence. The church has always needed "persons who are publicly and continually responsible for pointing to its fundamental dependence on Jesus Christ, and thereby provide, within a multiplicity of gifts, a focus of its unity". While "every charism serves to assemble and build up the body of Christ", each does so in a different way, the charism of the ordained minister doing so precisely by revealing these diverse charisms as forming *one* body.

21. (b) The Lima statement also rightly affirms that "the authority of the ordained minister is rooted in Jesus Christ, who has received it from the Father (Matt. 28:18) and who confers it by the Holy Spirit through the act of ordination". This means, first of all, that the ordained minister is by definition consecrated to *ministry*. He is not to "exercise lordship" but rather to be, like Christ, "as one who serves" in love (Luke 22:25, 27). His authority is authentic insofar as it conforms to this model. Authority thus understood is a gift in and for the community. At the same time, we must emphasize a point only briefly mentioned in the commentary to the statement: "The authority of ordained ministers must not be so reduced as to make them dependent on the common opinion of the community". Proper exercise of authority may sometimes involve confrontation, rebuke, and correction, expressed in preaching or in penitential discipline. The community must sometimes be reminded of its vocation to communion. Here too authority must be that of the loving God "who desires not the death of a sinner but that he should turn from his wickedness and live".

22. (c) As the Lima statement also reminds us, the act of ordination itself reveals the twofold nature of the ordained ministry. Ordination takes place within the believing community assembled for eucharistic celebration. Through ordination a new relationship is established between the one ordained and the body of the faithful. Here we see in practice both the

hierarchical and the conciliar character of church life which is so precious to the Orthodox tradition. At the same time, from the beginning of church history, the gestures and prayers of the ordination rite have drawn attention to God's initiative in what is taking place, a point made by the Lima statement when it declares that "the invocation of the Spirit implies the absolute dependence on God for the outcome of the Church's prayer". We Orthodox, as we ourselves pray in our rites, insist that it is the "grace divine" which "elects" the candidate for the ordained ministry, and "heals that which is infirm and completes that which is lacking" so that the ministry might be accomplished. Ordination therefore — though involving the consent of the candidate, his church community, and his bishop, all three of which are shown forth in the ordination ceremony — is never simply the community's formal acknowledgment that the person ordained already possesses the gifts and the powers needed to complete a particular ministry, which the Lima statement appears at certain points to imply (cf. §§ 44, 48 . . .). Orthodox believe that God himself bestows this unique gift upon the one ordained so that he might be able to bring the diverse gifts of the community into unity as one body.

23. In discussing the forms of ordained ministry in the church, the Lima statement draws attention to the historical development of the threefold ministry of deacon, presbyter, and bishop. Unlike Western Christians, we Orthodox have tended to take these three forms of ministry for granted since we have had to confront no major controversies on this issue in our history. We have deacons, presbyters, and bishops — and other ministers as well — but their significance for the life of the church has not been explored in depth. Living now in the West, being in daily contact with Christians who question and even reject the threefold ministry, and being asked now to respond to the Faith and Order Commission's statement on the ministry, we are compelled to ask the question: Is the threefold pattern of ministry to be regarded as normative for the church, a development inspired by God's Spirit to be dogmatically defended? Or is it simply an option for the church which, if adopted at this juncture (as the Lima statement appears to recommend) by those not having it, might expedite the reunion of divided Christians? By stressing the church's capacity for adapting its ministries to contextual needs, the Lima statement would seem to support the second alternative. Yet the statement also suggests that in the fulfilment of their mission and service, the churches need people who in different ways express and perform the tasks of the ordained ministry in its diaconal, presbyteral, and episcopal aspects and functions — whatever the titles given to the offices. We too would sense an "inner logic" of this sort at work within the church. For this reason we also welcome the assertion that "among the gifts (of the Holy Spirit) a ministry of *episkopē* is necessary to express and safeguard the unity of the body. Every church needs this ministry of unity in some form in order to be the church of God, the one body of Christ, a sign of the unity of all in the kingdom". At the same time, we take note of the challenge contained in these words. We must

re-examine the spiritual vitality and existential operation of those forms of ordained ministry which we have received and have for centuries taken for granted. For indeed, most of the Lima statement's observations — that "the collegial dimension of leadership in the eucharistic community has suffered diminution", that "the function of deacons has been reduced to an assistant role in the celebration of the liturgy", that "the relation of the presbyterate to the episcopal ministry" remains "an unresolved question" — call for a clear response not only from others involved in the ecumenical movement but from us Orthodox as well. Possessing the threefold ministry, we are faced with the task of elucidating its meaning for the life of the church today. We are grateful to the theologians of the Faith and Order Commission for calling attention to this task. For we must admit that our forms of ordained ministry have not always served effectively to proclaim and manifest Christ's victory over the divisions of this broken and fallen world. Instead of fostering unity in communion, all too often they have been misused in order to perpetuate old antagonisms, both within the church and in our relations with those outside.

24. The Lima statement asserts that "the primary manifestation of apostolic succession is to be found in the apostolic tradition of the church as a whole". While "apostolic succession of the ministry", i.e. "the orderly transmission of the ordained ministry", is a "powerful expression of the continuity of the Church throughout history", it must not be separated from other expressions of the church's apostolic tradition. Certainly this would hold true, we believe, for episcopal succession as well. We Orthodox insist that the succession of the apostolic tradition is actualized in the church through the laying-on of hands of the episcopate in apostolic succession. As in regard to the development of the threefold ministry, we would see an "inner logic" at work here, and not simply "the particular historical circumstances of the growing Church in the early centuries" referred to in the Lima statement. Can it really be possible that those charged with *episkopē* in the church, and thereby primarily responsible for "the orderly transmission of the ordained ministry", as well as the continuity of the church's essential faith and her necessary structures of communion, came to this position through fortuitous historical circumstances? We think not. Yet here too we find ourselves presented with a challenge. Too often we have separated the episcopate from its necessary, organic context of ecclesial communion, thereby compromising its value as a sign of the continuity, identity, and unity of the church. We Orthodox, particularly we bishops, must face this fact and do something to correct it, both for our own church as well as for the unity of all Christians.

25. We find the section of the Lima statement concerning the meaning and act of ordination and the steps towards the mutual recognition of ministries in the various church bodies to be too brief and too general. Not all of the recommendations and observations here are of equal weight and value. Certainly if the various churches followed the practice of ordination outlined

in the statement, many of the issues which have appeared to be divisive in the past might be more easily surmounted. At the same time, we are convinced that several of the conditions for ordination and mutual recognition which the document sets forth involve substantive issues of faith and should therefore not be treated as if they were merely of a disciplinary nature. For example, when the statement declares that in "recognition of the God-given charism of ministry, ordination to any one of the particular ordained ministries is never repeated", we are obliged to insist that to us this seems to touch upon the very nature of ordination and its meaning in and for the church. It should not be relegated to a discussion of the consequences of "leave of absence from service".

26. We also feel that the Lima statement fails to deal adequately with the qualifications for ordination to the various ministries in the church. The holy scriptures clearly teach, at least to us Orthodox, that not all baptized people, even those with marvellous personal charisms of the Holy Spirit, are necessarily called to episcopal, presbyteral, and diaconal ministries, but that certain formal — we might say "structural" — qualifications are demanded because of the nature of the service required. An examination of the pastoral epistles, together with the early canonical tradition, would be very helpful in correcting this defect in the Lima statement. We also believe that the specifically priestly nature of the ministry exercised by bishops and presbyters should be explored in greater depth.

27. The issue of ordination of women to the episcopal and presbyteral ministries is perhaps the most difficult issue of all. We find the Lima statement gravely deficient at this point. We believe that the question is far more serious and far more complex — and therefore a much greater obstacle to the mutual recognition of ministries — than the statement suggests. We cannot accept the Lima document, if we understand it properly, when it states that the "obstacles" which arise from the fact that "some churches ordain both men and women" while "others ordain only men" must "not be regarded as substantive hindrance for further efforts towards mutual recognition". Whereas the "hindrance" may not be "substantive" as far as "*efforts* towards mutual recognition" are concerned, the fact that women are being ordained to the priestly ministries at this time when the traditional, biblical understanding of the service is being more properly understood presents — at least in our minds — a truly substantive issue urgently needing clarification. We Orthodox Christians in America have investigated this issue thoroughly and honestly. We will continue to do so. The Lima statement is right when it calls all of us to admit that a "deeper understanding of the comprehensiveness of ministry which reflects the interdependence of men and women needs to be more widely manifested in the life of the Church". But we Orthodox Christians cannot admit that two thousand years of Christian practice in virtually all traditions should be changed without deep and serious reflection, prayer, and careful consideration of all aspects of the

issue. While we Orthodox may not have provided a clear and convincing presentation of our own views on the issue, we are not convinced by the arguments in favour of the ordination of women.

Looking to the future

28. Since its inception as an autocephalous church in 1970, the Orthodox Church in America has been officially involved in the World Council of Churches, holding membership in it. Even before 1970, the Russian Orthodox Church of North America and the Romanian Episcopate of America were members of the World Council of Churches. While our membership has often been questioned by our faithful people, and while we ourselves have from time to time reconsidered our church's participation in the World Council of Churches, we the bishops of the Orthodox Church in America have remained committed to membership in the Council, and have tried to ensure that our church would be represented in a competent and responsible manner.

29. It is well known to all who follow our church's involvement in ecumenical affairs that we have generally been highly critical of the social and political activities of the WCC, while supporting the work of the Faith and Order Commission. We have borne the criticisms of our participation in the Council because we have hoped — often "against hope" — that some good would come of the work of the theologians, which would move the various Christian groups into greater understanding and cooperation, and that one day there might even be the "unity of all" in one apostolic faith and one eucharistic worship.

30. We want Christian unity. We know that our Lord demands it. We believe that we are commanded to work for it. We affirm, God being our helper, that we must even be ready to die for it. We know that we are called to risk every misunderstanding — and every false accusation, calumny, and slander — to advance the cause of Christian unity, and we are not afraid of this or at least we pray not to be. What we are afraid of is that we might prove unworthy of our baptism, our participation in the holy eucharist, and our episcopal ministry in the church by our betrayal of Jesus Christ through a compromise of his divine truth.

31. Jesus Christ is the truth. The Holy Spirit is the Spirit of truth. The "church of the living God" is "the pillar and bulwark of the truth" (1 Tim. 3:15). There is unity in truth. This is the unity of the church of Christ. As we look to the future, we hope in the triumph of this truth. We salute the Faith and Order Commission of the World Council of Churches for forcing us to face the truth of the issues which confront us in our divisions. And we thank the Commission for furthering the cause of truth, which is the cause of Christian unity, through its work on "Baptism, Eucharist and Ministry". May this work continue, and, please God, may it bear fruit to the glory of his name and the unity of all of his people.

APOSTOLIC CATHOLIC ASSYRIAN CHURCH OF THE EAST

We have carefully and attentively studied the text "Baptism, Eucharist and Ministry", and would like to comment as follows:

The sacraments of the church, according to the divine scriptures, are seven in number: the priesthood, which is ministry of all the other sacraments; holy baptism; the oil of unction; the oblation of the body and blood of Christ; absolution; the holy leaven, namely, the king (Malka); the sign of the life-giving cross.

These are necessary because of the wants of man in this carnal world. In order for a man to be, and to exist in the world, he must be born of a carnal mother through a carnal father, though the figure and the perfection of a man come from the Father of Lights. In a like manner in order to belong to a world of immortality, it is requisite to be born of the spiritual womb of baptism, through the agency of the spiritual father which is the priest, not withstanding that form and perfection are imparted by the Holy Spirit and by the power of the Most High. Further, it is requisite for every one belonging to this world to sustain his temporal life by temporal food and earthly drink. So, in like manner, spiritual nourishment and divine drink are a means to him who is baptized for sustaining his external life in God.

Again, as everyone who is in the body, through the changes of the times and bad conditions, is subject to sickness and disease and is in need of physicians who will restore him to his former health if he follows their injunctions, so the man of God, through the effects of sin, his immoral living, falls into the disorder of iniquity, and receives health from the priests of the church, the spiritual physician, if he orders himself after their directions.

Should anyone from without inquire what constitutes the holiness and sacramental nature of each of these seven sacraments, we reply that these three things satisfy them. First, a true priest, who has attained the priesthood rightly, according to the requirements of the church. Secondly, the word and

---

• 550,000 members, 7 dioceses, 8 bishops, 77 pastors.

the command of the Lord of sacraments (1 Cor. 10:15–17), whereby He ordained each of them. Thirdly, right intention and confirmed faith on the part of those who partake of them, believing that the effect of the sacraments takes place by a heavenly power.

We shall now treat briefly the three sacraments, subject of your text, separately: baptism, eucharist and ministry.

Priesthood (Ministry)

Priesthood is the ministry of mediation (Num. 16–17; 26:9; 27:3; Jude 11) between God and man in those things which impart forgiveness of sins (John 20:22–23), convey blessings, and put away wrath (Num. 16:46–50; Acts 5:1–16). It is divided into imperfect, as that of the law; and perfect, as that of the church. The foundation of the priesthood in the church is laid on the declaration of the Lord of the priesthood to St Peter, in the region of Caesarea Philippi: "To thee I shall give the keys of the kingdom of heaven; whatsoever thou shalt bind on earth shall be bound in heaven; and whatsoever thou shalt loose on earth, shall be loosed in heaven" (Matt. 16:19 and 18:18; John 20:23). Its superstructure comes from that other injunction: "Feed my lambs. Feed my sheep. Feed my ewes" (John 21:15–17). Its completion and perfection from that he breathed on them saying: "Receive ye the Holy Spirit; if you forgive a man his sins, they are forgiven to him; and if you withhold forgiveness of a man's sins, they shall be held" (John 20:22–23).

The old priesthood was one of generation (Num. 16:40) and not one that was based upon manner of life and will, but the new priesthood by apostolic succession, and imparted in the church through the laying on of hands (1 Tim. 4:14, 5:22; Tit. 1:9; Heb. 6:2; Acts 6:6), is given to those who are deemed worthy of it after examination of their manner of life and thought. "Let these be first examined, and then let them minister being found blameless" (1 Tim. 3:10; Acts 6:3).

Therefore the perfection of this and the imperfection of that priesthood is evident, since we know that very many wicked children are begotten of righteous fathers, as Cain, Kham and the children of Lot, of Moses, of Eli, and others; and good children are begotten of wicked fathers, as Melchizedek, Abraham and others. Moreover, the former priesthood was conferred by material oil (Ex. 30:22–32, 29:7; Lev. 8:12), but this latter by the immaterial unction of the spirit, through the laying on hands (Acts 2:4, 6:6, 8:17).

As to the matter of the rules whereby he who desires the priesthood is to be tried, whether he be worthy or not, let him who wishes to know this attend to the words of St Paul, the tongue of the spirit; this is a true saying: "If a man desire the priesthood he desireth a good work. He who becomes a priest must be blameless, the husband of one wife, alert mentally, modest, of good behaviour, given to hospitality, apt at teaching, not given to wine, not hasty to strike, but patient, not quarrelsome, not greedy of lucre. One who rules well his own house, having his children under submission to bring them up with all purity. For if a man know not how to rule his own household, how can he take care of the church of God. Moreover, he must have a good report from outsiders: lest he fall into reproach, and snares of Satan."

Priesthood is the greatest and foremost sacrament in the church, through which all the other sacraments of the church are completed and perfected, and it is the greatest gift given by God to humanity by authorizing the man to forgive the sins of his fellow men and women (John 20:22–23).

Baptism

Baptism is the door through which a man enters into Christianity, and into God's kingdom (John 3:5). Baptism is the immersion in and the washing with water and this is divided into five kinds:
1. The washing off the filth of body, as is commonly done by all men.
2. The washing according to the law, whereby it was believed that purity towards God from all carnal uncleanliness was attained (Deut. 23:11; Lev. 15:5, 16, 17).
3. Those of the traditions of the elders, such as "the washing of cups and pots, brasen vessels, beds, and as when they come from the market, except they bath, they eat not" (Matt. 23:25, Mark 7:4,18–23).
4. The baptism of John, whereby he preached only repentance and the forgiveness of sins (Matt. 3:5–13; John 1:25–27; Acts 13:24, 19:4).
5. The baptism of our Saviour, which is received through the Holy Spirit (Matt. 3:11, John 3:5, John 1:33) for the gift of adoption of sons (2 Cor. 6:18; Gal. 3:29, 4:4–7; Eph. 1:5), for the resurrection from death, and for everlasting life (Rom. 6:3–5, 23; Col. 2:12), which is the circumcision made without hands, in putting off the body of the sins of the flesh by the circumcision of Christ (Col. 2:11).

For as the circumcision of the flesh was given for a sign denoting those who were of the family of Israel of the old according to the flesh, so the baptism of Christ is a sign of spiritual relationship to God. "But those who received him, to them he gave power to become the sons of God" (John 1:12).

The matter of baptism is pure water, and the form of baptism is immersion in water three times: "In the Name of the Father, Son, and Holy Spirit", according to the words of our Saviour (Matt. 28:19).

There is also a sixth baptism, that of blood, as our Lord has indicated: "I have a baptism to be baptized with, and I am oppressed until it is fulfilled" (Luke 12:50). There is also a seventh baptism, that of tears, as the saying of the fathers. The sixth and seventh baptisms are allied to the fifth, which is an emblem of death and the resurrection.

Eucharist (oblation)

The oblation is a service offered up by those below to those above, through material elements, in hope of forgiveness of sins and of an answer to prayer.

The old oblations consisted of irrational animals, and of the blood of bodies (Lev. 4:4 etc.), but with us the only-begotten of God (John 3:16) who took upon him the form of a servant (Phil. 2:6–7). He offered his own body as a sacrifice to his father for the life of the world (Heb. 9:14). And hence he is called by John "the Lamb of God which taketh away the sins of the world" (John 1:29). And again: "So God loved the world that he gave his only-begotten son" (John 3:16, Heb. 12:24), who was offered up to his father a living, rational sacrifice for all the created (Heb. 12:24) thereby reconciling the world with his greatness (Rom. 5:10, Eph. 2:16, 2 Cor. 5:19), and bringing salvation to angels and to men. Now seeing that it was impossible that his sacrifice upon the cross for the salvation of all could identically be enacted, in every place, throughout all ages, and to all men, just as it was, without any alteration, he beheld with an eye of mercy, and devised in compassion and with great wisdom; and in that night in which he was betrayed for the life of the world, he took bread into his holy, pure and immaculate hands, blessed, broke, and gave it to his disciples and he said into them: "This is my body which is being broken for the sake of life of the world into remission of sins." Likewise he blessed the cup and gave it to them saying: "This is my blood of the new covenant which will be shed for many for remission of sins. Take therefore, eat all of you of this bread, and drink of this cup, and do this whenever you shall meet together, in remembrance of me" (Matt. 26:26–29, Mark 14:22–25, Luke 22:14–20, 1 Cor. 11:23–25).

Throughout this divine command, mysteriously, the bread is changed into his holy body, and the wine into his precious blood, and they impart, to all who receive them in faith and without doubting, the forgiveness of sins, purification, enlightenment, pardon, the great hope of the resurrection from the dead, the inheritance of heaven, and the new life. Whenever we approach these sacraments, we meet with Christ himself, and him we bear upon our hands and kiss, and in partaking thereof, we are being united with him, his holy body mixing with our bodies, and his innocent blood mingling with our blood (1 Cor. 10:15–17), and by faith we know, him that is in heaven and him that is in the church, to be but one body, of our Lord Jesus Christ.

The matter of this sacrament Christ ordained to be of wheat and wine as being most fit to represent body and blood. The form he conveys through his life-giving word, and by the descent of the Holy Spirit.

We end here our comments on these three sacraments, and glorify God. Amen.

Mar Dinkha IV
Catholicos Patriarch

CHURCH OF ENGLAND

Responding to the Lima Text

22. The Sixth Assembly of the World Council of Churches in Vancouver invited all the member churches to prepare an official response to the text by December 31st 1985. The Faith and Order Commission intends to compare all these responses, to publish the results, and to analyse the ecumenical implications in a World Conference on Faith and Order in 1989. The response of the Church of England will go, as requested, directly to the Faith and Order Commission. It has also been suggested that copies of the final responses of Anglican Provinces be sent to the Anglican Consultative Council and to national and regional councils of churches. It is also hoped that the 1987 meeting of the Anglican Consultative Council will compare the provincial responses to the Lima Text bearing in mind also responses to other dialogues, such as the Anglican–Roman Catholic, Anglican–Lutheran, Anglican–Reformed and Anglican–Orthodox. Provinces of the Anglican Communion will differ in the method and timing of their responses to the Faith and Order Commission. The Church of England intends to follow the present debate in the General Synod with debates in Diocesan Synods and, in the light of their discussions, to produce a final response for the Faith and Order Commission.

23. As has already been suggested it is important when responding to an ecumenical text to bear in mind the claims made for its achievement by those responsible for producing the text. The Lima Text is not a comprehensive formulation on the three matters covered. Rather, it deals mainly with particular points of misunderstanding and disagreements which have led to division. Moreover while the text makes a significant achievement in the movement towards visible unity, it does not yet represent "full consensus". The Preface to the Lima Text says:

- 27,200,000 members, 17,460 congregations, 44 dioceses, 13,953 parishes, 18,376 clergy. This response was accepted by the General Synod in 1985.

Certainly we have not fully reached "consensus" (*consentire*), under-stood here as that experience of life and articulation of faith necessary to realize and maintain the Church's visible unity. Such consensus is rooted in the communion built on Jesus Christ and the witness of the apostles. As a gift of the Spirit it is realized as a communal experience before it can be articulated by common efforts into words. Full consensus can only be proclaimed after the churches reach the point of living and acting together in unity (The Lima Text, p. ix).

24. On the way to this goal the churches are discovering many promising convergences. The main part of the Lima Text demonstrates the major areas of theological convergence while the commentaries indicate either historical differences that have been overcome or identify disputed issues in need of further research and reconciliation.

25. We note also that the agenda of baptism, eucharist and ministry is itself only one part of a three part agenda that the Faith and Order Commission believes necessary for the visible unity of the churches. The other two parts are: a common expression of the apostolic faith, and common structures of decision making. It is the agenda of the Lima Text, the agenda of baptism, eucharist and ministry which is the most developed section of this three part agenda.

26. In responding to the Lima Text the Faith and Order Commission has asked the churches to answer four questions. The first is of particular importance and it has complex and significant implications:

the extent to which your church can recognize in
this text the faith of the Church through the ages;

We note that the question does not ask whether we can recognize in the text the faith of Anglicanism. It would therefore not be appropriate simply to compare what the text says with the historic formularies of the Church of England. We understand that the phrasing of the question directs us to consider how far the Lima Text reflects the apostolic faith of the universal Church: that is that faith which is "uniquely revealed in the holy Scriptures and set forth in the catholic creeds, which faith the Church is called upon to proclaim afresh in each generation" (The Declaration of Assent, *The Canons of the Church of England*, Canon C15). The question asked of us involves the identification and affirmation of the universal Christian tradition which has been mediated to us through the various traditions of all our churches.

27. For members of the Church of England, however, the statements of Canon A5 and the Declaration of Assent will have to be borne in mind. Canon A5 states:

The doctrine of the Church of England is grounded in the holy Scriptures and in such teachings of the ancient Fathers and Councils of the Church as are agreeable to the said Scriptures. In particular such doctrine is to be found in the Thirty-nine Articles of Religion, the Book of Common Prayer and the Ordinal.

This needs to be understood further in relation to the Declaration of Assent:

> The Church of England is part of the one, holy, catholic and apostolic Church worshipping the one true God, Father, Son and Holy Spirit. It professes the faith uniquely revealed in the holy Scriptures and set forth in the catholic creeds, which faith the Church is called upon to proclaim afresh in each generation. Led by the Holy Spirit, it has borne witness to Christian truth in its historic formularies, the Thirty-nine Articles of Religion, the Book of Common Prayer and the Ordering of Bishops, Priests and Deacons. (*The Canons of the Church of England*,Canon C15)

Subscription to the historic formularies of the Church of England is not required in all the provinces of the Anglican Communion. However, we note that at least in the provinces of Canterbury and York the Declaration of Assent both refers to the significance of the historic formularies for the Anglican inheritance of faith and also implies an openness to the need to proclaim the faith afresh in each generation. This allows, as the question of the Faith and Order Commission does, for a dynamic notion of the faith and a recognition that our appropriation of the Tradition has developed throughout history and continues to develop today. It does not ask us to deny the Anglican formularies as such. It is, however, in dialogue with others, in the broader ecumenical community, that we come nearest to the perception of "the faith of the Church through the ages", as we learn to correct and supplement each others' traditions. This does not require, however, a commitment to any and every secondary feature of the traditions of other churches, or indeed, even of our own.

28. The Faith and Order Commission also wants to know the *extent* to which the churches agree that the text expresses what each understands to be the "faith of the Church through the ages". Therefore the churches need to add to their responses an indication of where the Lima Text does not express the faith as it might, because it omits, over-emphasises, or otherwise needs to deal more adequately with particular issues.

29. The second question concerns the implications of what the text says for relations with other churches, in particular those who agree together that they can recognize it as an expression of what the Church understands to be "the faith of the Church through the ages":

> *the consequences your church can draw from this text for its relations and dialogues with other churches, particularly with those churches which also recognize the text as an expression of the apostolic faith;*

In answer to such a question we need to identify areas which need further refining and elaboration. In some cases our response to the text will suggest the need for further dialogue with one particular partner. The baptism text, for example, urges us to develop a discussion with Baptists while the ministry text suggests the need to discuss the question of the ordination of women to the priesthood with Orthodox and Roman Catholic partners. But this second question does not only call for further theological exploration, it challenges us to suggest certain steps which might appropriately be taken and celebrated with those who can agree substantial parts of the text with us. If we can agree the degree of convergence registered in the Lima Text with others this must demand a conscious drawing together in life and mission.

30. The third question concerns other practical implications of what the text says for our own church:

> *the guidance your church can take from this text for its worship, educational, ethical and spiritual life and witness;*

This question rightly recognizes that participation in any dialogue involves a process of commitment and openness. We do not do our own tradition justice by abandoning or denying it: we enter dialogue with a commitment to our tradition. Nevertheless we can only enter into serious dialogue if we are prepared at the same time to be open to the challenges and indeed the changes with which the process may face us. In the ecumenical quest in recent years a number of schemes have suggested changes which would be implemented in a united church, or have suggested changes needed on the way to that goal. The Church of England has found it difficult to respond to the need to change and be changed in the process. The Faith and Order Commission is right to ask us to examine ourselves and our attitudes in the light of the theological convergences of the Lima Text.

31. And the final question concerns the ongoing agenda of the Faith and Order Commission:

> *the suggestions your church can make for the ongoing work of Faith and Order as it relates the material of this text on Baptism, Eucharist and Ministry to its long-range research project "Towards the Common Expression of the Apostolic Faith Today".*

This question directs us to underline those issues raised in the Lima Text upon which consensus has not yet been reached and which we think need further work in the broad forum of the Faith and Order Commission. The Commission itself at its meeting in Lima indicated the need to look at the question of primacy, building upon all that is said about ministry and oversight in the ministry text. But this fourth question also points us in other directions to the other two parts of the three part agenda the World Council has suggested is necessary to support the visible unity of the churches, namely the common expression of the apostolic faith and common structures of decision making. The Lima Text inevitably raises the question of what faith it is which is confessed when baptism, eucharist and ministry are celebrated and practised. And, as we have already seen, the process of responding to the Lima Text forces us to raise questions about our own and other churches' structures of authoritative teaching and decision making and to consider what the appropriate structures might be in a visibly united church.

32. Bearing in mind the claims made for the text by the Faith and Order Commission itself, namely that it is a convergence text, we turn to consider the Lima Text in relation to each of the four questions asked of us.

Question 1:   The extent to which your church can recognize in this text the faith of the Church through the ages.

A. Baptism

(i) THE BIBLICAL BASIS FOR BAPTISM

33. The Lima Text on baptism begins with an understanding of baptism set forth in the Holy Scripture. It summarises the New Testament doctrine of baptism, administered in water in the name of the Father and of the Son and of the Holy Spirit, as being a participation in Christ's death and resurrection, a washing away of sin, a new birth, an enlightenment by Christ, a reclothing in Christ, a renewal by the Spirit, a liberation into a new humanity, an act of justification, God's gift of the anointing and promise of the Holy Spirit, a sign and seal of common discipleship and therefore a basic bond of Christian unity transcending all differences of sex, race and social status. Moreover, baptism is not only a decisive moment and act, but also the foundation of a process, of a life-long growth in witness, in personal sanctification, and in a continuing struggle to seek the realisation of God's will in every area of life. Baptism sets the disciple upon the way of the cross of the Suffering Servant. By baptism the whole Church receives the candidate into a fellowship grounded upon a shared discipleship in union with the one Lord of the whole Church. We welcome this biblical basis with which the text begins.

(ii) GOD'S GIFT AND OUR RESPONSE

34. The text maintains carefully the scriptural balance: "Baptism is both God's gift and our human response to that gift" (B8). In spite of the difficulty of maintaining this delicate balance in such a closely argued text, we believe that as a whole the text does achieve this. At the same time it is faithful to the stress on the prior gift of God in implanting new life and incorporating the baptised person into the already existing fellowship of the Spirit which is evident in the Church's faith through the ages. While the renunciation, the profession of faith and the vows are essential parts of the response of the believer, the prime initiative is understood to lie with the grace of God rather than with the decision of men and women.

35. The Lima Text does not work with a concept of baptism as an external mark or sign by which individuals may choose to signify conversion of heart. Rather, its concept of baptism is of a sign and instrument given by God whereby he incorporates men and women into the Church: it is a sacrament of new birth and life, to which are attached the divine promises of forgiveness of sins and of the gift of the Spirit.

(iii) INITIATION AS A PROCESS

36. We welcome the strong emphasis upon baptism as a decisive "beginning" in a process: "Baptism is related not only to momentary experience, but to lifelong growth into Christ" (B9). We also welcome the emphasis upon the relation of the individual to the community of faith in which he or she is baptised and confirmed. Since baptism is an act of the Church resting in the faithfulness of God, and since the congregation witnessing the act is also renewing its own pledges to foster and nurture the life of the newly baptised, we believe that Lima is right to suggest that baptism ought to be celebrated in the setting of the Christian community.

(iv) INFANT BAPTISM AND "BELIEVERS' BAPTISM"

37. The balance held in the text between God's gift and our response, the emphasis upon baptism as a decisive beginning in a process, together with the importance of the community of faith, are all important for the reconciliation between those who practise infant baptism and those who practise only "believers' baptism". The Church of England provides for both forms of baptism in its Book of Common Prayer of 1662. The Alternative Service Book, 1980, sets first in the order of initiation services an order of service for the baptism and confirmation of adults. In this it could be said to agree with the Lima Text that "baptism upon personal profession of faith is the most clearly attested pattern in the New Testament documents" (B11). This is followed in the ASB by provision for baptism of children. In this the custom which grew up very early in the Church's life and which may be reflected in Mark 10:13–16 is upheld. The prevenient character of God's grace is clearly manifested in infant baptism. Yet there also renunciation, profession of faith and vows remain essential and are made in the faith of the Church by sponsors. To the grace and forgiveness of God of which baptism is the sign and instrument the believer must respond in personal profession of faith, through conversion of heart and the acceptance of the ethical implications of baptism.

38. Those who stress "believers' baptism" and reject the baptism of infants lay the highest stress on the candidate's conscious choice and deliberate commitment. This stress is, or at least sounds, much greater than that placed on the priority of God's merciful grace and on the Church as the given, already existing instrument of the Gospel. Baptism may then come to be seen as no more than an outward badge or sign of profession, publishing to the congregation and to the world an inward decision or response, rather than as being in itself an effectual means of grace (cf. Article XXV Of the Sacraments, XXVII Of Baptism).

39. If acceptance of the practice of infant baptism runs the risk of obscuring the fact that without careful nurture the work of inward grace is imperilled, then rejection of the practice runs the risk of appearing to make

the gift of God contingent on the prior human acts of repentance and profession of belief.

40. The ecumenical duty of listening to and learning from each other is placed in the Lima Text on those who practise infant baptism and on those who practise "believers' baptism" alike. The text does not ask Baptists, or anyone else, to cease from deferring baptism either until adult life or at least until conscious choice is possible, nor to accept the practice of infant baptism as the standard pattern. Rather, it asks those who practise only "believers' baptism" to acknowledge that in those communions where, by very ancient tradition indeed, infants are admitted to the sacrament, those candidates are validly and effectively received into the Church of Christ and are made children of God, members of Christ, and inheritors of the Kingdom of Heaven. They grow up to know themselves to be personally committed to the Lord whose grace has here reached out in mercy to them. The Lima Text is right, we believe, to ask those who themselves reject infant baptism to accept the validity of the sacrament as true incorporation into the Body of Christ, and to ask that the act be not repeated in adult life.

41. We welcome the suggestion in the text that both practices are acceptable within the one Church of God, testifying to different aspects of the one baptismal truth. Lima challenges us to move towards one Church united in a common doctrine of baptism yet allowing for difference in baptismal practice.

(v) BAPTISM AND THE NATURE OF THE CHURCH

42. A church's baptismal practice will usually say something significant about its conception of the Church. The Lima Text consistently makes clear that baptism is a gift of God through which "Christians are brought into union with Christ, with each other and *with the Church of every time and place*" (B6, our italics). On this understanding, the practice of baptism implies a view of the Church as a continuing, historic and world-wide community of faith, empowered by Christ to preach the gospel and administer the sacraments of the Kingdom in his name, to declare his word to men and women and to act effectively towards them. If, on the other hand, the Church is conceived of as a local community of spirit-led believers, a "gathered" community of individuals who have each been led by an experience of the Spirit to confess Christ, then baptism can become primarily an occasion in which they testify to this experience. If taken to extremes, such a view may imply that the only real baptism is that of the Spirit and that the rite of water baptism is a churchly sign or testimony either to what has gone before or in anticipation of a future experience. It is a strong tradition among Anglicans that when rightly administered the sacraments are effectual actions of God through the ministry of his Church. That they call for a response is not to be doubted, but the ways by which a baptised person is led into obedience, witness and holiness, and the stages by which this will

happen, are left to the wisdom of God and will reflect that person's growth in grace as well as in personal maturity. In the future agenda of the Faith and Order Commission it will be important to draw out and develop this theme of the relation of baptism to the nature of the Church more fully.

43. The growing consensus on baptism illustrates something of the unity which already exists between churches which remain in separation. As the Lima Text says: baptism "unites the one baptised with Christ and with his people" (B2). Where separated churches are able to acknowledge each others' profession of faith there is already a wide mutual recognition of baptism. This both presupposes and implies some mutual recognition of ecclesial reality, for it is within the context of the life of separated churches that candidates are baptised. Such an ecclesial reality was recognised by Vatican II in its decree on Ecumenism para. 3. "All those justified by faith through baptism are incorporated into Christ. They therefore have a right to be honoured by the title Christian, and are properly regarded as brothers in the Lord by the sons of the Catholic Church" (see also *Dogmatic Constitution on the Church*, para. 15). Furthermore, in as much as "baptism is normally administered by an ordained minister" (B22), some would argue that such mutual recognition of baptism also implies a certain degree of ministerial acknowledgement. We recommend further explorations of the implication of the acceptance of each others' baptism for the recognition of ministries.

(vi) RE-BAPTISM

44. On the basis of the theological understanding in the text we believe it right to question, as the text itself does, the practice of re-baptism (B13). The decisiveness of baptism is shown by its unrepeatability. The Commission is right to warn against any practice that might be interpreted as re-baptism. This is not only because such an act is destructive of mutual brotherliness and charity between separated Christians, but because it can only obscure the biblical understanding of the sacrament and call in question the reality of God's act of grace which is not dependent upon human response.

(vii) INDISCRIMINATE BAPTISM

45. People will come forward for baptism at a time when their response to the Gospel (or that of their sponsors) is incomplete. It is a delicate matter to judge who should be baptised and who deferred, as no response is without ambiguity. On the one hand the text is right to warn of the offence which the indiscriminate practice of baptism can cause, where admission to baptism is granted to those who do not seem to have given any evidence of wanting to be identified with Jesus Christ and his Church. On the other hand, baptismal discipline may be so "over-discriminating" that those requesting baptism are required to provide unreasonable evidence of the authenticity of their faith. So called "indiscriminate baptism" reflects a view of the Church as a "mixed community"; a more rigorous policy emphasizes the "gathered" nature of the Church.

(viii) BAPTISM, CONFIRMATION AND FIRST COMMUNION

46. It is difficult for the text to be incisive on the subject of the relation between baptism, chrismation, confirmation and the proper point of admission to first communion, for Holy Scripture and ancient tradition allow the possibility of more than one answer to these questions and western practice reflected a diversity of view which the Church of England has inherited. The text illustrates this in §14:

> Christians differ in their understanding as to where the sign of the gift of the Spirit is to be found. Different actions have become associated with the giving of the Spirit. For some it is the water rite itself. For others it is the anointing with chrism and/or the imposition of hands, which many churches call confirmation. For still others it is all three, as they see the Spirit operative throughout the rite. All agree that Christian baptism is in water and the Holy Spirit (B14).

Anglicans would want to uphold the gift of the Spirit in baptism as an essential part of the faith of the Church through the ages. They would not necessarily want to make the distinction described in the commentary on §14 between baptism, described as conforming to Christ crucified, buried and risen, and chrismation as the reception of the gift of the pentecostal Spirit. Nevertheless anointing is frequently associated with the Spirit in biblical thought. It appears as part of the ceremony of appointment for kings and priests. As such some feel it is therefore an appropriate sign at baptism and/or confirmation. In the Church of England chrismation has been continued in coronation rites and we note is restored as an optional practice in the initiation rite of the Alternative Service Book.

47. Concerning the relation between baptism and confirmation in the Church of England, the 1966 report of the Liturgical Commission, *Baptism and Confirmation*, described three views. Although we quote these views we do not consider that the three are mutually exclusive.

> The first view is: Baptism in water is the sacramental means by which the Spirit is given to Christians. Confirmation is the occasion in which Christians renew the acts of repentance and faith which were made in their name, or which they themselves made, at their baptism. They do this in the presence of the bishop who solemnly blesses them; and this blessing may be regarded as an occasion of grace.

> The second view is: Baptism in water is the sacramental means by which the Spirit is given to Christians. Confirmation is a second sacramental act, consisting of prayer for the coming of the Spirit with the laying on of hands upon those upon whom the Spirit is asked to come. It effects a further work of the Spirit, to assist them against temptation.

> The third view is: Baptism in water and prayer with the laying on of hands together constitute the sacramental means by which the Spirit is given to Christians. If the two sacramental acts are distinguished in thought or separated in practice, the Spirit is thought to come in baptism

to effect cleansing from sin and the new birth and in confirmation to complete the divine indwelling. (*Baptism and Confirmation*, The Ely Report, 1966).

When confirmation is understood to signify the pentecostal completion of initiation, then the separation of the two rites (baptism and confirmation), or of the two parts of a single rite, cannot be carried far without at least appearing to divorce the gift of the Spirit from baptism in water in the name of the Trinity; a loss of coherence is almost inevitable. Clearly in the Gospel narrative of the Lord's baptism in Jordan, the anointing of the Spirit is linked quite immediately with the washing in water and Anglicans would want to uphold this and to affirm what the Lima Text itself says:

> God bestows upon all baptized persons the anointing and the promise of the Holy Spirit, marks them with a seal and implants in their hearts the first instalment of their inheritance as sons and daughters of God (B5).

48. However, each of the variant viewpoints illustrated above testifies to the importance of spiritual development, and confirmation itself ministers to the process of growth in grace. Confirmation gives firm testimony to the reciprocal relationship of divine grace and God-given faith in the corporate life of the Church; and, on the occasion of its ministering, to the believer's incorporation within it as part of the faithful Church, whose faith at that moment he or she affirms for himself or herself. Furthermore, the bishop's presence, and the laying on of hands, stress the universal nature of that ongoing corporate life of the Church, whose faith the candidate affirms that he or she shares, and the Church asks God to confirm in him/her the grace given at baptism as well as its present fruition. The laying on of hands by the bishop with prayer (and/or chrismation) effectively signifies that the candidate is a member not merely of a local congregation, nor indeed of one particular denomination or ecclesial body, but of a universal body in which the bishop is the visible sign of continuity.

49. Thus confirmation may be regarded as marking a stage in the process of growth in the Christian family. The "act of faith" is a response of the individual to the approach of God, through the mediation of other Christians in the Church, marking growth within the Christian family. The Christian moves into conscious and personally appropriated faith. Baptism, followed after some years by confirmation is, we believe, a feasible approach to sacramental initiation. Seen in this light, confirmation is not elevated to the dignity of being utterly necessary for salvation, but is a true means of grace and among God's gifts to his people, guiding them to rely not on their individual consciousness and feelings but on the faithfulness of God himself.

50. On this view, baptism itself can be thought the appropriate way into eucharistic sharing, though on grounds of expediency some may wish to defer regular participation in the eucharist until after confirmation. We would wish to see the relation between baptism and admission to the eucharist form part

of the ecumenical agreement on baptism, as indeed it appears to do in the eucharist text (E2).

51. The discussion of the relation between baptism, confirmation and first communion has continued within the Church of England with the publication of the Ely Report (1974) and the recent experimental admission of young people to communion before confirmation. At present these matters are being discussed by a working party on Christian Initiation set up by the Board of Education.

52. These discussions and experiments have widened the area of debate in the Church of England and clearly the exact relation between baptism, chrismation, confirmation and first communion is not yet evident. There is confusion in both belief and practice in the Church of England about which the Lima Text gives little guidance. However, the theological principles of the text together with the insistence on the process of initiation will, we believe, enable us in time to understand what is legitimate difference in practice within a united Church. We look forward to the help of the Faith and Order Commission in furthering ecumenical discussion in this area.

(ix) BAPTISM AND THE JUSTIFYING GRACE OF SALVATION

53. Baptism is traditionally seen as the sacrament of regeneration. This is fully recognised by the Lima Text and is in accord with Anglican tradition. The Lima Text also recognises the connection between baptism and justification (B4). This also is in accord with classical Anglican writers who, following Augustine, speak of baptism as "the sacrament of justification". This makes the important point that the justification of the believer is inseparable in reality from his or her sacramental incorporation into the fellowship of the Church. (We note that ARCIC II is discussing the relationship between the doctrines of justification and the nature of the Church).

(x) THE ETHICAL IMPLICATIONS OF BAPTISM

54. Finally, as we noted earlier, the Lima Text points to the ethical implications of baptism in a number of places. Baptism is said to be "the sign of new life" and a "sign of the Kingdom of God"; those baptised "are given as part of their baptismal experience a new ethical orientation under the guidance of the Holy Spirit" and finally, it motivates "Christians to strive for the realization of the will of God in all realms of life". Nevertheless, there might have been more emphasis on baptism, not only as the sign of a new reality and a new identity, but as the call to put into practice the values of the new age. Forgiveness, cleansing, sanctification, unity and hope — all sealed to the believer in baptism — are means, whose end is that "we too might walk in newness of life" (Rom. 6:4). Baptism is not only incorporation into the death and resurrection of Christ but also into his life of obedience to the

Father. The freedom made possible by Jesus' one sacrifice on the cross and his victory over death can become a living reality only in a life of sacrificial service in the struggle to overcome social circumstances that deny life. The response of faith to the message of Christ which issues in baptism is inseparable from a life of "good works". The life of obedience implied in following Christ and, where necessary, "bearing abuse for him" (Heb. 13:13) is a constituent part of faith and demonstrates the reality of grace. We may not ignore the fact that in certain contexts being signed with the sign of the cross in baptism will probably mean "completing what is lacking in Christ's afflictions . . ." (Col. 1:24). Identification with Christ involves ostracism, character assassination, loss of civil rights, harassment, physical violation, psychological coercion and even death in many parts of the world. This is the daily reality of incorporation into the crucified and risen Lord, as described by Paul in 2 Corinthians. "While we live we are always being given up to death for Jesus' sake, so that the life of Jesus may be manifested in our mortal flesh" (2 Cor. 4:11). Further, it is in this life of obedience that Christians are sent out in mission to the world; there is a missiological dimension to baptism. Although we should like a stronger emphasis on this to have been evident in the text on baptism, we welcome the importance it is given in the eucharistic text (cf. E19, 20, 21). We recognize also the problem raised when Christians agree on baptismal unity but disagree over ethical questions such as apartheid which is thought by some to be a decisive matter affecting the integrity of churches (cf. *God's Reign and Our Unity*, p. 28, para. 44).

(xi) CONCLUDING REFLECTIONS ON THE BAPTISM SECTION

55. We believe that the baptism section of the Lima Text, firmly based as it is in Scripture, does witness to the faith of the Church through the ages. We welcome in particular the balance between God's gift and our response which lies behind the text, the insistence on the priority of God's initiative, the emphasis upon baptism as a decisive beginning in a process, and the place and role of the community of faith. The text witnesses to a convergence in doctrinal understanding which we believe can support a diversity of baptismal practice. Building upon the text we believe it may be possible to deepen our understanding of the different stages in the initiation process. We look forward in particular to developing the ecclesiological implications of the text, to further work on baptism and justification and to an emerging picture of what diversity in practice can be supported by agreement in the essentials of faith. We recognise that baptism in the name of the Holy Trinity is at one and the same time a sign of our God-given unity and a challenge to overcome those divisions which continue to call in question that baptismal unity. We need to explore the implications of the mutual recognition of baptism (as is already expressed in England by the common baptismal certificate) for the reconciliation of churches, their members and their ministries.

B. Eucharist

(i) THE BIBLICAL BASIS FOR THE EUCHARIST

56. The three-part text treats of the institution, meaning and celebration of the eucharist. The first section firmly anchors the eucharist in the biblical record recalling the meals which Jesus shared with his disciples and the Lord's command to continue to eat and drink in remembrance of him. We welcome this biblical basis and with it the opening emphasis upon the eucharist as the gift of God.

57. A principal source of strength in the text is the central and longest section which sets forth the meaning of the eucharist in relation to the doctrines of the Trinity (as thanksgiving to the Father, as memorial of Christ, and as invocation of the Spirit), of the Church and of eschatology. This particular structure provides a welcome balance and harmony to eucharistic theology. In commenting upon the text this balance has to be kept in mind so that one aspect is not considered in isolation from the others, thus distorting the balance which the text itself is careful to keep. In this respect *The Final Report of ARCIC*, which deals explicitly only with issues of conflict between Roman Catholics and Anglicans, may need the fuller treatment which the Lima Text provides in order to provide a comprehensive statement of eucharistic faith.

(ii) EUCHARIST AND WORD

58. The text asserts that the eucharist "always includes both word and sacrament" (E3). Anglicans will welcome the emphasis upon the proclamation of the word in the eucharist. The reading of the Scriptures and preaching are part of this proclamation. Indeed, the entire action of the eucharist also proclaims the Word of God. As the Lima Text itself says: "Since the *anamnesis* of Christ is the very content of the preached Word as it is of the eucharistic meal, each reinforces the other" (E12).

59. The eucharist is, as the text rightly upholds, the central act of the Church's worship and ought therefore to be celebrated weekly on the Lord's Day (E31). Anglicans, in whose life the eucharist has not always played this central role, are in a position to testify to the enrichment which has resulted from the renewal of eucharistic life.

(iii) EUCHARIST AND SACRIFICE

60. In line with a prominent New Testament theme the text rightly describes the eucharist as the "great sacrifice of praise" (E4). The "spiritual sacrifice" in Israel's tradition gradually replaced the material sacrifices of the Temple and the Psalms are full of the idea of sacrifices of praise and thanksgiving. The Christian sacrifice of praise is made possible "only through Christ, with him and in him" (E4). In this benediction the Church responds in thankfulness for all God has done in creation and redemption, all God continues to do and will do in bringing the Kingdom to fulfilment.

61. We believe that the eucharist is, as the text says, "the living and effective sign of his sacrifice, accomplished once for all on the cross and still operative on behalf of all humankind" (E5). The Lima Text could hardly stress more emphatically that the sacrifice of Christ was once for all; "These events are unique and can neither be repeated nor prolonged" (E8). And yet, at the same time, the text underlines the fact that the once for all sacrifice of Christ is made present and effectual in the whole eucharistic celebration. The language is less emphatic than the *Final Report of ARCIC* but, like ARCIC, Lima leans upon the biblical concept of *anamnesis*. "The biblical idea of memorial as applied to the eucharist refers to this present efficacy of God's work when it is celebrated by God's people in a liturgy" (E5). What is remembered in the eucharist, that once for all event, is not repeated and yet the recalling of that event within the liturgy is the Church's effective proclamation of God's mighty act and promise.

62. In §§5–13 which deal with the memorial of Christ, both present communion with Christ and the anticipation of enjoyment of his promises are emphasised, and are explicitly related to the themes of thanksgiving and intercession. Both are embodied in the affirmation of the Church's union with Christ, the great High Priest. It is his intercession into which the eucharist enters, and upon which all Christian prayer relies. Thus "in the eucharist, Christ empowers us to live with him, to suffer with him and to pray through him as justified sinners, joyfully and freely fulfilling his will" (E9). By this sacrifice of thanksgiving the Church prays that, on the ground of the merits and death of Christ, not only the congregation present but the whole Church may receive remission of sins and all other benefits of his passion.

63. We believe that the use of the biblical concept of *anamnesis* here, as in other recent ecumenical texts, is useful. This concept, found in the Old Testament, important in the Passover celebration at the time of Christ and deepened and modified by Jesus in the Last Supper, has the merit of taking us back together to our biblical roots. The virtue of the language is that it shows that more than a simple recalling to mind of a past event is meant when in the sacrament of the eucharist the sacrifice of Calvary is recalled.

64. However, *anamnesis* on its own cannot take all the weight in healing past division on the eucharist and sacrifice. Indeed some discussions of *anamnesis* appear to suggest either that Calvary is repeated, or that we ourselves in the act of remembering make effective those benefits of Christ's sacrifice. Here we wish to draw attention to the elucidation offered by ARCIC of its own use of the term *anamnesis*. "The Commission believes that the traditional understanding of sacramental reality, in which the once for all event of salvation becomes effective in the present through the action of the Holy Spirit, is well expressed by the word '*anamnesis*'." (The *Final Report*, Elucidation, p. 19, para 5). The christological and pneumatological settings of eucharistic theology need careful correlation; and sections B and C of the Lima Text need to be read together.

65. Further, what is recollected in the eucharist, through the power of the Spirit, is not only the sacrifice of Calvary but the total Christ-event from the creation by the Logos to the consummation of the Kingdom. It is the recalling of the whole story in the eucharist that gives to the Church its Christian identity. We welcome the stress found in the text that the eucharist unites the past, present and future of God's act of salvation. This action brings into the present the once for all offering of Christ on Calvary and is also an anticipatory realization of the future fulfilment of the Kingdom.

66. We therefore welcome the use of the concept of *anamnesis* to bring together two hitherto opposing views, allowing us to use confidently the language of sacrifice in a context of the recital of all the mighty acts of God in Christ while relying on the power of the Holy Spirit to make efficacious the sacrifice offered once and for all on the cross. We believe the Commission is right on the basis of this to present the challenge it does and to ask whether "in the light of the biblical conception of memorial, all churches might want to review the old controversies about "sacrifice" and deepen their understanding of the reasons why other traditions than their own have either used or rejected this term" (Commentary, E8).

67. We would add to this discussion of the eucharist and sacrifice the further reflection that the biblical notion of sacrifice is exceedingly wide. It developed in a number of directions during the course of the Old Testament period. In a footnote to the *Final Report of ARCIC* on the eucharist this variety of meanings is referred to. "For the Hebrew sacrifice was a traditional means of communication with God. The Passover, for example, was a communal meal; the Day of Atonement was expiatory; and the covenant established communion between God and man" (the *Final Report*, E5). There is thus no single biblical view of sacrifice and the New Testament writers use the concept in different ways. So Paul, in Romans 3, talks of "expiation" and the effects of Christ's death as comparable to expiatory sacrifice; Hebrews 13 points rather to the Day of Atonement, likening the sacrifice of Christ to the sacrificial animal rather than the scapegoat; the Gospel of John uses the idea of the Passover sacrifice to elucidate the death of Christ on the cross. As the Lima Text does not draw out these various views of sacrifice it is never clear whether every view can equally appropriately be used to reflect on the sacrifice of Christ when it is called to mind in the eucharist. We would want to hold that a breadth of meaning is indeed possible and that it is important that the benefits of Christ's death are comparable to and far surpass the benefits of the whole of the Old Testament sacrificial system. The commentary observes that:

> It is in the light of the significance of the eucharist as intercession that references to the eucharist in Catholic theology as "propitiatory sacrifice" may be understood. The understanding is that there is only one expiation,

that of the unique sacrifice of the cross, made actual in the eucharist and presented before the Father in the intercession of Christ and of the Church for all humanity (Commentary, E8).

It is clear that further moves to find eucharistic consensus call for a renewed grasp of the meaning of sacrifice and the richness of the concept as applied to the eucharistic sacrifice.

(iv) EUCHARIST AND THE HOLY SPIRIT

68. The strong emphasis on the power of the Holy Spirit as active in the whole eucharistic celebration witnesses, we believe, to the faith of the Church through the ages. We welcome the way in which the central section of the text develops the pneumatological aspect of the eucharist as invocation of the Spirit. Here the relation of the Spirit to the Father and to the Son, the mutual indwelling of the persons of the Trinity, is never separated from the entire eucharistic action. The invocation of the Holy Spirit is rightly both upon the community and upon the elements of bread and wine. "The whole action of the eucharist has an 'epikletic' character because it depends upon the work of the Holy Spirit" (E16). This is an important balance bringing together the emphases of east and west and avoiding the presence of Christ being concentrated too narrowly upon the moment of consecration. Through the power of the Spirit the risen Lord is present in the whole eucharistic celebration.

(v) EUCHARIST AND PRESENCE

69. It is only within the context of the presence of the crucified and risen Christ in the whole celebration that the relation between the elements of bread and wine and that presence is discussed. Although the text talks of "the real presence of Christ" it never states any view of the unique mode of that presence in the eucharistic species. We note thankfully the very carefully balanced sentence linking together the presence of Christ and the faith of the individual. "While Christ's real presence in the eucharist does not depend on the faith of the individual, all agree that to discern the body and blood of Christ, faith is required" (E13). Here two hitherto opposing views are delicately held together in what we recognize as the faith of the Church through the ages.

70. We welcome also the very careful wording of §15. "It is in virtue of the living word of Christ and by the power of the Holy Spirit that the bread and wine become the sacramental signs of Christ's body and blood. They remain so for the purpose of communion" (E15). The text rightly does not demand any single theory of change in the elements of bread and wine. The commentary points to the existence of various views ranging from those who affirm the presence without attempting to explain it through to others who "have developed an explanation of the real presence which, though not claiming to exhaust the significance of the mystery, seeks to protect it from

damaging interpretations" (Commentary, E15). As Anglicans we are glad that, as in our liturgical texts, no one theory of change is set forward in the Lima Text: bread is broken, wine poured out, in representation of the Last Supper and we receive them not as bread and wine but as the body and blood of Christ.

71. It is at this point that the Final Report of ARCIC appears to go beyond this convergence of the Lima Text with its much stronger statement "Communion with Christ in the eucharist presupposes his true presence, effectually signified by the bread and wine which, in this mystery, become his body and blood" (Final Report, E 6). However, in the light of the Elucidation with its insistence upon Christ's presence in the elements never being divided from the encounter in the whole eucharistic celebration nor from the action of the Holy Spirit, the two texts may be seen not to be inconsistent. "What is here affirmed is a sacramental presence in which God uses realities of this world to convey the realities of the new creation: bread of this life becomes the bread of eternal life" (the *Final Report*, Elucidation, p. 21, para. 6). It would seem sufficient and faithful to the belief of the Church through the ages to uphold the real presence of Christ in the eucharist and his body and blood truly received in the bread and wine without demanding further agreement on the mode of that presence in the elements.

(vi) RESERVATION

72. What is believed about the relationship of the presence of Christ in the eucharistic elements finds its outward expression in the handling of the consecrated bread and wine, for instance in reservation (cf. para. 190). Here we acknowledge that differences exist within the Church of England as well as between the churches. We have already drawn attention to the very carefully worded §15. "It is in virtue of the living word of Christ and by the power of the Holy Spirit that the bread and wine become the sacramental signs of Christ's body and blood. They remain so for the purpose of communion" (E15).

73. Taking this up in §32, the text points to the diversity of practice that exists amongst the churches, as indeed within the Church of England. Some churches, stressing that Christ's presence does not depend on our subjective feelings but is linked to the objective act of his Church in obedience to his command, reserve the elements with the primary intention of distribution to the sick while others consume the elements in the act of communion. Reservation it seems is acceptable because it is seen as the extension of the eucharist itself. The text upholds a legitimate diversity of practice and piety pointing to the need to respect the practices of others. It recommends the practice of consuming any of the eucharistic elements not required for the purpose of communion — a practice which has enabled Anglicans of diverse views to maintain their unity.

(vii) EUCHARIST AND THE KINGDOM

74. A particularly fine example of the advantage of the five aspects of the central section of the eucharist text with its Trinitarian, ecclesiological and eschatological sections is seen in the constant echo of the incorporation of the world into the eucharistic action; from the standpoint of creation (E3, 4), redemption (E8) and mission (E17, 20, 21). The eucharist is the feast where the Church may recognize the signs of renewal already at work in the world, where, united with Christ in a special way, it prays for the world. The eucharist is the centre from which Christians go out renewed by the power of the Spirit to act as servants of reconciliation in a broken and divided world. This concern for the world is not an optional extra in our agreement on the eucharist but rightly belongs as an integral part of our common belief about the eucharist. The *anamnesis* of Christ which lies at the heart of the eucharist entails a new ethical stance for all who participate. The finality of Christ's mission in the reconciliation of all things determines the life and conduct of the Church and of the individual believer. "The eucharist is essentially the sacrament of the gift which God makes to us in Christ through the power of the Holy Spirit" (E2). As "the memorial of the crucified and risen Christ" (E5), "the eucharist opens up the vision of the divine rule which has been promised as the final renewal of creation, and is a foretaste of it" (E22). It is the celebration of those who, "fully identified with the death of Christ, . . . are buried with him and are raised here and now to a new life in the power of the resurrection of Jesus Christ" (B3). Thus the ethical implications which follow from baptism (B10) are equally relevant in considering the eucharist. While we wait in hope for the manifestation of God's new creation, we are also motivated to strive for the realization of the will of God in all aspects of life. This is a matter of imperatives which are entailed in the celebration of baptism and the eucharist and not merely a question of moral demands which follow from them. "For the Christian, therefore, the longing for the transformation of the world is inseparable from the lordship of Christ. The responsibility of Christians in the renewal of the world is simply another form of the radical claim engraved in them by baptism and renewed by the eucharist 'to live for God, in Jesus Christ' (Romans 6:10–11) so to act that God's plan for the world may be accomplished, that the event of the Cross and the Resurrection may shine in all its radiance" (J. M. Tillard, "The Eucharist, Gift of God" in *Ecumenical Perspectives on Baptism, Eucharist and Ministry*, ed. M. Thurian, Geneva, 1983, p. 113).

75. We welcome therefore the important statement: "All kinds of injustice, racism, separation and lack of freedom are radically challenged when we share in the body and blood of Christ. Through the eucharist the all-renewing grace of God penetrates and restores human personality and dignity. The eucharist involves the believer in the central event of the world's history. As participants in the eucharist, therefore, we prove inconsistent if

we are not actively participating in this ongoing restoration of the world's situation and the human condition. The eucharist shows us that our behaviour is inconsistent in the face of the reconciling presence of God in human history: we are placed under continual judgement by the persistence of unjust relationships of all kinds of our society, the manifold divisions on account of human pride, material interest and power politics and, above all, the obstinacy of unjustifiable confessional oppositions within the body of Christ" (E20). The text thus identifies various threats to the integrity of the eucharistic fellowship. Among these attention is correctly drawn to eucharistic division as subverting the essential sign character of the Church to the world and therefore making less effective the Church's witness and evangelism (cf. *God's Reign and Our Unity*, para. 32).

76. Integrity demands penitence for "inconsistent" behaviour before approaching the eucharist, and as a consequence of it renewed commitment to a world in process of transformation. In neither case is this a matter of adding to or making more perfect the self-offering of Jesus Christ, but of allowing this self-offering to be perfected in us. Without this our supposed participation in the new creation, defined as "a universal communion in the body of Christ, a kingdom of justice, love and peace in the Holy Spirit" (E4), is a mockery.

77. As the eucharist is itself a celebration of forgiveness it is important to avoid giving the impression that perfection is already required of worshippers. One aspect of the text which we should like to see strengthened is therefore what is said about the eucharist and the forgiveness of sins. In the eucharist we ask for the forgiveness of our sins and of the sin of the whole world. This theme is present but does not receive the emphasis it deserves in ecumenical agreement.

(ix) EUCHARIST AND THE CHURCH

78. Finally, as in the baptism section, so also in the eucharist section, the question of the relation of the eucharist to the nature of the Church is never far from the surface. It remains for future work to build upon the emerging ecclesiology. As each baptised Christian partakes in the eucharistic celebration, the central act of the Church's life, so the Body of Christ is strengthened and given new life. Further, it is in the eucharistic celebration, with the *anamnesis* of the Christ event, that the identity of the Christian community is formed. In the eucharist we are united with one another and with all the company of heaven. And, as the sacrament is shared with the sick and imprisoned, they are one with the worshipping community. We welcome the emphasis that "eucharistic celebrations have always to do with the whole Church, and the whole Church is involved in each local eucharistic celebration" (E19). Further the minister who presides, in the name of Christ, bears witness to the fact that each particular local community is related to other local communities in the one universal Church. In all of this we see the

way in which baptism, eucharist and ministry are integrally bound together within the mystery of the one Church. We recognise the implications of this for the communion of the churches. If each local community is part of the wider Church it cannot live its life disregarding the interests and concerns of other local churches. Consequently, on the basis of the converging theological agreement we must work harder for the unity of Christians in one eucharistic fellowship.

(x) CONCLUDING REFLECTIONS ON THE EUCHARIST SECTION

79. As with the baptism section of the Lima Text we have no hesitation in saying of this statement that in it Anglicans can recognize the faith of the Church through the ages. We welcome in particular the carefully balanced Trinitarian aspect of the text, the use of *anamnesis* held closely together with an understanding of the work of the Holy Spirit, the emphasis upon the real presence of Christ in the eucharist linked with the need of faith to discern that presence, the stress on prayer and intercession, the relation of the eucharist to the life of the world and the insistence on the centrality of the eucharist in the life of the Church. We acknowledge the remarkable degree of convergence in understanding registered in the text which goes further towards consensus than the sections on baptism and ministry. We believe the churches may be drawn even closer together as they develop a common understanding of the eucharist and sacrifice and will be forced to ask what consequences this theological agreement must have for eucharistic fellowship.

80. Further, emerging from this agreement we begin to see, as with the baptism text, what differences of practice may be carried by an underlying agreement in the faith. We look forward within an understanding of the doctrine of the Church to developing the relation between baptism and eucharistic sharing, the relation of the celebrant to the eucharist and the relation of the local eucharistic community to the whole Church. This inter-relationship concerns the eucharist particularly because the eucharist is where faith, life and worship meet in the context of the Christian community.

C. Ministry

(i) GENERAL REFLECTIONS

81. The subject of the ministry divides the churches more strongly than baptism and eucharist and consequently the ministry section of the text is longer and more discursive. The result is that the Faith and Order Commission thought it necessary to describe differing positions and register less agreement. Nevertheless the text does mark significant achievements and suggests to us that further agreement will be possible building on the convergences already registered in the text. We have been struck in particular by the close correspondence between the direction of the Lima Text and the 1938 *Doctrine Commission Report*, the *Ordinal* of the Anglican–Methodist

scheme, as well as FOAG's most recent statement on ministry, *The Theology of Ordination*, 1976 (*GS 281*). We hope that as members of the General Synod study the ministry section of the Lima Text and the *Final Report of ARCIC* they will refer in particular to *GS 281*.

(ii) THE CALLING OF THE WHOLE PEOPLE OF GOD

82. The ministry statement begins with the calling of all humanity to be God's people and moves to the bringing into being of the Church, that uniting into a single body by the Holy Spirit of all who follow Jesus Christ. That same Spirit keeps and guides the Church, which prefigures the Kingdom, providing gifts for building up the Church for service to the world. We welcome this setting of the statement on ministry for it recognises, as did *GS 281*, that the theology of ministry "requires the context of a theology of the Church, which in turn requires a theology of creation and redemption" (*GS 281, The Theology of Ordination*, para. 1).

83. The choice of the ecclesiological model of "the people of God" is only one of many models that might have been selected and, as the text develops, other models are rightly set beside it. No one model is exhaustive and each emphasizes different aspects of the one reality of the Church. The image of "the people of God" performs a similar function in the Lima Text to that of *Koinonia*, "fellowship", in the introduction of the *Final Report of ARCIC*.

84. Within the context of the people of God two hitherto apparently contrasting views of the ordained ministry are held together. In one model this ministry is seen as derived from the common priesthood of all believers, a delegation to the few of the functions which belong to the whole community of the faithful, while in the other model this ministry is seen as derived directly from the priesthood of Christ and itself forming a priesthood constitutive for the life of the Church. The Lima Text holds the two models together within the general concept of the calling of the whole people of God. The "people of God" has a "fundamental dependence" on Jesus Christ and the ordained ministry has been from the first moment of the Church's existence constitutive for its life and witness (M8). Both ordained ministry and community depend upon Christ and on each other in him. The Lima Text is concerned that there should be no over-simple distinction between ministry "in its broadest sense" (M7b), and the specifically ordained ministry, but equally no over-simple equation of the two. The Church is in its very nature built up by diverse and complementary gifts (M5). This echoes throughout the text: "The Church as the body of Christ and the eschatological people of God is constituted by the Holy Spirit through a diversity of gifts or ministries" (M23). The ordained ministry must be understood within the context of all the ministries. It must serve and focus them.

85. Throughout the text great emphasis is put on the interrelation of the ministry of the whole people of God and the ordained ministry: "All members of the believing community, ordained and lay, are

interrelated . . . Ordained ministers can fulfil their calling only in and for the community" (M12). Any view of a hierarchy separate from the laity is excluded: "the authority of the ordained ministry is not to be understood as the possession of the ordained person but as a gift for the continuing edification of the body in and for which the minister has been ordained" (M15). The power to teach and rule, given by Christ to the ordained ministry, is not to be understood in such a way that the Church is regarded as passively receptive. The ministry cannot be exercised without "the recognition and support and the encouragement of the whole community" (M12). Thus, the teaching of the ordained ministry is established as that of the whole community, not by reference to their own status or credentials, but by its reception in the life and witness of the community. The condition under which their authority is exercised is that it must conform to the model of Christ's own ministry for service and self-giving (M16). This excludes any notion that ministers can act as autocratic or impersonal functionaries.

86. We welcome this opening of the ministry section with its holding together of the two models of ministry within the concept of the ministry of the whole people of God. In this the Lima Text is very close indeed to the opening section of the 1938 *Doctrine Report* with its insistence that "the fundamental Christian ministry is the Ministry of Christ" . . . that "the Church, as the Body of Christ, sharing His life, has a ministerial function derived from that of Christ", and that "the particular function of the official Ministry can only be rightly understood as seen against the background of this universal ministry" (*Doctrine Commission Report*, 1938, p. 114).

(iii) CONTINUITY AND ORDER

87. The introductory section on the ministry of the whole people of God ends with the reflection that an answer needs to be found to the question: "How, according to the will of God and under the guidance of the Holy Spirit, is the life of the Church to be understood and ordered, so that the Gospel may be spread and the community may be built up in love?" (M6). The text contains the basis for the churches to discover a common answer to this.

(a) The New Testament

88. The text emphasises that the New Testament is clear about the need for set-apart persons for ministry. Jesus chose Twelve, representing the New Israel, and commissioned them to preach the word, to feed the flock, to care for them in both doctrine and discipline, etc. . . . These same Twelve, after the resurrection, are among the leaders of the community. These apostles prefigure the Church as a whole and also prefigure those set apart for ministry. But their role as witnesses to the resurrection is unique and marks a difference between them and those ordained ministers "whose ministries are founded on theirs" (M10).

89. Although the basic reality of a set-apart ministry was there from the beginning the text goes on to make quite clear that the question of the ordering of the historic ministry cannot be determined by a purely historical enquiry. Appeal to the text of the New Testament or to the history of the apostolic age has failed to establish a form of ministry which corresponds precisely to that of any of the modern churches.

90. The question then becomes what is the nature of the link, if any, between what is to be found in the New Testament, and the ministry as it had developed by the time of the Council of Nicaea, and to what extent should this early history be normative for the Church through the ages? The Lima Text appears to lay much stress on the idea that there has been a development from this early variety, and that the development has embodied basic characteristics of the Christian community. "As the Holy Spirit continued to lead the Church in life, worship and mission, certain elements from this early variety were further developed and became settled into a more universal pattern of ministry" (M19). In saying this the Lima Text would command the support of most Anglicans and is in line with *GS 281*. Indeed the Church of England has consistently ascribed a high authority to the primitive Church which settled the Canon of Scripture, gave us the ecumenical Creeds, and articulated the ministry and sacraments on the basis of Scripture. This authority is not exempt from scrutiny and needs to be appropriated in every age. The Lima Text and the *Final Report* may be said to provide a twentieth century endorsement of that authority and the main lines of that early clarification. How specific one may then be is a legitimate question, and some Anglicans would wish to make stronger claims than the Lima Text is able to make about the transmission of apostolic authority in the New Testament period.

(b) The threefold order of ministry

91. The Lima Text appears to be saying that the development of the threefold order of ministry was, under the guidance of the Holy Spirit, the way of exemplifying and building up the basic characteristics of the Church. The text acknowledges the many changes the threefold ministry has undergone throughout history and hesitates to commit itself to the proposition that the threefold historic ministry has become obligatory for all. It speaks of "points of crisis in the history of the Church" when "the continuing functions of ministry were in some places and communities distributed according to structures other than the predominant threefold pattern" (M19); it insists that "other forms of the ordained ministry have been blessed with the gifts of the Holy Spirit" (M22) and that "there have been times when the truth of the Gospel could only be preserved through prophetic and charismatic leaders" (M33). The reference to "points of crisis" no doubt includes the Reformation which, whatever its positive results, shattered the

unity of the Church in the West and introduced the contrast between the traditional structure of the ministry and the structures which developed from the Reformation, which are among the principal ecumenical problems of today. The Lima Text appears to be saying that the historic threefold ministry is not essential but is the norm, departure from which has to be justified by an emergency situation in which the existing ministry actually destroys some essential characteristics of the Church rather than builds them up. This leaning in the direction of a threefold order of ministry in the Lima Text is a significant shift from the earlier *Accra Text* (1974).

92. On the basis of this estimate of the threefold order Lima invites a challenge to those who have departed from it to consider whether "the threefold order of bishop, presbyter and deacon may serve today as an expression of the unity we seek and also as a means for achieving it" (M22). But the challenge goes also to those churches, like our own, which have retained the threefold order "to ask how its potential can be fully developed for the most effective witness of the Church in this world" (M25). It is important that the threefold order should increasingly be seen as adaptable in use to a wide variety of historical and cultural contexts. This estimate of the threefold order as not prescribed by Holy Scripture and yet desirable for unity is a position members of the Church of England will welcome. It is in line with the reflections of the Doctrine Commission of 1938.

93. But, for some, the question of the desirability of a threefold order of ministry is still not determined simply by reference to the fact that it emerged in the very early years of the Church's life and has continued to be accepted by a very large number of Christians. The Lima Text adds a further argument to this: that the threefold ministry of bishops, presbyters and deacons has a special role in effecting unity out of diversity, a diversity which is moreover both legitimate and life-giving (M22–23). This is perhaps Lima's most important teaching on the ordained ministry. The threefold ministry is presented as exercising a unitive function in a number of different ways.

(a) It brings together into unity the many kinds of ministry which exist in the Church. The text is committed to the view that "the community which lives in the power of the Spirit will be characterised by a variety of charisms" (M32). The ordained ministry is included among these but has a special function towards them. It is specially charged with fostering the gifts of all the faithful; it must not seek to hinder or repress them. But it also has a regulative role: it must bring differing gifts into complementarity and exercise oversight to see that all is done within the apostolic tradition. The threefold ministry itself exhibits this character of unity-in-diversity. Bishops, presbyters and deacons have different but complementary functions but find unity under their bishop and in collegiality with each other.

(b) It gives unity to the diversity that exists in any local community. The text sees the threefold ministry as best serving the personal, collegial and communal aspects of church order, with the bishop providing a "focus of unity" for all, ministers and laity alike.

(c) Further the threefold order gives the local churches in all their diversity of situation and culture a relationship to the wider universal Church. In §29 the text reveals its basic teaching about episcopacy. The bishop of a local church brings all his people, presbyters, deacons and the whole community into communion with the universal Church: he represents them to a wider community and it to them.

94. In these ways the Lima Text upholds the desirability of a threefold order of ministry, while recognizing that its manner of expression stands evidently in need of reform (M24). The argument moves away from the notion that the threefold order is one amongst many possible patterns to the notion that it is the most obvious candidate for a church visibly united: it may serve both as an expression of unity and the means for achieving it.

95. Anglicans will welcome the direction of the Lima Text as witnessing to the faith of the Church through the ages. At the same time they will be aware of the challenges to their own understanding and use of the threefold order that this gives. Measured by the standards described in the text bishops have not always been "representative pastoral ministers of oversight, continuity and unity" (M29). Indeed the current use of episcopacy by the Church of England, with bishops suffragan outnumbering the diocesans by 64 to 44, is at variance with the theology of the office set out in its own official rite as well as with the arguments it has used to commend episcopacy to other churches. Further, as was recognized in *GS 281*, the Anglican use of the diaconate is open to criticism. In spite of many discussions on the subject in the Church of England there has been no reform or reconstitution of an effective diaconate. The Lima Text points to the need for the sharing of insights on diaconal service. "As the churches move closer together there may be united in this office ministries now existing in a variety of forms and under a variety of names" (M31 commentary). We believe that the Anglican–Reformed dialogue, *God's Reign and Our Unity*, has a significant contribution to make at this point. (*God's Reign and Our Unity*, paras 91–97).

96. We note that although Lima stresses the notion of development from the early New Testament varieties of ministry to the emergence of the threefold order of bishops, priests and deacons, it says nothing about the development of the papacy and does not reflect on whether there is a need for a ministry in the universal Church which provides a "focus for unity" and which could combine the personal, collegial and communal dimensions at that level. Although, we believe, this subject was raised at Lima, it was thought that to prepare a considered statement would involve too great a delay in the publication of the text. We look forward to further work in this area, which will provide a valuable context in which to view the work of the *Final Report of ARCIC* on the papacy.

(c) Apostolicity and Apostolic Succession

97. The idea that the ordained ministry maintains the Church in its essential characteristics is important in allowing the Lima Text to offer an agreed statement on the meaning of apostolicity and apostolic succession. This is not conceived primarily as succession in ordination traceable back to the apostles themselves. The role of the apostles was unique and unrepeatable; their relationship to the ordained ministry is that of type and analogy; they "prefigure both the Church as a whole and the persons within it who are entrusted with the specific authority and responsibility" (M10). The basic succession is in the apostolic tradition. Anglicans will welcome this emphasis on continuity of the apostolic tradition. This continuity in the Lima Text is described as "continuity in the permanent characteristics of the Church of the apostles: witness to the apostolic faith, proclamation and fresh interpretation of the Gospel, celebration of baptism and the eucharist, the transmission of ministerial responsibilities, communion in prayer, love, joy and suffering, service to the sick and the needy, unity among the local churches and sharing the gifts which the Lord has given to each" (M34). To be apostolic is necessarily to share in the great mission to which the Church is called and also to abide in the fellowship of the unity of God's universal Church. Such a succession in a historic community preserving down the ages its distinctive life of faith and love points, we believe, to the faith of the Church through the ages.

98. To this understanding of apostolicity and apostolic succession in life and teaching the Lima Text, in line with its strong emphasis on development, adds that: "under the particular historical circumstances of the growing Church in the early centuries, the succession of bishops became one of the ways, together with the transmission of the Gospel and the life of the community, in which the apostolic tradition of the Church was expressed. This succession was understood as serving, symbolizing and guarding the continuity of the apostolic faith and communion" (M36). In this the Lima Text rightly recognizes the emphasis in the earliest times on the need for continuity, for the orderly transmission of the Gospel and for the need to safeguard the tradition. As the Church sought to give expression to visible unity in faith and life, the ministry was understood as a sign of that unity and continuity. In all of this Lima is again close to the 1938 *Report of the Doctrine Commission*:

> The Church has been called apostolic primarily in that it preserves the essential tradition of the apostolic preaching and teaching, and maintains, as a safeguard of that tradition, a duly appointed order of ministers, who derive their commission in historical succession from the original apostolate. The Church may also be called apostolic as being charged with the mission to bear witness to Christ and to declare His Gospel before the world. By its apostolicity, therefore, the Church of today is linked to the Church of primitive times through an essential identity of doctrine, a

continuity of order, and a fellowship in missionary duty. (*Doctrine in the Church of England: The 1938 Report*, ed. G. W. H. Lampe, 1982, p. 111).

Clearly the Doctrine Commission lays greater emphasis upon an "order of ministers, who derive their commission in historical succession from the original apostolate". In *GS 281* we quoted the work of the French Roman Catholic and Protestant Group of les Dombes with its distinction between the "fullness of the apostolic succession of the whole Church" and the "fullness of the apostolic succession in the ministry". "This succession, in fact, as a ministerial sign, bears witness to the apostolic character of the Church . . . " (*Modern Ecumenical Documents*, pp. 95, 96).

99. Although the Lima Text points to the development of an episcopal order in the early church as one of the ways of expressing apostolic tradition, it is clearly very cautious indeed about it. Paragraph 36, quoted above, is a statement of historical fact: "Under the particular historical circumstances of the growing Church in the early centuries, the succession of bishops became one of the ways, together with the transmission of the Gospel and the life of the community, in which the apostolic tradition of the Church was expressed" (M36). When taken with the reflections in the section on the reconciliation of ministries (M53), the Lima Text is seen to be advocating the acceptance of an episcopal ministry. It is suggested that those churches without episcopal succession, and living in faithful continuity with the apostolic faith and mission, should realize "that the continuity with the Church of the apostles finds profound expression in the successive laying on of hands by bishops and that, though they may not lack the continuity of the apostolic tradition, this sign will strengthen and deepen that continuity. They may need to recover the sign of the episcopal succession" (M53b). Nevertheless it is also clear that episcopal succession does not of itself guarantee continuity. What is important is the implication that both episcopal and non-episcopal churches are lacking unless their faithfulness to the apostolic tradition in life and teaching is linked to a common sign of that faithfulness in a single ministerial succession. We consider that the Lima Text is moving in a significant direction and in line with what Anglicans will understand as the faith of the Church through the ages.

100. We note that although the Lima Text does not contain a systematic treatment of the theology of episcopacy its paragraph on the functions of bishops is an important statement:

> Bishops preach the Word, preside at the sacraments, and administer discipline in such a way as to be representative pastoral ministers of oversight, continuity and unity in the Church. They have pastoral oversight of the area to which they are called. They serve the apostolicity and unity of the Church's teaching, worship and sacramental life. They have responsibility for leadership in the Church's mission. They relate the Christian community in their area to the wider Church, and the universal Church to their community. They, in communion with the presbyters and

deacons and the whole community, are responsible for the orderly transfer of ministerial authority in the Church (M29).

To this can be added other important reflections in the text as, for example, §36 with its emphasis upon the bishop as the one who symbolizes and guards the continuity of apostolic faith and communion. This estimate of episcopacy is very close to that expressed in the *Ordinal* composed in connection with the Anglican–Methodist Scheme of Unity which contains a statement on the duties of a bishop. This statement was accorded the assent of Roman Catholic and Orthodox theologians as well as Anglicans and Methodists and is an explication in more detailed terms of episcopacy:

> A Bishop is called to be a Chief Minister and Chief Pastor and, with other Bishops, to be also a guardian of the faith, the unity, and the discipline which are common to the whole Church, and an overseer of her mission throughout the world. It is his duty to watch over and protect the congregations committed to his charge and therein to teach and to govern after the example of the Apostles of the Lord. He is to lead and guide the Presbyters and Deacons under his care and to be faithful in ordaining and sending new ministers. A Bishop must, therefore, know his people and be known by them; he must proclaim and interpret Christ's Gospel to them: and lead them in the offering of spiritual sacrifice and prayer. He must take care for the due ministering of God's Word and Sacraments; he must also be diligent in confirming the baptised and whenever it shall be required of him, in administering discipline according to God's holy Word (*Anglican–Methodist Ordinal*, pp. 30–31).

These same sentiments lay behind the Covenanting Proposals (*Towards Visible Unity: Proposals for a Covenant*, pp. 18–19). They are also expressed in the Ordinal in the *Alternative Service Book*.

(iv) MINISTRY AND PRIESTHOOD

101. Anglicans will be grateful for the very carefully worded §17 on ministry and priesthood, together with the accompanying commentary. A private member's motion in the General Synod in February 1984 drew attention to the need for members of the Church of England to seek agreement in this area amongst themselves before entering any further union negotiations. In clarifying their position, members of the Church of England will find help from conversations with those of other churches. We believe that both the Lima Text and the *Final Report of ARCIC* help us here. Paragraph 17 distinguishes between the unique priesthood of Jesus Christ, the priesthood of the whole Church and ordained ministers who "are related, as are all Christians, both to the priesthood of Christ, and to the priesthood of the Church". Further, Lima says that ordained ministers "may appropriately be called priests because they fulfil a particular priestly service by strengthening and building up the royal and prophetic priesthood of the faithful through word and sacraments, through their prayers of intercession, and through their pastoral guidance of the community". The commentary adds to this the historical fact that, "in the early Church the terms

'priesthood' and 'priest' came to be used to designate the ordained ministry and ministers as presiding at the eucharist". It continues to say that when the words are used of the ordained ministry they differ in meaning from the sacrificial priesthood of the Old Testament, from the unique redemptive priesthood of Christ and from the corporate priesthood of the people of God. It is worth noting that §17 of *GS 281*, after a short reference to the way in which *hiereus* came to be used of ministers in the early Church says:

> Three elements in the traditional Christian use of the language of priesthood are thus discernible:
> (i)   The unique priesthood of Christ himself.
> (ii) The corporate priesthood of the whole Church.
> (iii) The priesthood of those ordained to the proclamation of the word, the administration of the sacraments and the pastoral care of the faithful.
> While it is true that ministers of word and sacrament are not excluded from the corporate priesthood, and that all Christian priesthood must derive from Christ, it is not possible to equate these three elements nor even to move without great care from speaking of one to speaking of another. While Christian piety has used these elements to enrich each other, it is necessary theologically to keep them distinct (*The Theology of Ordination, GS 281*, para. 17).

102. It should also be noted that although the first two of these elements are to be found in the New Testament, the third is a development of the late second century. We endorse the statement contained in the Preface to the *Anglican–Methodist Ordinal*, which like the Ordinal itself had widespread approval.

> The royal priesthood which the whole Church has received from Christ her Lord, and in which each member of his Body shares, is exercised by the faithful in different ways. The distinctive Ministry is a special form of this participation. It is in this way that the priesthood of bishop and presbyter should be understood.

> The Ministry is thus a divinely appointed organ which acts in relation to the whole Body in the name of Christ and which represents the priestly service of the whole Body in its common worship. Ministers are, as the Methodist Statement on Ordination says, both Christ's ambassadors and the representatives of the whole people of God. (*Anglican–Methodist Unity*, The Ordinal, p. 12)

103. We note that although the *Final Report of ARCIC* treats the subject of the relationship of the ordained minister as priest to the presidency of the eucharist more fully than does the Lima Text it does not contradict what is said in the Lima Text. (Cf. *The Final Report*, Ministry and Ordination, para. 13, p. 35 and Elucidation, para. 2, p. 40). What is certain in the *ARCIC* text and commentary 17 of the Lima Text is that the eucharist is not made a sacrifice because the celebrant is given the title of priest. The argument moves rather in the reverse direction. Further, the content we put into the word priest in relation to the presidency of the eucharist is affected by our

understanding of the eucharist as sacrifice (cf. the discussion of eucharist and sacrifice, para. 60ff and especially the discussion of *anamnesis*). The theological convergence registered in the understanding of the eucharist as sacrifice has implications for an understanding of the priesthood of the ministry.

104. We believe that the Lima statement on the ministry and priesthood is carefully prepared and in accord with the faith of the Church through the ages, and not contrary to the beliefs of the Church of England.

(v) PERSONAL, COLLEGIAL AND COMMUNAL ASPECTS OF ORDAINED MINISTRY

105. We welcome the insistence in §26 on the personal, collegial and communal aspects of ordained ministry but recognise that there are puzzles raised by these paragraphs. The Lima Text makes no attempt to define what it means by the local community in which the personal, collegial and communal aspects of ministry have to be expressed; it does not describe the sort of structures through which the views of the people of God can be expressed and heard; it does not indicate what it means by regional level and the relation of a bishop to that; it does not proceed beyond the regional to the international with the implications that might have for the personal sign at the international level. Clearly it is here that the agenda of the ministry section moves into the agenda of the third part of the Faith and Order Commission's task, the work on common structures of decision-making. The *Final Report of ARCIC* has already demonstrated the importance of this interlocking agenda while the Anglican–Reformed dialogue has a significant contribution on the understanding of the local church (*God's Reign and Our Unity*, para. 111).

106. Closely related to these principles for the exercise of ministry are the reflections on the ordained ministry and authority. Here, as we already noted, the essential connection between the bestowal in ordination of the authority given by Jesus Christ and its exercise in the community is duly recognized. Further, this authority is exercised with the co-operation of the whole community (M15). Presumably this is a statement of intention and not of historical fact. A further important point is made when the text takes the life, death and resurrection of Jesus as the paradigm for the exercise of authority by the ordained within the community and says "authority in the Church can only be authentic as it seeks to conform to this model" (M16). There are challenges here to the exercise of authority in the structure and life of the Church of England and to our attempts to hold together in our structure and life the inter-relatedness of ordained and the community in the exercise of authority. How can we find a better relationship between the ordained and the community in the exercise of authority?

(vi) ORDINATION

107. The Lima Text sets out the meaning of ordination in §39, emphasising that it is in the name of Christ, by the invocation of the Spirit and with the

laying on of hands. The description is similar to that given in the Preface of the *Anglican–Methodist Ordinal*:

> Ordination is a solemn act by which one who is acknowledged to have received God's call is brought into a particular Order of Ministry within the Church. Central to it is the action of the Holy Spirit in bestowing upon the person being ordained that which makes him a minister. The words of the Ordination Prayer indicate what that is in respect of each Order. As Hooker says: "The power and authority delivered with these words is itself charisma, a gracious donation which the Spirit of God doth bestow." Those who voice the prayer are themselves already ministers with authority to ordain, and they accompany it by laying their hands on those who are being ordained. Both Churches present their candidates in the belief that the Holy Spirit will act in response to this prayer. Thus, for both, prayer with the laying on of hands is the outward sign whereby the ordinand receives the gift of the Spirit making him a minister (*Anglican–Methodist Ordinal*, p. 12).

108. We believe that what is set out in §39 is in accord with the faith of the Church through the ages. We note also, and would agree with what is said in the commentary, that it is consistent with what is said about the sign of apostolic succession in the episcopal ministry that it should be the bishop who ordains, but with the participation of the community, expressed in the process of selection as well as formally at the ordination.

109. We welcome the emphasis that ordination is both an act of God through the power of the Holy Spirit and also an act of the community which has called forth the gifts in the individual, acknowledges those gifts, prays for them, and commits itself to be open to those gifts.

110. The ordained are those called by the Holy Spirit, who receive a special gift of the Holy Spirit and whose ministry is for life. Furthermore, in §§41 and 43 the term "sacramental sign" is used of the act of laying on of hands and the act is deemed to be unrepeatable. We note that the text makes no use of the word "character" to describe this ministerial distinctiveness, a phrase which in the past has been the subject of much misunderstanding (cf. the discussion of this in *GS 281*, para. 28).

(vii) LAY CELEBRATION

111. The Lima Text describes the chief task of the ordained as building up the body of Christ. This is done through a ministry of word, sacrament and guidance in worship, mission and caring. Anglicans will welcome the way in which the ministry of word, sacrament and guidance are held together in contrast to the view that places the sole emphasis upon eucharistic celebration. "It is especially in the eucharistic celebration that the ordained ministry is the visible focus of the deep and all embracing communion between Christ and the members of his body" (M14). It is Christ who presides but that presidency is signified and represented, in most churches, by an ordained minister. Here the text is merely descriptive, leaving open the question of lay celebration. There is no agreement on this point in the broad

ecumenical community involved in the preparation of the Lima Text. The accompanying commentary makes the point that very early on in the Church's life it was the ordained minister who presided over the eucharistic celebration, appropriately providing a focus of unity. This was the view supported in *GS 281* which we regard as faithful to the belief and practice of the Church of England:

> Since the eucharist is more than just the rite of a particular community, each celebration involving in principle the whole Church, it seems clearly most fitting that the president should be one who shares in the (potentially) universal ministry . . . it is precisely this potentially universal aspect which is characteristic of the ordained ministry, and therefore it would follow that in the event of a particular community wishing to celebrate the eucharist either it should be sent (permanently or temporarily) someone who has this universal character, or that universal character should be given to one of the community's own leaders by ordination (*GS 281*, para. 55).

(viii) WOMEN AND THE ORDAINED MINISTRY

112. As we have noted, the ministry section works with the primary concept of the ministry of the whole people of God and only within that considers the ministry of the ordained. The text urges that the Church discover the ministry that can be provided by women as well as men. It must also discover "a deeper understanding of the comprehensiveness of ministry which reflects the interdependence of men and women" (M18). We consider that this is an important area for consideration in all the churches. However, on the subject of the admission of women to the ordained ministry the text is much more cautious than the earlier *Accra Text*. The Lima Text notes that an increasing number of churches do ordain women to a full ministry of word and sacrament while others maintain that the tradition of the Church may not be changed. All else is relegated to a carefully balanced commentary describing the positions of those who do ordain women and those who do not (M18, commentary). Ecumenical discussion of practical and theological issues relating to the ordination of women is encouraged. It is suggested that "openness to each other holds the possibility that the Spirit may well speak to one church through the insights of another. Ecumenical consideration should encourage, not restrain, the facing of this question" (M54).

113. It may be considered, as in the *Elucidation* of the ministry statement of *The Final Report of ARCIC*, that on this matter neither text is describing who can or who cannot be ordained, rather what is the nature of the ordained ministry. It is hard to press this argument too far when the text is concerned elsewhere with precisely this question of who can be ordained (M50). The text appears to treat the question as a matter of doctrine rather than church discipline. This is clearly a major question facing the Anglican Communion and Anglicans in their relationships with other churches in England. It will be

important to develop this discussion within the broad ecumenical forum of the World Council of Churches.

114. We note that the Lima Text treats the question as if the ordained ministry were simply one thing. It does not recognize that some churches, for example parts of the Anglican Communion, ordain women to the diaconate but not to the priesthood and episcopate. Further, it does not acknowledge that some churches refrain from ordaining women to the priesthood and episcopate on the ground that parts of the Church do not have the authority to make such a major change without ecumenical agreement.

115. The question of the ordination of women to the priesthood goes beyond the agenda of the Lima Text. It penetrates the other two parts of the interlocking agenda of the Faith and Order Commission. The ministry which Christ entrusted to the Church is not carried out only by individual men and women; the Church has, as the Lima Text recognises, a corporate ministry carried out through councils and synods. If women are excluded from these structures by not being ordained then it might be thought that the wholeness of the Church's ministry is impaired. The agenda of the ministry text passes here into the agenda of the search for common structures of decision making.

(ix) MINISTRY AND THE CHURCH

116. The ministry section of the Lima Text, like the preceding sections on baptism and eucharist, contains important insights about the nature of the Church. The text holds together the christological, pneumatological and eschatological dimensions of the Church. The Church is the place of the foretaste of the Kingdom still to come. As such it is a sign and sacrament of the Kingdom in the world. But there is also the human face of the Church and because of the fall there is always a gap between the ideal and the actual. The chief model used for the Church is the people of God, though side by side with this are set the body of Christ, the eschatological people, the priestly community. Each local church is a manifestation of the universal Church and the ordained ministry is vital for building up and strengthening that community. As we have already noted Lima has not defined the meaning of the local church and the relation of the threefold ministry to it. However, the ministry expresses in the local situation the continuity and unity of the Church through time and across the world. The threefold ministry, and episcopacy in particular, is the appropriate sign of the Church's unity and continuity. Within the Church the ministry of the whole people of God and the ordained ministry depend on Christ and on each other in him. The Church is built up and strengthened by the diverse and complementary gifts of all, ordained and lay. The ministry section points to the need for right structures of the Church, structures that can witness to personal, collegial and communal aspects of ministry. The development of this lay outside the scope of the Lima Text. It remains for the project on common structures of decision-making to develop this further.

(x) CONCLUDING REFLECTIONS ON THE MINISTRY SECTION

117. Although there is less agreement registered in the ministry section of the Lima Text than the other sections we are encouraged by the convergences that are presented and the direction in which the text is pointing. The text does mark a significant stage in the ecumenical dialogue on ministry and we believe that it will be possible to deepen agreement on the basis of this text. We welcome in particular the recognition that the theology of ministry requires as its context the theology of the Church and we look forward to the development of the ecclesiological insights in this text within the Faith and Order project on the expression of the apostolic faith today. We are encouraged by the emphasis throughout on the interrelation of the ministry of the whole people of God and the ordained ministry, the estimate of the threefold order as important both as an expression of unity and a means for achieving it, the agreement on the meaning of apostolicity and the need for a sign of apostolic succession, and the recognition of episcopal ministry as an appropriate way of expressing apostolicity. In all of this we recognize challenges to the Church of England's expression of ministry particularly to its expression of diaconal and episcopal ministry. We welcome also the very carefully worded section on ministry and priesthood and hope that it will form a starting point for the reconciliation of our own internal divisions on this matter. In all of this we believe that Lima Text does witness to the shape of the faith of the Church through the ages. The text contains helpful insights for the deepening of a theology of episcopacy which will be important for the reconciling of ministries. What is said about the personal, collegial and communal aspects of ordained ministry is also crucial and we look forward to the development of these aspects in Faith and Order's project on common structures of decision-making. We ask in particular for a more realistic facing of the question of the ordination of women to the priesthood in order to test further the comment in §54 of the Lima Text that differences on this issue must not be regarded as a substantial hindrance for further efforts towards mutual recognition of ministries.

Question 2: The consequences your church can draw from this text for its relations and dialogues with other churches, particularly with those churches which also recognise the text as an expression of the apostolic faith.

A. General consequences

(i) THE GOAL OF VISIBLE UNITY

118. The preface to the Lima Text re-affirms the goal of "visible unity in one faith and one eucharistic fellowship" (p. viii). In light of the decision of the Church of England not to accept either the Anglican–Methodist Scheme for Unity or the Covenant Proposals we need to find ways of convincing others that we do indeed desire the visible unity of the people of God. We must support attempts to renew the British Council of Churches in such a

way as to encourage the Roman Catholic Church to become a full member of the Council; support the initiative of the British churches in an ecumenical consideration of the nature and purpose of the Church; enter bilateral conversations with those churches where particular divisions persist between us and encourage the growth of local ecumenical initiatives (the proposals contained in the Derby Report GS 642, we consider of special importance in the present stage of relationships in England).

(ii) TOWARDS A COMMON EXPRESSION OF THE APOSTOLIC FAITH

119. In the introduction to our response to the Lima Text (§25) we made reference to the three part agenda of the Faith and Order Commission of the World Council of Churches: the common expression of the apostolic faith; agreement in baptism, eucharist and ministry; the search for common structures of decision making. As well as receiving the convergences of the Lima Text, we hope that the British churches will share in the other two projects of the broader agenda. Already work has begun towards a common expression of the apostolic faith. We recognise that many of the discussions, formal and informal, taking place in Britain might helpfully be developed within the context of that study, (e.g. the work of the Church of England Doctrine Commission and the British Council of Churches work on the doctrine of the Trinity).

120. A necessary basis for the reconciliation of the churches is that the churches should have confidence in one another that they hold the same faith. This does not mean there ought to be a rigid verbal uniformity but rather a unity in the Tradition at the level of faith which allows for a rich and proper diversity in traditions. Already at a formal level this was acknowledged in the process which led to the Covenant Proposals. However, this never communicated itself to the churches at large. While it may be adequate for negotiation of agreement that one party should be asked to produce statements to the satisfaction of another (this is what the Church of England, through its Faith and Order Advisory Group, asked of the other covenanting churches) such a procedure hardly seems that spiritual process which is needed for the reconciliation of churches. Rather, what is required is that the churches should jointly and explicitly confess their common faith for only in this way will the churches convince one another of their readiness to change and be changed in the process of reconciliation. Moreover, confession of faith is inadequately understood if it is thought of merely as assent to statements of belief. Properly understood, the Church's confession of faith is an act of obedience and an expression of praise addressed to God in response to his deeds of mercy and love. Accordingly, attempts to reconcile the churches will be hopelessly inadequate if they are undertaken merely at the level of doctrinal or institutional agreements. They must grow out of prayer and be carried by prayer and be expressive of the life of communities which are growing together.

(iii) ECCLESIOLOGY

121. In our earlier reflections on the three sections of the Lima Text we pointed to the importance of building upon the ecclesiological insights of those texts. Even if ecclesiology is not deemed to be central to Christian faith (a point which many would want to disagree with) it is certainly crucial if the subject in hand is the unity of the churches. Only an explicit common understanding of the nature of the Church and its role as a credible and effective sign, instrument and sacrament of salvation will provide a secure foundation for the reconciliation of churches. It is within such an ecclesiological framework that the doctrinal convergences on baptism, eucharist and ministry will have to be set. We hope that in the new work on the "nature and purpose of the Church" the British churches will find a way of bringing together and deepening the ecclesiological insights of the Lima Text, the other bilateral dialogues, the Anglican–Methodist Scheme for Unity, the Covenant Proposals as well as the experience of local initiatives in growing together. As we said in commenting upon the baptism text, we recognise that baptism in the name of the Holy Trinity is at one and the same time a sign of our God-given unity and a challenge to overcome those divisions which continue to call in question that baptismal unity. We need to explore the implications of the mutual recognition of baptism (as is already expressed in England by the common baptismal certificate) for the reconciliation of churches.

(iv) UNITY AND MISSION

122. Throughout the three sections of the Lima Text, the sacramental life of the Church is related to the vocation to mission. In baptism we are committed to a life of obedience and sent out into the world; in the eucharist we are strengthened and renewed by the power of the Spirit to act as servants of reconciliation in a divided world; and the ordained ministry is given to the Church to build up the ministry of the whole Church to the world. Thus throughout, the Lima Text reminds us that unity and mission belong together. The unity of the Church is not an end in itself but for the service of God and for mission to the world. Further moves towards the unity of the churches in Britain need to be set more firmly within the context of the Church's vocation to mission. Moreover, unless the work of Christ bears fruit in the reconciliation of Christians at an institutional as well as a personal level, the Church cannot function as an effective and credible witness to the gospel of reconciliation in a divided world.

(v) THE LUND PRINCIPLE

123. The degree of theological convergence registered in the Lima Text, while not yet sufficient to support the full visible unity of all the churches, does challenge us to work more faithfully with the Lund principle: the churches should "act together in all matters except those in which deep differences of conviction compel them to act separately". The churches in

Britain need to find ways of recommitting themselves to this principle and acting upon it, in for example, matters relating to interfaith dialogue, questions of justice and peace, human rights, education, mission and evangelism. A greater sharing in life and mission is needed to support the growing theological agreement.

(vi) JOINT STUDY OF THE LIMA TEXT

124. Joint study of the Lima Text should be encouraged wherever possible. A text produced in an ecumenical forum is often best discussed and received within an ecumenical group where it can more readily be used as a convergence instrument. In particular joint study of the text, together with other bilateral texts, should form a part of the training of women and men for the ordained ministry.

B. Baptism

(i) THE BRITISH COUNCIL OF CHURCHES WORKING PARTY ON CHRISTIAN INITIATION

125. In 1984 the British Council of Churches set up a working party on Christian initiation with the following tasks:

> to consider the varying understandings and practices of the British and Irish churches . . .

> to receive submissions from Local Ecumenical Projects, the Association of Inter-Church Families, the Covenanted Churches in Wales on dual/multiple/extended membership . . .

> to follow up discussions in the churches about the WCC Lima Text and what they imply for questions of membership . . .

> to review earlier discussions in the BCC and elsewhere (e.g. the Consultative Committee for Local Ecumenical Projects work on joint confirmations . . .)

> to pick up questions which may arise from the discussions and practice in regard to the proposed second part of the baptism certificate.

We consider it important for the British churches to support this group, to build on the convergences of the Lima Text and especially to face the particular questions raised by that text which we have referred to in §55: namely, the relation of baptism, confirmation and first communion; "indiscriminate baptism"; rebaptism; the question of whether different baptismal practices may be held within a visibly united Church and the implication of our mutual recognition of baptism for the reconciliation of churches, their members and their ministries.

(ii) CONVERSATIONS WITH THE BAPTIST UNION

126. We recognise that the baptism section of the Lima Text raises in particular the question of our relationship with the Baptist Churches. In 1979–80 an informal conversation took place between members of the

Church of England and the Baptist Union on baptism and episcopacy. In those conversations much common ground was discovered between the two traditions. It was recognised that both Baptists and Anglicans place high value on nurture within the Christian family and within the family of the worshipping congregation. Both bodies value careful and long preparation, among Baptists before baptism, among Anglicans before confirmation. Neither the Anglican nor the Baptist theologians were happy with any attempt to isolate a particular moment at which faith begins. Just as among Anglicans there is some variation in the recommended age for confirmation, so also among Baptists there are some who baptise children when they are six or seven. No one was willing to defend "indiscriminate baptism", and the Baptist participants were glad to note that today more Anglicans are being baptised, confirmed and receiving first communion in a single rite as adult believers.

127. We note with concern the increasing tendency of house-church groups to "rebaptize" converts from the main-stream churches. The Lima Text provides us with an appropriate context in which to discuss rebaptism with those who practise believers' baptism especially members of the Baptist Union as well as a framework in which to deepen the convergences between our two traditions which were registered in 1979–80. The ecumenical duty of listening is imposed by the Lima Text on paedo-baptists and Baptists alike. We note that the Lima Text does not call Baptists or anyone else to cease deferring baptism until conscious choice is possible, nor to accept the practice of infant baptism as the standard pattern. It asks Baptists to acknowledge that those churches, where by very ancient tradition indeed infants are admitted to the sacrament, are validly and effectively receiving them into the Church of Christ. This is a sensitive and difficult matter but any future bilateral conversation must consider whether the theological convergences in the Lima Text, especially the emphasis on initiation as a process, means that the two baptismal practices can be contained within a truly united Church.

(iii) JOINT CONFIRMATIONS

128. Our observations on the meaning of confirmation (§§46–52) have a bearing on the practice of confirmation in Local Ecumenical Projects. It may be argued that the practice of "joint confirmations" obscures the meaning of the rite. Whatever our particular understanding of the relation of confirmation to baptism, we all agree that it takes its meaning from its relation to baptism as the sacrament of initiation into the one, holy, catholic and apostolic Church. "Joint confirmations" can obscure this by appearing to use the rite as a ceremony of admission to membership of two or more denominations, thereby reducing its proper significance. Against this it may be argued that, even if "joint confirmations" are an anomaly, the fact of Christian division is a still greater anomaly, and that it is therefore right to use "joint confirmations" as a sign of the need for closer unity and as a means

towards the fuller sharing of a common life. At all events when "joint confirmations" take place, we believe that there should be a clear distinction made between the primary significance of the rite as a confirmation of initiation into the one Church, and any secondary function it may have as conferring "full membership" of any particular denomination or congregation.

129. It may be asked how far Anglicans themselves are responsible for causing confirmation to be perceived as a ceremony conferring admittance to a particular denomination through their custom of using the service of confirmation as a means of admitting into their Communion baptised and communicant Christians who have not received episcopal confirmation in another body. Would it not be preferable to use a distinct ceremony other than confirmation for this purpose, as already happens when (confirmed) Roman Catholics and Orthodox are admitted to communion in the Church of England? It should be remembered that, in the English conversations between Anglicans and Methodists, as in the proposals for the English Covenant, Anglicans never made episcopal confirmation a requirement for those already baptised and admitted to full communion in other churches. Further, now that the Roman Catholic Church allows the administration of confirmation by presbyters, albeit with the use of episcopally consecrated chrism, it may be asked whether all confirmed Roman Catholics have been "episcopally confirmed". The same question arises of course in relation to the Orthodox, who have no rite of "confirmation" other than the chrismation which accompanies baptism.

C. Eucharist

(i) EUCHARISTIC SHARING

130. As the churches move more closely together the question of eucharistic sharing becomes more important. Beyond the provisions of Canon B15A for individual action, there are also provisions for congregational inter-communion under the direction of the bishop. The report of a Church of England working party set up under the chairmanship of the Bishop of Derby was published in the summer of 1984 and presented to the General Synod in November 1984. It contains suggestions for changes in canon law which we believe will make clearer the Church of England's present position on eucharistic sharing. The recommended changes in Canons A and B would make it lawful in certain circumstances and with the permission of the local diocesan bishop for an Anglican clergyman to preside at a eucharist using the rites of another church approved by the bishop. It also makes it lawful for an ordained minister of another church to preside at a eucharist in a Church of England building. In each case the eucharist would be deemed to be a eucharist of the church of the presiding minister. The effect

of such a change in canon law will be to recognise the degree of shared ministry which already exists in the British churches, while recognizing that the ministries are not yet interchangeable. The theological undergirding of the Bishop of Derby's Report makes clear that the eucharist may not be understood in isolation from the ministry, and neither may be divorced from the doctrine of the Church. This is in line with the position of the Lima Text which we have endorsed in our comments. We quote as an appendix to this section the theological reflections of the Derby Report.

131. Both within the Church of England and with our ecumenical partners we look forward to widespread discussion of the proposed changes in canon law and to the examination of the theological reasons for such changes set out in the Derby Report.

(ii) JOINT CELEBRATIONS

132. In addition to our reflections on the proposals of the Derby Report, the Faith and Order Advisory Group has recently commented upon the question of "joint celebrations" of the Holy Communion. Two practices are distinguished. The one a service in which the whole service is celebrated in common, including the saying of the prayer of thanksgiving and the consecrating of one set of elements from which all communicants communicate. In the U.S.A. this has been called, *common joint celebration.* (*Anglican–Lutheran Relations:* Report of the Anglican–Lutheran Joint Working Group, 1983, Appendix II.) The other, a service in which the whole service is performed in common except that the prayer of thanksgiving is said in parallel and separately by ministers of two or more churches over two or more sets of elements from which the ministers communicate their own members separately. This can be called *parallel joint celebration.*

133. This second practice enables those who share a common faith to have a joint celebration where one or more partners are unable to recognize the validity of the ministry of one of the other participating churches. It is recognized that there could be a theological objection to this practice on the understanding of communion itself, since there is a serious anomaly in having two sets of elements which are not interchangeable at one eucharist.

134. FOAG believes, however, that this practice could be permitted in certain circumstances where a joint celebration was desired, where the churches involved share a common faith, where they are committed to the search for unity with one another, where they share some common life and mission, and where no other solution is at the present acceptable to all parties. In the Church of England the decision on what might constitute an appropriate occasion for this should be left to the diocesan bishop.

135. A common joint celebration of the eucharist could occur at a stage in relationships between designated churches beyond mutual hospitality at one another's eucharists on the one hand, and short of interchangeability of ministries on the other. It would presuppose:

(i)   A common apostolic faith.

(ii) Mutual recognition of one another's Churches as Churches.

(iii) Mutual commitment to the search for full visible unity, including ongoing theological discussions upon points not yet agreed.

(iv) Sharing in a common life and mission.

(v)   Mutual recognition of the efficacy (but not necessarily the interchangeability) of one another's ministries.

136. In a common joint celebration the ministers of all the participating churches stand side by side at the altar (but not replacing one another) as a sign of growing unity which yet falls short of full acceptance of one another's ministries. It becomes a growing point of unity rather than its culmination in full communion. In this way ministry is not separated from Church and eucharist.

137. FOAG wishes to emphasise that genuine Local Ecumenical Projects (LEPs) are proper places for such common joint celebration, since in them the discovery of the gift of unity and of the reality of one another's ministries comes from experience and is not imposed from outside. Moreover the existence of a Sponsoring Body at county level and of the Consultative Committee for Local Ecumenical Projects in England (CCLEPE) at national level are testimonies to the fact that the LEP is not simply a local reality, but that it has the authorisation of the respective Church authorities at county (diocesan etc.) and national levels.

138. FOAG also wishes to emphasise that where only one minister is present at the altar, this should not be regarded as a common joint celebration of the eucharist, but as the eucharist of the Church of the presiding minister. Until there is mutual recognition and interchangeability of ministries (i.e. full communion), the minister of one Church cannot replace the minister of another at the altar. In these circumstances the Church of the presiding minister is exercising hospitality towards the members of other churches at the eucharist.

139. FOAG notes that its view of common joint celebrations has much in common with the interim eucharistic sharing agreement which already exists between Anglicans and Lutherans in the United States. However, in the U.S.A. the agreement has preceded the experience of a common life, rather than following it (cf. Anglican–Lutheran Relations, Report of the Anglican–Lutheran Joint Working Group, 1983).

140. We have quoted these developments in full because both the Derby Report and the FOAG reflections on joint celebrations underline the relationship of the eucharist to the ministry and relate both to the nature of the Church. Further, both texts strive to make sense of a genuine commitment to the visible unity of the Church and the reality of the degree of shared life which exists amongst the English churches while acknowledging at the same time that there is still further agreement to be reached and a richer life to be sought on the basis of that agreement.

(iii) THE CONSUMPTION OF THE EUCHARISTIC ELEMENTS

141. As we have already noted, the Lima Text asserts that in the eucharist bread and wine become the sacramental signs of Christ's body and blood and "remain so for the purpose of communion" (E15). It also recommends that, while "the primary intention of reserving the elements is their distribution among the sick and those who are absent", it should be recognized "that the best way of showing respect for the elements served in the eucharistic celebration is by their consumption, without excluding their use for communion of the sick"(E32). This recommendation accords with Anglican practice, and should be followed in all common joint celebrations in which Anglicans participate. Indeed, Anglicans will wish to ask other churches to follow this practice. For unless this practice is observed, many Anglicans who would otherwise wish to communicate with Christians of other churches, will find their understanding of Christ's presence in the eucharist excluded.

(iv) LAY CELEBRATION

142. We noted in our comments on the Lima Text that reference is made there to the fact that there are differences of practice concerning lay celebration. We also quoted the view of the Faith and Order Advisory Group that the eucharist is most fittingly celebrated by an ordained minister as a person who shares in the universal ministry (GS 281, para. 55). In the light of what appeared to some to be the unresolved position over this matter in the Covenant Proposals, the Church of England should pay particular attention to what other churches in England say on this in their response to the Lima Text.

D. Ministry

(i) THE RECONCILIATION OF MINISTRIES

143. Recognizing the challenges of §§51–55 of the ministry section of the Lima Text and acknowledging the difficulties encountered in the attempts of the British churches at the reconciliation of ministries we hope that further discussions in England will be carried out in the context of the convergences of the Lima Text and in relation to other bilateral dialogues. However, we believe that questions relating to the recognition of ministries and their eventual reconciliation may no longer dominate the agenda, as they have done in recent English moves towards unity, but must be set within a wider ecclesiological framework.

144. The churches in Britain still have much to learn from each other's practice of ministry about the personal, communal and collegial expressions of ministry at every level of the Church's life. The recently published Anglican–Reformed dialogue, *God's Reign and Our Unity*, for example, has some very important suggestions on how a threefold order of ministry might be reformed in a united Church (*God's Reign and Our Unity*, paras 112–

119). We look forward to a widespread discussion of this report and believe it would be appropriately studied where our two churches already share together in Local Ecumenical Projects.

(ii) THE MINISTRY OF OVERSIGHT

145. As we seek together a way of reconciling ministries the sharing of oversight, as experienced in meetings of Church leaders in many dioceses and in particular in new insights in Milton Keynes and Thamesdown, is particularly significant. The suggestion from Thamesdown for an "ecumenical bishop" for the Thamesdown area is an imaginative one although we recognize it raises complex theological issues.

(iii) WOMEN AND MINISTRY

146. We noted in an earlier paragraph that the ministry section works with the primary concept of the ministry of the whole people of God and only within that considers the ministry of the ordained. The text urges the churches to discover the ministry that can be provided by women as well as by men, but it is very cautious indeed on the subject of the ordination of women to the priesthood. We note that the experience of the covenanting discussions in England showed clearly that the ordination of women to the priesthood continues to be a "grave obstacle" to the reconciliation of churches. We welcome both the Lima Text's encouragement to engage in ecumenical discussion of practical and theological views relating to the ordination of women and also its suggestion that the Spirit may speak to one church through the insights of another. We recognize that this is not a discussion that will go away and that if the churches and their ministries are to be reconciled we must face the question of whether reconciliation to full communion is possible while we hold different views on this subject. Again, *God's Reign and Our Unity* has some sharp observations in this area. Members of the Church of England need to encourage the Free Churches to speak more about their experience of women in the ordained ministry and invite those women to take part in Anglican services. Equally we must attend to the reservations expressed by both the Roman Catholic and the Orthodox churches.

(iv) PARALLEL ORDINATIONS

147. The question of parallel ordinations is a much more recent development. The Faith and Order Advisory Group has not dealt with this in its work so far. The question of whether parallel ordinations for those who are to share closely in the exercise of their future ministries are appropriate needs investigation. Any such parallel service would need to be most carefully devised to avoid any possible confusion that might suggest that the candidates were being ordained into two communions. How far is it possible to devise a service which unambiguously recognises the degree of ministry in which the candidate would share but which also recognises the disunity

which still exists, is a difficult question. As we have emphasised throughout our reflections, the Church's ministry cannot be divorced from the Church: the reconciliation of ministries belongs within the context of the reconciliation of the churches. Parallel ordinations need to be thought of in this context.

(v) CELEBRATION OF CONVERGENCE

148. Although we have nothing immediately to suggest in relation to the celebration of convergence, we nevertheless believe it important locally, regionally and internationally to find imaginative ways to claim and celebrate the theological convergence of the Lima Text if it is affirmed by the churches. Symbolic acts can have a lasting significance in the relationships between hitherto divided communions. The occasion of Pope John Paul II's visit to Canterbury with the remaking of baptismal vows illustrated this as did the Lutheran celebrations in Germany in 1983 with their ecumenical dimension. It may be that some appropriate celebration might take place in England within the context of the new initiative of the British churches on the nature and purpose of the Church. Internationally the occasion of the World Conference on Faith and Order in 1989, which will commemorate both the last of the truly ecumenical councils and the undertaking of the "Lima agenda" in Lausanne might provide an opportunity to celebrate the theological convergence on a wider scale. All too often we are left recounting failures rather than celebrating the signs of hope which are already here.

Appendix 1 (See para. 130 above) taken from "Local Ecumenical Development: the Derby Report GS 642", paras 24-26

Theological considerations

24. These developments suggest that LEPs need to be helped to express visibly that unity which they are already experiencing. In searching for the necessary legislation to make this possible, the following points ought to be taken into account:

the importance of supporting and encouraging local unity, for the expression of unity in LEPs is truer to the nature of the Church than the anomaly of separated denominations.

the need to prevent an unbearable strain being put upon the unity that already exists within any single communion.

the importance of safeguarding those theological agreements already reached between the English Churches which are beginning to appear in the convergences in international bilateral and multilateral dialogues (e.g. the Final Report of the Anglican–Roman Catholic International Commission and the Lima Text of the Faith and Order Commission of the World Council of Churches, Baptism, Eucharist and Ministry), while at the same time not disregarding issues relating to the ministry that still remain unresolved.

25. The particular theological issues that need to be borne in mind are:

(i) The ordained ministry cannot be divorced from the Church. The proposed service for the making of the Covenant recognised that the reconciliation of ministries must be set within the context of the reconciliation of the Churches. This was also true of the earlier Anglican–Methodist proposals.

(ii) Local unity within an LEP ought not to be understood in isolation from a wider unity Structures of authority and communion wider than the local have a task of maintaining unity within and between local churches and also of expressing it visibly. Here episcopal and conciliar elements both have their part to play.

26. We recommend that the reality of shared ordained ministry that is already exercised in local situations ought to be affirmed in Canon Law. The changes suggested in what follows are an attempt to make legal a degree of shared ministry between the Churches without as yet implying full interchangeability of ministries. Full reconciliation of ministries and thus complete interchangeability between the ministries of hitherto separated denominations can only be reached within the context of the reconciliation of Churches and within a commitment to ministerial and conciliar forms which express unity wider than the local level. The visible expression of ministry at the local level is inextricably bound to its expression in the wider Church. Already the existence of Sponsoring Bodies in which the local bishop shares together with other Church leaders points to the need for local unity to be related to wider structures and to the exercise of wider episcopal oversight.

Question 3: The guidance your church can take from this text for its worship, educational, ethical and spiritual life and witness

(i) THE CHURCH OF ENGLAND AND THE WILL FOR UNITY

149. As we have already noted, the preface to the Lima Text re-affirms the goal of "visible unity in one faith and one eucharistic fellowship". In the past the ecumenical movement was assisted by many pioneering Anglican initiatives. Today we recognize that, for whatever reasons, Anglicans in many countries have often been the cause of breakdown in union schemes (cf. ACC 3 Trinidad 1976). In England the refusal of the Church Assembly and the General Synod to give adequate majorities to Anglican–Methodist unity was more recently followed by an inadequate majority of votes in the General Synod in support of the Covenant Proposals. Whatever our judgement on the adequacy or inadequacy of these earlier projects members of the Church of England need to ask themselves, how sincere, and if sincere, how important is our desire to seek "visible unity in one faith and one eucharistic fellowship"?

Have we, perhaps implicitly, surrendered this goal for something less? Is there a general belief that because we are ourselves divided over issues such as priesthood and the ordination of women to the priesthood, we can never agree on terms of union with any other church: any attempt therefore at the union going beyond intercommunion and collaboration is not to be pressed for, for it is not possible to achieve. It is in this context that we need to respond to the challenge of the preface to the Lima Text recalling us to our previous goal of visible unity, a vision held by the New Testament, by the Catholic tradition, by the English Reformers, and by the Tractarians. The insights of the Lima Text, together with those of other bilateral dialogues, may help us both to overcome our own internal divisions and also to renew our understanding of how visible unity in one faith and one eucharistic fellowship might be expressed.

(ii) THE BAPTISM TEXT

150. There is evidence that in the Church of England most of those baptised never become communicants and it is highly probable that their personal religion is not of the "converted" kind described in the Lima Text. The paragraphs on the meaning of baptism (B2–7) speak of the sacrament in language so high that it has little apparent connection with the lives which will be lived by the majority of babies brought for baptism in the Church of England. The Lima Text challenges "many large European and North American majority churches" who practise baptism in an "apparently indiscriminate way". If the sacrament of baptism is expected to yield the fruits described in the Lima Text, is there enough determination on the part of ministers and people to nurture all those baptized into membership and to help their growth ethically and spiritually? Is the religious education of children and young people strong enough, particularly now that religious education is weak in so many schools? Is adult education taken with anything like sufficient seriousness in the Church? Do questions relating to faith, the key to commitment in the Church, feature enough in our Synods?

151. Further, although the Lima Text is not decisive on the question of the relation of baptism, confirmation, chrismation and first communion, it does challenge us to clarify our own understanding of the various parts of the initiation process and in particular to think of the admittance of baptized children to communion. Some experiments are taking place in the Church of England but the discussion is less active than in, for example, the Episcopal Church in the U.S.A. The explanation of this may be our tradition of giving a place to confirmation beyond anything affirmed in the Lima Text (cf. §49 above). The question of children's participation in the "Family Communion" which has become the chief, often only, service is still on the Church of England's agenda. We look forward to the contribution on this matter which the working party under the Bishop of Knaresborough on Christian initiation will make.

152. Finally, the theology and practice of baptism in the Lima Text are far more corporate than has been the practice of the Church of England in the past, or indeed is today. The stress is on membership of the body of Christ, the community of the Church, with all the implications for relationship with all who are baptized in whatever denomination and with all the implications for active church membership that goes with this. What is the relation between membership of the Body of Christ and that membership as it is expressed in a particular denomination and how is the anomaly of one baptism and different denominations to be overcome?

(iii) THE EUCHARIST TEXT

153. In the Lima Text the eucharist is significant as the feast where the Church recognizes the signs of renewal already at work in the world, where, united with Christ in a special way it prays for the world, and is the centre from which Christians go out renewed by the power of the Spirit to act as reconcilers in a broken world. In any further revision of the Alternative Service Book, we hope the world transfiguring and the eschatological dimensions of the eucharist and the intercessory character of the eucharistic prayer will find greater stress.

154. We recognize also the challenge to us raised in the commentary on §15 about the mutual recognition of ministries and members in churches becoming "one eucharistic fellowship". We welcome, as we have said in earlier paragraphs, the attempt of the working party under the Bishop of Derby to enable the Church of England to move a little closer to the goal of eucharistic sharing.

155. Finally, some members of the Church of England are asking for guidance on the authority of the Lima Liturgy finding it an appropriate service for ecumenical occasions. We note that the Lima Liturgy, celebrated by the Faith and Order Commission at their meeting in Lima was not a text prepared or voted upon by the whole Commission. It is not an "agreed text" in the sense that Baptism, Eucharist and Ministry is agreed. Nevertheless it has been used on significant ecumenical occasions, as at the Vancouver Assembly at which the Archbishop of Canterbury presided. It is proving an important liturgical text for ecumenical occasions and the Church of England might consider endorsing and authorizing its use.

(iv) THE MINISTRY TEXT

156. Although the ministry text achieves less of a consensus than the other two texts its theological convergences still contain challenges for us. First, the view expressed on the priesthood of the ordained ministry, which closely resembles that put forward in the 1938 Doctrine Report, and expressed in the Ordinal of the Anglican–Methodist Scheme, challenges the Church of England to consider whether the two apparently irreconcilable views of priesthood held by some of its own members cannot now be brought together within the theological convergence of the Lima Text. Unless we are able,

helped by recent ecumenical texts, to clarify our understanding of the priesthood of the ordained ministry all attempts at unity with others are likely to flounder. This is of course also highly relevant for the question of the ordination of women to the priesthood.

157. Secondly, what the Lima Text has to say about episcopacy suggests that we need to undertake a fundamental reconsideration of our own theology and practice of episcopacy. Recently in the Church of England many changes affecting bishops have been made or are under study; for example the method of episcopal appointments, the responsibilities of area bishops. However, the motivations have been pragmatic rather than theological. Further, the often voiced criticism that dioceses are too large and that the creation of suffragan bishops makes little sense theologically has never been seriously answered. If the Church of England is to commend episcopacy to the Free Churches then a clear and defensible theological case for bishops needs to be articulated and the practice reformed to make the benefits of personal oversight obvious.

158. Closely related to this, though going beyond the agenda of the Lima Text, is the need to work out the relationship between the personal, collegial and communal exercise of oversight. What, for example, in the Church of England, is the relationship of the House of Bishops to the Standing Committee of the General Synod and indeed to the General Synod itself, and what is the relation between the bishops and the diocesan synods? Further, the Church of England, together with the Anglican Communion as a whole, needs to consider the structures of oversight that properly belong to the Communion and the relation of personal oversight, primacy and collegiality appropriate at a level above the provincial.

159. The ministry text, pointing as it does in the direction of a threefold order of ministry, suggests that Churches which retained this ancient pattern need to clarify their understanding of the diaconate. We recall that the most recent working party of the Church of England on the diaconate recommended its abolition. In spite of the fact that this was never adopted by the Church of England there has been little attempt to clarify our position in spite of repeated calls to do so by members of the General Synod. We note that the Portsmouth Diocese is experimenting with training men and women for a permanent diaconate. Again we recognize that, as with the discussion on the priesthood of the ordained ministry, this is particularly relevant for an understanding of the ministry of women, especially as it can be argued that most professional diaconal ministry is exercised at present in the Church of England by deaconesses.

160. Finally the ministry text suggests that "a deeper understanding of the comprehensiveness of ministry which reflects the interdependence of men and women needs to be more widely manifested in the life of the Church" (M18). We welcome the recent reports of ACCM on the role models for women in training and shared ministry between husbands and wives who are

both ordained. We look forward to a more general discussion of "complementary ministry" as well as a widespread consideration of the ordination of women to the priesthood. In particular the Church of England must consider whether it is possible to live in full communion with other provinces which do already ordain women to the presbyterate and, if we agree it is possible, whether we shall continue to refuse to allow those women priests to preside at eucharists when they visit this country. We need to test out the assertion of the Lima Text that differences on this issue "must not be regarded as substantive hindrance for further efforts towards mutual recognition" (M54).

(v) ADDITIONAL REFLECTIONS

161. There are three further reflections to add to the consequences that the Lima Text has for the Church of England. The first relates to what is said in the text about the guiding principles for the exercise of ordained ministry, namely the personal, collegial and communal aspects. The Lima Text gives no clear guidance on how these aspects are to be put into practice. The Church of England might well wish to reflect on the ways in which personal, collegial and communal aspects of ordained ministry are expressed in its own life (cf. *God's Reign and Our Unity*, Paras 92ff and 110ff).

162. Secondly, we note that the language of the Lima Text is inclusive. This is in contrast to the exclusive male language used in the ASB. We understand that the present Liturgical Commission is sensitive to this issue and has devoted attention to the relevant linguistic principles. In all its new work it has attempted to use inclusive terms where possible, while recognising that classical texts must be treated with integrity.

163. The final reflection relates to the educational process which has to be undertaken if the theological convergences of the text are to be received by clergy and laity. This raises questions of how a report which is necessarily couched in language familiar to theologians can be popularised and disseminated. We welcome the study guides that have already been published and we hope that dioceses and parishes will be encouraged to produce their own study materials, particularly in conjunction with other churches in their areas.

Question 4: The consequences your church can make for the ongoing work of Faith and Order as it relates the material of this text on Baptism, Eucharist and Ministry to its long-range research project "Towards the Common Expression of the Apostolic Faith Today"

164. In the course of our report we have drawn attention to those areas which we consider need further study in relation to baptism, eucharist and ministry. For example, the relation of baptism, confirmation and first communion, the personal, collegial and communal aspects of ministry, the ordination of women to the priesthood, primacy etc. We look forward particularly to the development of the ecclesiological and missiological

insights of the Lima Text within the study on the apostolic faith. This would provide an important international context for the British Churches' study on the nature and purpose of the Church, as well as a multilateral text against which to consider the convergences and agreements of the bilateral dialogues. We hope also that the Faith and Order Commission will resume its work on common structures of decision making, building upon what is said in the Lima Text about the personal, communal and collegial aspects of ministry.

165. Finally, we consider it important to develop each of the three parts of the inter-related agenda which the Commission has itself indicated as necessary for the visible unity of the churches within the overarching framework of the unity of the Church and the renewal of human community.

* * *

The motion "That this Synod to the extent described in GS 661 recognizes in 'Baptism, Eucharist and Ministry' the faith of the church through the ages" was carried following a division of the whole Synod. The voting was as follows:-

Ayes	383
Noes	12
Abstentions	1

* * *

Supplementary report by the Board for Mission and Unity of the General Synod of the Church of England, 1986

(18) The voting in diocesan synods confirms the view of the General Synod that there is an overwhelming agreement that members of the Church of England are able to recognize in the Lima text "the faith of the Church through the ages". This does not imply that every point in the Lima text is expressed in precisely the terms Anglicans would wish to use nor that there are not further areas concerning the doctrines of baptism, eucharist and ministry that need further reflection in the multilateral forum of the World Council. Indeed GS 661 drew attention to these areas: on baptism in §55; on eucharist in §§79 and 80 and on ministry in §117.

(19) Although the second and third motions on the Lima text passed by the General Synod in February 1984 were not referred to diocesan synods the dioceses did acknowledge that to recognize the faith of the church through the ages in the text raises the question of changes that need to be made both internally in the life of the Church of England as well as in our relations with other churches. In particular the Lichfield diocesan Synod requested that in the light of the Lima text on baptism a national review of the Anglican practice with regard to baptism be undertaken. The Wheathampstead deanery synod, in the diocese of St Albans, urged that steps be taken in the light of the Lima text to permit duly commissioned ministers of other traditions to preside at the eucharist in the Church of England. Similar questions relating to the baptism text were raised in the Birmingham diocesan synod. FOAG would remind the Synod that the proposed Ecumenical Canons currently before the Church of England are based upon the theological convergences of the ecumenical dialogues. Further, the ongoing debates about the reform of the diaconate and the nature and role of episcopacy can also be seen in part as our response to the dialogues (cf. *The Nature of Christian Belief*, §76).

CHURCH IN WALES

Background note

Four international dialogues are now before the churches for decision and the Anglican communion is engaged in receiving and responding to the texts. These are "Baptism, Eucharist and Ministry", the document of the Faith and Order Commission of the World Council of Churches (BEM); the "Final Report" of the Anglican/Roman Catholic International Commission (ARCIC); "Anglican/Lutheran Relations" from the Anglican/Lutheran Working Group 1983; and "God's Reign and Our Unity" from the Anglican/Reformed International Commission 1981–84. A fifth, the Second Report of the Anglican/Orthodox Joint Doctrinal Discussions, is expected soon.

The oldest of the dialogues, and comprising the widest range of Christian traditions, is that of the Faith and Order Commission of the World Council of Churches. This brings into theological conversation Eastern Orthodox, Oriental Orthodox, Roman Catholic, Old Catholic, Lutheran, Anglican, Reformed, Methodist, United, Disciples, Baptist, Adventist and Pentecostal Church traditions. This remarkable multilateral text (BEM) is a reminder of the oneness of the ecumenical movement and provides a context in which to view the convergences in any of the bilateral dialogues. "Baptism, Eucharist and Ministry", Faith and Order Paper No. 111, published in 1982, was preceded by these two earlier reports of the WCC Faith and Order Commission:

— "One Baptism, One Eucharist and a Mutually Recognized Ministry", Paper No. 73, 1975.
— "Towards an Ecumenical Consensus — Baptism, Eucharist, Ministry", Paper No. 84, 1978.

The first of these contained three agreed statements on baptism, eucharist

---

• 132,000 Easter communicants, 632 benefices, 6 dioceses, 693 full-time pastors, 59 non-stipendiary.

and a mutually recognized ministry, on which the WCC Faith and Order Commission requested reactions from member churches by 1 April 1976. The statements did not represent a consensus in the full sense but a summary of the measure of agreement achieved, of shared convictions and perspectives.

At the request of the Bench of Bishops, the Doctrinal Commission prepared a short response on behalf of the Church in Wales. While it welcomed the WCC statements, it drew attention to possible omissions. Its comments were forwarded to the WCC Faith and Order Commission as part of the process of sharing in the expression of views on the way towards ecumenical consensus.

The WCC Faith and Order Commission received over one hundred replies from member churches. It distributed in 1978 its second report (Paper No. 84). This was an evaluation of, and a response to, the comments received. It pointed out that agreed statements "seek to express the convergences between the churches. Thus, inevitably, they will never fully correspond to the particular views and the terminology of any one church."

The Doctrinal Commission commented to the Bench on Paper No. 84 in July 1978. The Provincial Council for Mission and Unity also responded to "Towards an Ecumenical Consensus" from its own perspective. These reports were forwarded to the WCC Faith and Order Commission.

The third report is entitled "Baptism, Eucharist and Ministry", known as the Lima or BEM document. It was received by member churches in mid-1982. The bishops asked the Doctrinal Commission to prepare responses to the four questions addressed to member churches (see page 82). Meanwhile, the Provincial Unity Committee disseminated the findings within the Church in Wales as widely as possible and prepared its own response.

The BEM report was studied (in conjunction with the ARCIC "Final Report") in the dioceses in 1984 with the help of a questionnaire and BCC booklets. Representatives of the Church in Wales have attended national, regional and local interchurch meetings to explore its implications.

The Bench of Bishops has brought together in this leaflet the responses of the Doctrinal Commission (Part I) and of the Provincial Unity Committee (Part II) to the BEM report. Motions will be placed on the agenda-paper and moved on behalf of the Bench to enable the governing body to commend their contents as the response by the Church in Wales to the four questions put to member churches by the WCC Faith and Order Commission.

Part I: The response of the Doctrinal Commission

INTRODUCTION

The Doctrinal Commission has already submitted observations on two precursors of the Lima statement (Faith and Order Paper 73, 1975, and Faith and Order Paper 84, 1977). The present paper (No. 111, Lima statement = BEM) marks a further stage in the fifty-year process of study and consultation which has achieved such a notable degree of agreement on baptism, eucharist and ministry among widely different traditions within the Christian family.

Our response follows the threefold division of the paper and we have addressed ourselves directly to the four questions posed in BEM on page x. The first three questions form the basis of the separate responses given in each of the three sections, but our response to the final question is reserved for a paragraph at the end.

For ease of reference we reproduce here the first three questions, which concern:

— *Question 1:* The extent to which your church can recognize in this text the faith of the church through the ages.

— *Question 2:* The consequences your church can draw from this text for its relations and dialogues with other churches, particularly with those churches which also recognize the text as an expression of the apostolic faith.

— *Question 3:* The guidance your church can take from this text for its worship, educational, ethical, and spiritual life and witness.

The fourth question is reproduced at the head of the paragraph which responds to it on page 88.

BAPTISM

Question 1

The statement on baptism is clear and concise, and we believe that the Church in Wales should find little difficulty in recognizing in this text the faith of the church through the ages.

Question 2

We appreciate what is said in the statement about the implications of Baptism for Christian Unity (§6). Perhaps we have tended to focus too narrowly on issues related to the eucharist in this regard, and failed to take the full advantage of the opportunity for progress offered by the understanding of baptism as involving incorporation into membership of the church universal. Those who share this understanding of baptism should consider the implications of such an understanding for their relationships one with another.

Important, too, is the recognition that baptism is related not only to a momentary experience but to life-long growth into Christ (§9). This, together with the insistence that every baptism (whether of an "infant" or of a "believer") is within the context of the community of faith, offers a positive and constructive meeting point for churches whose practice has long differed on this point.

Question 3

Our positive response to the statement on baptism should not be taken to imply that the Church in Wales has succeeded in freeing itself of the ambiguities of faith and practice which are consequent upon the break up of the unity of the rite of Christian initiation. Nevertheless, as a Commission we are glad to find that the statement's analysis of the meaning of baptism and its insistence on the essential unity of the rite accords closely with the thinking expressed in the Doctrinal Commission's report "Christian Initiation" (1971). This report was subsequently received by the governing body of the Church in Wales and commended for study in the Province. However, the matter appears to have rested there, despite continuing unease in many quarters over our present understanding and practice of baptism and over the precise significance of confirmation as we now have it in relation to water baptism and admission to holy communion. These issues raised in the 1971 report now come to us afresh in the Lima statement. This presents a challenge to the Church in Wales to face up boldly to a re-examination of the theological, practical and pastoral issues which are bound up with our present practice of Christian initiation and to be ready to act upon the results of such re-examination.

EUCHARIST

Question 1

The following points indicate ways in which the Church in Wales recognizes in this text the faith of the church through the ages:

i) The eucharist is a gift. It is something the Church receives from her Lord. The eucharist is a continuation of the fellowship meals of Jesus during his early life, culminating in his last meal, where the fellowship of the kingdom was connected with Jesus' suffering and death, but now viewed in the light of the resurrection. It is an anticipation of the final messianic banquet and therefore points to the future as well as to the past and present. It is the central act of the church's worship.

ii) The eucharist consists of both word and sacrament and proclaims and celebrates the whole of God's work. It is a thanksgiving to God for everything he has done. "It is the Father who is the primary origin and final fulfilment of the eucharistic event" (§14). It is a celebration of God's chief work of reconciliation in the life, ministry, death and resurrection of Jesus. In response to that unique sacrifice of God in Jesus Christ we can only offer ourselves and our praise and thanksgiving.

iii) In the controversies of history the notion of the mass as sacrifice has been highly divisive. Here the starting point is that there can be no repetition of the sacrifice at calvary. "What it was God's will to accomplish in the incarnation, life, death, resurrection and ascension of Christ, God does not repeat" (§8). Yet there is agreement that the sacrifice of Christ is effectively present in the whole eucharistic celebration. In expounding this understanding of the word *anamnesis*, one commentator puts it in these words: "In the eucharist, we recall the sacrifice of Christ in a dynamic way that puts us in touch with God's saving act. In and through the proclamation of the once occurring sacrifice the effects which are eternal are experienced anew and become effective through the power of the Spirit."

iv) The presence of Christ is connected with the entire eucharistic celebration and is not seen as being confined to the elements. It is also stressed that this presence is not dependent on the faith of the individual, although to discern that presence, faith is required. In this total eucharistic context the bread and wine become "sacramental signs of Christ's body and blood".

v) The eucharist is seen as having social implications. "The eucharistic celebration demands reconciliation and sharing among all those regarded as brothers and sisters in the one family of God and is a constant challenge in the search for appropriate relationships in social, economic and political life. All kinds of injustice, racism, separation and lack of freedom are radically challenged when we share in the body and blood of Christ" (§20).

Question 2

i) The Church in Wales needs to ask to what extent the eucharist is really regarded as the "central act of the Church's worship" (§1) by other churches and whether it does take place every Sunday (§31).

ii) In our response to Faith and Order Paper 84 we expressed our concern over the disposal of consecrated remains and would wish to put this to other churches. "It would do much to allay unnecessary suspicions if churches engaged on the quest for unity had a more or less uniform practice with regard to the disposal of the consecrated elements remaining over. The need is for a reasonable measure of local and/or denominational flexibility combined with a proper reverence for the sacramental elements. In Anglicanism, it is the practice for the priest (and such lay persons as he may invite to help him) to consume reverently what remains either immediately after the administration of holy communion or straight after the blessing or dismissal. If the latter alternative is chosen, the consumption takes place either at the altar or in the vestry. This type of practice seems entirely appropriate in a joint service."

Question 3

i) The Faith and Order Commission in approaching baptism and the eucharist starts by expounding the theology of these sacraments. The Church in Wales in authorizing new liturgical services did not involve the Doctrinal Commission or ask it to produce a theological statement on them. It entrusted full responsibility to the Liturgical Commission to produce baptismal and eucharistic services. Since the prime function of that body is to produce draft services, it was hardly able to examine as fully as the Doctrinal

Commission some of the theological and doctrinal principles underlying those services. Is that the right way to proceed? The effect is that since *lex orandi* is *lex credendi* the Liturgical Commission has charge of doctrine as well as liturgy.

ii) If the eucharist is to include both word and sacrament (§3) and is the main service on a Sunday and often the only one that most Christians will attend, the Church in Wales ought seriously to consider offering a wider choice of readings, with perhaps a two or three year cycle of readings. Furthermore, if a "eucharistic faith does *not* imply uniformity in either liturgy or practice" (§28) should not the Church in Wales allow more variety in its eucharistic provisions?

iii) If the eucharist is a "proclamation and a celebration of the work of God" (§3) (i.e. past, present and future) the liturgy needs to reflect this. Our prayer of thanksgiving gives the impression that God's creative activity lies in the past alone.

iv) The direction re manual acts by indented rubrics in the Welsh rite together with the rubric about what to do and say if the bread and wine run out seem to pinpoint the institution narrative as being the moment of consecration. This seems to be at variance with what BEM says on p.13 and indeed with current liturgical understanding of the eucharist. This suggests that the Church in Wales should look again at its understanding of what is meant by consecration.

v) BEM stresses that the main object of reserving the elements is for distributing them to the sick. Is that how the Church in Wales understands reservation?

vi) The Church in Wales is challenged to take seriously the fact that the unity of the church in its sacramental and ministerial life can never be an end in itself but has to be bound up with the church's mission.

MINISTRY

Question 1

The Doctrinal Commission agrees that it is possible for the Church in Wales to recognize in this text the faith of the church throughout the ages. The indication in §§1–5 that the ordained ministry is to be seen within the context of the calling of the whole people of God is consonant with what has been said in the Commission's earlier response (1978) to Faith and Order Paper 84 (see §16). At the same time, we are pleased to note what the present document says about the church's need for ordained ministers (see, e.g. §§8 and 12), and its evident appreciation of the threefold ministry of bishops, priests, and deacons (see §§19–25). The claim that "ordained ministers are representatives of Jesus Christ to the community" (§11), that their presence "reminds the community of the divine initiative" (§12), and that in the eucharist the ordained minister signifies and represents the presidency of

Christ (§14) would seem to be in agreement with the statement in the 1978 document (§18) that the ordained ministers of the church have been set apart "to represent God to the faithful in worship".

Question 2

We should wish to know how these other churches would propose to give practical effect to the document's recognition of the value of episcopacy (§§22 and 29), if they do not at present possess an episcopal order themselves.

Question 3

i) It is possible also, however, that a question is posed to the Church in Wales itself. Are we prepared genuinely to accept the statement (§37):

> . . . a continuity in apostolic faith, worship and mission has been preserved in churches which have not retained the form of historic episcopate?

The forms of the covenant into which the Church in Wales has entered with other churches include the statement (5a):

> We recognize the ordained ministries of all our churches as true ministries of the word and sacraments.

The present document offers a further challenge to consider what this means: the Lima statement and the covenant statement are in agreement. Can the Church in Wales any longer maintain the (tacitly accepted) view that whilst, e.g. a Methodist celebration of communion is a valid sacrament only for Methodists, an Anglican celebration is valid for Methodists (and others) as well as for Anglicans? This question will become more acute if the section on the eucharist in the report is accepted by the other covenanted churches.

ii) The report calls attention (§12) to the inter-relation of word and sacrament. At the same time, these two means of grace are not identical (cf. §13). If conclusions may be drawn for the form of the ordained ministry, are we to stress the inter-relationship or the non-identity? Emphasis on the former would suggest that the minister of the word should be authorized as the minister of the sacrament also (and vice versa). This is what the present ordination of priests in the Church in Wales clearly implies (symbolized in the giving both of the Bible and of the chalice and paten). Stress on the latter might be held to justify the ordination of women to the diaconate only, i.e. to the ministry of the word (symbolized in the giving of the Bible). And it could be said that this would be constant also with the Pauline teaching that within the unity of the one body various members have different gifts and functions.

There are several considerations which suggest that the inter-relationship is of more significance than the non-identity, and that it is of such a kind as to imply that, in point of theological principle, a person authorized by ordination to exercise the ministry of the word may be authorized also to act as a minister of the sacrament. First, if one looks at the form of the sacrament, it is the words spoken in the eucharistic prayers and culminating in the words of institution as the words of the Lord himself (cf. §13) which play the primary part in designating and interpreting this particular act of sharing and consuming bread and wine as the sacrament of Christ's death and resurrection, thus making the eucharist what it is. Secondly, one might find NT warrant for this in John 6, which in all probability is intended to have eucharistic significance. Signs, in the Fourth Gospel, need to be interpreted by Christ's discourses, if they are to be effective. In this instance, those who eat the "uninterpreted" loaves are simply eating ordinary food: it is those who receive Jesus's interpretation — his *words* which are the "spirit" and "life" — who eat the bread as the flesh of the Son of Man given for the life of the world. Even in the process of sacramental action, it is the interpretative word of Christ which makes the action effective.

As regards Paul's teaching on varieties of functions and gifts, it has to be observed that nowhere does he speak of the gift or function of being a "baptizer" or a "eucharistizer". From this one might draw one or the other of the following conclusions: either no special gift is necessary to preside at the eucharist (which would logically lead to lay celebration), or this vocation is subsumed under one or more of the other gifts. Possibly Paul himself held the former view. But (obviously) he would not have disallowed the function to those whose specific gifts might appear especially appropriate to it. What gifts might these be? Perhaps the gift of service (Rom. 12:7), which would seem highly appropriate to the representative of the Son of Man who came to serve and to give his life for mankind (Mark 10:45). In present terms, service is specifically, though not exclusively, the function of the diaconate. Or possibly one should think in terms of the feeding of Christ's flock (John 21:25). But this "feeding" must be the feeding with the bread of life which is talked of in John 6, where it is the word of Christ which is ultimately seen as primary. Hence it is the minister of the word who is to do the feeding. Perhaps the function of ministerial forgiveness (John 20:23) would be appropriate, since this is one of the benefits of the death of Christ. In that case, the appropriate vocation is that of those who are called to continue the apostolic ministry of the proclamation, on behalf of Christ, of the *word* of reconciliation (2 Cor. 5:18–21). Thus, it would seem that a vocation to the diaconate and thus to the ministry of the word carries with it, theologically speaking, the possibility of vocation to the ministry of the sacrament.

Those arguments suggest that the present practice of the Church in Wales of ordaining men to the diaconate for one year only and thereby confining them to the ministry of the word alone is called in question, and that it is not defensible to confine women to ordination to the diaconate only. In point of theological principle, they may be ordained also to celebrate the eucharist. The Church in Wales has already allowed order to be conferred on women as regards the diaconate: there therefore seems no logical reason why they should be precluded from receiving either of the other two orders.

iii) There is a clear recognition in the report (§11) that ordained ministers proclaim the word of God: they are spoken as "heralds and ambassadors" who represent Christ and "proclaim his message of reconciliation", and here there is a reflection of 2 Cor. 5:20 where Paul sees himself quite literally as the spokesman of God/Christ (cf. 2 Cor. 13:3 and 1 Thess. 2:13). One consequence and one question follow from this.

1. The sermon is to be taken seriously, both by those called to preach and by those who hear, as the apostolic gospel which is the word of God.
2. What is the position (in point of theological principle) of licensed readers? They are licensed to "preach". Does this mean the same thing as the "preaching of the word of God" to which deacons are ordained? If so, and if this is a continuing commission (as in most cases it is), is it not anomalous that they are not commissioned to do this by ordination? If not, what *does* preaching mean? Would there be a case for ordaining readers to the non-stipendiary ministry?

Question 4

This asks for the suggestions your church can make for the ongoing work on Faith and Order as it relates the material of this text on "Baptism, Eucharist and Ministry" to its long-range research project "Towards the Common Expression of the Apostolic Faith Today".

The project referred to has three emphases: (a) recognition of the Nicene Creed as the common ecumenical symbol of the apostolic faith; (b) explication of the Christian faith in contemporary situations; (c) movement towards a common confession of the apostolic faith today.

The main working method is research and study undertaken by a number of regional and international working groups (at least one of these is to be based in Europe).

Recognition of the Nicene Creed is something the Doctrinal Commission has urged on the Covenanted Churches in Wales (see our response to "Principles of Visible Unity in Wales"), so we are gratified that the Faith and Order Commission sees the Nicene Creed as an "ecumenical symbol of the apostolic faith". We have also spent some time discussing the *filioque* clause, and one of our number is a member of a BCC working party studying this question with representatives of the Orthodox Church. In one way or another we have contributed, we hope, to the promotion of (a) at our own local level. Perhaps we should also add that the Nicene Creed is and always has been part of our liturgy, so that we have no difficulty, as a church, in recognizing it as a common expression of faith.

The Church in Wales has done much less that is directly relevant to the second and third aspects of the project, though our hope is that study and discussion relating to BEM may lead to more serious attention being given to contemporary articulation of the Christian faith insofar as it involves church order as well as promoting the kind of consensus on these matters at a local level that properly reflects the consensus achieved by the Faith and Order Commission at an international level.

We are anxious to cooperate with those engaged in this project in any way, though our most fruitful contribution may prove to be rigorous re-examination of our own structures and practices in the light of BEM.

December 1983   Elwyn Roberts (Convenor)
                                                 D. P. Davies (Secretary)

Part II: The response of the Provincial Unity Committee

Our response follows the threefold division of the paper, and is based on the first three questions posed in BEM (see text in the report of the Doctrinal Commission on page 82).

BAPTISM

Question 1

There are many aspects of this statement which we welcome warmly. The first two sections re the institution of baptism and its meaning and the last section on the celebration of baptism are helpful summaries which we believe express the traditional faith of the church and even enrich our understanding of it by placing it in a wider and fuller context than we tend to do normally. In the sections on baptism and faith (III) and baptismal practice (IV) a number of questions are raised for us. In particular we think that §14 on the relation between baptism and confirmation needs further treatment (see response to Question 2) and that it would also be helpful to have an analysis of what is meant by church membership. We also think that the case for infant baptism is not adequately presented, and that the brief reference in §11 to "while the possibility that infant baptism was also practised in the apostolic age" is a somewhat minimal admission in the face of the fact that it has been the common practice of the vast majority of churches from early times.

Question 2

In considering our relation with other churches we note the importance of §6 with its reference that "our common baptism which unites us to Christ in faith is thus a basic bond of unity". If this is taken seriously it would lead to a revaluation of the place of confirmation. The practice of the Church in Wales has been to insist on episcopal confirmation before admitting members of other churches to full membership. This insistence will need reassessment if the position taken in §6 is accepted. In undertaking such a reassessment we would welcome a fuller treatment of the role and purpose of confirmation, as indicated above.

We welcome the attempt to reconcile the positions on infant and believers' baptism by emphasizing God's initiative in both and by placing them in the context of the faith of the community, and of the need for nurture and growth. The attempt could have been sharpened, however, by analyzing more clearly the processes which lead to full communicant membership and arguing that since the end product is the same then mutual recognition could be possible. This is dealt with too briefly in the last paragraph of the Commentary (12).

We also welcome the statement that baptism is an unrepeatable act. It is a matter of regret that some churches, while paying lip service to the principle of recognition of other churches' baptism, in actual practice do not act upon it and insist on "conditional baptism" as it is euphemistically called.

Question 3

The statement challenges the practises and even the thinking of the Church in Wales on questions of initiation. The reference to indiscriminate baptism in §16 and Commentary 21 needs to be taken seriously, as does the recommendation that baptism should be administered in the public worship of the church. The same point is expressed differently in §8, where we are reminded of the "necessity of faith for the reception of the salvation embodied and set forth in baptism". In our practice we should pay more attention to the faith of the parents who bring an infant for baptism. Both practice and thinking is further challenged by sub para (b) of Commentary 14 asking us to consider whether the failure to admit baptized children to the eucharist indicates an adequate understanding of the consequences of baptism.

In common with all other Anglican provinces we are reconsidering the relation of confirmation to baptism and this document will stimulate us further in this process. A challenge to us and probably to other churches is the factor which can be described as the gap between the "ought" and the "is". The language of Section II describes what baptism is meant to be and implies that it "effects", brings about what is described. In so many cases this does not appear to happen and so those questions regarding our practises, both sacramental and pastoral, referred to above are strongly reinforced. The final sentence in §8, "personal commitment is necessary for responsible membership in the body of Christ", is one that has to be taken very seriously.

EUCHARIST

Question 1

This statement was found to be very acceptable — a full and rich treatment of the subject. We particularly welcomed the way it linked the eucharist to the Trinity in Section II, and the irenic way in which it dealt with the controversies of the past, dealing very well with the two traditional problems of the eucharistic sacrifice and real presence, elucidating the former in terms of *anamnesis* and the intercessory aspect of the eucharist, and with the latter indicating the different views that have been held not so much between the churches but within them. As Anglicans we have come to recognize and accept that there are a number of diverse interpretations of the eucharistic presence. We welcome in BEM a similar recognition and also the readiness to relate the presence of Christ to the whole eucharistic action.

Question 2

In considering the document in relation to our dialogue with other churches we note five matters of varying significance:

i) We would wish to know if the other churches accept the full teaching on the meaning of the eucharist given here and especially if they attach the same importance to the eucharist as is given in BEM.

ii) Following from this, we would also ask if they accept the emphasis on the centrality of the eucharist in their worship, as is recommended in §§30 and 31 concerning the frequency of celebrating the eucharist and its appropriateness as taking place at least every Sunday.

iii) An important question is that relating to the celebrant of the eucharist. This is discussed very briefly in §29 and it would have been helpful to have had a further treatment. It is good that the statement avoids the terminology of validity and efficacy. Yet the questions pinpointed by this language concern many of our clergy and laity in the Church in Wales. To many of them the validity of the celebration is closely linked to that of the celebrant (and this is linked to the question of orders), and they would find the very brief discussion in §29 inadequate.

iv) The question of the right elements is important to us. The suggestion in Commentary 28 that the choice of bread and wine is culturally conditioned and is perhaps open to change in another culture would be unacceptable to the large majority in our church. Many are made very uneasy by the use of non-alcoholic substitutes for wine within the free churches. The traditional elements of bread (normally under the more convenient form of wafers) and alcoholic wine are invariably used in the Church in Wales, and in our relation with others who do not attach the same importance to the question it has been and could be a contentious and significant issue.

v) A similar important and emotive issue is the disposal of the consecrated elements after the service. This question is again dealt with too briefly in §32. Some of the churches with which we are in dialogue have in the past attached no importance to the consecrated elements. They have seen no need to consume them reverently, but dispose of them quite haphazardly, thereby causing offence to Anglicans. Since the use of an eucharistic rite for joint celebrations between the covenanted churches, the Anglican position has come to be better understood and the response is more sensitive and careful, but there still needs to be some further growth in understanding and sympathy on this issue.

Question 3

We see the text as particularly useful in the many-sided, positive teaching of the meaning of the eucharist, particularly in the helpful way in which it links the Trinity as thanksgiving to the Father, memorial of Christ and invocation of the Spirit. There is much useful teaching also in Section D on communion of the faithful and in Section E as meal of the kingdom, stressing as they do the ways in which the eucharist creates the Christian community and stimulates the ministry of reconciliation in the world. The way in which the eucharist focuses and leads to mission and witness in society is an important point and saves us from seeing it as a purely religious act, taking place within the four walls of the church building.

The outline of the elements of an eucharistic liturgy is one that is fully acceptable to our church and lays down similar guidelines to those we have applied in our liturgical revision over the last twenty years, although perhaps we need to take more seriously the place of proclamation of the word in the eucharist.

In our own province, it would be widely agreed that primary intention of reserving the elements is for distribution to the sick (§32) but we acknowledge that in some parishes it would not be seen purely in these terms. As already mentioned in the section on baptism, the point made regarding the admission of baptized children to communion (Commentary 19) is one that will receive careful consideration in our church.

MINISTRY

Question 1

We recognize the following aspects of the text as expressing the faith of the church:

i) We recognize that the text begins in the right place with the calling of the whole people of God and that the primary understanding of ministry is that of the ministry of the whole people. This has not always been clearly understood in the past, but is one of the basic truths grasped anew in our time.

ii) The text rightly places the ordained ministry in the context of the whole people but also distinguishes the role of the ordained ministry and sees it as essential for the whole body.

iii) While agreeing that there is no single clear pattern of ministry in the New Testament, we would see the emergence and development of the threefold ministry as more than just a historical accident but as necessary for the wellbeing of the church. At the same time, as a Reformation church, we would agree that the threefold pattern stands in constant need of reform and that the three guiding principles referred to in §26 have to be recovered again and again and renewed in the life of the church. Because of its centrality, we agree with the view that "the threefold ministry of bishop, presbyter and deacon may serve today as an expression of the unity we seek and also as a means for achieving it".

We would concur with the view in Commentary 31 that considerable thought has to be given to the question of the diaconate. The emergency of the role of women in the ordained ministry is something new in the twentieth century, and our own church, in common with most other churches, has still not fully responded to it. We continue to wrestle with the issues raised and the division of views described in commentary 18 is reflected in our church, although our "synod" has clearly expressed the view that there is no fundamental objection to the ordination of women.

iv) We welcome the description of apostolic succession in the life of the church and agree that the episcopal succession is "one of the ways in which the apostolic tradition of the Church was expressed" (§36).

v) The section on ordination is helpful in holding together the different aspects of ordination — the inner call, the outward sign, the invocation of the Spirit and the commitment of both ordinand and congregation. The section outlining the conditions for ordination has a balance and scope which we also welcome.

Question 2

In our relation with other churches the following points in the text on ministry seem to us the most important:

i) We would hope that the argument which places the ordained ministry in the context of the church's general ministry would be acceptable to all churches. We stress that the ordained ministry must not be divided from the Christian community. It has its raison d'être in and for the community (§12). We agree with the emphasis on the indispensability of the ordained ministry (§§8–11).

ii) We would strongly support the argument in §22 that the threefold ministry "may serve today as an expression of the unity we seek and also as a means for achieving it", and see this as the guiding principle by which the ministries of different churches can be reconciled, while at the same time accepting the argument in §26 that the threefold ministry should be exercised in a personal, collegial and communal way, and acknowledging the argument in §24 that reform is necessary.

iii) In particular, we see the importance of giving more thought to "the need, the rationale, the status and functions of deacons" (Commentary 31). It is here perhaps that a constructive dialogue can be entered into with other churches who have a lay diaconate or eldership or permanent diaconate as an integral part of their ministerial order. We feel that the brief reference in that paragraph needs much fuller study.

iv) The same is true on the question of the ordination of women, briefly alluded to in §18 and Commentary 18. The latter recognizes that churches are divided on this issue and only briefly lists the main arguments for and against. As a church we have to face this issue and seek some resolution of it, particularly in the light of the fact that our partners in the Covenant in Wales all practise the ordination of women and would not be prepared to change their position.

v) In the discussion on "Succession in the Apostolic Tradition" (Section IV), we shall have to give careful consideration to the argument in §37 "that a continuity in apostolic faith, worship and mission has been preserved in churches which have not retained the form of historic episcopate" and draw out the consequences for our relations with such churches, while at the same time urging them to "appreciate the episcopal succession as a sign, though not a guarantee, of the continuity and unity of the Church" (§38).

vi) Regarding ordination, we welcome the fullness of the statement in §41 and its explication in succeeding paragraphs. This encourages us to urge that this view of ordination be accepted by all churches, noting particularly the point in Commentary 39 that traditionally it is the bishop who ordains, with the participation of the community.

vii) We recognize the importance of the last section. We shall have to give serious consideration to §53(a), asking us to "recognize both the apostolic content of the ordained ministry which exists in churches which have not maintained such succession and also the existence in these churches of a ministry of *episkopé* in various forms". The steps by which the reconciliation of ministries is brought about and the service to mark the reconciliation will require much more extensive study; the brief consideration given here needs much fuller treatment.

Question 3

The following aspects of the text could usefully be incorporated into our thinking and our educational programme:

i) the need to educate our laity to grasp that they share in the calling and ministry of the whole people of God and to help them to realize their vocation;

ii) we shall continue to study the question of the ordination of women and seek a common mind on it;

iii) the reference in the text to the need to exercise the ministry in a personal, collegial and communal way calls for further exploration and thought;

iv) the reference to the need to clarify the role of the diaconate is one that is already engaging our attention and will continue to do so, since we now have permanent deacons (women deacons) as a feature of our ministry; in our dialogue with the churches of the Reformed tradition in Wales we have begun to consider how the diaconate can be reconciled with the eldership found in those churches;

v) the content of the section on ordination is on very similar lines to the teaching in our church on this subject and has been incorporated, for instance, into our modern revision of the ordinal.

Question 4

The following is the concluding question put to member churches:

> The suggestions your church can make for the ongoing work of Faith and Order as it relates the material of this text on "Baptism, Eucharist and Ministry" to its long-range research project "Towards the Common Expression of the Apostolic Faith Today".

We have already indicated in our response to the first three questions, the subjects which we think are dealt with too briefly in the text and need further study and discussion. They can be summarized thus:

A.
  i) the relation between baptism and confirmation and the place of the latter in the process of initiation into membership;
  ii) a study of the different meanings attached to church membership within the churches;
  iii) a clearer analysis of the process of initiation, especially as contrasted in believers' and infant baptism;

B.
  i) the role and status of the celebrant of the eucharist;
  ii) the choice of elements in the eucharist;
  iii) the use of the consecrated elements outside the immediate context of the service;

C.
  i) the ordination of women;
  ii) the role and status of the diaconate;
  iii) steps to reconciliation of churches and ministries, and the means for achieving reconciliation.

CHURCH OF MELANESIA

Baptism

Question: The extent to which your church can recognize in this text the faith of the church through the ages?

Response: We believe that this comprehensive statement on baptism contains the substance of our faith and is consonant with the historical faith of the church throughout the ages.

Question: The consequences your church can draw from this text for its relations and dialogues with other churches, particularly with those churches which also recognize the text as an expression of the apostolic faith?

Response: It can give us common ground to initiate dialogues and establish relationship with other churches that recognize the text on baptism as the expression of the apostolic faith.

Question: The guidance your church can take from this text for its worship, educational, ethical, and spiritual life and witness?

Response: As a guide the text gives us enlightenment on our church worship, Christian living, teaching and witness. However we give room for contextual diversity of our culture (i.e. Melanesian).

Question: The suggestions your church can make for the ongoing work of Faith and Order as it relates the material of this text on baptism, to its long-range research project "Towards the Common Expression of the Apostolic Faith Today"?

Response: We suggest the following as an application of this text:
a) that the Faith and Order Commission of the WCC draw up or cause to draw up a common "rite of baptism" based on the teaching of this text;

- 140,000 members, 5 dioceses, 5 bishops, 200 priests.

b) that a common catechism based on this text be disseminated for use among the churches who recognize the text as an expression of the apostolic faith.

Eucharist

Question: The extent to which your church can recognize in this text the faith of the church through the ages?

Response: We appreciate the balanced treatment of the different aspects of the eucharist in this text, but we cannot recognize in it the faith of the church throughout the ages as eucharist has been the centre of bitter controversy.

Question: The consequence your church can draw from this text for its relations and dialogues with other churches, particularly with those churches which also recognize the text as an expression of the apostolic faith?

Response: This text can open up new avenues for dialogues with other churches which might lead to deeper and common understanding. However the dialogue may produce unexpected negative results which may frustrate the goals of Christian unity.

Question: The guidance your church can take from this text for its worship, educational, ethical and spiritual life and witness?

Response: This text can stimulate us to clarify our stand on the eucharist in relation to other churches with regard to our worship, teaching, Christian living and witness.

Question: The suggestions your church can make for the ongoing work of Faith and Order as it relates the material of this text on eucharist to its long-range research project "Towards the Common Expression of the Apostolic Faith Today"?

Response: We appreciate the attempt of the Commission to bring about a common understanding of the apostolic faith in relation to the eucharist, but we suggest that the Commission will be more precise in its use of liturgical terms lacking in the text.

Ministry

Question: The extent to which your church can recognize in this text the faith of the church through the ages?

Response: We appreciate the work the Commission has done, but we regret to say that we cannot recognize in this text an adequate elucidation of the faith of the church in so far as ministry is concerned because:

a) there seems to be a complete silence on the sacramental aspects and sacramental function of the ordained ministry, e.g. "ministry of forgiveness" (reconciliation);

b) the text does not fully express the catholicity of the "threefold orders of ministry";

c) we would like to refer you to the final report of the ARCIC agreed statement on ministry and ordination.

Question: The consequence your church can draw from this text for its relations and dialogues with other churches, particularly with those churches which also recognize the text as the expression of the apostolic faith?

Response: As expressed in our answer to the preceding question, we fail to see from this text any help that may promote our relations and dialogues with other churches.

Question: The guidance your church can take from this text for its worship, educational, ethical and spiritual life and witness?

Response: We cannot take any guidance from this text for our use in Christian worship, teaching, and Christian living for we profess more than what this text contains.

Question: The suggestion your church can make for the ongoing work of Faith and Order as it relates the material of this text on ministry to its long-range research project "Towards the Common Expression of the Apostolic Faith Today"?

Response: We suggest that the Faith and Order Commission review the whole content of the text on ministry and in so doing reference should be made to the apostolic succession, authority, and the sacramental aspects and functions of the ordained ministry.

HOLY CATHOLIC CHURCH IN JAPAN (ANGLICAN)

The significance of the Lima text for the divided churches striving for visible unity is considerable.

1. We recognize in this text an appropriate expression of the faith of the church handed down through the ages from the apostles' time.

2. The text shows an attitude of mutual respect for each church's tradition and a willingness to fill the deficit of each other if necessary.

3. We can find in this text a pertinent guideline for a revitalization of worship, Christian education, moral and spiritual life in each church.

4. The HCCJ will continue to study the text together with the forthcoming WCC document "Towards a Confession of the Apostolic Faith".

- 55,570 members, 324 parishes, 11 dioceses, 11 bishops, 348 pastors and active church workers.

CHURCH OF THE PROVINCE
OF SOUTHERN AFRICA

A. Churches have been asked to respond to the following matters:
1. The extent to which your church can recognize in this text the faith of the church through the ages.
2. The consequences your church can draw from this text for its relations and dialogues with other churches, particularly with those churches which also recognize the text as an expression of the apostolic faith.
3. The guidance your church can take from this text for its worship, educational, ethical, and spiritual life and witness.
4. Suggestions your church can make for the ongoing work of Faith and Order as it relates the material of this text on baptism, eucharist and ministry to its long-range research project "Towards the Common Expression of the Apostolic Faith Today".

B. The Southern African Anglican Theological Commission has produced the following guide to assist the response of the Church of the Province of Southern Africa, which is to be made by the Provincial Standing Committee in November 1985.

Introductory
1. The first question is difficult to answer, since it depends on the interpretation given to the faith of the church through the ages. The texts deal with three of the most controversial issues facing the church and cannot hope to mention all the different views which have been held by the church through the ages. There are different views even within the Anglican Church since the Reformation, and not all would be represented in these texts.
2. It is important to note the qualifications mentioned in the Preface.
a) "Full consensus can only be proclaimed after the churches reach the point of living and acting together in unity" (p. ix). "The faith of the church

---

• 2,200,000 members, 731 parishes, 17 dioceses, 1,210 bishops and priests.

through the ages" is to be expressed not in doctrinal statements but in Christian living in the bond of the Spirit. The texts all show the remarkable overlap in theological understanding between the participating churches, and this is prima facie evidence of their being an expression of "the faith through the ages".

b) The texts do not pretend to be "a complete theological treatment of baptism, eucharist and ministry", but are concerned only with "those aspects of the theme that have been directly or indirectly related to the problems of mutual recognition leading to unity" (p. ix).

Baptism

1. The CPSA recognizes in this text the faith of the church throughout the ages. It wishes particularly to emphasize the following points:

a) Baptism is a gift of God (§§1,8).

b) The meaning of baptism in pp. 2–7, and especially the understanding of baptism as the basic bond of unity. This means that our unity in Christ is itself a gift of God, so that baptism indeed is "a call to the churches to overcome their divisions and visibly manifest their fellowship" (§6).

c) The relation between baptism and faith (§8). Further explanation of the relationship seems to be necessary. Baptism as God's gift is God's reaching out to man which needs to be accepted by man to effect the new relationship which baptism entails (grace and faith).

d) The unrepeatability of baptism (§13). If baptism is seen as God's gift, its reality may not be denied, and therefore any form of rebaptism is theologically impossible.

e) Baptism as a corporate act (§§12,23).

f) The relation between baptism and eucharist (§14, especially as described in commentary 14c).

g) The unity that baptism gives across all divisions of class, race or nation (§6).

The CPSA recognizes with the Lima statement the divergencies which exist in the understanding of the relationship between baptism and confirmation, which is intimately connected with the relation between baptism and faith. In line with the faith of the church and with the teaching of Vatican II, it is baptism in the name of the Trinity which incorporates a person into Christ and therefore makes him a member of the church. The personal expression of faith is necessary for the establishment of a full relationship between the believer and God. In the case of adults, baptism, personal profession of faith and confirmation occur together as different parts of a single rite. In the case of infants, the reality of God's gift may not be doubted, but the personal expression of faith, necessary for the completion of the relationship between the believer and God, is to be made later. This traditionally occurs at confirmation, when God can be trusted to strengthen the believer with his grace for his life of discipleship. Admission to the eucharist may be granted to those baptized but not confirmed on the grounds that by God's gift they are members of the body of Christ, and such admission may be refused only on the grounds that the reality of baptism depends on the faith of the candidates.

2. *Consequences arising from the statement on baptism*
   If the Lima report is accepted:
   a) Readiness to accept as communicants of the CPSA, communicants of other churches who have been baptized in the name of the Trinity.
   b) Readiness to accept the sacramental integrity of other churches and consequently to recognize their rites of admission of members to communicant status.

   Further discussion is needed on the relationship between baptism and confirmation, and the ministry of the bishop in this regard.

3. *Guidance of the church from the statement on baptism*
   a) The need to ensure in those baptized a growth in personal commitment and holiness. If baptism is to be taken seriously, it is the beginning of a life of discipleship and of growth in the Lord.
   b) The need to avoid indiscriminate baptism.
   c) The need to ensure that no one is baptized without adequate preparation for Christian discipleship, and, in the case of infants, that parents or guardians are made aware of the meaning of baptism and the responsibility which they incur.
   d) The need to help members of the church to understand that the eucharist is (inter alia) the occasion for their reaffirmation of their baptismal vows, and to ensure that this is not only taught, but also expressed in the liturgy.
   e) As incorporated into Christ by baptism and sharing in his life, the believer has the duty to display in his own life, the unity which the Lord has given him with all other baptized persons, of whatever sex, race or culture.
   f) Baptism into Christ implies a new style of living, modelled on the example of Christ himself.

Eucharist
   1. The CPSA accepts as biblical and as representing the faith of the church throughout the ages, the following articles of the Lima statement. In this it does not deny the truth and validity of other parts of the statement but draws attention to the special significance of the points mentioned:
   a) the eucharist as "the gift of salvation" (§2);
   b) the eucharist as the action of God himself (§2);
   c) the eucharist as "the proclamation and celebration of the work of God" (§4);
   d) the eucharist as the church's act of thanksgiving (§§3–4);

e) the eucharist as *anamnesis* of Christ's unique sacrifice (§8);
f) the eucharist as anticipation of the parousia (§6);
g) the eucharist as the occasion when the sacrifice and offering of Christians is associated with the once-for-all sacrifice of Christ (§10);
h) "Christ's real, living and active presence in the eucharist" (§13);
i) the eucharist as the expression of the participation of the believer in the ongoing life and mission of Christ in the world, thereby involving him in the struggle against all forms of injustice and separation (§§20,25);
j) the dependence of the whole eucharistic action on the Holy Spirit (§§14–18); this item represents the recovery of an element in eucharistic theology often neglected in the West.

2. A further comment: The importance of the person of the president at the eucharist needs to be underlined. In view of the acceptance of the eucharist as having "to do with the whole church" (§19) and the stress (§29) on the fact that "the rite is not the assemblies' own creation or possession", the president of the eucharist needs to be seen as one who acts on behalf of the whole church. It is in this sense that ordination takes on a special importance.

3. The consequences for ecumenical relations:
a) Further discussion between the churches is needed on the nature of the presidency of the eucharist, and the theological significance of ordination in this regard.
b) Further discussion is needed on the presence of Christ in the eucharist so that churches may take seriously the reality of each other's eucharistic celebrations.
c) Attention is drawn especially to the remarks in Commentary 28 (p.17). To what extent are features in the eucharist immutable?

Ministry
1. The CPSA accepts the following articles as especially reflecting the faith of the church throughout the ages.
a) The ministry of the church is derived from the ministry of Jesus Christ. The whole church is called to ministry "reflecting Christ's love for the world, and the power of the Spirit given to the church" (§§1–6).
b) The ordained ministry derives from the ministry of Christ himself, in and through his church (§§7c, 11).
c) Ordained ministers point to the church's "fundamental dependence on Jesus Christ, and thereby provide, within the multiplicity of gifts, a focus to its unity" (§8).
d) Ordained ministers function as "representatives of Jesus Christ to the community" as leaders and teachers and as pastors (§11).
e) The main function of the ordained ministry is to "assemble and build up

the body of Christ by proclaiming and teaching the word of God", and by presiding at the liturgical celebrations of the church (§13).

f) The authority of the ordained minister is to be seen as a gift from God, for the building up of the church (§15).

g) The representative nature and function of the ordained minister is essential to the understanding of the ministry. Ordained ministers represent both Christ and his church. As representatives of the church they address the world.

2. Some possible reservations:

a) In affirming the need for *episkopé*, the text is not dogmatic on the forms of the other orders of ministry or even of the nature of the *episkopos*. While this is a true reflection of the historical position, further elucidation of the nature of *episkopé* is needed.

b) While recognizing that it is not necessary to have precisely the same view of ministry in order to recognize each other's ministries (§28), some definition is needed in order to present the visible reality of the church. Agreement on the content of the Lima statement would seem to be the minimum requirement.

3. The consequences for ecumenical relationships:

a) The churches are called to re-examine the meaning of "apostolic ministry", and their understanding of *episkopé* and *episkopos*.

b) They need clarity about the nature of priesthood and diaconate, and their place in the ministry of the whole church.

c) They need to re-examine the nature of authority and ways of exercising it.

d) They need to consider the place of the "travelling ministry" within the church and its relation to the authority of the local church (§21 and commentary 21).

e) In view of the Lima statement, especially §28, the CPSA needs seriously to consider ways in which it can recognize ministries of other churches without a ceremony which may seem to imply reordination.

f) The CPSA needs to consider the possibility of recognizing the orders of women ministers and the obstacles to union which they appear to constitute.

4. Guidance from this text for the worship, educational, ethical and spiritual life of the CPSA

a) Expectations demanded of clergy in fulfilling all the various ministries of the church seem to demand the gifts and insights of the different denominational traditions.

b) Consideration of ways to help the clergy to take seriously their role as trainers, leaders or servants of the laity.

c) The vocation of clergy, as representatives of Christ and his church, to holiness of living needs to be taken very seriously.

5. *Suggestions for the ongoing work of the Faith and Order Commission in relating this text to its long-range project*
Nothing is suggested in this respect.

July 1985   Provincial Synod

EVANGELICAL–LUTHERAN CHURCH OF DENMARK

The following statement has been compiled by four university teachers of theology. They were given the task of drawing up a draft reply from the Church of Denmark to the Faith and Order Commission of the World Council of Churches. This draft was to be submitted to the bishops at their annual meeting in January 1985. The reply is thus an expression of well-founded opinion in the Church of Denmark as represented by the four co-signatories. An official reply to the questions posed (where problems of canon law are not entailed) can only be given by the bishops, possibly making references to the statement which follows here.

Introduction

The established Evangelical–Lutheran Church of Denmark understands itself to be part of the one Christian church reaching back to the apostles, from which we ourselves have received the gospel.

We wish to express our gratitude to the Faith and Order Commission for the significant work which has gone into the convergence declarations concerning "Baptism, Eucharist and Ministry" now issued. These declarations allow us to see the breadth of the Christian witness with regard to baptism, eucharist and ministry in such a way as makes it possible to understand also those formulations, which are alien to us as expressions of the faith of the Christian church through the ages, without, as far as we can see, these expressions being in conflict at any decisive point with the confession of our own church.

Nevertheless, we wish to make clear that we understand the expression "the faith of the Church through the ages" more as a description of a

---

• 4,684,060 members, 2,101 parishes, 2,029 pastors. This response, which has been obtained from the two theological faculties at the Danish universities, has been submitted by the bishops of the Evangelical-Lutheran Church of Denmark.

historical context than as a credal norm, even though we also hear in that expression the questionings to us of other churches as to the sufficient biblical foundation for the confessional position of our church. The faith of the Christian church in the proper sense of the phrase is for us: to believe in the gospel of Jesus Christ as God's unconditional grace and to confess that the Triune God works upon us through creation and redemption, as is proclaimed in baptism. For us this confession of faith also involves confessing that it is the same God who works upon us in the proclamation of the gospel, in the baptism and the eucharist, and in the reality of the church. But we do not find ourselves able to see in the mutual recognition of one another's baptism, eucharist and ministry a *presupposition* for the reality of the baptism, the eucharist or the church among us, for it is our conviction that this reality is rooted solely in Jesus Christ's own institution and promise. On the other hand we gladly acknowledge the mutual recognition of baptism, eucharist and ministry as a visible sign of the unity of the church which is given solely in Christ.

From this standpoint we are in a position to reply to the questions put by the WCC Commission on Faith and Order:

1. That we find ourselves able to see in the published convergence texts concerning baptism, eucharist and ministry an expression of the faith of the church through the ages and that we can recognize the baptism, eucharist and ministry of those churches who understand these matters within the framework of declaration, always presupposing that no human doctrinal understanding or particular church order is understood as a requirement of salvation on a par with the gospel.

2. That we recognize with gratitude the enrichment of our own understanding of baptism, eucharist and ministry when we see the reality of our own church in the light of faith of the Christian church through the ages, as formulated in this declaration.

3. That we are willing to be inspired by the declaration in the teaching and theological training of our own church and in endeavours towards church and liturgical renewal, and to allow the declaration to correct our view of baptism, eucharist and ministry of the other churches.

4. That we call upon the WCC Commission on Faith and Order to prepare and publish a detailed account of the answers and critical reservations received, and we would urge the Commission to continue its study project "Towards a Common Expression of the Apostolic Faith Today". We also declare ourselves willing to participate in this study.

Baptism

1. With regard to *the institution of baptism* (section I) we find — despite a generally "pre-critical" use of the Bible — that the formulation of the sacraments as rooted in Jesus Christ's own ministry, death, and resurrection and his present working in the congregation corresponds happily both with

modern historical-exegetical insight and with the witness of the New Testament and the confession of our own church.

2. The presentation of *the meaning and content of baptism* (II) corresponds with our own teaching on baptism. We note particularly that baptism is clearly founded on God's saving action in Christ and that emphasis is placed on the Triune God as the real subject in baptism. The emphasis on the eschatological and the paranetic aspect, stronger than in more traditional Lutheran teaching on baptism, corresponds with our biblical understanding and is an enrichment of our baptismal perspective. The same is true of the emphasis on the fellowship of the church as the context for baptism. Baptism has a prominent place in the consciousness of the Danish church: this is an inheritance from the Grundtvigian revival of the last century, which laid particular emphasis on baptism as entry into the congregation.

3. The presentation of the relationship between *baptism and faith* (III) is also a point with which we find ourselves by and large in agreement, although this expression is foreign to our tradition. We understand the description of baptism as being "both God's gift and our human response to that gift", on the basis of the emphases in the text on the inclusive character of baptism as it embraces the whole of human life, a viewpoint in harmony with the tradition of the Reformation. It is an indelible part of Lutheran baptismal understanding that "faith in baptism" (i.e. in God's promise given in baptism) belongs to baptism itself: we understand faith both as the faith of the baptizing congregation and as the faith-life grounded in baptism of the one baptized. We, too, are able to speak of a growth in the life of faith of the Christian in the congregation, and we understand this faith to be the gift of God.

4. We acknowledge that it is fruitful to approach the question of the relationship between *baptism of believers and infants* from what has been said above and to see these as two forms of one and the same baptism. We can by and large concur in the presentation given (section IVA). Nevertheless we miss in §11 a clear *reason for infant baptism*, which for us rests on the constitutory significance of baptism for the life of the Christian. As a Lutheran church we maintain the legitimacy of infant baptism based on God's action towards us, and we understand it as a consequence of the transition from missionary baptism to congregational baptism, even though we, too — increasingly — have examples of the baptism of adults, particularly in connection with confirmation, but also in cases of conversion from a non-Christian environment. We are in agreement with the emphasis on (a) the positive parental wish for baptism, (b) the faith and intercession of the congregation as a presupposition for infant baptism, and similarly the emphasis on (c) the significance of baptismal instruction as a task for both parents and congregation (§§11–12). On this basis we can embrace the solemn injunction to take seriously the responsibility for the growth in a Christian context of the baptized, even although the danger of "indiscriminate baptism" is in our view not only a problem for national churches

practising infant baptism but a problem for all churches (16 and 21 commentary). We have chosen the expression "growth in a Christian context", as we wish to emphasize that no Christian upbringing can or should guarantee that a person comes to faith, just as little as we ourselves can guarantee that we shall remain in the faith: both can only be object for prayer. On the other hand, we acknowledge that a positive attitude towards an "instruction in the Christian teaching for children" must as a matter of course be a prerequisite for infant baptism, and we admit that this is a pastoral problem for us. With regard to confirmation (see §12 commentary) many in our church today understand confirmation more as being a completion of the church's baptismal instruction and an introduction into the worship of the congregation — these things being seen as an affirmation of the faith of the congregation rather than as a personal confession of faith. Nor is there an insistence on confirmation as a pre-condition for receiving communion, if children participate in the eucharist with their parents or while they are receiving instruction.

5. With regard to the *positive directions* (IVC, §§15–16 see opening to commentary 12), it goes without saying that we recognize the baptism of "believer baptists" to be Christian baptism, since we presuppose the confession that it is God who gives faith, and that this will always be in need of growth, and since we *also presuppose* that they in their turn recognize the infant baptism of believing Christians as a complete Christian baptism and desist from what we would adjudge to be "rebaptism". For us it is crucial that no one who has been baptized as an infant and who later comes to a consciousness of faith or to a doubt about his faith should ever be in any doubt about his baptism. This is why we emphasize that baptism is valid by virtue of God's promise, while faith takes baptism to itself and lives life in the strength of baptism.

In our own church, it is a matter of course that we regard adult baptism as having the same status as infant baptism, and there are many in our church who would say that the church should accept a postponement of baptism where the preconditions for infant baptism are wanting. On the other hand we are *not* able to view the introduction of a "service of blessing for a child" as a possible alternative to baptism in our church, since we take our specific stand on infant baptism as an expression of the child's membership of the congregation. This does not prevent us from recognizing a legitimate intention in those churches which find themselves unable to practise infant baptism.

6. Concerning *confirmation* (IVB) we have already stated that it belongs to baptism just as instruction in Christian faith and in the personal confession of that faith, finding expression in participation in worship, belongs to Christian living. On the other hand we do not regard a special (sacramental) confirmation as a precondition for participating in the eucharist of the congregation, since baptism itself is in our view "to receive the Holy Spirit"

and to be incorporated into the congregation which is joined together in eucharist. We find the explicit reference to this (§14 and commentary) important, but on the contrary we do not find that the text offers any real help to a consideration of the place of confirmation in an "Evangelical Lutheran" context (see 4 above with reference to §12).

7. With regard to the *baptismal rite* (V) we also baptize in the name of the Father, the Son and the Holy Spirit as a confession that the Triune God himself is the one who baptizes; and we confess that to be baptized is "to receive (i.e. to receive the promise of) the Holy Spirit together with the forgiveness of sins and eternal life" and "to be grafted into the congregation of believers (i.e. the congregation which confesses belief in the Triune God)". We do not therefore regard anointing with oil or sacramental confirmation respectively as a necessary dimension of Christian baptism (initiation), but we acknowledge it in other churches as part of the tradition of the ancient church. The same is true of references made in the text to other symbolic dimensions of the baptismal rite. In the Church of Denmark it is usual for baptism to take place in the context of the common worship of the congregation, and we — like the Lima text — place emphasis on this.

Eucharist

1. Concerning *the institution of the eucharist* (I), in our eyes the text combines in a sober manner historical and confessional statements without confusing the two. The tradition of 1 Cor. 11:23–24 plays a central role, and rightly so, in the eucharistic liturgy of the Lutheran church. Reference to Jesus' table fellowship with his disciples and with the multitude, to the experience of the presence of the Risen One in the meal after Easter, as well as reference to the Last Supper as the background to the eucharist, and finally emphasis on the eschatological perspective of the eucharist corresponds with our understanding of the New Testament and is a valuable and necessary enlargement of perspective by comparison with the classical and over narrow conception of the eucharist as a repetition of the Last Supper. The eucharist is also a paschal experience. We, too, regard the eucharist of other churches — despite critical reservations — as being in intention a celebration of the one "Lord's Supper", and for us, too, the eucharist — indissolubly linked with the verbal proclamation of the gospel — is the "central act of the church's worship" (§1 — see also §12).

2. In the presentation of *the meaning of the eucharist* we take positive note of the clear emphasis on the eucharist as *God's gift* and Christ's action with his congregation (§2, see also §1 opening and §§4, 6, 7, 9, 13 and 29).

The same is true of the reference to "the forgiveness of sins" (Matt. 26:28) and the promise of eternal life (§2) as a reminder that the eucharist is celebrated this side of the parousia, a reminder which in our view is important to underline. The emphasis on the work of the Spirit and on the Trinitarian aspect of the eucharist respectively and the relationship to creation (§§3 and 23) are an enrichment of our understanding of the eucharist as is also the eschatological perspective (§§6–8 and section IIE, §22). This is also true of the emphasis on the relationship between the eucharist and the fellowship of the congregation (including the paranetical dimension section IID, §19) which for us is a recovery of some aspects of our Reformation heritage.

3. To have the content of the eucharist presented in terms of the liturgical concepts of the early church: *"eucharist, anamnesis and epiclesis"* (IIA,B,C) is alien to the tradition of our church especially to our Danish tradition — despite the fact that we are familiar by virtue of the worship and hymn tradition of our own church with all the themes mentioned as also with the *fellowship motif* (IID) and the eschatological vision of the *"meal of the kingdom"* (IIE). Nevertheless we have the impression that this text — to a greater extent than the text on baptism — views the eucharist from the point of view of the congregation's response and action in worship. This is not necessarily incorrect, of course, as long as the eucharist also and primarily (§2) is viewed as God's gift; but we feel it important here to spell out the relationship between the liturgical action of the congregation and God's action. We note with approval that nowhere does the Lima text give expression to the thought that the congregation (not to mention the minister) *by* its thanksgiving, remembrancing of invocation of the Holy Spirit "effects" the presence of Christ, but confesses, as we do, that *in* this act of worship Christ himself *is* present, *inviting* us to his supper and *giving* us a share in his work (§§4,6,7,14,15,29).

4. Concerning *the presence* (real presence) we understand the emphasis on Christ's personal presence as the subject who acts in the eucharist and on the presence of Christ's own saving action (as an anticipation of eschatological fulfilment), both indelibly linked to the physical meal, as a significant corrective to the often all too narrow, traditional Western understanding of the real presence. We mean in addition by this that such an understanding — maintaining the intrinsic connection between the real presence and the material gifts of the eucharist as the "sacramental signs of the body and blood of Christ" (§15) — allows us to recognize certain intentions of our Reformation heritage which we can see more clearly today in the light both of the early church and of ecumenical perspectives. However we do not find the formulation in §13 sufficiently exact, recognizing as we do that it has not here been possible to arrive at a clear consensus (commentary on §§13,14 and 15). For us it is essential to emphasize the constitutive dimension of *"Christ's promise" in the words of institution*, which we understand as *gospel*, as the present declaration of fellowship with him (cp "the living word of Christ", §§15 and 14). We find this covered to some extent by the emphasis given to the invocation of the Holy Spirit taken to mean prayer for the fulfilment of Christ's promise (§14), and we should wish to emphasize this aspect. We find it makes a valuable link between the eucharistic prayer of the early church,

addressed to the Father and including a prayer for the descent of the Spirit, and the intention underlying the eucharistic conception of the Lutheran Reformation: the possibility by faith in Christ's own promise and undertaking of receiving the gift of communion in this physical meal. We recognize that an understanding of the eucharistic consecration as *prayer* can offer a valuable corrective to a too narrow understanding of (the moment of) "consecration" (commentary 14). Moreover this prayer should also be a prayer for the receiving of communion in faith.

5. With regard to "*making remembrance*" (the *anamnesis*) we, too, from a Lutheran standpoint are in principle able to speak of "the presence of the sacrifice of Christ" (§§6–8), of the thanksgiving of the congregation as a "sacrifice of praise" (§4) and of a "sacrifice of ourselves" in daily service for which we are strengthened in the eucharist (§10), even though we in our church seldom speak in this way directly in connection with the eucharist, and although it must of course be a presupposition that *the unique character of Christ's saving work* is clearly maintained, (cp. §8). The Reformers, too, are able to emphasize that Christ "makes intercession for us", just as all prayer is prayer in the name of Jesus. Moreover we note with satisfaction that the Lima text nowhere speaks of the eucharist as a "sacrifice", a form of language which would at best be open to misunderstanding.

6. Thus, although the Lima text on the eucharist uses a language with which very few in our church are familiar, we are able to read the text as a witness to "the faith of the church through the ages" and to hear it as a call to view our own church's tradition in the light of the greater, common tradition of the whole church — not least the liturgical tradition of the early church — in which our Lutheran Church of Denmark also stands. Perhaps this may be an inspiration to us for a liturgical renewal which in addition to respecting our own Danish church tradition would maintain *the connection between the eucharist and the proclamation of the word* as a governing idea.

It is on this basis that we judge the text's liturgical directions (§27). These in our view suffer to some extent by having such an abundance of motifs that there is a threat of obscuring the clear structure of the eucharistic liturgy and the central location of its content in Christ's own word and institution as *the only absolutely necessary element*. We are in agreement with the text in emphasizing the eucharist as a necessary part of the worship of the congregation (the Danish "high mass"). In many of our churches, and in an increasing number, it is usual to celebrate the eucharist every Sunday. It is, however, an absolute rule that the eucharist cannot be celebrated without communion. For us, too, it goes without saying that the eucharist is presided over by an ordained minister.

7. Concerning intercommunion the Church of Denmark takes the same position as the other Lutheran churches in Scandinavia: we regard *all Christians* who are able to participate in the eucharist in their own church and who wish to receive communion in our Lutheran church, trusting in that

which Christ has instituted, as being *welcome at the Lord's table*. Mutual access to each other's communion table is in our opinion a consequence of mutual recognition of each other's eucharist.

Ministry

1. For us the text on ministry is set apart from the others, in that we do not see a particular ministerial function or a particular structure of ministry as being constitutive for the church in the same way as baptism and eucharist are. Nevertheless we also take the view that, together with the proclamation of the gospel, baptism and the eucharist, there has been "given a ministry" (C.A.*V*). In this sense we, too, can acknowledge the ordained ministry as "constitutive for the church" (§8). Moreover we find it proper and valuable that the text has "the vocation of the *whole people of God*" as its point of departure, since all are called to witness to the gospel and to serve their neighbour (including the service of intercession). We see this "universal priesthood" of the individual and of the congregation as being *grounded in baptism*. We would underline those sections in the text which emphasize the mutual dependence on each other of minister (bishop) and congregation (§§12,26,32–33), and we regard it as helpful for our understanding that also the ordained ministry is seen as an "office of service" in the congregation (§7). On the other hand we are in agreement with the text that there is to be found in the church "*a special ministry*" with the fixed task of attending to the public proclamation of the gospel, to the administration of the sacraments and to pastoral care in the congregation, and which in this way has a care for and represents "the unity of the church", both in the local congregation and — in the person of the bishop — at a regional level (§8). But we are not of the opinion that the leadership of the congregation rests *exclusively* with the ordained ministry.

2. With regard to the question of the "*authority*" of ministry and its character as a "*priestly* ministry" (sections IIB and C), we think it is right that the minister in his/her preaching and administering the sacraments (in so far as it is the gospel which is proclaimed) speaks and acts with the authority of Christ and as a mediator of or servant for the "priesthood" *of Christ* vis-a-vis the congregation, whereas he or she as leader of the worship of the congregation, and especially of their intercession, together with the congregation and on their behalf is charged with the "(universal) priesthood" *of the congregation*. The authority of the minister is thus the authority *of the gospel* alone. Only as mediator of and servant to the priesthood of Christ and of the congregation is he or she a "priest". We find this understanding is expressed in the text (§§15–17).

3. In the Church of Denmark the equal access of men and women to the ordained ministry is recognized (section IID). We acknowledge no divisiveness in this matter for the church (§54) since we presuppose that mutual

recognition of one another's ministry also includes women ministers in those churches which ordain women.

4. Concerning the *structure of ministry* (section III) we are agreed in emphasizing that the New Testament does not recognize only one structure of ministry, but speaks of a range of different "ministries" (§19) and also that the differing functions which find expression in "the threefold ministry" *de facto* are taken care of in those patterns of ministry, which have not adopted the episcopal system (§24). From the standpoint of our own church's tradition we would therefore be in a position to recognize "the threefold ministry", all the more so as we have preserved the office of bishop; but we are *not* able to recognize it as necessary (*de iure divino*) for the unity of the church (cf the three reservations in the opening to §22). We find the considerations in the text on the content of "the threefold ministry" instructive (§§25–26 and section IIIC), but (going along with the commentary to §32) we do not find it obvious that every ministry in the congregation can be incorporated into this pattern, nor is it obvious what in this case separates the ministries requiring ordination (the deacon's office) from other ministries in the congregation (cf. §32). On the other hand, we find the references made by the text to the differing ministries and to a differentiation of the tasks of ministry highly relevant as questions to our own tradition and practice.

5. In the question of *the succession* (section IV) we find it right that continuity in the apostles' tradition, which we understand as agreement with the apostolic gospel, should receive precedence over continuity of ministry, especially given a functional understanding of ministry. We, too, place weight on this latter continuity, but we cannot see an unbroken succession in the transmission of the ministry either as a guarantee for the agreement of a church's preaching with the apostolic gospel or as a prerequisite for exercising the church's ministry. On the other hand we could perfectly well assume it as a visible sign of the mutual recognition of one another's principal offices of ministry, even if it is not on our side a presupposition for such recognition (cf §38).

6. We find the emphasis on *ordination* as an action of the *whole congregation* and not just of the ordaining person extremely valuable (§41). We too ordain ministers to their particular office "in the manner of the apostles" with prayer and the laying on of hands by an already ordained person given authority for this task (the bishop or the bishop's representative). For us, too, ordination means (a) a recognition on the part of the congregation of the minister's vocation and a handing over of the ordinand to God for a particular ministry: namely on behalf of Christ to proclaim the gospel and administer the sacraments, (b) a prayer for the help and guidance of the Holy Spirit, and (c) an undertaking on God's part to fulfil this prayer, since we emphasize the proclamatory character of this undertaking (cf. 42 "the freedom of the Spirit"). Ordination means therefore for us not the taking up of someone into a higher spiritual state in relation to the

congregation but the placing of that person into the particular mutual relationship which exists between God, congregation and minister (cf point 2). For us, too, ordination is in principle ordination for the whole of life and to the whole church. We do not therefore repeat ordination at a transfer to a new ministerial post or when a person takes up his or her ministry again after other work. Nor do we today as a general rule reordain persons ordained in another church, if, after taking the priestly vow to maintain the church's confession, they become ministers in the Church of Denmark.

7. Concerning a mutual recognition of one another's ministries enough has been said above (points 1 and 5). We can acknowledge the significance such a step would have, together with a recognition of one another's baptism and eucharist, as a visible sign of the unity of the church, which the churches would thereby confess.

Copenhagen/Aarhus	Leif Grane*	Mogens Müller
December 1984	Lars Thunberg	Erik Kyndal

---

* For my part the positive statements which appear (enrichment, gratitude, etc.) must be given the minimum content possible.

EVANGELICAL LUTHERAN CHURCH OF FINLAND

Introduction

The Evangelical Lutheran Church of Finland has carefully familiarized itself with the paper "Baptism, Eucharist and Ministry", prepared by the Faith and Order Commission of the World Council of Churches, and issues the following reply.

"Baptism, Eucharist and Ministry" is a noteworthy ecumenical document, which should continue to be studied in the churches even after the official replies have been given (31 December 1985). Our church views with pleasure the ecumenical convergence demonstrated by the document and regards the BEM paper as offering a useful starting point for theological discussion between the churches on the subjects of baptism, eucharist and ministry.

Evaluation of the document is difficult because it can be interpreted in many different ways. Many points in the text can be understood and interpreted in such a way that they are in harmony with Lutheran tradition, but the same points can also be interpreted differently. Our answers to the questions formulated in the preface of BEM will become apparent in the statement.

Our church's statement is divided into three main parts. The structure of the statement in each of these main parts is the same: Firstly (A) we shall state those points where in our opinion our church can recognize the faith of the church through the ages. Secondly (B) we shall state those challenges and questions which the document presents to our church and also to its relations and discussions with other churches. Thirdly (C) we shall state certain reservations and critical questions, which in the opinion of our church demand further explanation or are contrary to the teaching of our church. This statement contains replies to the first three questions posed by the Faith and Order Commission. The Church Council for Foreign Affairs will reply to the fourth question.

- 4,642,500 members, 8 dioceses, 598 parishes, 8 bishops, 1,300 pastors.

Baptism

A. Total agreement

In the section of the BEM document concerning baptism the Evangelical Lutheran Church of Finland recognizes the basic factors of the "faith of the Church through the ages":

1. Baptism is administered because our Lord Jesus Christ has so commanded (§1).

2. Baptism mediates salvation, eternal life and blessedness (§§2, 3, 4).

3. Baptism is a gift of God which can be truly received only by faith (§8).

4. Baptism is a means of grace. It unites man with Christ and with the salvation given to the world in him (§§3 and 4).

5. God bestows the Holy Spirit in baptism (§5).

6. Baptism is the basis and starting point of the life in faith. It means at the same time a lifelong process of growth into Christ and in Christ (§7).

7. Baptism also has important ethical dimensions, and there are ethical consequences connected with it (§§4, 10).

8. Baptism is an act which cannot be repeated. There is only one Christian baptism (§13).

9. Christian baptism is baptism in water and the Holy Spirit (§14).

10. In baptism the decisive factor is not the age of the baptized person. Our church can also accept and recognize as true baptism the baptism administered in such communities as reject the baptism of infants, provided that it is a question of a previously unbaptized person, and baptism takes place using water and in the name of the Triune God, Father, Son and Holy Spirit (§12, with its related commentary, and §15).

11. The administration of baptism is the task of an ordained minister although baptism performed by a layman in case of emergency is valid (§22).

B. Challenges/questions for our church

The section of the document concerning baptism gives the Evangelical Lutheran Church of Finland ample grounds for self-examination and rethinking. The text presents to our church and present practice, among other things, the following challenges and questions:

1. The statement of the document that "baptism is . . . connected with the corporate life and worship of the Church" and the recommendation based on it that "it should normally be administered during public worship" (§23), together with its explanation, gives our church grounds for complex consideration of this question. The administration of baptism in premises consecrated for divine service has clearly increased in our church in the last few years. The present service book of our church contains the form for a baptismal service, and baptisms are also performed in main services, but this is not usual, however. According to the teaching of our church both types of

baptism — in church and in homes — are equally acceptable. In both cases it is a sacrament of the church and a service of worship by the assembled congregation.

2. The statement that the administration of baptism is also appropriate to the great festivals of the church year (§23) is correct. Baptismal practice, as far as possible, can be guided in this direction.

3. The remembering of the symbolic meaning of the baptismal water and the related statement that baptism by immersion symbolizes the Christian's participation in the death, burial and resurrection of Christ (§18) are in agreement with the teaching of the confessions of our church. Practical reasons have led to the establishing of baptism by pouring as almost the sole practice in our church. In that case it is possible and advisable to emphasize in baptismal teaching and preaching, in the manner of Luther's Shorter Catechism, that baptism is the immersion of our old man and the resurrection of the new man.

4. It is important to emphasize the close connection between baptism and confirmation (§14). The document here gives support to an explanation of our own confirmation practice and of its theological bases.

5. The emphasis on baptism being a lifelong process of growth into Christ (§9) reminds us of the teaching of our confessions according to which baptism, as an act of God, endures and takes continual effect. Baptism is thus not only a momentary experience, but a lasting gift, to which the believer returns every day. It is the foundation of our faith and of our Christian life and endeavour. By preaching and Christian education the members of our church should continually be reminded that the precious treasure of baptism is given to us as a source of daily joy and power.

6. The emphasis on the communal nature of baptism is correct. Those things bestowed in baptism — union with Christ, mutual fellowship between Christians and membership in the church of Christ — are central to our faith (§6). The communal and congregational dimensions of baptism have not received sufficient mention in practical teaching about baptism and its administration. The document thus gives us a healthy reminder of the fundamentals of our own confession.

7. The work and the educational programmes of the Evangelical Lutheran Church of Finland are based on baptism. Such anchoring of Christian education to baptism is part of the Lutheran tradition. In practice, however, the task and duty of nurture connected with baptism has not always been sufficiently emphasized (§12).

8. The emphasis on baptismal practice which is conscious of the content of baptism and on the responsibility for nurture connected with baptism (§16) is legitimate in our situation. Forms of activity have been developed in our church in which baptism and its related teaching are carried out together. Baptismal visiting — the discussion before baptism — has increased in our congregations. Experiences have been encouraging.

9. The document offers excellent material for discussion with some churches and Christian communities. For example, the emphasis on baptism being baptism "in water and the Holy Spirit" (§14) offers a natural basis for meeting with other Christian communities in our own country.

C. *Reservations/critical questions*

Our church has reservations with regard to certain expressions concerning baptism used in the document. The following points require further clarification:

1. The necessity of baptism for salvation is not given sufficiently clear expression in the document.

2. The necessity of baptism for salvation and its nature as an unconditional gift are partly explained by the fact of original sin, which doctrine the document does not sufficiently bring out.

3. The position of baptism as a means of grace alongside the word of God is not made clear in the document.

4. The following statement of the document deviates from the teaching of our church: "Baptism is both God's gift and our human response to that gift" (§8). Baptism as such is God's gift, to be received by faith.

5. The treatment of the relation between baptism and faith lacks any mention of the fact that faith also is in reality a gift and act of God. Baptism is a means of grace, whereby the Holy Spirit produces faith.

6. The statement that "baptism needs to be constantly reaffirmed" (Commentary 14c) may obscure the uniqueness and unrepeatability of baptism. Baptism is given to strengthen our faith.

7. While the document rightly stresses the continuing meaning of baptism for the Christian's whole life, attention should also be paid to the fact that this does not only mean growing in Christ (§9), but also returning in repentance to Christ and to his perfect gift in baptism. The enduring meaning of baptism is living by this gift.

8. The nature of baptism as a washing of regeneration and as reception of the Holy Spirit is not brought out sufficiently in the document.

9. The work of the Holy Spirit in man begins, according to the teaching of our church, at baptism and in baptism.

10. The decisive meaning of the act and initiative of God in baptism — irrespective of the age of the baptized person — should be emphasized more strongly than is done in the document.

11. The theological basis of infant baptism is inadequately presented in the document.

12. One easily gains the impression from the document that infant baptism and adult baptism are placed on an equal footing, so that there is no difference as to which is used. This does not correspond to the understanding of our church. In addition infant baptism is, according to the teaching of our church, also believer's baptism. It must be stated that in this respect the

document demonstrates that only very limited convergence has been achieved and not consensus.

13. From the point of view of interchurch fellowship baptism is an unsolved problem, for the reason that most churches which reject infant baptism do not regard the baptism of adults who have been baptized as infants as re-baptism. Therefore the wish expressed in the document (§13 and commentary 13) is in this respect for the time being an objective for the future.

Eucharist

A. Total agreement

The Evangelical Lutheran Church of Finland is in agreement with the section of BEM dealing with the eucharist on the following points:

1. The eucharist is a sacrament instituted by the Lord Jesus Christ. It is a sacramental meal which mediates to us God's love in Jesus Christ (§§1 and 2).

2. Jesus Christ is himself truly present in the eucharist (§§13 and 15).

3. The bread and wine blessed during the celebration of the eucharist are the body and blood of Christ (§§13 and 15).

4. "The eucharist is the sacrament of the unique sacrifice of Christ." The celebration of the eucharist includes the memorial of Christ and God's great acts of salvation in him. The incarnation, life, death, resurrection and ascension of Christ are "events" which "are unique and can neither be repeated nor prolonged" (§8).

5. The presence and influence in the eucharist of the sacrifice of Christ, who died once-for-all upon the cross, is an essential part of the church's worship (§§5–7).

6. The emphasis on communion in the eucharist is important: "The sharing in one bread and the common cup in a given place demonstrates and effects the oneness of the sharers with Christ and with their fellow sharers in all times and places" (§19). Communion is not, however, considered as being lessened by the fact that the eucharistic bread is separate nor by the fact that the wine in the common cup is distributed to each communicant in different vessels.

7. The eucharist emphasizes the universality of the church. "Eucharistic celebrations always have to do with the whole Church, and the whole Church is involved in each local eucharistic celebration" (§19).

8. The eucharist is a means of salvation on the basis of the unique sacrifice of Christ (§2).

9. Christ, who is truly present in the eucharist, is also present in the preaching of the word of God. Word and sacrament are both instruments of God's grace and salvation. The eucharist, as a visible word, and the preached

word of God belong together: "The celebration of the eucharist properly includes the proclamation of the Word" (§12).

10. The document with reason emphasizes the work of the Holy Spirit. The emphasis on the "epikletic" interpretation of the eucharistic act reminds us of the fact that the Holy Spirit is present in the whole of salvation history and makes Christ and his work of redemption present in us through the word and sacraments. The invocation of the presence of the Holy Spirit belongs to the eucharistic celebrations (§§14, 16, 17 and 18).

11. The eucharist is a foretaste of the kingdom of God and in it the Lord's second coming is anticipated (§§6, 18 and 22).

B. *Challenges/questions for our church*

The section of the document on the eucharist furnishes many impulses for our church and raises important questions:

1. The content and meaning of the *epiklesis* in the eucharistic liturgy should be explained in our church. The epikletic prayer in our present eucharistic liturgy contains the petition that Almighty God should send the Holy Spirit to the recipients of the eucharist, so that they should in faith receive Christ's body and blood for their salvation (§§14 and 27).

2. The exhortation to treat the eucharistic elements in a worthy manner after the eucharistic celebration (§32) is justified. The real presence of Christ in the consecrated elements during the eucharist calls for a respectful attitude towards this sacrament after the celebration of the eucharist too. The solution proposed in the document is not, however, in accord with the present practice of our church.

3. The emphasis on the cosmic significance of the eucharist — touching the whole of creation (§22) — gives our church cause for remembering a dimension which belongs to our eucharistic theology, but which is often forgotten.

4. The conciliatory significance of the eucharist and the eucharist as a meal of forgiveness (§2) is an essential part of the Lutheran faith. In emphasizing these points the document calls our church to live fully within our own spiritual heritage.

5. The idea that the celebration of the Lord's Supper deepens Christian faith, and the recommendation that the eucharist should be celebrated frequently (§30) are correct. The number of communicants in our church has continually increased. Celebration of the eucharist every Sunday (§31) does not take place in all our congregations, but development is clearly moving in this direction. We agree that every Christian should be encouraged to receive communion frequently (§31).

6. The emphasis on the character of the eucharist as a thanksgiving (§§3 and 4) has often remained in the background in Lutheran eucharistic theology. By reminding us that the eucharist is a great sacrifice of praise, "by

which the Church speaks on behalf of the whole creation", the document draws attention to an important dimension of the eucharist.

7. The eucharist has an organic connection with the need of the world (§20). This emphasis calls our church to check its own eucharistic teaching and attitude towards international diakonia.

8. The social dimensions of the eucharist and its renewal of the life of individuals (§§22 and 24) have not always been given sufficient attention in the eucharistic teaching of our church. In this respect the challenge posed by the document is timely and justified.

9. The reference in the document to the diaconal dimension of the eucharist (§24) is a challenge for our church and gives it cause for theological deliberation.

C. Reservations/critical questions

Our church has reservations with regard to certain expressions used in the section of the document dealing with the eucharist:

1. The term "sign", which appears frequently in the document, acquires many different meanings. The exact content of this term is often unclear and needs defining more precisely. When our church speaks of the eucharist as a "sign", it means the nature of the eucharist as a means of grace.

2. The real presence of Christ in the eucharistic bread and wine is expressed in a manner which our church can accept and interpret according to its own doctrine. The text is not, however, unambiguous, but it can also be interpreted in a manner which is in conflict with Lutheran eucharistic doctrine (§§14 and 15).

3. The doctrines of justification and sanctification, which are integrally connected with the eucharist, are not explained sufficiently in the document. Nor is it evident that the eucharistic gift can be summed up as the forgiveness of sins. Thus the forgiveness of sins, life and blessedness, that is, the real presence of Christ now and in the fulfilment form a whole.

4. The task of the Holy Spirit in the eucharist is described in the document in such a manner that differing interpretations are possible. Our church has reservations with regard to such an interpretation and form of *epiklesis* where the certainty of the divine institution and promise would be obscured. Our church emphasizes that the *epiklesis* must not obscure the character of the eucharist as a gift of God nor give the impression that the subject of the eucharist is man.

5. Our church understands the eucharist in such a manner that the words of institution are the active and creative word of God. From this basic point of departure the celebration of the eucharist as a whole derives its meaning.

6. The statement that the bread and wine become the body and blood of the risen Christ (commentary 13) is too restricted. According to our own

spiritual heritage the eucharist is precisely communion with the sacrificial body of the crucified and risen Christ.

Ministry

A. Total agreement

The Evangelical Lutheran Church of Finland is in agreement with the following points in the section of the document concerning ministry:

1. The calling of the whole people of God is a decisive factor for the understanding of the church and its ministry (§6).

2. The church, as the body of Christ, is called to proclaim and anticipate the kingdom of God. All the members of the church are called to carry out this task (§4).

3. All Christians are participants in the common priesthood. The different gifts given to Christians by the Holy Spirit are intended for the building up of the church and for the service of the world to which the church is sent (§5).

4. The ministry of the church belongs to its permanent basic structure (§8).

5. The person called to the ordained ministry of the church (§§11, 15, 16 and 45) receives his ministry in ordination through the invocation of the Holy Spirit and the laying on of hands (§7).

6. The ministry of the church is by its nature apostolic. It differs from the unique ministry of the apostles, but is based on it and continues the apostolic task of assembling, building up and guiding the church (§§10 and 11).

7. The continuity throughout history of both true faith (doctrine) and the church's ministry belongs to the apostolic tradition of the church (§§34–38). Our church holds to the apostolic tradition in both of the aforementioned forms. Without the continuity of true faith and doctrine the church's ministry cannot be authentic.

8. The apostolicity of the church means, in the opinion of our church, faithfulness to the task, message and service inherited from the apostles (§34).

9. There is mutual dependence between ministers of the church and other members of the congregation (§12). The ministry and congregation belong together in such a way that the ministry exists in the congregation and precisely for the congregation. There is no ministry without the congregation nor congregation without the ministry.

B. Challenges/questions for our church

The section of the document on ministry gives our church food for thought on, for instance, the following points:

1. The threefold pattern of the church's ministry should be studied afresh in our church (§25). According to our confessions the ministry is one, but they know and can accept the threefold pattern of the ministry as a human institution.

2. The basis, nature and practical applications of ministry demand

continual study. Discussion of ministry in our church can gain impulses from the document and especially from those paragraphs explaining the guiding principles for the exercise of ministry in the church (§§26 and 27).

3. The questions raised in the document (§25) and the description of the diaconate (§31) issue a challenge to our church to give a thorough explanation of the servant nature and tasks of the diaconate as well as the church's ministry.

4. Ecumenical discussion as to the admission of women to the ordained ministry is useful from our church's point of view and should be constantly followed.

C. *Reservations/critical questions*

Our church has reservations with regard to the following ideas in the document:

1. The structure of the document gives cause for asking to what extent the document places baptism, the eucharist and ministry side by side. It is more in accord with the teaching and confession of our church to speak of the word, baptism and eucharist as means and gifts of grace, in which Christ himself is truly present. God has instituted the church's ministry to administer these things. Thus the character of a means of grace applies only to the word and sacraments. Whereas the church's ministry is a good gift of God and an ordinance for the generation of saving faith through the means of grace.

2. The church calls its ordained ministers to strive to live in such a way that their lives are an example to the congregation, but the statement in the document that ordained ministers are regarded as "an example of holiness and loving concern" (§12) contains an emphasis alien to our tradition.

3. The statement that in the celebration of the eucharist the church's ministry represents in a visible manner the communion between Christ and the members of his body (§14) may move the focus of attention away from the objective means of salvation, the word and sacraments.

4. Although our church respects the episcopal succession as one sign of the church's continuity and unity, it does not, however, consider it a guarantee of the unity, apostolicity and continuity of the church (§38). According to the teaching of our church the Holy Spirit uses the word and sacraments as means of creating faith in those who hear the gospel (Augsburg Confession V).

5. The deacon's ministry described in the document (§31) does not correspond to the present diaconate of our church.

6. The threefold pattern of the ministry in the manner described in the document (§§29–31) does not fully correspond to the understanding of the church's ministry to be found in the Lutheran confession.

7. In the commentary on the admission of women to the ordained ministry (§18) the opinions of both defenders and opponents of the ordination of women are explained briefly and at the same time deficiently.

8. The relation of ministry and authority (§§15–16, 26 and 27) remains an open question in the document.

4 November 1985   Archbishop: John Vikström
                                   Secretary of the Synod: Sinikka Pylkkänen

Church Council for Foreign Affairs

TO THE FAITH AND ORDER COMMISSION OF THE WORLD COUNCIL OF CHURCHES

At the suggestion of the Bishops' Conference of the Evangelical Lutheran Church of Finland our church's reply to the BEM document has been prepared by the Synod. In addition, the Bishops' Conference has asked the Church Council for Foreign Affairs to prepare a reply to those questions in the preface to the BEM document where enquiry is made into the relation of the document to the apostolic faith and the ecumenical implications of the document and also the church's attitude to the forthcoming work of the Faith and Order Commission, in particular to the Commission's apostolic faith project. In answering these questions special attention has been paid to the methodology of both the document and the forthcoming work of the Commission.

The document and the apostolic faith

The questions put to the churches in the preface of the document, in so far as it is a question of the content of the document, have been answered in the statement of the Synod. This naturally also applies to the relation of the document to the apostolic faith. Our church has found ample material in the sections on baptism, the eucharist and ministry which from the point of view of its own spiritual heritage it regards as "an expression of the faith of the Church through the ages", that is, apostolic.

The evaluation of the ecumenical significance of the findings and the drawing of practical conclusions are made more difficult, however, firstly by the fact that there are no generally accepted standards of the content of the "apostolic faith". "Apostolicity" continues to appear concretely only as a concept as interpreted by the different confessions. The evaluation of the document is made difficult, secondly, by the fact that the exact position and task of the document from the point of view of ecumenical theology is not stated. In the preface to the document there are statements defining the document's character, but they remain ambivalent. Also the official status of the preface is unclear. Mainly as a result of this it is not possible to give clear answers to the questions asked at the end of the preface. Thirdly, problems of interpretation are caused for our church by the fact that in the document it is unclear how a distinction is to be made between those matters which are essential for unity and those which are non-essential. With this is connected the fact that the basic concepts "convergence and consensus" are not adequately defined. Consensus as to the doctrine of the gospel and the administration of the sacraments is, from our position, a prerequisite for full church unity and corresponding full pulpit and altar fellowship.

Evaluation of the ecumenical range of the document requires a wider context (for example, a complete interpretation of the Nicene Creed), from which alone the document can find its final factual significance. For this reason our church considers the Faith and Order Commission's project "Towards the Common Expression of the Apostolic Faith Today" of great importance.

The document demonstrates convincingly how important questions as to the content of doctrine and faith are, from the point of view of both the unity of the church and also church life. This is a challenge to the forthcoming Faith and Order work and to other ecumenical activity. Also as a guide for the whole ecumencial movement the document is important in this sense. For it demonstrates how making a deep study of faith and doctrine can also make a contribution to the church's diaconal service in the world. The diaconal tasks of the church and Christians in the present-day world is in organic relationship to the Lord of the church, his sacrifice, presence and gift.

The BEM document is important to the churches not only because it contains many important individual insights and impulses, but also because it is a noteworthy step towards a common expression of apostolic faith and doctrine. The document is not, however, sufficient to form such a common confession or consensus of the churches, which in itself would be sufficient to restore the broken unity of the church. The document is, however, as it is and especially because of its process of reception, a notable step on the path to the rapprochement of the churches.

The forthcoming Faith and Order work

The fourth question in the preface to the document asks for our church's suggestions for the future work of the Faith and Order Commission, when the convergence attained on baptism, eucharist and ministry is related to the project "Towards the Common Expression of the Apostolic Faith Today".

Our church regards it as very important that the attempt visible in the BEM document to attain convergence on the basis of apostolic faith and doctrine should continue. Sections A and B of the Synod's statement demonstrate that this line is fruitful. The reservations which we have stated in section C are not in conflict with this fact; rather they underline its importance. Although a profound experimental dimension forms an essential part of faith, it is rooted above all in the apostolic witness, doctrine and tradition.

An even more profound joint explanation of the apostolic character of the church's faith and doctrine holds a key position in any further work. Just as important is to explain how the experience of unity depends upon an increase in doctrinal consensus. Certain statements in the preface to the BEM document in which there is mention of the communal experience as a gift of the Holy Spirit, "before it can be articulated by common efforts into words", and where it is stated that "full consensus can only be proclaimed after the churches reach the point of living and acting together in unity", could also lead to mistaken interpretations, according to which common doctrine would only be a product of common experience. This interpretation of the ecumenical process does not, in the view of our church, correspond to the pattern which appears in the text of the document itself. In any case it is important that in the work of the Faith and Order Commission thought should be given not only to questions of doctrinal content, but also distinctly to methodological questions.

28 November 1985   Church Council for Foreign Affairs

John Vikström   Mannu Sinnemäki
Archbishop   General Secretary
Chairman

LUTHERAN CHURCH IN HUNGARY

1. The Lutheran Church in Hungary declares itself a part of the one church of Christ, and therefore — on the basis of common mission-mandate given by Christ and in the awareness of common responsibility towards all humankind — tries to make all efforts to unity in faith and service among the churches. With this engagement we have taken part in the ecumenical endeavours of the churches and we gladly welcome all the steps which bring us nearer to church unity.

2. After studying all the aspects of the Lima document at various levels in our church, with gratitude to God, we state that this document is not only one among many other documents but it certainly indicates a new phase in the unity endeavours of the churches. It really finds much agreement of approach among the churches in the understanding of baptism, eucharist and ministry. By doing so this document has made the ecumenical dialogue more lively, deepened it and made it more substantial. Consequently, it has given rise to much joy among wide circles of our believers; sometimes it has even caused exaggerated hope, also.

3. We consider, on the basis of our experiences in the last decades and of a knowledge of inner possibilities of the churches, that a long and difficult way is ahead of us in realizing the visible unity of the churches. We take, however, an aim to be realized within a reasonable time for the churches, i.e. to recognize mutually one another as parts of Christ's universal church and to acknowledge each other as real churches. Therefore we accept the Lima document as an adequate basis to carry negotiations further to both bilateral and multilateral talks in order to achieve mutual recognition but we take it as nothing more than such a basis for negotiations, e.g. we do not accept it as a common confession or as a document which may be decisive in our relation to other churches. We do not believe that relations of the various churches depend on whether one or another church accepts this document or not.

● 430,000 members, 320 parishes, 2 dioceses, 320 pastors.

4. The Lima document reveals various agreements among the churches in such a measure that we may — on the basis of the New Testament scriptures and the Lutheran confessions — regard them as satisfactory for the mutual recognition of the churches. However, the document also contains statements which are not necessary — in our opinion — to consensus for the unity of the churches, for example the *anamnesis* and *epiklesis* in relation to holy communion. On the other hand, it does not take some principles into consideration which may make ecumenical unity difficult or impossible, e.g. the teaching on the authority of the papacy. Furthermore, a fourth part could be added to the document, i.e. a mutual understanding of the common apostolic faith, as in our opinion this is certainly necessary for church unity. It may not be an agreement only on the sacraments but also on the common apostolic faith, as our confessional writings put it: we must agree on the evangelical principles, too.

5. We fully agree with the Lima document in respect to baptism when it emphasizes the importance of baptism by the Spirit and the spiritual renewal by the Spirit. To our great regret, however, it fails even to mention the consequent ethical teaching task of the church which was given by Christ to the disciples as a mandate, together with baptism and, in equal measure with it, the commandment to mission.

6. We are ready to admit that our church people should take part in holy communion more intensively and with a deeper understanding of the richness of the eucharistic communion as it corresponds to the holy scriptures and to the confessional writings. It is useful that the Lima document calls our attention to this. We notice, however, that forgiveness of sins — connected with the holy communion — does not appropriately appear in the document. In addition to this we do not know how to interpret the part of the document which deals with *anamnesis*, the memorial of the crucified Christ, as well as the *epiklesis*, the invocation of the Holy Spirit. In our opinion this interpretation in the document is not based on the apostolic tradition as might be required. After thorough study and analysis we cannot help feeling that in the text of the document the stress is laid upon the activity or action of either the congregation or the minister instead of on the active presence of Christ; this may be indicated by using exclusively the word "eucharist" instead of Lord's supper.

7. We accept that the Lima document emphasizes the service character of the ministry. We appreciate the moderation in which the threefold pattern (bishops, presbyters and deacons) has been treated and the fact that it has not been taken as a condition for unity although it was recommended somehow. We cannot recognize this order of hierarchy on the basis of the Lutheran Reformation or the teaching of the New Testament, in spite of the arguments in the document. Similarly, we cannot accept the idea according to which the apostolic succession as a historical continuity must be a decisive factor of church unity or a guarantee of validity of the church ministry. We live in the

firm belief, however, that the continuity of the apostolic faith is of crucial importance and we confess — on the basis of the holy scripture and the concordant witnesses of our confessional writings — that our church lives in this continuity of the apostolic faith.

8. We cannot leave undisputed the radical challenge of the Lima document connected with the eucharist, with respect to a worldwide diakonia in the social, economic and political life (§§20–21). We can fully agree with this, while making two remarks: (1) This diaconal way of life is certainly based upon forgiveness and reconciliation experienced. (2) This prompting motive may be received not only from the eucharist but also from the proclamation of the gospel. Therefore the document should have said something more and emphasized forgiveness and the proclamation of the word of God.

9. In Christ not only the unity of the church is given but Jesus Christ is actively present in the world as well as in the church by his Holy Spirit. He converts people and gathers together his own people who are divided and lack unity — that is our firm belief based upon the witnesses of the holy scripture and the confessional writings, and on our own experience. The Lima document definitely speaks about the present, living, active Christ in connection with the ministry; it mentions the same only once in the section on eucharist, and not at all in the section on baptism. The theses of the Lima document — drawn up after lengthy theological study and work — scarcely reflect the experiences of the believers who lived over and over again the power of Christ working for unity. However, we see the real guarantee of church unity in this active and uniting presence of Christ. When we — the representatives and members of various denominations — are together in the name of Jesus we gladly experience the reality that the living Jesus Christ himself unites us even in the proclaimed word of God and also in prayer.

The churches in the ecumenical movement must be determined to work towards eucharistic communion for the unity-forming work of the living Lord. This decision must not be put off to the end of the way towards unity, it must not be postponed, but on the basis of open community we must proceed forward to a fuller unity of the churches. Our church — believing in the living Lord Jesus Christ and in the power of his gospel — is ready for this open community.

10. Our church is willing and ready to be in dialogue in the future with any church on the basis of the Lima document or even going further than this document, in order to achieve mutual recognition. For the success of such dialogues in the days to come we do not cease to pray, together with the Lord of the church, that his will may be realized and "that they may all be one".

Budapest
10 December 1985   The General Presbyterium

LUTHERAN CHURCH –
MISSOURI SYNOD

"Baptism, Eucharist and Ministry", distributed by the Faith and Order
Commission of the World Council of Churches, is the culmination of some
fifty years of labour by leaders and scholars from many communions. It asks
for a response from the churches of the world. Four specific questions are
posed in the preface which are to guide the churches in preparing their
responses:
— the extent to which your church can recognize in this text the faith of the
  church through the ages;
— the consequences your church can draw from this text for its relations and
  dialogues with other churches, particularly with those churches which also
  recognize the text as an expression of the apostolic faith;
— the guidance your church can take from this text for its worship,
  educational, ethical, and spiritual life and witness;
— the suggestions your church can make for the ongoing work of Faith and
  Order as it relates the material of this text on "Baptism, Eucharist and
  Ministry" to its long-range research project "Towards the Common
  Expression of the Apostolic Faith Today".
Two additional points made in the preface are important to bear in mind:
(1) "Readers should not expect to find a complete theological treatment of
baptism, eucharist and ministry. . . . The agreed text purposely concentrates
on those aspects of the theme that have been directly or indirectly related to
the problems of mutual recognition leading to unity." (2) The text does not

---

• 3,051,417 members, 6,157 parishes, 8,724 pastors. In June 1982 the then general
secretary of the WCC, Dr Philip Potter, in a letter to President Ralph Bohlmann,
invited The Lutheran Church-Missouri Synod to respond to BEM. In response to
this invitation President Bohlmann asked the Commission on Theology and
Church Relations to coordinate the preparation of an evaluation of this document
for the synod. After soliciting and receiving reactions and suggestions from the St
Louis and Ft Wayne seminary faculties, the Commission has prepared this
response.

claim to represent a consensus of the theologians involved, but rather "the significant theological convergence which Faith and Order has discerned and formulated". Both of these points represent judgments which are not always self-evident and which make the document more difficult to evaluate.

We shall first make some general comments, and then consider baptism, eucharist and ministry individually.

General observations

1. The text, well argued and presented, merits serious consideration and response.

2. We welcome the serious attention here given to doctrinal/theological matters. This represents a positive change in the WCC. In recent years it seems that Faith and Order concerns have been subordinated to activistic ones, and we hope that BEM represents a permanent turn towards serious theological study.

3. We applaud the frequent use of biblical language and formulation. (Churches with a strong confessional or doctrinal heritage easily replace, in practice, biblical expressions with later dogmatic ones.) At the same time, this procedure raises concern. Biblical language is subject to interpretation: later dogmatic formulations arose precisely because biblical language was misunderstood or, at least, understood differently. Unless it can be demonstrated that these varying understandings no longer exist, a resolution of disagreements will not be achieved simply by reverting to the use of biblical language.

4. The churchly or corporate perspectives of the document are to be applauded, especially in contrast to the individualistic outlook we often confront in contemporary contexts.

5. The ultimate hermeneutical or theoretical basis of the document is unclear. The question as to whether or not we can "recognize the faith of the Church through the ages" in the document seems itself to be an inadequate formulation of the task at hand. At worst, it sounds reductionistic to some "least common denominator" approach to unity in the church. And if not that, it appears to put the accent on the church's faith or tradition rather than on an objective norm. We believe that the ultimate criterion for the church's confession of faith is the inerrant scriptures, always viewed in the light of the gospel of Jesus Christ. It does not suffice to use scripture only as a "witness" to the gospel. The gospel "interprets" scripture, and scripture "interprets" the gospel.

Other formulations in BEM are similarly weak or misleading. The "tradition of the gospel" sounds strange to our ears. We are aware that "tradition" can be used neutrally, but the document's use of this phrase appears to accent human receptivity and activity unduly. It appears to us that at times tradition assumes normative status in this document. Moreover, "apostolic faith" is never defined. Similar questions arise with respect to the juxtaposition of phrases such as "experience of life" and "articulation of faith" in seeking doctrinal consensus. Not only does BEM appear to place the accent on human activity, but it seems to concede to experience a place alongside of scripture as a source and norm of faith.

6. Not surprisingly, then, the gospel itself appears to be muted in the document. Themes such as "justification by grace through faith" and "vicarious atonement" are attested only weakly and indistinctly. We understand that these topics are not BEM's primary concerns as such, but their centrality in the Christian faith makes discussion of any article of faith deficient without them. The themes of sin and grace in relation to baptism and eucharist are conspicuous by their near absence, as we shall note.

7. The division of the document into (1) the main text, which asserts "major areas of theological convergence", and (2) added commentaries, which should "either indicate historical differences that have been overcome or identify disputed issues still in need of further research and reconciliation", is helpful. However, concern must be registered about the way in which the distinction has been carried out. First of all, it is less than clear at times that certain differences have actually been overcome. Secondly, the language of the text is frequently ambiguous, thereby suggesting that it may have resulted from a search for a "least common denominator". It is often not clear when the document intends to be descriptive and when prescriptive. Although each of the three sections of the document must necessarily take up liturgical activity as well as doctrinal matters, it is often not made clear whether BEM is referring to the church's "service" and grateful response, or whether the subject is God's prior activity, when the church's proper response must be passivity and receptivity.

Because elasticity of language may be used to conceal continuing divisions rather than point towards emerging unity, confessional statements have historically included negative as well as positive statements in order to indicate as clearly as possible what is *not* meant as well as what is. BEM would also be immeasurably strengthened if theses were accompanied by antitheses as well.

8. The repeatedly stated goal of BEM "to realize the goal of visible church unity" is not developed adequately. We recognize this goal as desirable, even mandated by the scriptures, to the degree possible. However, the scriptures also forbid us to sacrifice truth (full, actual agreement in doctrine) for the sake of external union. Moreover, the spiritual unity of the church already exists in the body of Christ. The *una sancta* is always ultimately hidden; its extent is known to God alone. This church becomes accessible to us through its true marks, the purely preached gospel and the rightly administered sacraments (AC VII). To seek the external unity of the church elsewhere is to attempt to walk by sight, not by faith. It may be that full visible unity will not be realized before our Lord returns.

Baptism

1. Much in this section of the document is commendable. For example, the dominical institution of baptism and its meaning as a participation in Christ's death and resurrection is clearly linked with key biblical passages. We fully agree that baptism "in the name of the Father, the Son, and the Holy Spirit" (B1) is unrepeatable (B13), and that the Holy Spirit incorporates all the baptized into the body of Christ (B6). That baptism "should normally be administered during public worship" (B23) is another laudable point.

2. That the one baptism "constitutes a call to the churches to overcome their divisions . . ." (B6) is also to be affirmed. At the same time, the false impression is left that churches must "visibly manifest their fellowship" before it is possible to make "a genuine Christian witness".

3. We fully agree that baptism is related to "life-long growth in Christ" (B9) and that churches which practise infant baptism "must guard themselves against the practice of apparently indiscriminate baptism and take more seriously their responsibility for the nurture of baptized children to mature commitment to Christ" (B15). In that context, we can agree that a periodic rite of renewal of baptismal vows (B14 Comm.) can be helpful.

4. Certain corollaries of the preceding statements are developed unsatisfactorily in BEM, however. The initial (B1) reference to baptism as a "rite of commitment" and a later reference to the sacrament as "both God's gift and our human response to that gift" (B8) signal a confusion between the monergism of divine grace and our human response which is never clarified in the document.

5. Closely related to the foregoing point is the document's attempt to countenance both infant baptism and believer's baptism. The claim that "the real distinction is between those who baptize people at any age and those who baptize only those able to make a confession of faith for themselves" does not adequately recognize that the most important difference is between those who understand baptism itself as sheer gift and actual means of grace (sacrament) and those who make conversion and confession of faith a prerequisite to the symbolization of that gift.

6. Likewise, a serious caricature results from BEM's failure to clarify the connection between baptism and original sin. It is misleading to classify the "washing away of sin" (1 Cor. 6:11) as merely one "image" among many of the meaning of baptism (B2).

7. The document concedes, but appears to gloss over, the seriousness of the fact that "Christians differ in their understanding as to where the sign of the gift of the Spirit is to be found", whether in the "water rite itself", in chrismation, in confirmation, or in all three, as well as in the question of infant communion (B14 and Comm.).

8. The description of baptism as "a liberation into a new humanity" (B2) and reference to its ethical implications as including motivation "to strive for the realization of the will of God in all realms of life" (B10) can be understood

unobjectionably. However, these formulations appear to leave the door wide open for a praxis or stance that is determined more culturally or ideologically than scripturally.

9. In that light, the cautions stated against "confusion between baptism and customs surrounding name-giving" (B21 Comm.) appear to be misfounded. The stated concerns are cultural, not theological: "the baptized are required to assume Christian names not rooted in their cultural tradition . . . alienating the baptized from their local culture through the imposition of foreign names". No cognizance seems to be taken of the frequent close connection between "cult and culture", that is, that names easily in many cultures witness to a non-Christian tradition. One cannot claim scriptural mandate for this custom, but it is our judgment that more, not less, needs to be made of the "christening" aspect of baptism, and that our "Christian names" may be a powerful and continuing witness to the fact that baptism also calls us *out* of this world and sets us on the road to the next. Both biblical and ecclesiastical tradition attest to the antiquity and widespread adherence to this practice.

Eucharist

1. Much in this section is congenial to us. Especially commendable, from a functional standpoint, is the recommendation that, because of its centrality, the eucharist be celebrated frequently — "at least every Sunday" — and that the faithful should be encouraged to receive it frequently. We must admit that our own contemporary practice falls short of meeting this ideal, which the Lutheran confessional writings also encourage. Other themes are laudably accented which often receive insufficient emphasis in practice: the essentially celebrative or joyful ("eucharistic") character of the sacrament, its eschatological import, and others. The following observations are not intended to negate this positive judgment, but we must express reservations about many of the same types of doctrinal ambiguities here as under "Baptism".

2. The text begins with a clear accent on the gift character of the eucharist (E1 and E2, although in E2 the phrase "sacrament of a gift" is obscure), but this implied accent on "*sola gratia*" is not carried through unambiguously in the rest of the section.

3. Lutherans are not very familiar with some of the language and/or accents of BEM in this section. This causes us to desire greater clarity and precision. For example, the very word "eucharist" (thanksgiving) has not been our usual term for this sacrament, although our own liturgies normally surround the sacrament with hymns and prayers of thanksgiving. "Eucharist" is by no means intrinsically objectionable to us. Nevertheless, the use of this term for the sacrament of the altar implicitly suggests a shift in accent from God's gift to what the church does. Greater precision is needed to underscore the theological distinction between God's unmerited gift and the church's grateful response.

4. Closely related is our concern with the description of the eucharist as a "sacrifice". The text does specify it as a "sacrifice of *praise* . . . possible only through Christ, with him and in him" (E4) whose self-sacrifice has been "accomplished once and for all on the cross and [is] still operative on behalf of all mankind" (E5, cf. E10). We have no problem with such formulations, but we are still desirous that the priority of "sacrament" over "sacrifice" and a clear theological distinction between the two be unambiguously spelled out. Acceptable and even laudable though it is in one sense, the Lord's Supper, we believe, should not primarily or ordinarily be referred to as a "sacrifice". The attempt of E8 (Comm.) to explain sacrifice as propitiatory "in the light of the significance of the eucharist as intercession" is, at best, only a bare beginning to the resolution of that problem.

5. The concepts of *anamnesis* (traditionally: "memorial" or "remembrance") and "re-presentation" are also problematic. E7 emphasizes that it is Christ who "acts through the joyful celebration of his Church", but much of the subsequent discussion appears to concentrate on what the *church* does. In the light of persistent misunderstandings, precise logical sequences and distinctions are necessary here too. The two terms or concepts themselves, though undeniably biblical as such, need to be defined with greater clarity. "Memorial" or "remembrance" is too easily and commonly understood in merely symbolic terms of the church's obedience to an ordinance and as simply an affirmation of its faith. "Representation", on the other hand, needs to be more clearly distinguished from the false notion of "repetition" accomplished by the ritual action of an ordained minister. The impression left in E1 is that the eucharist is only a continuation of other meals shared by Jesus during his earthly ministry, and that it was merely "prefigured" in the Passover. Stress is needed both on the uniqueness of Jesus' final meal on earth and a genuine sense of its typological continuity with Old Testament meals (fulfilment). The latter would also clarify the sense of "re-presentation".

6. Not unrelated to these concerns are questions regarding section IIC on the "*epiklesis*" or invocation of the Spirit. Many of the assertions in this section, if heard in a general sense, are acceptable (e.g. that it is the Holy Spirit "who makes the historical words of Jesus present and alive" — E14 Commentary). What is lacking is clarity about the relation of the Spirit to the word, and to the dominical words of institution. The concession in E28 Commentary that possibly "local food and drink serve better to anchor the eucharist in everyday life" raises the question whether the word is considered normative at all. The accent of E12 that the preached word should normally accompany the eucharist is laudable, but nowhere are the deeper issues of word in relation to sacrament plumbed. The initial assertion in E14 that "the Spirit makes the crucified and risen Christ really present to us in the eucharistic meal, fulfilling the promise contained in the words of institution" is a model of ambiguity, and, in spite of qualifying statements, runs the risk of identifying Christ's presence with a particular moment or action within the

rite rather than with the sacrament as a whole. The appeal of Commentary 14 to early liturgies where "the whole 'prayer action' was thought of as bringing about the reality promised by Christ" appears to place undue weight on the church's action or ritual.

7. At the other end of the spectrum of views is the "reservation" of the elements (implying that "Christ's presence in the consecrated elements continues after the celebration") considered in E32. It is one thing to "respect the practices and piety of the others" in this and other respects; it is something else to allow contradictory understandings to stand side by side. The notation that the "primary intention" of this practice was the "distribution [of the elements] among the sick and those who are absent" is helpful. But we cannot pretend that serious differences in belief and piety in worldwide Christendom on this point are thereby overcome.

8. A major problem throughout this section is BEM's ambiguity about the nature of Christ's presence in the sacrament. Even though expressions such as "real presence" and "the sacrament of the body and blood of Christ" are used, the document never clearly articulates more than the presence of the *person* of Christ, nor does it speak of a physical eating of his body and blood other than by faith. More than some *purely* "symbolic" meaning is affirmed, but it is not clear how much more. The addition of adjectives such as "effective", "unique", "living", etc., does not go far enough. We appreciate the attempt to avoid philosophical speculation about the precise nature of the mystery (precisely the intent of Lutheranism's traditional "in, with, and under"), but that may not become a cloak for a pluralism of incompatible theological views. The question posed in Commentary 13 whether confession and denial of the presence of Christ's body and blood can be accommodated must be denied. In the light of all of this, it is not surprising that nothing at all is said about the *manducatio impiorum* (that also the unbelieving receive Christ's body and blood, but to their judgment), nor about its sequel, the necessity of church discipline and of "close(d) communion".

9. Possibly the most serious deficiency of this section is the almost complete absence of discussion about what we regard as one of the major benefits of the eucharist, namely, that in it God graciously offers "forgiveness of sin, life and salvation". Conversely, disproportionate accent is placed on horizontal (this-worldly) relations. It is not clear in what sense the whole "world" is present in the celebration (E23) or that the eucharist is a "representative act . . . on behalf of the whole world" (E20). If these words are meant eschatologically, this should be specified. Otherwise, an indefensible universalism and an ideologically driven activism will be indicated. That the latter is, indeed, in view seems clear by many unfocused assertions in E20 about the eucharist as "a constant challenge in the search for appropriate relationships in social, economic, and political life", that "all kinds of injustice, racism, separation and lack of freedom are radically challenged", or

that we must be "actively participating in this ongoing restoration of the world's situation and the human condition".

Concerns similar to these had to be expressed about BEM's discussion on baptism. When regarded from this perspective, therefore, the concern with "above all, the obstinacy of unjustifiable confessional oppositions within the body of Christ" (E20), while valid as such, is inappropriate in this context.

Ministry

1. The title of this section invites questions. Does "ministry" refer to a calling of all Christians, to a called and ordained clergy, or to both? And if the latter, when does it refer to each, and what is their relationship to each other? In our own church, as in others, the use of this term is by no means consistent. M7 specifies a usage in BEM where "ministry" refers to "the service to which the whole people of God is called", whereas "ordained ministry" is employed for "persons who have received a charism and whom the church appoints for service by ordination through the invocation of the Spirit and the laying on of hands". Our own tradition has generally made use of "the (holy) ministry" instead of "ordained ministry". We have usually referred to the calling of all Christians as "the *priesthood* of all believers", while "ministry" in the generic sense has only recently become familiar. It must be admitted that the use of the same word — either "priesthood" or "ministry" — for both lay people and clergy only through the use of qualifying terms, can be helpful in summarizing what both share as well as what distinguishes them (M17 and Commentary on "priesthood" for "ordained ministry" is well done.) However, the issues do not inhere in any terminology as such, but in the way it is understood and applied.

BEM's over-riding interest is plainly in what it calls the "ordained ministry". Only M1 is devoted primarily to "ministry", although its relation to the "ordained ministry" is touched on repeatedly throughout this section, especially in M26–27. Hence, some other title might have been more accurate.

2. On the whole, section I, entitled "The Calling of the Whole People of God", will probably command as much universal assent in all churches as anything in the entire BEM. Our only regret is that it is so brief. Nevertheless, unguarded, ambiguous terminology appears here too. That God "calls the whole of humanity to become God's people" is subject to universalistic misinterpretations (M1). M4 almost invites "liberation theology" caricatures of "Gospel" and "Kingdom of God". M5 on the "gifts of the Spirit" glides over a host of problems and disagreements.

3. On the whole, our problems with this section are few, precisely because of our fundamental agreement with the assertion that "the New Testament does not describe a single pattern of ministry which might serve as a blueprint or continuing norm for all future ministry in the Church" (M19). Hence, the issue is, as such, an adiaphoron. Ministerial ordering or structure is

contingent on and can ultimately be judged only by its usefulness in the proclamation of the gospel.

4. It does not appear to us, however, that BEM is content to leave the matter at that. There appears to us to be a definite tilt in a certain hierarchical direction, especially on the basis of "tradition" in the early centuries of the church. Lutheranism has always regarded tradition highly, also with respect to the doctrine of the ministry, but utmost care is required that it not be conceded a *de facto* authority alongside of scripture.

5. The precise meaning of "ordination" or of the relation between the "ordained ministry" and the "priesthood of all believers" is given short shrift in this section. Lutherans themselves have not always been of one mind on the issue, and BEM apparently tries to have the best of both worlds. On the one hand, to speak of ordained ministers as having received a "charism" (M7 and M32, "variety of charisms"; cf. M28–31) appears to want to accommodate congregationalistic, if not "charismatic", views of the ministry, where ordination is either repudiated or conceded only a formal, nominal role. On the other hand, to speak of the act of ordination as "conferring" authority on the ordained ministry (M15), or as a "sacramental" sign, where the church "enters sacramentally into contingent, historical forms . . ." (M43) points in a sacerdotalistic direction. We are aware that "sacramental" (especially if put in quotation marks) can be used in an acceptable generic sense (God's use of *any* external forms), but to many this terminology will signal much more than this. Other statements, however, seem to maintain an acceptable balance. We welcome statements affirming both that "the authority of the ordained minister is rooted in Jesus Christ" (M15) and that his "call must be authenticated by the Church's recognition of the gifts and graces of the particular person" (M45). It would have been helpful, however, if BEM had spelled out more clearly wherein that "authority" consists, namely, the "power and command of God to preach the Gospel, to forgive and retain sins, and to administer and distribute the sacraments" (AC XXVIII, 5).

6. The discussion of "the Forms of the Ordained Ministry" (section III) focuses largely on the development of the threefold pattern of bishop, presbyter and deacon. We have no problem in principle with that type of structure. We are not accustomed to the term "bishop", but as long as it is clear that his *episkopē* or "oversight" differs only in extent or degree, not in quality, from that of the "presbyter" or local pastor, there is no intrinsic objection. The "considerable uncertainty" about the diaconate, of which M31 Commentary speaks, is also true of our church.

7. Nevertheless, it appears to us that BEM makes more out of the ancient tradition of a threefold pattern than scripture will sustain. It is debatable whether it "may serve today as an expression of the unity we seek and also as a means for achieving it" (M22). There is no evidence that a common form of ministry bespeaks a unity of doctrine, and no evidence that its common adoption would hasten genuine unity of faith. Ironically, part VI at the end of

the document ("Towards the Mutual Recognition of the Ordained Ministries") seems to say that forms do not ultimately matter. As regards "the mutual recognition of ministries" (M51), the Lutheran church has always recognized the validity of the public ministry in historic Trinitarian churches.

In general, there seems to be a tendency to interpret the "ordained ministry" and its ordering in a hierarchical direction. (We note in passing that no mention whatsoever is made of the papacy, surely the most serious ecumenical issue with respect to "ministry" today.) On the one hand, it is clearly affirmed that "the authority of the ordained ministry is not to be understood as the possession of the ordained person but as a gift for the continuing edification of the body in and for which the minister has been ordained" (M15). But on the other hand, we have talk of the ordained ministry as reminding "the community of the divine initiative" (M12; cf. E29) or as being the "visible focus of the deep and all-embracing communion between Christ and the members of his body" (M14).

8. What is said about "apostolic succession" in part IV appears to be quite moderate. The document attempts a distinction between the "succession of the apostolic ministry" and the "apostolic tradition of the whole church" (M34 and Commentary). The accent is laudably placed on the latter, defined as primarily "an expression of the permanence and, therefore, of the continuity of Christ's own mission in which the Church participates" (M35). There is much to be said for the historical continuity and accountability implied, but the statement would have been strengthened by greater attention to definition of the concept as faithfulness to scriptural doctrine. In development of this theme, more appears to be made of tradition than is supportable, however. It may go too far to describe episcopal succession "as a sign, though not a guarantee, of the continuity and unity of the Church" (M38). To assert that it "not only points to historical continuity; it also manifests an actual spiritual reality" (M36, Commentary) has no scriptural basis. The laying on of hands, though surely a laudable and biblically attested custom, cannot be urged as necessary for transmission of the succession on the basis of "apostolic tradition" (M52; see the helpful discussion, however, in M40, Commentary).

9. In a major inconsistency and radical departure from "tradition", BEM leaves undecided, although it does not require, the ordination of women. The major argument cited against it again appears to be only tradition. The two viewpoints are simply set side by side (M18 and Commentary). On the one hand, "an increasing number of churches have decided that there is no biblical or theological reason against ordaining women"; in fact, they do so "because of their understanding of the Gospel and of the ministry", and "reinforced by their experience . . . none has found reason to reconsider its decision". On the other side are churches which "consider that the force of nineteen centuries of tradition against the ordination of women must not be

set aside" and which "believe that there are theological issues concerning the nature of humanity and concerning Christology which lie at the heart of their convictions. . . ."

BEM itself, however, introduces the topic by appealing to Gal. 3:28 (in Christ "neither male nor female") with the apparent implication that thus the church will be faithful to its call "to convey to the world the image of a new humanity" (M18). In any case, "differences on this issue . . . must not be regarded as substantive hindrance for further efforts towards mutual recognition. Openness to each other holds the possibility that the Spirit may well speak to one church through the insights of another" (M54).

It is our judgment that BEM has not adequately summarized the weighty biblical and theological arguments against the ordination of women, nor does it recognize what serious barriers these are to full doctrinal unity.

Conclusion

As noted above, BEM has positive features. At many points the "faith of the Church through the ages" is clearly set forth and we rejoice at the progress that has been made in achieving a common expression of some aspects of that faith.

At the same time, we must also register serious reservations about BEM. The document frequently bases its conclusions on tradition, the faith or experience of the church, or the like, rather than on the clear teachings of the scriptures. As a result, it leaves critical questions undecided, or resorts to artfully ambiguous language which can be read or understood in many different ways. Such ambiguity in the confessing of the "faith of the Church through the ages" is not acceptable to a confessional church.

Furthermore, this document does not provide a solid basis for external unity in the church. Throughout the assumption seems to be that there can be unity at all costs by means of a "reconciled diversity" despite pluralism of doctrine and practice. This is an assumption which we cannot accept.

Thus, both in relation to other churches as well as in our internal use of BEM for "worship, educational, ethical, and spiritual life and witness", we judge that BEM will prove more helpful as a guide for discussing the vast gulfs of disagreements still dividing Christendom, especially on the issues of baptism, eucharist, and ministry, than as a basis for overcoming them by reaching a full, common understanding of gospel and scripture.

Commission on Theology
and Church Relations

STANDING COUNCIL OF THE LUTHERAN AND REFORMED CHURCHES OF FRANCE

Message to the churches of the Standing Council

Brothers and Sisters,

1. Having assembled at Lyons to prepare our churches' response to the text of the Lima agreement, we invite you to perceive in this event, modest as it is, God's promise for the progress of his people. This document is addressed to us by the representatives of all the great Christian confessions included within the Commission on Faith and Order of the World Council of Churches. We are conscious, to be sure, of the limitations and occasional ambiguities of this text, and we cannot ignore the fact that the future of the world challenges our faith in other urgent ways. In numerous directions, Christians of every confession are participating in a common witness and in shared struggles, and are discovering therein the joy of unity as a gift, extending even to martyrdom. The ecumenical movement itself is taking an active part in this, being the first to tell us that the quest for unity cannot be separated from missionary witness, evangelization, and ethical and socio-political considerations. It also reminds us of the link between the historical breaches which caused divisions to arise in the church, and those which split modern society and divide even Christians.

Nevertheless, we cannot neglect the specific elements Christ gives us to make his gospel manifest; that is, baptism and the Lord's Supper on the one hand, and the ministries on the other. The findings of the Faith and Order Commission call upon us to see whether, on these points, we can transcend age-old rifts so as to be more prepared for the "today" of the kingdom. The text on "Baptism, Eucharist, Ministry" (BEM) should help us to break out of our constraints, especially in view of our sensitive position in France as a minority church compared to Roman Catholicism, which is itself a minority within a society in evolution. We have a fresh opportunity to enter into the promise of a common church life and to place our energies and our ministries at each other's service, with no loss of individual identity.

2. It is obvious that the ecclesiological, sacramental and patristic language of BEM is not our customary language and does not express our thought-structures. Even so, we do not reject it, because we are convinced that we should not aim to arrive at uniformity of language. We wish to hear each person "telling in his [or her] own tongue the mighty works of God" (Acts 2:11). We are encouraged to try to understand this language not with a view to replacing our own, but in order to see if the other Christian traditions express, in their own tongues, the same faith and the same Christian convictions as we do. We know already at this point — BEM demonstrates it well — that on many points we confess, albeit in different ways, the same faith.

We nevertheless request the Commission on Faith and Order to make this language more explicit, so as to remove all ambivalence in the use of terms affecting the present text of BEM. It is important for the language of the Reformation Churches to be taken into fuller consideration, so that other churches and traditions may, on their side, come to an understanding of our expression of faith in Christ, which represents one particular way of setting out priorities in understanding the gospel of Jesus Christ. In addition to the three themes presented (baptism, eucharist, ministry), we await a study on certain articles of faith which are fundamental for our churches, such as the understanding of salvation in Christ, the authority of scripture, the relationship of word and faith, Christian commitment. . .

3. After study of BEM at various levels of our church life, three theological questions arise out of the documents's three chapters. They are characteristic of our fundamental convictions and express our understanding of the gospel's demands. In the name of faithfulness to that gospel, we cannot be happy with positions which are too divergent, and we request the Commission on Faith and Order to supply additional definitions:

A. *Scripture and tradition*: We know that we are all heirs to a tradition and a history which affect our interpretation of holy scripture and the manner in which we ascribe authority to it. Tradition and history remain always secondary for us, and can never become the authorized interpreter of the biblical message.

B. *Word and sacrament*: The unique word of God has been given to us in the form of proclamation (preaching) and in the celebration of sacraments. By these two means God draws near to people and grants them his grace. All unilateral insistence upon a single one of these two poles seems to us regrettable. One should neither give priority to the sacrament over the spoken or written word, nor reduce the sacrament to a mere confirmation of that word.*

---

* To avoid all ambiguity, "word" here is intended by the authors to be understood as the preached word (e.g. sermon).

C. *The role of the church*: We maintain, with BEM, the necessity of structures for all ecclesiastical life. We think, however, that the church and its ministries are never in themselves dispensers or sole purveyors of grace. Every activity of the church and ministries has to be simply a means for the clear discernment of an activity which is God's alone.

These three theological questions are not new. They have been part of the ecumenical dialogue for years. They are points which are incidentally on the agenda of our internal debates, and they emerge as the background to all the specific questions we should like to put to the authors of BEM. Their emergence is not fortuitous, but a clear indication that fundamental features of our identity are at stake. Clarification of these points will lead us to a better understanding of "those churches which . . . recognize the text as an expression of the apostolic faith" (preface p. x, BEM).

4. In receiving BEM we are personally questioned not only on our principles and practices, but also on the destination of our churches in present-day France. They are rooted in the message which the Reformation received from God for the universal church: the proclamation of grace, the declaration of the justification in Christ accorded to unrighteous man. This message is not limited in time; persons and nations have more need than ever of this news, which could free them from the grip of secularization and theocracy, economic and ideological powers, and fatalism, all of which oppress and paralyze them.

But we recognize in ourselves a strong temptation to use this heritage to justify what we ourselves say, our negative reactions, and our own brand of paralysis. We appeal to you, brothers and sisters, to discover in the gospel of grace, with renewed conviction and fresh inspiration, the power of God. He wants to make us into free men and women, released from reflexes of fear, sectarianism and self-defence, removed by faith from all protection other than that of Christ, and placed by love at the service of others.

This is when the agreed statements will have allowed us not only to hear what others have to say about BEM, but also to tell them, with humility and truth, what we ourselves have received.

Symposium and Common Assembly
Lyons–Francheville, 8–10 March 1985

EVANGELICAL CHURCH OF THE AUGSBURG CONFESSION OF ALSACE AND LORRAINE

The High Consistory of the Evangelical Church of the Augsburg Confession of Alsace and Lorraine receives the Lima document on "Baptism, Eucharist and Ministry" (BEM) with gratitude. It rejoices at the new opportunity this document provides for dialogue between the various member churches of the WCC and the stimulus it gives to a thorough study of themes which have long been a matter of controversy in the different churches and have for too long been grounds for divisions preventing a genuine ecclesial communion between them.

We do not share the reservations of those who would have preferred to see more immediate economic, ethical, social and economic problems being tackled, since, in our view, BEM does tackle fundamental problems touching the life of our congregations at the very centre and whose study could lead to the deepening and consolidation of our common faith and in this way create the possibility of a revival and fresh dynamic which would enable the various churches to pursue their mission in the world more effectively.

As requested by the Faith and Order Commission we propose here to follow the sequence of its questions in the preface to the Lima document itself.

Recognize the faith of the church

The High Consistory recognizes the Lima document as a sign of unity between the WCC member churches.

The Lima document provides a broad framework in which an attempt is made to press forward beyond the different ecclesial traditions. It is therefore a compromise statement which is not without its ambiguities and consequently requires a certain number of clarifications.

The Lima document employs a language which is not our own. In large measure the terminology (faith of the church, eucharist, sacramental sign,

---

● 225,000 members, 206 parishes, 246 pastors.

etc.) is sacramental and patristic. It requires us to make a special effort to listen in a fraternal spirit to what it is saying as well as a process of translation (exegesis), since it requires us to take seriously the anxieties, preoccupations, and also the riches, of other ecclesial traditions.

Ecumenical consequences

The High Consistory sees the Lima document as an invitation to dialogue with other churches of the kind which has already taken place between the different branches of French Protestantism, and which cannot but be enriching for us all.

This dialogue opens up new vistas for us and will produce definite convergences, though these are not to be equated with a consensus necessarily entailing a total ecclesial communion. The Lima document is certainly a fruitful instrument for the ecumenical dialogue, indeed, this is its outstanding positive aspect, but the ambiguities it contains demand the prolongation of this dialogue. In this sense, the Lima document is a serious challenge to our church, stimulating us to review our own positions and to re-examine carefully certain of the questions to which it addresses itself so as to clarify our own confessional identity. Only on the basis of such a thorough reflection and a clearly defined identity will it be possible for us to engage in a fruitful dialogue with others.

Consequences for the life of our church

The Lima document can certainly not be accused of confining its attention to secondary problems, of complacently accepting a certain status quo by failing to tackle genuine contemporary questions affecting the mission of the church.

It is interesting to note that in recent years the High Consistory of our church has itself examined both the problem of baptism and that of the eucharist as well as the thorny question of ministries in the church, which remains one of the main difficulties in the present ecumenical dialogue.

The Lima document prompts us to reconsider our baptismal and eucharistic liturgies and to update them by making full use of the wealth of the universal tradition.

It also invites us to re-examine our catechetical instruction and our theological training of future pastors while at the same time not neglecting the repercussions such reflections could have for the life of our various congregations at the parish level.

Suggestions for Faith and Order

But the problems tackled by the Lima document raise numerous questions and we have to ask ourselves whether certain divergences still retain a divisive role in relations between the churches.

We request the Faith and Order Commission:

1. To spell out the relationships between scripture and tradition (since the Lima document is largely influenced by the post-apostolic period).

   To resume the study on the authority of scripture and the relationship between scripture and faith.

   To define more clearly the key to the exegesis of the biblical message and so avoid also the double danger of the primacy of the church, on the one hand, and subjectivism, on the other.

2. To define also the relationship between word and sacrament. Are word and sacrament equivalent expressions of one and the same presence of God?

   What is meant when it is said that the eucharist "continues as the central act of the Church's worship"?

   What are we to make then of the phrase "the service of the Word"?

   In what way is the presence of Christ in the eucharist a "unique presence"?

3. To reconsider the problem of ecclesiology, since the doctrine of ministries is closely connected with ecclesiology.

   Does the Lima document not tend to see the church as God's co-worker in the salvation of human beings?

   Are the ministries divinely instituted? Or are they defined solely on the basis of the organization of the church and by the functions of those who exercise them?

   The role of the *episkopé* would need to be redefined. Does it not loom too large in the Lima document?

   These are only some of the questions which still need fuller exploration and clarification.

   The High Consistory draws attention to the Commentary of the Theological Commission of the National Alliance of Lutheran Churches of France (ANELF) which voices its satisfaction with the Lima document but which also lists many questions which need to be examined further and which do indeed call for fuller explanation.

   The Lima document is undoubtedly a document of hope. Because it contains many compromises which demand clarification, however, it cannot be more than a first step towards deeper ecclesial communion. It is the responsibility of our churches to pursue this work of reflection with a view to the consolidation of the faith and a more complete unity which will enable them to continue and intensify the mission entrusted to them by our Lord in this world.

NATIONAL ALLIANCE OF LUTHERAN CHURCHES OF FRANCE

At the request of the National Committee, the document presented by the Faith and Order Commission of the World Council of Churches on "Baptism, Eucharist and Ministry" (Lima document, January 1982) was studied in detail by the Theological Commission of the National Alliance of Lutheran Churches of France (ANELF). Following various studies and working sessions, the Theological Commission submitted the following commentary to the National Committee on 20 March 1984. Having gratefully received the commentary, the Committee of ANELF offers it to the churches and their members who may wish to study the Lima document as an aid to their reflections.

Baptism
A. It is with gratitude that we receive the text on baptism, noting its fundamental accord with the Lyons Thesis on Baptism in the Name of the Father, the Son and the Holy Spirit. Faithful to the credal documents of the sixteenth century, this Thesis was ratified by our Lutheran churches as well as by most of the Reformed churches of France. The Lima text on baptism is also concordant with existing regulations governing the dual practice of infant baptism and adult baptism presupposing the responsible choice of families or individual persons in communion with the church and its baptismal ministry.

a) We appreciate the breadth of the text, its theological and spiritual richness, its ecumenical dimension, and, above all, its determination to make the truth of the various baptismal practices mutually accessible and in this way to give each of them, where necessary, a greater plenitude in accordance with that of the biblical teaching. In particular, we endorse the affirmation that baptism is fundamental for the Christian life and therefore relevant for the whole of life in the church and in the world; we also endorse the text's affirmation of the significance of water in unity with the action of the Holy Spirit. We recognize the capital importance of a personal and community preparation for baptism and of a complete and joyful liturgy as the setting for its celebration. All these aspects present our churches with a challenge to make their baptismal preaching and practice — and, supported by it and supportive of it, a baptismal life — a living and central reality. For what in fact is involved in baptism is our communion in Christ and in the Triune God and our incorporation into his church.

b) We invite our churches to examine their theory and practice of baptism in the 'light of the Lima text. In particular, we invite them to consider ways and means of ensuring that the mutual recognition of baptism between churches which find their own understanding of baptism reflected in this text may become effective in practice and that the ecclesial implications of this recognition may be seen and respected.

B. Against the background of this recognition, we draw attention to certain points which need clarification, greater precision, or exploration when a final revision of the text is undertaken.

B.A. *Points calling for clarification and greater precision*

a) The text gives a general impression of *repetitiveness* which is symptomatic of a failure fully to systematize its contents. In a text of this kind it would be helpful and desirable to aim for greater conciseness.

b) In what is said about the institution of baptism, we regret the absence of any *reference to the baptism of Jesus by John*. There is indeed a reference to it subsequently, but what is involved here is the very foundation of Christian baptism inseparable from the death and resurrection of Christ and the gift of the Holy Spirit (cf. Lyons Thesis 1).

c) The statement in II A3 that baptism means participating in the life, death and resurrection of Jesus Christ needs to be completed in the sense of the statement in IV B14 that baptism signifies and *effects* this participation in Christ's death and resurrection. For baptism accomplishes what it signifies.

d) The statement in IV A concerning the dual practice of adult and infant baptism as alternative equivalents for entry into the church invites not only pedobaptist churches to recognize the baptism of churches which practice adult baptism but also the latter churches to *recognize the baptism of pedobaptist churches*, providing the full meaning of baptism is recognized on both sides.

e) We regret the absence of any development of the relationship between *baptism and penitence* as an actualization of baptism throughout the entire life of the baptized person (cf. below B.B.b.).

B.B. *Further investigations*

a) The root of Christian baptism is in Christ and, in a central way, in his death and resurrection and in the gift of the Holy Spirit. To make its full significance for concrete daily life comprehensible and to avoid any appearance of its being merely tacked on to daily life from the outside without really being organically part of it, it seems to us vital to relate baptism to the lifelong experience of death and resurrection (of "dying to become") which in Christian baptism is "recapitulated" in Christ, i.e. attested for faith as a presence and action of Christ's death and resurrection which here confer their benefits.

In this sense, and along the lines indicated in §§18 and 19 of the text, we would like to see what is said about the *symbolic value of* water, in unity with the action of the Spirit, related more directly to the fundamental human experience of death as transition to life. (In particular, immersion could enhance the symbolism of baptism.)

b) Baptism, as a once-for-all ecclesial act, is entrance upon and even *initiation into a baptismal existence* extending over the whole of the baptized person's lifetime. Throughout this lifetime, *penitence* is the actualization of baptism. We would like to see this connection as well as its practical ecclesial implications made more explicit. We ought to be able to find again in our churches some private or public penitential act including, on the one hand, the confession of sins and individual absolution, and, on the other hand, the profession of faith and commitment in the presence of the church. In this way a suitable personal and ecclesial expression could be provided for whatever is of authentic spiritual substance in the motivation which leads some Christians to ask for re-baptism in the wake of some radical spiritual experience.

C. Several of these comments and recommendations are addressed not only to the Lima text on baptism but equally validly to our churches themselves, constituting a challenge to them too. We very much hope that the Lima text may provide firstly our own churches and then also all other churches with a stimulus to a more deeply-rooted, more thoughtful and living, catechetical and baptismal practice and baptismal Christian ethic. We also hope that baptism, as the foundation common to all our churches, may be for their relations with each other as well as for their mission in the world, a powerful ferment of unity and a dynamic spur to evangelism, by directing their attention to everything which exists as a baptismal reality in the deep-seated spring of human hope.

Eucharist

A. We welcome with interest and gratitude this text on the eucharist. It provides us with a whole series of prospects and stimuli which if translated into the life of the churches could greatly enrich our eucharistic celebrations. We would also like to underline the convergences between this Lima text and other recent ecumenical approaches.

a) We note the central place given to *thanksgiving* in the eucharist. The emphasis is not exclusively on the "downward" action (God's pardoning action in Christ) but also on the "upward" action of the community towards God with and through Christ. We note that the prayer envisages not only the act of redemption in the narrower sense of the term but embraces also the act of creation and consummation. The question this addresses to us is how this plenitude is embodied in our liturgies and the extent to which our celebrations are doxological in character (praise).

b) The eucharist as invocation of the Spirit

The part played by the invocation of the Holy Spirit in the Western liturgies has traditionally been fairly meagre. Lutheran liturgies have often restricted it to the prayer for a blessed (or believing) communion. Some part seems also to have been played by fears of spiritualization, as if reference to the Spirit (which in this case would suggest the Greek "spirit" rather than the Holy Spirit) might cast doubts on the real presence!

Here we have to face the challenge of the text and let it remind us that the entire eucharistic celebration is epicletic in character (in other words, the *epiklesis* can equally well be placed before as after the words of institution). We invoke the Holy Spirit, praying that he may himself fulfill the promises of Christ. The eucharist is not simply the prolongation of the incarnation nor is it a "magic and automatic act", but set within the framework of a prayer. In the Lutheran-Reformed Liebfrauenberg Theses (France 1981), the Protestants of France declare: "The presence of Christ is not the work of subjective human piety but the work of the Holy Spirit."

From this perspective, the *epiklesis* concerns both the action of the Holy Spirit in us human beings (the assembled community) and his action on the elements. This can be given visibility by the act of blessing the elements, although on this last point there is still a certain difference between Lutherans and Reformed.

c) Communion of the faithful

Here, too, all recent eucharistic statements share a common concern: namely, to give proper emphasis to the community dimension of the eucharist. Three sets of questions are addressed to us by the Lima text on the eucharist:

— How can we express more fully in our liturgies the fact that we celebrate the eucharist "in communion with all the saints and martyrs" (§11), i.e. with the church of all the ages? Is there agreement on the need to open the eucharist to all the baptized (§19)? How, then, can we advance in our intercommunion practices and theologies? To what extent can the admission of children also be extended?
— How can the ethical implications and consequences of the eucharistic celebration be more fully expressed (§20)?
— What form are we to give to communion during and after the eucharistic celebration (the sign of peace, taking communion to the sick, etc.)?

d) The celebration of the eucharist

It would be beneficial if our worship were enriched by the various elements mentioned in §27. Heed should also be paid to the challenge to a more frequent celebration of the Lord's Supper (§30). Finally, like other documents of a similar kind, the Lima text on the eucharist refers to the problem of preparatory education for the Lord's Supper as well as to the problem of liturgies. At the level of our congregations as well as in our catechetical practice (not to mention the training of our pastors), there are obvious gaps of which we often take too little notice.

B. Having registered our agreement and our gratitude, we wish nevertheless to offer some *critical observations*. In some cases, these are more in the nature of requests for explanation; in others a more fundamental questioning is involved, and even disagreement.

B.A. *Request for explanation*

a) We cannot see the precise point of an affirmation in §2: "In accordance with Christ's promise, each baptized member of the body of Christ receives in the eucharist the assurance of the forgiveness of sins (Matt. 26:28) and the pledge of eternal life (John 6:51–58)." Is this simply meant to make it clear that only the baptized are called to communicate? Including baptized infants? Is it the intention to assert that, at this level, faith (which is not mentioned here) does not enter the question? Or is the intention simply to say that the baptized, who remain sinners, need the declaration of pardon?

b) In respect of the *use of the elements after the eucharistic celebration*, the Lima text seems to us a little ahead of itself in affirming that "each church should respect the practices and piety of the others" (§32). Are there no questions to be posed and correctives to be applied on the basis of a common vision of the eucharist?

c) The meal of the kingdom

This is a frequent theme of ecumenical documents of this kind. Once again the emphasis is placed on mission, service in the world, etc. What is missing here is *a dimension of consolidation*: it is "bread and wine for pilgrims" (§26), certainly, but not only in view of their apostolic exodus into the world; also in view of Christ's return. In this intermediate time of tribulation, the church is comforted and consolidated by the eucharist. The statements of the Arnoldshain Theses and the Lyons Theses on this question are to be preferred.

d) §29 affirms that the "presidency" of Christ is signified by the presence of an "ordained minister". Believing as they do that Christ's sovereignty is expressed by the gospel as such rather than by the ministry, the churches of the Reformation often have reservations about such expressions as this. The Liebfrauenberg Theses viewed the ministry only as "bond between the local community and the other communities in the universal Church" (a theme also expressed in Lima, §29). It should also be noted that, unlike the Liebfrauenberg Theses, the Lima text does not envisage the possibility of the eucharist's being presided over by "a person commissioned by the Church" (Liebfrauenberg 7) but not really ordained. It would doubtless be necessary for us on our part to revise certain of our practices in this respect.

B.B. *Three important and more critical questions* need to be posed, it seems to us.

a) Eucharist — word/sacrament

According to the Reformation tradition, God uses different means to approach human beings: the spoken word, baptism, the Lord's Supper, the power of the keys, brotherly comfort. This perspective, which is evoked by the Smalcald Articles (1537), is more often than not reduced to the polarity of word/sacraments.

"Word and Sacrament are for us comparable to the two foci of an ellipse" (Liebfrauenberg Thesis 1). The perspective in the Lima text on the eucharist seems to us to be a different one: "Its (*sc.* the eucharist's) celebration continues as the central act of the Church" (§1).

Admittedly the term "eucharist" sometimes seems to be used more broadly to denote worship in its entirety: "The eucharist always includes both word and sacrament" (3); it "properly includes the proclamation of the Word" (§12). We are still left with the impression, however, that it is almost always used in the restrictive sense of the celebration of the sacrament. Protestant sensibilities and Protestant theologians (including Lutherans) are naturally uneasy about this. Though wholeheartedly recognizing the need to restore to the eucharist a much more important role in our liturgical practice, we are nonetheless not prepared to neglect the role properly assigned to the preached word.

Another question arises in the context of this whole problem area. On several occasions the Lima text on the eucharist speaks of the mode of Christ's presence in the eucharist as "unique" (§§13, 15). It will obviously be agreed that Christ gives himself differently in the eucharist or in baptism than he does in the word. What we must avoid, however, is the suggestion that there is another type of the presence of Christ (more intense?) in the eucharist in comparison with his presence in the word. Otherwise we abandon the Reformation tradition.

Finally, there is the question of the extent to which the eucharist constitutes the church. Certainly it does so in the broader sense of the term (worship, polarity of word and sacrament) but then it would be necessary also to remember the action of the word in the constitution and creation of the church (cf. Luther's phrase: *ecclesia creatura Verbi*). Here, too, there is a biblical and Reformation tradition to be maintained.

b) The question of the real presence

In our view, there is a real danger of drowning problems in words when we speak of "presence" or even of "real presence". We need to remember the dominant concern of Luther and Lutherans: the presence and the gift of Christ in his body and blood (synonyms of salvation!) are tied to the actual gift of the elements. We receive Christ's body and blood by the act of eating and drinking (*manducatio oralis*) and this gift is so real that it even affects unbelievers (though in a non-saving manner).

This view appears to be respected in the Lima text: "in the eating and drinking of the bread and wine, Christ grants communion with himself" (§2). But it is watered down again in the subsequent text. Certainly "Christ's real presence in the eucharist does not depend on the faith of the individual" (§13). But can it also be said that the communicant is really reached by the gift independently of his or her faith? Possible doubts here are strengthened still further by the Commentary which also introduces a dangerous pluralism:

some churches "do not link that presence so definitely with the signs of bread and wine". Is this not to downgrade the elements and to invite a spiritualism which negates the very notion of sacrament? The eucharist would then seem to be no more than a symbol of human action.

If the matter had to be left there, it would seem to us difficult and even impossible to speak of agreement.

c) The church and Christ

What troubles us is the way in which the church is constantly associated with the action of Christ and represented as sacrificing with him (§§4, 8, 9, 23). Certainly the inclusive aspect of Christ's sacrifice had to be emphasized in order to restore balance to the Protestant approaches. "Christ unites the faithful with himself" (§4). This view of the matter seems to us correct. But an obvious danger emerged: the church is so united with Christ that it is on the way to becoming a cooperator in salvation. What we miss here is the *extra nos* of justification by faith. In our view, the point is far better stated in Thesis 4 of the Liebfrauenberg Theses which begins as follows: "Having been made the beneficiaries of the unique and perfect sacrifice of Jesus Christ who died on the cross and rose again from the dead, a sacrifice actualized in the Lord's Supper, we give thanks to God and to Christ . . . With confidence we approach God our Father through Jesus Christ present in our midst as High Priest and Intercessor . . . "

Ministry

A. We receive with interest the Lima text on the ministry. As Lutheran churches we are challenged by it since it stimulates us to rethink our view of ministry in our own churches.

We accept the Lima text's *emphasis on the necessity of the ministry for the very being of the church*. The church is the assembly of saints in which the gospel is taught purely and the sacraments are administered rightly in accordance with the word of God (Augsburg Confession VII). But it was not the purpose of the Augsburg Confession to reduce the notion of the church to a simple meeting of believers. The ministry is necessary for the proclamation of the gospel and the administration of the sacraments, even if this ministry (these ministries) must always remain subordinate to word and sacraments. A church without a ministry (ministries) is inconceivable. It is also important, moreover, to recognize, with the Lima text, that the church has *not just a single ministry but ministries*. We find a special challenge in the emphasis placed by the Lima text on the diaconal ministry. This has too often been neglected in our churches and in ecumenical dialogues.

Realizing the vital ecumenical importance of the question of ministries, we are grateful to the Faith and Order Commission for having provided a first draft of a document which could some day be the expression of a consensus between the Christian churches leading to ecclesial communion between them. We invite our member churches and their local congregations to reflect on their practice of ministry in the light of the Lima text.

B. Against the background of this acknowledgment, we feel bound to mention *certain questions* which remain unresolved in reading the Lima text or which are posed for us by our relationships and dialogues with other churches in our particular geographical context. These questions transcend this specific context and require to be articulated at international level.

B.A. On the basis of the Leuenberg Agreement, our churches are in ecclesial communion with the Reformed churches and specifically with the two Reformed Churches in France (the Reformed Church of Alsace and Lorraine and the Reformed Church of France). The Leuenberg Agreement is one of the few ecumenical documents which does not tackle the question of ministry (ministries) or the problems of ecclesiology. This was no oversight but an ecumenical translation of the fact that these questions are not of primary importance for ecclesial relationships between Reformed and Lutheran churches.

Our Reformed brothers and sisters in France have theological positions on the question of ministry (ministries) which we do not share (cf. for example, the most recent statement of the Commission on Ministries of the Reformed Church of France, Valence Synod 1982). Questions concerning the ministry (ministries) remain open and form the subject of discussions between us. But this does not call our ecumenical communion in question.

This being the case, we consider it vital that the following points be clarified in respect of the Lima text on ministry:

a) What *place is assigned to the question of the ministry* in the ecumenical efforts of the Faith and Order Commission? Does the presentation of this text on the ministry *alongside* the texts on baptism and the eucharist signify that it is assigned analogous theological importance?

b) What is the precise *relationship between the ministry and the ministries*? What is the real place of all "the other ministries" in the church? Are we entitled to separate them from the ordained ministry in the way the Lima text does in its section II, where this ordained ministry seems to be far more important than all these other ministries?

c) Is the *text on the ministry merely an example of a theology of ministry* or does it claim to be in its main outlines the definition of the ministry to be accepted by all the Christian churches together?

In addition to these comments, there is also *the question of authority* in the church, a point which is not clarified in the Lima document. This additional clarification seems to us to be needed because it is decisive for relations between churches (as well as for our ecclesial communion on the basis of the Leuenberg Agreement).

B.B. Our churches are also engaged in doctrinal discussions on the ministry (ministries) with the *Roman Catholic Church* through the bilateral discussions conducted by the Lutheran World Federation. One recent discussion on the ministry reveals a number of points still unresolved between Rome and the Lutheran churches. The Lima text on the ministry does not tackle these questions but ignores them. This troubles us, since evading the real questions is no way of solving them. Two churches which are divided on the question of the ministry can thus quite easily endorse the main lines of the Lima document and see in it a possible expression of a theology of ministry without each being led to reopen the question of its practice at the local and confessional level. By failing to tackle this thorny question, this document is in danger of *freezing the status quo*. To show what we have in mind, we point to the following five considerations:

a) *The precise relationship between universal priesthood, ministries in the church, and ordained ministry*. What precisely is this distinction? Does it involve a difference of essence or only of degree (Vatican II, *Lumen Gentium* §10)? The question has remained in dispute in the international Lutheran/Roman Catholic dialogue (L/RC 17). The Lima text does not deal with the problem; it fails to clarify the relationship between the ordained ministry and the ministry of all. Surprisingly enough, moreover, the expression "universal priesthood" does not occur. Are not all the baptized a priesthood? Is it not the case that this term is reserved for those ordained to the special ministry whereas believers have primarily functional ministries?

b) Every church needs ministries in order to fulfill the mission of Christ. The unanswered question is *to what extent the ordained ministry is decisive for the definition of the very esse of the church*. In the Lutheran/Roman Catholic dialogue, the Catholics can speak of a local church only if there is an episcopal ministry, whereas the Lutherans, while not denying the importance of this ministry, define the church without reference to the *episkopé* (L/RC 68). The Lima text uses the term church without defining it. The real question thus remains open. Is a small assembly of Christians a church in the full sense? Is a community without a bishop a church (Lima §23)?

c) The Lima text refers to the "powerful claim" which "*the threefold pattern* (*sc.* of ministry)" as developed in history has on the acceptance of the churches (§25). This threefold form exists in our churches but for us it is a distinction based on human law. There is divergence on this point in the dialogue with Rome (L/RC 47 and 48) for it is in the bishop alone that the plenitude of the ministry in which priests and deacons share pertains. Here again, the Lima text leaves the question open. Is the threefold form of ministry a mere example or is it essential for the faith of the church? (Lima §28 can be interpreted as making this threefold form an example, whereas other passages speak a different language.)

d) In respect of *ordination*, two points are left open in the Lutheran/Roman Catholic dialogue: the question of its sacramental character and the question of its indelibility (L/RC 33). The Lima text speaks of its being a "sacramental sign" (§41) but gives no explanation of what this means. Does this mean that it is a sign, a blessing on the transmission of priesthood, or a sacrament? All these interpretations remain possible. The question of indelibility is not dealt with at all.

On the other hand, we welcome the definition the Lima text gives of the *"apostolic succession"* as the apostolic succession of the whole church (§§35, 36, 38), since this point was left open in the Lutheran/Roman Catholic dialogue (L/RC 59–65).

e) We regret, finally, that at no point does the Lima text tackle the question of the *papal ministry*, though this is a fundamental question for the doctrine of the ministry and a subject of controversy between the churches (L/RC 50–55). Directly related to it are the questions of the magisterium and of doctrinal authority. Can we possibly speak of the ministry (ministries) and at the same time remain silent on these key issues?

C. Our criticisms are not to be taken as a simple repudiation of the Lima text. Quite the reverse. We welcome this as a first draft of a consensus document but now wish to push forward beyond this stage and tackle the really controversial points between the churches. This seems all the more necessary to us since the question of the ministry is only a form of an even more fundamental question still, namely, that of what we mean by the church (its sacramental character, its constitutive elements, etc.). This point seems to us to be on the agenda of the future dialogue.

9–10 November 1985   High Consistory

EVANGELICAL LUTHERAN CHURCH OF FRANCE

I. Introduction

I.1. With our church's reception of the BEM text, we feel a need to recall the essential element in our preaching. On the basis of scripture our church aims above all to proclaim the certain truth that the true and essential conversion is that of the human heart touched by divine grace. Thus the preaching of the all-powerful grace of God is central to its theology and teaching. Consequently it must reaffirm that the unity of the church of Christ is not a task to be achieved in itself, but is the free gift of the action of the Holy Spirit. That is the context within which our church must today experience baptism, eucharist and ministry, and this must be recalled before any discussion or reception of the Lima text is undertaken.

Despite its limitations and omissions, we acknowledge that this document represents an important contribution to the witness of the churches, since we should continually give an account together of the hope that is in us. BEM thus permits us to clarify the historical divergences which have contributed to division among Christians. It offers real convergences which can create and strengthen a deep ecclesial fellowship between different confessions. We thus note with satisfaction the process of theological discussion at all levels in our church which has arisen out of the dynamic of BEM. This development is most valuable, not only in acknowledging a Christian tradition other than our own, but also for a new and clearer realization of our own identity.

I.2. We have in France an effective ecclesial fellowship between four Lutheran/Reformed churches. This is the context in which we make this response, all the more so since other doctrinal agreements[1] link us together within French and European Protestantism. We have, as would be expected, contributed the report on discussions undertaken by various groups in our church to the Francheville consultation, which brought together these four churches in France.

- 40,000 members, 45 parishes, 50 pastors.
[1] These agreements are: the document known as "The Theses of Lyon", 1968; the Leuenberg Agreement, 1973; and "The Lord's Supper", Liebfrauenberg, 1981.

I.3. It is in this context that the Evangelical Lutheran Church of France welcomes with great interest many of the statements in BEM; it views other statements in the text as a challenge to express its desire for ecclesial fellowship in time and space with other traditions; and, lastly, it puts forward some points which would make for a greater recognition of the Protestant tradition. That tradition is also a gift to be shared with other Christian traditions.

I.4. It goes without saying that we consider as the basis for ecclesial fellowship the necessity for a common understanding of the gospel, which "must be further deepened, tested in the light of the witness of holy scripture, and continually made relevant in the contemporary scene".[2]

II. What we welcome

II.1. On the subject of *baptism*, we are in basic agreement with BEM on this point. We acknowledge that baptism is on the initiative of God, Father, Son, and Holy Spirit. We accept in their entirety the four meanings of baptism set out in the text: death and resurrection with Christ; conversion, pardoning and cleansing; the gift of the Spirit; and the sign of the kingdom. It is because baptism is incorporation into Christ that it is also incorporation into the messianic community. We rejoice with BEM, following Paul, that we can declare that there is only one baptism, and we associate ourselves with the ecumenical challenge implicit in the unrepeatable nature of baptism.

As for the practice of baptism, we recognize ourselves in the BEM text, which indicates the possibility of a dual practice: the baptism of infants and the baptism of adults. Both forms of baptism involve faith: prospective faith in the case of infants, and personal faith in the case of adults. But, as BEM emphasizes, the whole of one's life is involved with a view to an ever-deepening mature understanding of the baptismal experience. We therefore, with BEM, reject "re-baptism".

II.2. As regards the *Lord's Supper*, we appreciate the balance of the text, on the one hand centring the sacrament again on the person and work of Christ, and on the other giving a constant reminder of its being rooted in the Trinity, and, more particularly, the importance of the Holy Spirit. We recognize ourselves in many of the points in the paragraphs which deal with the meaning of the Supper: the praise given to the Father for the gift of salvation; the memorial of the person and work of the Redeemer; the role of the Holy Spirit in the conscious thanksgiving for the salvation both achieved and constantly promised; and, lastly, the expectation and anticipation of the kingdom — these are basic points to which we adhere, and do so quite apart from certain sacramental interpretations and deductions which are discern-

---

[2] The Leuenberg Agreement, art. 38; cf. *Recherches ecclésiales*, study booklet No. 4 of the Lutheran-Reformed Standing Council, Paris, 1981, pp.17 ff.

ible in the text. Like BEM, we insist on the dimension of praise which should necessarily be present in any celebration of the Lord's Supper, since, in his word, God reveals his salvation to us and pressingly invites us to accept it. We are glad to see that the unique nature of Christ's sacrifice, and hence of our salvation, is explicitly set out in the BEM text. We are in essential agreement with BEM on the presence of Christ under the visible signs of the bread and the wine. However, out of earnest desire that God's absolute freedom should be given its place, we shall later state our reservations and concern about the mode of that presence. We welcome with satisfaction the statements which see the Lord's Supper as an anticipation of the messianic banquet: in that regard, both for its own and the world's sake, the church, as it gives thanks to the Father, should also seriously consider at the same time the historic and contemporary divisions, antagonism and hatred in humankind. Finally, we accept with BEM that "the affirmation of a common eucharistic faith does not imply uniformity in either liturgy or practice".

II.3. Concerning *ministry*, in this section we take the BEM statements as open questions and challenges addressed to the majority of the churches arising out of the Reformation. But it is important in itself that these questions should be raised so that we can reach a deeper common understanding and mutual recognition of our respective traditions. It is along these lines that we are unable to reject this section of BEM.

III. Things which challenge us

III.1. In the section on *baptism*, as in that on the Supper, we wish to make the effort to understand better, in the truth of the gospel, the true nature of the sacrament and all it means for the life of the Christian and the mystery of the church. While we accept that baptism achieves what it symbolizes, we do so on the sole and exclusive basis of the word of God. Our absolute confidence in the promises and in the infallible faithfulness of God enables us to accept that sacramental view of the signs. Now, the question addressed to us is whether we acknowledge the objective efficacity of the sacraments. Our church needs to deepen its sense of mystery before it can have a more satisfactory sacramental understanding in the eyes of those traditions which are more sensitive to this issue than we are. But in the very insight in which we can perhaps most easily recognize ourselves, a challenge arises: the essential deep relationship emphasized by BEM between baptism and confession of faith as a commitment of one's life reminds us of an important dimension of baptism in the Christian tradition. It has, regretfully, to be admitted that, even if not in the church's teaching (catechism, confession of faith, preaching), at least in practice, the baptism of infants and their consequent confirmation are increasingly emptied of meaning in our churches. This is a challenge to us. It thus seems desirable to us to seek an appropriate liturgical sign, non-sacramental in nature, to meet the desire expressed by those who have experienced a revival or "rebirth" in their baptismal life.

III.2. Concerning the *Lord's Supper*: one of the challenges of BEM consists in our church's more marked rediscovery of the dimension of praise and the celebratory aspect of the Supper. But that applies to worship as a whole. It is thus difficult for us to regard the Lord's Supper as "the central act of the Church's worship". The increased emphasis placed on this sacrament should not be obtained at the expense of the recognition of its relationship with the proclamation of the word. Moreover, the strengthening of the link between what God accomplishes for us on the one hand, and our thanksgiving and intercession on the other, opens up for us a more inclusive vision of the church as a "sacramental" reality or mystery. While we permit ourselves to be challenged by this perspective, we cannot fail to mention a risk attendant upon it, i.e. that the church is so much one with Christ that it appears to be cooperating with him in the salvation of humankind. How can we receive the idea of increased emphasis on the Supper without ending up with a kind of a "super-sacralization" of this sacrament?

III.3. As for *ministry*, our church is at present engaged in redefining its ministries, and is thus challenged by several points in BEM on this matter. While we wish to avoid confusing the *esse* of the church with its *bene esse*, we do accept that the church needs ministries to accomplish its mission. BEM seems to give the "ordained" ministry a privileged position over other ministries. Similarly, the text presents a hierarchical model of ministry (bishops, presbyters and deacons) in connection with presiding at the "eucharist". While we propose to go into all these matters more thoroughly, we also wonder whether this implicit sacralization of the ministry and its hierarchical structure are essential for mutual recognition of ministry. Protestantism places great stress on the church's prophetic mission, the ministry of the word. The pattern put forward in BEM consists almost exclusively in the function of presidency at the Supper. That raises the whole issue of the nature and role of the church.

IV. What we propose

IV.1. On the *sacraments*: It seems important to us to seek a clearer and more fruitful balance between the "visible Word" of the sacraments and the "audible Word" of the preaching of the gospel. Any increased emphasis on the sacraments which did not take into account this sensitivity to the gospel seems to us to run the risk of, in our eyes, sacralizing the sacraments, with the real danger of superstition and magical reactions in popular piety.

IV.2. On *ministry*: It is our strong desire that this section should be rewritten. We are really asking the following questions:[3]

---

[3] We here follow quite closely the reactions of the ANELF Theological Commission; cf. "Une prise de position luthérienne au sujet du document Baptême-Eucharistie-Ministère", in *Positions luthériennes*, No. 3, July/September 1984, pp.11 ff.

— Is the model presented by BEM just one example of the theology of ministry, or is it rather a definition of ministry as it should be among the churches with a view to eventual ecclesial fellowship?

— What is the exact relationship between the priesthood of all believers and the "ordained ministry"?

— Does BEM acknowledge adequately the "ordination" of women to "particular ministry"?

— To what extent can ministry (which for us is a matter of human law) define the *esse* of the church?

— What is the meaning of the phrase "representatives of Jesus Christ" as applied to the "ordained ministers"?

— Is it possible to avoid consideration of the primacy of the Bishop of Rome in discussion on the overall issue of ministries?

V. Conclusion

Our church receives BEM. We request Faith and Order to take our comments into account for a wider examination of the points at issue. Finally, we wonder whether this approach, with its somewhat backward-looking approach to our traditions, will really further the conversion to unity which we all seek. It seems to us, in effect, to be a matter of urgency that our convergences and our divergences alike should be tested at the level of contemporary witness and obedience to the gospel in face of the major issues of today's world.

REFORMED CHURCH
OF FRANCE

The National Synod has been informed of the request of the Commission on Faith and Order of the World Council of Churches for an official response to the text "Baptism, Eucharist and Ministry"; and is acquainted with the findings of the consultation organized by the Lutheran-Reformed Standing Council at Francheville on 8–9 March 1985 (see pp. 142–144).

1. Without prejudice to the position of this document with regard to the Statement of Faith of the Reformed Church of France (1938) and to the confessions of faith to which it refers, the National Synod considers the Faith and Order text to be an important milestone on the ecumenical journey; its production, the thinking it is provoking in the churches, and the conversations arising from it are all part of the process of mutual recognition with a view to the visible unity of the church.

2. The National Synod recalls that, at its meeting at Angers in 1977, it indicated the limits it sets to taking the production of such statements of agreement as bonds of ecumenical fellowship.

3. The National Synod receives the findings of the consultation ("Message to the Churches" and "Reception of the BEM Document") as expressions of the emphases and differences which have come to light in the course of study of BEM. It forwards it without amendment to the Commission on Faith and Order.

4. In particular, and in accord with the consultation, the National Synod states that, in order to recognize in the BEM text the faith which the Reformed Church of France confesses in these matters and to progress in its relationships and conversations with churches which will also recognize this text as an expression of the apostolic faith, further clarification is needed on the following points:

— *Scripture and tradition*: We would be unable to accept tradition as the authoritative interpretation of the biblical message.

• 400,000 members, 500 parishes, 600 pastors.

— *Word and sacrament*: We would be unable to accept a diminishing of the primacy of the word to give priority to the sacraments.

— *The role of the church*: We would be unable to accept that the church and ministers, whose calling is to serve God and the work of his grace, might seem to be dispensing or controlling that grace.

Our understanding and reception of the three parts of the BEM text depend on the answers we receive to these points. These theological issues are part of our fundamental convictions and understanding of the gospel and we consider that in them our faithfulness is at stake.

5. The National Synod reaffirms its commitment to ecumenical dialogue with a view to the visible unity which is Christ's gift.

It insists on the prime importance, in this ecumenical endeavour, of the gospel witness to contemporary men and women, in faithfulness to the mission entrusted by Christ to his people.

It emphasizes the connection between the various aspects of this endeavour, none of which should be minimized: theological investigation, missionary activity, a concern for evangelism, social solidarity, defence of human rights, etc. Thinking and sharing in each of these areas is all part of the same movement towards unity.

It calls to perseverance and progress, including within our local congregations, in listening to each other and sharing in service, while welcoming diversity and discerning convergence.

It gives thanks to God for the signs of unity and the enrichment already received in the course of these endeavours.

6. The National Synod instructs the National Council to ensure that the investigations and conversations initiated during the study of BEM continue, both within our local congregations and in the bilateral and multilateral relations of the Reformed Church of France with other churches.

REFORMED CHURCH OF ALSACE AND LORRAINE

The Synod of the Reformed Church of Alsace and Lorraine, meeting 2–3 November 1985, welcomes BEM ("Baptism, Eucharist, Ministry", 1982) as an important stage in our progress towards church unity. Parishes and groups who have received this text as a working document have become aware that ecumenical deliberation on the themes it tackles is important, and ought to be continued.

BEM caters in part for the impatience of many Christians who profoundly desire to make progress in their convergences. Such progress, however, necessitates the testing of each individual's convictions; sincere humility; and acceptance of our differences. Study of BEM seems to have made this open attitude possible.

The symposium on BEM organized by the four Lutheran and Reformed Churches of France (Francheville, 8–9 March 1985) drew attention to the existence of texts common to these four churches, which formulate a number of convergences:

— The "Lyons Theses" (1968) on "Word of God and Holy Scripture", "Baptism in the Name of the Father, Son and Holy Spirit", and "The Lord's Supper".
— The agreement among the churches derived from the Reformation in Europe, known as "The Leuenberg Agreement" (1973).
— The text on "The Lord's Supper" of Liebfrauenberg, 1981. The Synod of RCAL accepts the conclusions of this consultation, and stresses the necessity of a clarification from the ecumenical standpoint of three points there raised: scripture and tradition; word and sacraments; role of the church.

As a Reformation-derived church, for which scripture remains the sovereign authority, we rejoice in the generally biblical inspiration of BEM.

• 45,000 members, 53 congregations, 54 pastors.

However, three aspects present a problem:
—the questionable use of certain Bible citations;
—the scarcity of Bible references in the chapter devoted to ministry;
—in the same chapter, the excessive importance of tradition relative to scripture.

Baptism

The emphasis on baptismal catechetical instruction and on the communal nature of baptism is, in our opinion, a very positive element.

Section III rightly emphasizes the importance of faith and the existential and ethical consequences of baptism.

On the other hand, it would be advisable to explore in greater depth the relationship between baptism, forgiveness, conversion and the gift of the Spirit, and to clarify the chronological order of these elements. We observe, in fact, that an increasing number of believers who received baptism in their infancy are searching, in genuine spiritual need, for a way of demonstrating their personal acceptance of the new life. Our Reformed churches remain attached to the laying-on of hands (confirmation). An approaching synod of the RCAL will attempt to clarify this question.

Eucharist

Though aware of the importance of eucharistic celebration within the context of worship, we cannot accept that the eucharist constitutes the central act of worship. For us, word and sacrament form an indivisible whole, the gift of the new covenant.

It is Christ alone who presides over the eucharist; the presidency of the person who officiates should be defined on the basis of this statement.

We receive as a challenge the content of subsection 31 on the place and frequency of the celebration of the eucharist.

Ministry

We have some reservations to record.

The title alone of this document could give the impression that the ministry is conceived of as a third sacrament.

We think that, according to scripture, the ministry is not a constitutive element of the church, but that diverse and complementary ministries are bestowed by the Lord upon the church for its upbuilding and its mission. We acknowledge that the beginning of this chapter conveys a certain receptivity towards a diversity of ministries, but we regret that this richness later boils down to the three ministries of the bishop, the presbyter and the deacon. We are convinced that in the situation that exists today one cannot reduce the calling of the church to these three ordained ministries alone.

The exercise of ministry is collegial, in the call addressed to the church in its entirety. It is through this vision that we understand the concept of apostolicity. The text of BEM tends to limit it too strictly to historical continuity.

* * *

We hail with gratitude this first draft of a text on convergence leading us towards unity. We discover therein the richness of the faith and practice of numerous churches. The hope of unity in Christ invites us to accept our divergences as challenges, and to advance in mutual comprehension and recognition.

Some remarks on the format:
— It would have been preferable to have distinguished the commentaries by a different typographical presentation (this concerns the French edition).
— Certain unexplained terms or expressions make the document occasionally somewhat incomprehensible to "ordinary" Christians, even instructed ones. The final version should be more accessible to lay people.

UNITED PROTESTANT
CHURCH OF BELGIUM

Statement on baptism

I. First question

Of the three statements of the Commission on Faith and Order, the one relating to baptism seems to have a claim to priority for possible adoption.

Theologically, we welcome its Christological, pneumatological, ecclesiological and eschatological approach.

The endeavour to reconcile the divergences of centuries, particularly as to paedobaptism (which is regarded as expressing the gift of divine grace) and adult baptism (which represents the response of the human being) undoubtedly represents a positive contribution to the dialogue both within and between the churches.

The important fact must also be noted that baptism has not been treated in isolation but is rather looked on as a process of continued growth in the believer's existence in and with Christ, with ethical implications for every sphere of life.

We consider that the statement on baptism is a good, broad reflection of the church's teaching through the ages.

Nevertheless, the following three caveats were regularly in evidence during discussions of the report:
a) scripture yields too readily to tradition;
b) current theological differences do not receive enough attention;
c) the covenant idea is not sufficiently explored.

II. Second question

From our standpoint, an important consequence arising from this text is our church's will to go forward to interchurch recognition of baptism, especially with the Eastern Orthodox and the Anglican churches, always

---

● 35,000 members, 103 parishes, 105 pastors.

provided that our hesitation about some of the statements is recognized and that these can be made the subject of later discussions.

These points are:

a) The idea of baptism as having a saving power in itself, so that it then becomes indispensable to salvation.

b) The interpretation of §22 regarding administration by an ordained minister.

On this we should like to observe that:

1) the meaning of the words "in certain circumstances" must be given greater clarity;

2) it is necessary to keep §53 on the ministry, dealing with recognition of baptism administered by an ordained Protestant minister.

c) Dissociation of baptism and confirmation in some churches raises serious problems, especially in so far as confirmation is regarded as a sacramental act conferring the "fullness" of the Holy Spirit and completing baptism.

From this angle: is the fullness of the Holy Spirit therefore not conferred by baptism but solely through the laying on of hands by the bishop? And is it only through confirmation that one becomes fully a member of the body of Christ?

III. THIRD QUESTION

For our church, the statement on baptism can be valid only in part as a directive, because of the reservations already stated in I and II.

In our church it is very important, for the *pastoral* element in baptism, to accept child baptism and baptism of adults as two modes of baptism both equally valid.

Very serious note must be taken of the caveat entered on several occasions against "indiscriminate" baptism. In practical terms, one could consider consultation on baptism, possible refusal to baptize, relating baptism to confession of faith, and concern for religious education and catechesis.

Paragraph 13 on "rebaptism" is presented too unilaterally from the standpoint of respect for the baptismal practices of the other churches. It goes without saying that mutual recognition of baptism would have to exclude "rebaptism" of members of other churches.

But it can happen that a believer baptized "thoughtlessly and indiscriminately" as a child may wish for adult baptism. Would it not be possible to apply to such a case the last part of §11, regarding baptism of those "from unbelief who accept the Christian faith and participate in catechetical instruction", without ipso facto inconsistency with §13. It is necessary to keep before us the recognition of child baptism in churches which practise adult baptism, in so far as the person concerned looks on that baptism as a true one; it may be that this recognition could be in the form of a confirmation of the baptism received at an early age.

In the *catechetical* sphere, the stress laid on continuing training of the baptized person seems essential to us.

In the *liturgical* sphere, we have objections to §19 and the many supplementary signs accompanying the gift of the Spirit. In this context we would refer to §14, on the differences of opinion which exist as to understanding where the sign of the gift of the Spirit should be found.

IV. Fourth question

1. Formulation

Taking into account the theological style of language which is addressed explicitly "to the people of God on every level of church life" (see introduction), we would suggest a different formulation, to take into consideration the following comments, among others:

a) The document ought to be based to a greater extent on the authority of scripture, including the Old Testament.

b) It is desirable to use simple, contemporary language which is within the grasp of all parishioners.

c) In the expression of the common faith, it is necessary also to state frankly and clearly the divergences.

2. The theological angle

In this sphere, study of the arguments adduced for or against another form of baptism (paedobaptism or adult baptism) may be very illuminating. For instance, the role of the doctrine of original sin; ecclesiology — state church or missionary church, or a church of *imitatores*; liberty of conscience; custom and tradition; etc.

3. The liturgical angle

a) Liturgically, the question should be raised whether we can know if the New Testament texts and the practice of the primitive churches, which presuppose baptism of adults, are actually compatible with child baptism. We cannot ignore certain hermeneutical problems that belong here.

b) Is it possible to accept the Orthodox model of child baptism as it stands, i.e. by immersion (§18)? There are differences of meaning and function between child baptism and the baptism by immersion in the New Testament. These differences must also show up in the liturgy.

4. Rebaptism

It seems worth commending deeper study of the ways and means for "rebaptism", suggested in III, above all with a view to dialogue with the free churches.

Statement on the Lord's Supper

I. FIRST QUESTION

Faith is something which has to be lived out and celebrated by believers before it can be thought out and given theological formulation.

If only for that reason, theological definition and ecclesiastical styles have a merely relative right to exist.

The *church's* faith always implies the faith of Christians, in the absence of which there will be the suspicion that that faith is formalist and institutionalist.

BEM's statement on the eucharist, in attempting to remove and relativize some historic Western controversies, has recourse systematically to certain theological ideas of the Eastern Orthodox church. For the rest, this statement prefers to use the vivid language of the primitive church.

In §§1, 2, 19 and 24 we rediscover important elements of what may be called "the common experience of the faith" as regards the Lord's Supper: it is a "gift from the Lord"; "in the eating and drinking of the bread and wine, Christ grants communion with himself"; this participation in Christ clearly implies "at the same time communion within the body of Christ which is the Church"; "reconciled in the eucharist, the members of the body of Christ are called to be servants of reconciliation" (French: forgiveness) "among men and women and witnesses of the joy of resurrection".

When the text as a whole has been read, however, there remain a fair number of questions. Here are some of them:

1. What is the authority of the scriptural texts quoted, if different and indeed contrary theologies interpret them by applying their own particular hermeneutical principles?

2. What convergence is desired or can be achieved, given the great lack of precision persisting as to not only the use of scripture but also the content of fundamental theological concepts such as:

— *Anamnesis*: does this apply to the entire history of salvation or to the work and life of Christ?

— Sacrifice: personal or in the context of worship?

— Is the presence of Christ a matter of transubstantiation or of "transignification"?

— Does *epiklesis* extend to gifts and/or to persons?

— Is it the mark of the eucharistic community to convey a sign or to perform a function?

3. The meaning of the eucharist and the question of the ministry (apostolic succession, consecration) are handled separately. Will it be possible to go on in this way in the current dialogue?

4. Could there not have been a clearer affirmation that worship and the ministry are both in the service of the word, in its dual sense of preaching and sacraments, which are both equally important?

Here, finally, are some comments and objections for study:

1. From the standpoint of the Reformed tradition, which stresses the ministry of the word, the "eucharistic" character of the report seems to be highlighted too much.

2. As the term "eucharistic" is too loaded, it would be better to use the expression "the Lord's Supper".

3. Alongside the elaborate celebration there has also been in the course of the church's history a simpler form of fraction (breaking of the bread), with a more clearly community character.

4. We would put a question mark against the commemoration of martyrs and saints.

5. In this document, reference is missing to the Jewish roots of holy communion. This cannot fail to have both theological and practical consequences.

The question of the extent to which our church can "recognize in this text the faith of the church throughout the ages" is to our mind too general and at this stage of the dialogue it is only with some difficulty that a reply can be given.

II. Second question

This statement, which is strongly influenced by Orthodox eucharistic ecclesiology, offers themes and points of view which are important for the current dialogue and for the endeavour to build up a convergence or consensus between the non-Roman Catholic churches which are members of the WCC.

An effort must be made to clarify the problems listed under I.

Recent statements of the Roman Catholic Sacred Congregation for the Doctrine of the Faith and those of Pope John Paul II indicate a hardening of the positions alluded to in part I. This will hardly make the dialogue with the Roman Catholic Church any easier.

The problem of intercommunion is not investigated with adequate care in BEM.

From the Reformed standpoint, participation in the Lord's Supper is accorded in principle to all baptized believers.

Although in our view no intrinsic significance should be attached to the bread and wine apart from the celebration of holy communion, we do not consider the practices and piety surrounding the elements in other churches to be reasons for ecclesiastical divisions.

III. Third question

The statement on the eucharist contains dimensions which enrich our traditional celebrations of holy communion and are capable of in some way correcting and supplementing them.

On this subject we may mention:

1. The dimension of praise and joy (§§3, 4, 7, 24) contrasting with the sometimes too exclusive emphasis on the sufferings of the Lord and human unworthiness.

2. The aspect of "communio" with the Lord and among the faithful (§§19, 20, 21, 24) as a corrective to a somewhat individualistic way of understanding the encounter with God.

3. The link-up with the world and creation and with ethical implications, as against an over-emphasis on justification.

BEM presupposes celebration of holy communion at regular intervals, if possible weekly.

Currently, in many Belgian congregations, holy communion is celebrated once a month, and this represents a considerable increase in relation to past practices. We are convinced that it is not possible to exert pressure on congregations as to the frequency of their celebration of holy communion. Quantitative gain does not of necessity mean qualitative gain. There might also be reason to fear a liturgical monopoly and a backward step towards a magical view of the sacrament.

In large centres of population where several churches are sited, the suggestion could be made that holy communion be celebrated by turns in each church so that all wishing to participate in the celebration might do so.

Holy communion is not an optional extra to the preaching of the word any more than preaching is optional in a very elaborate eucharistic celebration.

Preaching and celebration of holy communion are two expressions, equal in value, of the same effective logos.

IV. FOURTH QUESTION

Remembering the work under way in the Commission on Faith and Order, we wish to give forceful expression to the wish that the problems be given a fundamental re-examination. This will involve giving serious consideration to the Jewish roots of holy communion.

We are convinced that the words and purpose of Jesus cannot be understood apart from their Jewish context.

Scriptural data will be exegetically understandable only from their setting in the life (*Sitz im Leben*) of the church. This is a prerequisite for their ultimate theological interpretation and for living them out in the liturgy.

Paragraph 28 suggests "the renewal of the eucharist itself . . . in regard to teaching and liturgy" as "the best way towards unity in eucharistic celebration"; consequently a radically new approach — through the Jewish roots, in fact — seems to be the only means of escape from the "obstinacy of unjustifiable confessional oppositions" (§20) — despite BEM's conciliation techniques.

We have now brought forward enough questions and points of dispute on I, II and III to make plain our doubts on the subject of possible convergence or consensus.

A practical compromise as suggested in §27, playing down or ignoring the exegetical and theological problems, seems to us to be difficult to defend and to lack realism.

Statement on the ministry

I. FIRST QUESTION

From the Reformed standpoint, priority has been given through the centuries to the preaching of the gospel. The question of *the* faith of the church can be answered only if appropriate distinctions are drawn. Through the ages, the faith has experienced the constraints imposed by historical circumstances, and there have been excesses and errors. We therefore have to speak both of continuity *and* of discontinuity. In this context, the problem relating to how the ministry and church structures are to be understood is in our eyes only of secondary importance.

Nevertheless we do consider discussion on the ministry to be of first-class importance as BEM seems to uphold a clerical view of the ministry which is liable to channel the saving work of the word and the Spirit into confined traditional courses, leaving no freedom for the prophetic dynamism of renewal.

BEM shows us quite plainly the ministerial structure of the majority of churches, especially those tied to the doctrine of apostolic succession. However, through the centuries, there has always existed a minority, visible more or less, which has not conformed and has rested its case on scripture.

Zwingli and Calvin in particular commended a view of the church which would leave maximum freedom for the activity of the word and the Spirit and would give most scope for a *conciliar* structure as the instrument for taking decisions, in virtue of the elements of participation and inclusiveness which it implied.

When we speak of the *ministry of the church* (its service and mission) we are talking about the proclamation of the gospel by word and deed. That ministry is entrusted to all Christians.

We regard as legitimate any ordination of ministries in so far as it matches up to the supreme ministry which is the preaching of the gospel, and in so far as it takes account of the biblical witness and current social realities.

In all ecumenical dialogues of the last few decades, the calling of the whole people of God has been the starting-point for the debate regarding the ministry. So it is for BEM (§§1–7). We wonder, however, whether this doctrinally correct view has been sustained throughout the entire statement on the ministry, in view of the disproportionate attention given to the ordained ministry. In this report there is an almost unbearable tension between ministry and community. A chapter is lacking on the non-ordained ministry and the priesthood of all believers.

All the churches are agreed that the calling of all Christians does not exclude special, particular ministries and services; §7 offers various clarifications of ideas relating to this.

We are in agreement with the intention to describe the ministry in *functional* (§8) rather than classical, ontological sacramental terms (*repraesentatio*).

On the other hand, we consider the last part of §8 untenable, and inconsistent with what precedes it, i.e. in its claim that the ministry is constitutive of the life and witness of the churches. All the misconceptions relating to ordination, the structure of the ministry and the apostolic succession can be traced back to this opinion.

The theological basis of the ministry cannot be dissociated from the exegetical and historical data. Paragraphs 9, 10, 19 and 21 give expression to a broad consensus in this field.

Paragraph 10, speaking of the calling of the Twelve to be "representatives of the renewed Israel", makes a reference to the calling of the whole people and not to the institution by Jesus of an ordained ministry. The role of the apostles, as a primitive form of the ecclesial ministry, is unique and cannot be repeated.

"Since very early times" there have been persons called to the holy ministry (§8).* From a variety of primitive forms (§19), "during the second and third centuries, a threefold pattern of bishop, presbyter and deacon became established". Paragraph 21 mentions modification of their roles. But nowhere do we find any theological interpretation or justification of the later development and the geographical expansion of the ministry of the "episkopos"!

In this context, §22 is completely illogical: a threefold "although" (as to the primitive multiplicity of ministries, the matching of ministries to the church's needs and ministries other than the three mentioned but also furnished with gifts — charismata — of the Holy Spirit) is followed by a conclusion which is not explained: the triple ministry is "an expression of" and also "a means for" achieving "the unity we seek".

The theological shift from the original content to the later hierarchical and cultic "bishop — priest — deacon", which arose moreover out of the post-Nicaean, secular power structures of the Roman Empire, and the division of the church into clergy and laity, are accepted as they stand by BEM — but by what right and on what basis?

Below are the fundamental questions which are a precondition for sincere convergence and consensus:

---

* The French text quoted in the present document does not correspond to the French of BEM, which would read ". . . The ministry of such persons, who since very early times have been *ordained* . . ." —Translator's note and italics.

1. Are the three ministries mentioned a functional expression of the *unique* ministry (the preaching of the word, and the sacraments) and therefore in principle theologically and doctrinally *equivalent*?

2. Or is there a hierarchical structure in the ministry on account of which ministerial fullness (episcopal consecration) would belong only to the bishop, and presbyters and deacons would merely be taking part to a lesser degree in this episcopal ministry and doing so in dependence on it? Paragraph 24 sidesteps this decisive question, which will thus continue to be a focal point for the current dialogue.

The titles we would propose are pastor-elder-deacon. The translation "priest" (N.T.: *hiereus*, i.e. sacrificer) for the N.T. term *presbuteros* is not compatible with this. The idea that the *presbuteros* can offer a sacrifice is contrary to the New Testament.

Neither is the tripartite terminology pastor-elder-deacon the sole valid way of categorizing divisions of the ministry, for according to the New Testament the primitive church knew of other ministries and services which could well come to exist again within the Christian community today.

The following objections could be made to the idea that the bishop represents the "focus of unity" (§20):

a) The distinction to be drawn between bishop and presbyter is not biblically, theologically and ecclesiologically straightforward. The two terms sometimes appear as synonyms in the New Testament.

b) The "Jesus movement" was at the start a lay movement and Jesus himself never functioned as a cleric.

c) Alongside the pastor and teacher, who is made responsible by virtue of charisma and of training for presiding at worship, the secular dimension of the church must also be represented by ministries of elders and deacons — just as much in the liturgy and witness of the church as in its service to the world.

In BEM the church and the ordained ministry are central. In the Bible the focus is on God's covenant with Israel and the nations — with the world!

II. Second question

After more than fifty years of discussions on church unity and on mutual recognition of ministries it may not be unprofitable to recall that for scripture there is a divided world which is reconciled in Christ. In the New Testament, the relation with Israel and the nations makes itself constantly evident (Matt. 28:19–20; John 21:11; Rev. 21:12–14). The church must be one church if the world and creation are to have unity. This profoundly Jewish political and social New Testament dimension — which embraces the world as a whole and is characteristic of the covenant idea — is much less than adequately aired in BEM.

One of the reasons behind the constitution of the United Protestant church of Belgium was the will to embody more fully our unity in Christ. Our church, however small and weak it may be, represents the WCC in Belgium. As such it is the ecumenical partner of the church of Rome. This little church of ours is flexible and pliant and may have the appearance of an experiment for the future, for our Roman Catholic brothers and sisters in Belgium and — who knows? — even a little for the coming world church.

Given the freedom of the Holy Spirit to operate in a variety of very different structures, the church may — or rather must — pattern the ministry in the light of its task (of proclaiming the gospel) and of the needs of present-day society — remaining faithful to scripture, but at the same time having a capacity for innovation.

In ecumenical dialogue, the Reformed view of the church shows itself to be a very open one, with an absence of prejudices as to the theory and the practices prevailing in the constitution and ministry of other churches.

For us, recognition of the ministries of the other churches must not represent an insurmountable problem, even if we do not accept either their form or their theological content, for it is not the ministry in itself but the proper preaching of the gospel that guarantees the unity of the church.

An immediate and practical consequence of the above would be that from now on there should be no further reconsecration of ministers who, being responsible for worship in the other churches, might wish to be accepted in ours. It is enough for them to be inducted (*installer*) into their new functions if they wish to go on exercising their ministry, provided they fulfil the conditions laid down by our church relating, e.g. to a probationary period and to training.

Out of a concern for frankness in dialogue with the non-Reformed churches, we must raise a certain number of theological questions which in our view are liable to cause difficulties in working out a consensus or convergence theologically and ecclesiastically.

1. Apostolic succession and tradition

Ecumenically speaking, the distinction of principle made in BEM between "the apostolic tradition in the Church" (i.e. continuity in the apostolic faith, in worship and in mission etc., §37) and "the apostolic succession in the apostolic ministry", e.g. bishops (§36), seems to us to represent progress.

It suggests that there can be an apostolic tradition apart from the apostolic succession, and that the succession of bishops is only one way among others of expressing the apostolic tradition of the church.

Unfortunately, this view is not presented with historical or theological backing, nor is it adhered to with any consistency in the report. The absence of any theological distinction between "episkopos" and "presbuteros" amounts to no more than a highly doubtful "argument from silence".

In its reference to Clement of Rome and Ignatius of Antioch, §38 seems to be claiming that only the bishop is Christ's representative and the successor of the apostles. Why not (for instance) the presbyter also?

Here in fact we have the Roman Catholic and Orthodox idea that consecration of the bishop is an essential for the episcopal succession tacitly underlying this context. The result is that thoughts about ordination, ministry and church, etc. are at once given ontological and hierarchical status. For this reason the compromise solution proposed in §53 will not work in practice: churches which already have bishops would pass over in silence the question of the historical and theological basis for the episcopal ministry, while those without bishops would accept the figure of the bishop, but without accepting its traditional theological implications.

2. Ordination

According to §30 the episcopal ministry is, if not a guarantee, at least a sign, of the continuity of the apostolic tradition; and this is not stated regarding the presbyter and the deacon.

It must therefore be asked how one is to know what the significance is of the laying on of hands and of *epiklesis* (§§39–44).

At all events it will be necessary to think of ordination as an act of God and an act of the church.

What, however, is the gift (§§39,43; charisma: §48) or the gifts (§§41,44,45) relating to the act of ordination?

Must ordination be looked upon as a "sacramental sign" of the "giving of the Spirit", or is it enough to think of *epiklesis* and the laying on of hands as signs of intercession and of promise so that there may be the gift of the Spirit? The second of these hypotheses we can accept.

Again, the main objection to these paragraphs on ordination is their lack of clarity. Because of an anxiety to avoid misunderstanding on ontological categories, BEM emphasizes only the functional-relational aspect of the ministry. Likewise, it avoids defining the "gift".

These questions must however be raised, especially with the Orthodox and Roman Catholic churches. These churches, in fact, consider the ministry as a "special participation in the priesthood of Christ" because of an indelible sacramental character through which special ministerial powers are conveyed to the priest. In these churches, the ordained priesthood is distinguished essentially, and not merely as a matter of degree, from the rest of the faithful, for the consecrated priest can, *in persona Christi*, make the sacrifice of Christ "present".

Such an ontological, hierarchical and cultic view of the priesthood, culminating in the episcopal ministry, is, of course, unacceptable in the Reformed churches.

3. Ordained and non-ordained ministries (communities)

After chapter I (the calling of the whole people of God), the community is again discussed in this report in §16 (interdependence of ordained ministers and the faithful) and in §§26 and 27 (on the active participation of all members in the life of the community and the management of the church).

The conclusions we should have liked to see being drawn from these general statements are not there. Different churches have very divergent or even opposed views regarding "active participation" of the laity in the life and management of the community.

Thus, to the Roman Catholic church, the council of the laity has only a consultative role and has no right of decision except for matters of secondary importance. Magisterium and management belong only to the bishop or are dependent on his authority; priests are the bishop's representatives; synods and councils are assemblies of bishops.

For their part, the Reformed churches do not recognize this hierarchy; the congregations take part in the ministry of the word and sacrament through elected representatives. In the presbyterial-synodal system, alongside ministers ordained for the conduct of worship, lay people also take part in management of the congregation — in the session, presbytery, synod and general assembly (or terminological equivalents). It is our conviction that this is the best way of expressing the calling of the whole people of God.

BEM devotes only one sentence to this system (§27). It does not even explain what a synod is; yet in almost all the churches the synod has a function. The WCC had at one time proposed a "*conciliar* community" as the aim of unity! Convergence to us seems impossible without participation of the non-ordained members in the magisterium and management of the church. It is also our view that the functions of episkopos, presbuteros and diakonos exist also in churches with a presbyterial-synodal system, even if these functions are exercised there collegially.

4. Ministry of unity

Paragraphs 13 and 14 deal with the ministry of the church as a focus of unity for the life and witness of the church. Paragraphs 21, 23 and 29 mention the bishop on this subject.

Is there then nothing else to be said, according to BEM, on the universal face of the church? For instance, would the WCC not have a part to play here? And what is the significance of the synod?

We should like to think of the WCC as an effective structure for the universal community of Christians — as a provisional ministry for unity. Evangelicals really do have an interest in a worldwide organization of Christendom.

Any debate with the Roman Catholic Church which leaves the pope out of account is unrealistic. For that church the papacy counts as a "ministry of unity". Even after Vatican II, visible communion with the pope is part of the "internal structure of the faith and is constitutive for the essence of the Church".

Now, BEM says nothing on this. As a Reformed church, we can accept an ecumenical council if it is made up of ordained ministers and laypeople commissioned by their churches.

5. Ordination of women

Paragraph 18 deals with the various attitudes to a female ministry. A minority is of the opinion that our church is disobeying scripture in opening all its ministries to women. The majority considers the emancipation, or liberation, of woman, even in church matters, to be a form of obedience to what the Holy Spirit is saying to the Christian communities.

As to the commentary on §18, we are entitled to ask whether reference to nineteen centuries of tradition is enough to constitute a formal criterion. Neither is the theological appeal to "human nature and Christology" any more convincing. Christ as the new Adam represents the *human person* without distinction of sex.

Summary

We consider that acceptance of BEM as it stands would give the impression that the present church structure of the presbyterial-synodal Reformed churches is not legitimate. Underlying the report there is an interpretation of the ministry which makes its starting point the existence of a certain continuity, because of the laying on of hands, between the apostles and today's church where that is governed by bishops. If so, then as Protestants we would still feel that we are "separated brethren", cut off from the "true" church.

III. THIRD QUESTION

In reply to the question on the amount of guidance our church can take from BEM, we would make the points below, which follow from what has been said above.

1. Our church is in principle prepared to continue taking part in the inter-church dialogue on the church's ministry.

2. This implies our willingness to adapt or even change our own church structures if the conclusions of this dialogue lead us to do so. To that end we place our trust in the Holy Spirit which "will lead us into all truth" (John 16:18).

3. This readiness within our own church is also strengthened by our free acknowledgment that the reform of the church has not led to unified witness and action in the church of the West. Fragmentation among the Reformed churches is doubtless the cause of a sizeable weakening of the evangelical witness.

4. For the most part, the Christian churches are separated from their Jewish roots. Lack of biblical (i.e. Jewish/Christian) thinking is evident throughout BEM.

As to the ministries, this comes out among other things in the non-biblical interpretation of the laying on of hands, which should be considered not as a sacramental consecration *ad vitam*, but rather as a "dynamization" (dunamis = power) or confirmation for a concrete, specified task.

This comes out clearly too in the false interpretation of the term *presbuteros* — properly an official in the synagogue — and above all of the "priesthood of all believers", which is diametrically opposed to the levitical temple cult.

The biblical preaching of the prophets and apostles, which is the criterion not merely for the organization of the ordained ministry but also for the liturgy, for catechetics, for ethics, for the spiritual life and for witness, never had "the church" as such as its focus or *raison d'être*. Its focus is Israel, and the world of nations around Israel; its *raison d'être* is the new humanity. Our main quarrel with the BEM from this angle is not directed so much against "church-centredness" as against lack of orientation towards the world as a whole.

IV. FOURTH QUESTION

In the light of the work being done by the Commission on Faith and Order, we would therefore wish to press for a new starting-point and for a new perspective and method.

1. New starting-point

We would refer to what has already been said under Question III on a scriptural interpretation which takes account of the Jewish and Christian roots of the New Testament. The calling of the whole people of God has not been clearly present as a starting-point throughout the statement as a whole (cf. I).

Jesus did not found a "church", or any "ministry of the church". He wanted to recall his people to the unity of the Covenant. That is why he appointed the twelve as representatives of the whole people (the twelve tribes) and not as a new clergy. On the contrary, the lay movement of Jesus opposed fossilized clerical domination and the baneful alliance between state religion and the powers that be.

2. New perspective

The New Testament picture of an Israel reconciled with the nations has as its outcome a new humanity and a renewal of the world. The church must be considered from that universal standpoint.

The situation of the poor and of those discriminated against, of the oppressed and those subjected to colonization does not receive enough attention in BEM. To be sure, the church is not simply the bringer of a message of liberation, but it serves the action of the Spirit which does indicate paths to reconciliation and liberation. The task of deacons and the dimension of diakonia in the church are also aspects which can be endowed with new vigour and new inspiration: the church is the servant (diakonos) of the world!

3. New method of working

Raising the question of starting-point and perspective means that a new interpretation of the ministry is also needed — a new method of working and new ministerial structures.

This is how we interpret §51: it is not enough to enter into doctrinaire ecumenical agreements on the ordained ministry when the real question is the diakonia of preaching the gospel (word and actions). Much more is needed in terms of an ecumenical renewal of the ministry.

On the basis of scripture, guided by the history of the church, and enriched by the experiences of other churches, all the churches must, in their response to the challenge of this age and this world, "examine" with one accord "their forms of ministry" which in a changed world will be closer to the original intention. BEM, however, gives us very few concrete suggestions in this field.

In a mobile and increasingly complex society such as ours, the services offered by the church must undergo a process of adjustment and differentiation. Alongside stable, territorially defined traditional communities, increasing importance will be given to the idea of a community of persons. In this society, the ministry will require specialization of an increasingly significant kind, particularly as to:

— the training of infants and adults; religious education, theology for adults;
— the church's social work: the sick, prisoners, diaconate;
— regional responsibilities and functions: coordination among communities, districts, and on a national level; tourism, etc.

Renewal of the church's ministry also presupposes a revision of traditional roles, e.g. the possibility of exercising a temporary or part-time ordained ministry.

As a matter of course, a reform of ministries requires a reform of communication and of the management arrangements within church communities. Every exercise of a ministry must be understood collegially. Democratic structures, acceptance of responsibility, joint management and communication must come to characterize church policy in a changing world. The convergence which — at least so far as its treatment of themes is concerned — BEM has seen fit to circumscribe in the past is in our view something for the future.

22–23 November 1985   Synod

PRESBYTERIAN CHURCH
OF RWANDA

Baptism

In general, our church is in agreement with what is stated in this chapter.

We should, however, have liked to find in it some special emphasis on the idea of God's covenant with his people (cf. Rom. 4:16, 17; 6:1ff.; Col. 2: 11–12, etc.).

We have difficulty in limiting the sacrament of baptism solely to the notion of sign and seal of our common discipleship. For our part we understand baptism in a deeper sense as sign and seal of the grace of Jesus Christ towards us.

As regards chrismation, we would advise against any gesture that might be construed as a magic action. The text gives the impression that without anointing with chrism, baptism would not be complete.

In our view, the celebration section omits the aspect of participation by the community.

Eucharist

The name "eucharist" designates only one part of the sacrament of the Lord's Supper. The central action is the presence of God in the word of Jesus Christ. Worship is not merely a cultural action, but the means whereby God intervenes in our lives and involves his church in mission in the world. If the eucharist is placed at the centre of worship, that will mean that the word of God merely prepares for the essential, the eucharist. *Sola fides, sola gratia*!

We find the deep meaning of the sacrament in the Lord's words: "Do this in memory of ME." The memorial, *anamnesis*, constitutes for us the most essential part of the sacrament, since it places Christ in the centre of the Lord's Supper as gift of God to humanity and not vice versa. That means that for us the content of section A (§§3–4) is not in accord with the gospel. When

---

• 70,000 members, 45 parishes, 71 pastors, 110 evangelists.

the basis of the sacramental meaning is a biblical one, we do not understand how the world could be capable of offering the sacrifice to God.

We note in general that an ecumenical reading (interpretation) of the Bible on which the sacramental statements might be based, is lacking.

The heading of section C does not correspond to the content of the text. The text is more acceptable than the title. The real presence of Christ does not occur at the precise moment of the invocation. It is not a magical action of man that brings God into the eucharist.

As for children's communion, baptized children belong to the church and the family of believers by grace and by the covenant, so why forbid them to receive holy communion?

The dynamic consideration in §25 (p.15) is fundamental. We would have wished it to be decisive throughout the commentaries.

The view of the contextualization of the elements of the Lord's Supper in section E is very restrictive and even colonialist. It ignores the universality of the church through cultures and nations.

The idea that "Christ's presence in the consecrated elements continues after the celebration" is not biblical. Christ is present in the worship and not in the wine and in the bread. We emphasize, however, that the consecrated elements of the eucharist demand respect from all. Provided that respect is shown, the deacons who serve the table may deal with the elements which remain over as they choose.

Ministry

We have the impression that the holy scriptures are not the basis of this chapter. The distinction between laypersons and ordained ministers in the mission of the church is not a biblical idea. The ministry of the apostles is not tied to the sacraments, so why tie it to the ordained ministry? The apostolicity of the church is not based on episcopal succession but on apostolic preaching. We consider that ministry is bound up with the community and with the function fulfilled in, by and in the name of the community. Ordination cannot therefore confer on an individual a position separated from the community to serve as representative of Jesus Christ. To make such a claim would be to contradict the noble consideration of section I (pp. 20–21) — which presents the mission of the church as a community — and there is no biblical authority for so doing. The ordained ministry receives authority from the word of God which it faithfully serves, and not from ordination.

The text on pages 21f. reconciles positions which are hard to reconcile, and so ends up by contradicting itself through wishing to please everyone. As regards apostolic succession, we consider that it should not be tied to human persons because the gifts of God are not tied to human beings.

The text of section VI, "Towards the Mutual Recognition of the Ordained Ministries," is in contradiction with the title and leads to an exclusive conclusion which involves a danger of refusing ecumenical dialogue, namely that non-episcopal communities are not members of the apostolic church. How can it be maintained that continuity with the church of the apostles finds profound expression in the successive laying-on of hands by bishops, which strengthens and deepens that continuity, and still think of the prophetic and charismatic aspect of the ministry or the dynamism of the ministry which may lead the church to suffering? With such an understanding of the ministry we are no longer placed under the cross but in a theology of glory in relation to ministries.

Conclusion

We are extremely appreciative of the ecumenical effort which led to the existence of this document. We are convinced that theological foundations such as this provide a sound approach to the ecumenical future of the churches. We encourage this undertaking and recommend that we should start from joint reading of the Bible among the various families of the church, so as to be able to arrive at theological considerations. The Bible can unite us, whereas tradition disunites.

Having said that, the document on baptism, with a few modifications, meets with no difficulty in receiving our approval. Those on eucharist and ministry would have to be fundamentally revised before we could accept them.

Kigali, 1 March 1984

CHURCH OF JESUS CHRIST
IN MADAGASCAR

General remarks

The BEM document is a work for which we may well praise God. We are very grateful to those who took part in producing it and thank them warmly.

BEM is an excellent working tool which can help the various churches to get to know one another better, by assisting them to understand and listen to one another and discuss the points they have in common and those that still divide them in regard to baptism, eucharist and ministry.

The availability of the BEM document is a valuable aid for the church in its task of educating the faithful to be open-minded, to perceive, receive and accept the ideas of others when these are ideas whose accuracy in terms of holy scripture and the doctrine of the apostles they cannot deny, even if that fact has unfortunately long been hidden from them.

However, the BEM text is not an end in itself but an important step making it possible to move forward towards more perfect communion between the churches. The remarks and suggestions we make here have been formulated and brought together round the four questions which Faith and Order put to the churches.

To what extent can your church recognize in this text the faith of the church through the ages?

BEM's basis for explaining baptism is well defined, in simple, clear language, which takes account of the traditions inherited by the churches through the generations. Thus we have: institution (ch. I), meaning (II), relation to faith (III), practice (IV), celebration (V). This, it can be said, corresponds to the Christian faith since the days of the early church.

The former CJCM liturgy for the eucharist chiefly stressed Jesus' passion and death. The BEM text has completely changed that. This is why the

---

• 1,250,000 members, 76 regional synods, 3,000 parishes, 15 synodal presidents, 935 pastors.

current liturgy includes all the essential points in the history of salvation
which most churches have already included for centuries, namely:

— *thanksgiving to the Father* for all he has done as Creator, Saviour and
Sanctifier;
— *memorial of Christ* and of all He has done: incarnation, teaching, service,
suffering, death, resurrection, ascension, sending of his Holy Spirit, return
to establish the kingdom of God;
— *invocation of the Holy Spirit* for the faithful who are present and for the
bread and wine;
— *communion of all believers* to demonstrate communion with Christ and
with believers throughout the world, sharing the bread and wine in a
particular place;
— *the feast of the kingdom of God*: the eucharist symbolizes the marriage feast
of the Lamb in the future kingdom.

*The consequences your church can draw from this text for its relations and
dialogues with other churches, particularly with those which also recognize the
text as an expression of the apostolic faith.*

BEM makes known to us the viewpoints of the various churches. Even if
this knowledge runs the risk of offending some, we also recognize that the
authors of the document are endeavouring not to give needless provocation,
but on the contrary are trying to lead the different parties to admit their
mistakes and jointly to seek the points they have in common. Faith and Order
should continue this way of working.

The consequence of the BEM text here in Madagascar has been to confirm
"mutual recognition of baptism". In our opinion this "mutual recognition",
not only of baptism but of many other points of the Christian faith, is the true
way for ecumenism to follow.

The BEM text has brought about a lessening of the conflicts which
formerly existed in Madagascar between Christians of the various churches,
especially between Protestants and Catholics.

BEM has facilitated local, regional and national relations between the
different churches and has contributed to the progress of ecumenism in
Madagascar.

BEM has encouraged Christians' enthusiasm for collaboration to improve
and consolidate points of agreement and for a joint quest in search of
solutions to what still divides them.

As a Reformed church, accepting the Presbyterian synodal system, the
CJCM is ready for its part to study and grasp more profoundly what is
involved by "succession in the apostolic tradition".

*Guidance your church can take from this text for its worship, educational,
ethical and spiritual life and witness.*

Formerly many congregations of the CJCM celebrated the Lord's Supper only on the first Sunday of each month. At present, thanks to BEM, the CJCM accepts the principle of celebrating the eucharist every Sunday. For the preaching of the word of God should not be separated from the sacraments. Similarly, the celebration of the eucharist is encouraged on Ascension Day and at Christmas if it does not fall on a Sunday.

As for the ministry of women pastors, the CJCM has had experience of them since its foundation in 1968.

In general, the CJCM uses bread and wine or grape juice for the eucharist. In some places where these elements are not available, elements are used which are obtainable locally.

Suggestions from your church for continued work by Faith and Order on the relation between the material of this BEM text and its proposed long-term research into a "common expression of the apostolic faith today".

Faith and Order should explain that the following points are well-founded:
— infant baptism;
— baptism of adults;
— communion offered to those who have just been baptized, even to children;
— the fact of not conferring the sacrament of baptism except on the great Christian festivals such as Christmas, Easter, Pentecost.

Matters concerning ministry occupy too much space in the BEM document. It is obvious that the total number of pages and theses devoted to baptism and eucharist together only amount to the same as those on ministry alone.

The scriptural references in all the commentaries in BEM are quite inadequate. It is very striking, for example, to see only a single verse (Luke 4:18) in explanation of the calling of the whole people of God. Where are Eph. 4:11–12 and 1 Pet. 2:9 etc.?

BEM attaches too much weight to the ordained ministry, almost as though it alone ensured the perfection of the sacrament and not Christ who is the master of the feast.

In our view it is the whole of the church, pastors (or priests) with all the faithful who take part in the act of ordination (§41).

18 April 1986   For the National Council
                                                 Paul Ramino
                                                 Secretary general

PRESBYTERIAN CHURCH (U.S.A.)

A. Background
31.193
The Faith and Order Commission of the World Council of Churches has transmitted to the member churches the paper adopted in Lima in 1982, entitled "Baptism, Eucharist, and Ministry" (Faith and Order Paper No. 111) and has requested the official response of the churches "as a vital step in the ecumenical process of reception." This official response is to be authorized "at the highest appropriate level of authority," which for the Presbyterian Church (U.S.A.) is the General Assembly.
31.194
The response is to include the following four matters:

1. The extent to which your church can recognize the faith of the Church through the ages;

2. The consequences your church can draw from this text for its relations and dialogues with other churches, particularly with those churches which also recognize the text as an expression of the apostolic faith;

3. The guidance your church can take from this text for its worship, educational, ethical, and spiritual life and witness;

4. The suggestions your church can make for the ongoing work of Faith and Order as it relates the ongoing work of Faith and Order material of this text on Baptism, Eucharist and Ministry to its long-range research project "Towards the Common Expression of the Apostolic Faith Today."
31.195
This response is presented to the 198th General Assembly of the Presbyterian Church (U.S.A.) for adoption and transmission to the Faith and Order Commission of the World Council of Churches.

● 3,131,228 members, 11,662 congregations, 18,969 pastors.

31.196

A description of the process followed in preparing this official response is provided in Appendix A.

B. Response and recommendations

It is recommended that the 198th General Assembly (1986)

31.197

1. Adopt as amended the "Response of the Presbyterian Church (U.S.A.) to the World Council of Churches' Faith and Order Commission on Baptism, Eucharist and Ministry".

31.198

2. Forward the Presbyterian Church (U.S.A.) response to the Faith and Order Commission of the World Council of Churches, with copies to the World Alliance of Reformed Churches and the Consultation on Church Union.

31.199

3. Commend the "Response" for study by congregations and especially presbyteries, synods, and seminaries.

31.200

4. Make single copies of the "Response" available, without cost upon request through Program Agency/General Assembly Mission Board budgets.

5. Commend those persons listed in §31.281.

Response of the Presbyterian Church (U.S.A.) to the World Council of Churches' Faith and Order Commission on "Baptism, Eucharist and Ministry"

BAPTISM

31.201

1. The extent to which the Presbyterian Church (U.S.A.) can recognize in this text the faith of the church through the ages:

31.202

We agree that the text on Baptism is a valid expression of the faith of the Christian church through the ages, especially as that expression emphasizes areas of ecumenical convergence related to mutual recognition of the various branches of the church. The treatment of the diversity in the faith of the church represented by the baptism of "infants" and of "believers" assists in our agreement.

31.203

Our response raises questions as to the formulation of some matters, as we comment on the ecumenical text through our own confessional tradition and practice. We reserve these questions for treatment in Part 4.

31.204

2. The consequences the Presbyterian Church (U.S.A.) can draw from this text for its relations and dialogues with other churches. . .:

31.205

The Constitution of the Presbyterian Church (U.S.A.) states:

There is one church. As the Bible speaks of the one body which is the church living under the one Spirit of God known through Christ, it reminds us that we have "one Lord, one faith, one baptism, one God and Father of us all." (Ephesians 4:5–6). . . .[W]hile divisions into different denominations do not destroy this unity, they do obscure it for both the church and the world. The Presbyterian Church (U.S.A.), affirming its historical continuity with the whole church of Jesus Christ, is committed to the reduction of that obscurity and is willing to seek and to maintain communion and community with all other branches of the one, catholic church. . . .(G-4.0202–0203)

31.206

Accordingly, we heartily concur with the text that

Our common baptism, which unites us to Christ in faith, is thus a basic bond of unity. . . . Therefore, our one baptism into Christ constitutes a call to the churches to overcome their divisions and visibly manifest their fellowship. (B.6)

31.207

We recognize the integrity and validity of baptism administered with water in the name of the Father and of the Son and of the Holy Spirit by other churches and in consonance with this ecumenical text. We affirm that this text can become the basis for bilateral and multilateral denominational conversations and local conversations.

31.208

Arising out of our unity in baptism is our further affirmation that we need to work toward a united witness in mission.

31.209

One consequence of the reception of this text could be joint participation in services of baptism as a visible expression of the welcoming of the baptized person into the church universal.

31.210

3. The guidance the Presbyterian Church (U.S.A.) can take from this text for its worship, educational, ethical, and spiritual life and witness:

While our tradition has always affirmed that baptism is incorporation into Christ (our confessional tradition often describes this as "engrafting" into Christ), we have emphasized "washing and cleansing of sin" more than "participation in the death and resurrection of Christ". We welcome the text's reminder of the many biblical images of baptism, especially that of Romans 6.

31.211

Since our confessions have affirmed that "the sacrament of Baptism is but once to be administered to any person" (Westminster Confession of Faith

XXX. 7 Cf. Second Helvetic Confession XX), we welcome the text's assertion that "baptism is an unrepeatable act" so that "any practice which might be interpreted as 'rebaptism' must be avoided" (B.13). This reaffirms our historical theological statements and positions of polity. Yet we recognize that the text has pastoral implications for us, since recent studies have shown that our profession has not been matched fully in our practice.
31.212
We welcome the text's reminder of the ethical implications of baptism (B.4) because it stresses that "baptized believers" have "a common responsibility, here and now, to bear witness together to the Gospel of Christ" and that the "context of this common witness is the church and the world" (B.10). This parallels the reminders in our Book of Order that baptism "heralds a new beginning of participation in the ministry of Christ" (S-3.0200). But the text strengthens this emphasis by stating that baptism "embraces the whole of life, extends to all nations, and anticipates the day when every tongue will confess that Jesus Christ is Lord to the glory of God the Father" (B.7). Moreover, because so often the practice of baptism expresses an individualistic and limited understanding of God's saving purpose, we welcome the text's reminder (in keeping with the image of I Peter 3:20f.) that "the use of water, with all its positive associations with life and blessing, signifies the continuity between the old and new creation, thus revealing the significance of baptism not only for human beings but also for the whole cosmos" (Commentary B.18).
31.213
Our tradition, like the text, has stressed the importance of Christian nurture. We need to be reminded of the importance of this element as a most needed safeguard against "indiscriminate baptism" (B.16) and against an offer of cheap grace. Similarly, the text's stress that baptism is related "to life-long growth into Christ" (B.9) is paralleled by our tradition's historic conviction that the "needful but much neglected duty of improving our Baptism, is to be performed all our life long" (Westminster Larger Catechism, 167). The stress on Christian nurture has a new importance as our church now invites baptized children to the Lord's Supper.
31.214
Our Directory for the Service of God affirms with the text that baptism "should normally be administered during public worship so that members of the congregation may be reminded of their own baptism and may welcome into their fellowship those who are baptized and whom they are committed to nurture in the Christian faith" (B.23). We can learn from the text (B.20) the importance of the full liturgical celebration of the Sacrament of Baptism.
31.215
Since in our church we are discovering afresh the liturgical importance of the Christian year, we appreciate the text's reminder as to the appropriateness of linking the symbolism and celebration of baptism with the great festival occasions of the Christian year. It may lead us to develop a complete service

focused on the Sacrament of Baptism to be used on festival days. We also are instructed by the document's testimony to practices in other Christian groups, such as the laying on of hands and chrismation, and we receive it as prompting a reconsideration of practices in our own tradition. The document is guiding the work of drafting a new directory of worship for the Presbyterian Church (U.S.A.).

31.216

4. The suggestions the Presbyterian Church (U.S.A.) can make for the ongoing work of Faith and Order as it relates the material of this text . . . to its long-range research project . . .:

31.217

Even as we affirm the text as a valid expression of Christian faith through the ages, we believe that our tradition has important reminders to contribute to a common expression of the apostolic faith. Accordingly we point to some reminders of matters which we do not find dealt with in sufficient clarity in the text.

31.218

We note that the present form of the text has sought to respond to Presbyterian and Reformed critiques of an earlier draft by including in Paragraph B.1 a reference to "the New Covenant between God and God's people." We suggest that our tradition's stress on "the covenant of grace" would find more adequate expression if covenant were included among the biblical images for baptism (B.2). We do not wish to overstate, as our tradition has often done, the analogy of baptism with circumcision, but we believe that *covenant* imagery and understanding are essential to an adequate interpretation of the baptism of infants as well as of adults.

31.219

We suggest that further study is needed for a more clearly articulated understanding of the relationship between grace and faith in baptism and in the Christian life. We note that the text speaks of baptism as "the sign of the new life through Christ" (B.2), but we are not sure whether the text understands baptism as a sign both of faith and of God's prior grace. For example, the text suggests that the baptism of infants "emphasizes the corporate faith and the faith which the child shares with its parents" (Commentary, B.12). Our tradition rests the baptism of infants not so much on "corporate faith" as on the prevenient grace of God. We read that "baptism is a sign and seal of our common discipleship" (B.6), whereas our tradition has stressed that sacraments "are holy signs and seals of the covenant of grace" (Westminster Confession XXIX.1; cf, Heidelberg Catechism 66, Second Helvetic Confession XIX). We know there are in the document synonyms for grace such as "God's initiative in Christ" (B.12), but we ask whether grace is sufficiently emphasized as the ground of faith. We are concerned to focus also on the continuing dependence on the sustaining grace of God of the life of the baptized person in its ethical expression.

31.220

While B.5 states that "The Holy Spirit is at work in the lives of people before, in and after their baptism," we suggest that the implications of this statement have not been sufficiently developed. Our tradition affirms that the "efficacy of baptism is not tied to that moment of time wherein it is administered" (Westminster Confession, XXX.6). This statement has biblical warrant, for in Acts the sign of the gift of the Holy Spirit sometimes precedes baptism (10:44f.), sometimes attends baptism (9:12), sometimes follows baptism (19:6). Recognition of the freedom of the Spirit makes clear that baptism like the eucharist is "not a magical or mechanical action" (Cf. Commentary on E.14). The reality of new life is initiated by God and is manifested in and through baptism (Cf. B.5, 7). To be reminded that the efficacy of baptism is not tied to the moment of its administration also has pastoral relevance when dealing with persons who ask for rebaptism on the basis of some cultural, denominational, or "charismatic" understanding or experience. Such a reminder strengthens the affirmation that "Baptism is related not only to momentary experience, but to life-long growth into Christ." (B.9)

31.221

The text rightly cites the biblical reminder that there is "one baptism" (B.6). We believe, however, that the expression "infant baptism," especially when this is contrasted with "the baptism of believers," may suggest that there are two baptisms. It would seem more appropriate to avoid the expression "infant baptism" altogether. The Church would be more consistent if it spoke, as the text sometimes does, of the baptism of children of believers or of infants and of the baptism of those making their personal profession of faith.

31.222

We are also constrained to point out that Galatians 3:27, 28, as B.6 and Commentary on B.10 note, is a baptismal passage: "For as many of you as were baptized into Christ have put on Christ. There is neither Jew nor Greek, there is neither slave nor free, there is neither male nor female: for you are all one in Christ Jesus." The implications of baptism for the inclusiveness of the Christian community and the inclusiveness of the ministry to which the community is called need to be taken more carefully into account in the life of the Church.

31.223

We note that the text gives particular prominence to the symbolic meaning of immersion (B.18). With John Calvin (Institutes IV, 15.19) we do not question that "the rite of immersion was observed in the ancient church." Our tradition affirms that the meaning of baptism is not dependent upon its mode. We believe that each of the traditional modes of baptism has important symbolic significance. The text stresses that "the act of immersion can vividly express the reality that in baptism the Christian participates in the death, burial and resurrection of Christ" (B.18), as Romans 6 suggests. In ongoing ecumenical discussion it would be appropriate to point to the symbolic meaning of pouring and sprinkling as well. Pouring, for example, calls to mind the imagery of Joel 2:28 (appropriated in Acts 2:18, 33) of the pouring out of the Holy Spirit. This imagery is explicitly linked with baptism in Titus 3:5, "by the washing of regeneration and renewal in the Holy Spirit, which he poured out upon us richly through Jesus Christ, our Savior." Sprinkling calls to mind the prophetic promise that God "will sprinkle clean water upon you and make you clean" (Ezekiel 36:25), an imagery which the New Testament links with the sprinkled blood of Christ in baptismal allusions, such as I Peter 1:2 and, more explicitly, Hebrews 10:22, "with our hearts sprinkled clean from an evil conscience and our bodies washed with pure water." We suggest then that the ecumenical church can increase its appreciation for the "variety of forms" (B.11) that have developed, all expressing various images in the rich portrayal of baptism's meaning.

EUCHARIST
31.224
   1. The extent to which the Presbyterian Church (U.S.A.) can recognize in this text the faith of the church through the ages:
   We acknowledge that the text on the eucharist contains the historic faith of the church through the ages and is to be commended for its excellent work in this problematic area of life and theological controversy in the church. We would particularly acknowledge the five-fold explication of the meaning of the eucharist in Sections I and II and would note:
31.225
— the Eucharist as Thanksgiving to the Father and especially the connection of the eucharist with the faith of Israel through the *berakah* (blessing) and the passover;
— the Eucharist as Anamnesis or Memorial of Christ and the discussion of the "real presence" in terms of the reality of the presence rather than upon the "how" of the occurrence;
— the Eucharist as Invocation of the Spirit and the emphasis upon the eucharistic ministry of the Holy Spirit, in the presence of Christ as host, in the efficacy of the word, and in the bond between sacramental sign and communion;
— the Eucharist as Communion of the Faithful and the recognition of the presence of the whole church in any eucharistic celebration;
— the Eucharist as Meal of the Kingdom and the linking of eucharist with ethical responsibility in the presence of injustice, racism, separation, and bondage and with the mission of the church in relation to the coming of the Kingdom.

31.226

There are also matters about which we shall comment from our particular tradition and understanding of the faith of the church in the sections that follow.

31.227

2. The consequences the Presbyterian Church (U.S.A.) can draw from this text for its relations and dialogues with other churches:

From the Reformed perspective, the statement will surely enhance our relations and dialogues within the church catholic. Of immediate importance is the anticipated development of mutual recognition of ministries and full intercommunion between Lutheran and Reformed Christians of North America. This text is in considerable congruity with the reports of those conversations.

31.228

The text serves also as stimulus to consider our own tradition and what it can contribute to the ecumenical dialogue. Even more it gives impetus to our learning from other traditions about the mystery of the divine presence in the eucharist and in worship. The text also raises and poses for discussion questions about the relation of ordained ministry to the eucharist and about the ministry of the whole people of God in respect to the sacrament.

31.229

Above all, the text in its focus upon what is agreed and common sets a tone for discussions that begin not with differences of history, particular tradition, and practice, but with the central affirmation of the eucharist as God's gift to the people of God as a nurturing in Christ and a form of loyalty through the Holy Spirit.

31.230

The increased mutual understanding expressed in the text encourages us in intercommunion and in the development and use of common liturgies and ecumenical liturgies (e.g., the COCU liturgy and the Lima liturgy).

31.231

3. The guidance the Presbyterian Church (U.S.A.) can take from this text for its worship, educational, ethical, and spiritual life and witness:

The careful treatment of the shape of the eucharistic liturgy (E.27) is serving as a helpful guide to the discussion presently going on in the Presbyterian Church (U.S.A.) about the Service for the Lord's Day and the proposed new Directory for Worship. In our practice we have not paid sufficient attention to the understanding of the liturgy from the perspective of the eucharist and so have impoverished our worship life.

31.232

The call for eucharistic celebration as frequently as each Sunday (E.31) supports the increasing emphasis upon more frequent communion evidenced in our Book of Order (S-3.0500). The text reminds us: "Many differences of theology, liturgy and practice are connected with the varying frequency with which the Holy Communion is celebrated" (E.30). We in the Presbyterian Church (U.S.A.) should enter into the study and discussion of our own varying local practices and traditions to explore what doctrinal issues may be at stake.

31.233

The text throughout presents the Lord's Supper as a means of grace, an understanding familiar to our tradition. The potential of this understanding for the educational and nurturing activities of the church is very great, for the observance of the Supper is an occasion for the remembering and renewal of baptismal vows, both on the part of adults and on the part of children. The observance of the Supper is also a reminder of the dependence upon the nurturing grace of God on the part both of children and of adults.

31.234

We need to hear that the eucharistic celebration demands reconciliation and sharing. Everyone is to be challenged as to readiness to come to the Table (E.20). No one is to be excluded from the Table.

31.235

The encounter with the risen Lord in the power of the Holy Spirit at the Lord's Table should become a more prominent feature of our church's efforts in spiritual renewal. Eucharistic celebration is a powerful and radical element in the life of the company of believers.

31.236

To speak of the Lord's Supper as "the great sacrifice of praise" (E.3) and as an offering is not usual among us. We have been more likely to see ourselves as receivers than givers in the celebration of the Eucharist. We need to consider that we also offer ourselves and that the bread and wine are brought as our offering to the table, where they then are the means of Christ's offering for us and to us. Not incidentally we need to pay heed to the concerns expressed in E.32 about the way in which the elements are treated, for our practice often can offend Christians of other communions.

31.237

The way in which the Eucharist is grounded in the creation and the created order (E.4) as well as the striking characterization of it as "precious food for missionaries, bread and wine for pilgrims on their apostolic journey" (E.26) and as part of "the responsible care of Christians for one another and the world" (E.21) bids us to see the sacrament as connected to the daily life and special calling of the church and of each Christian. Then we are reminded that:

31.238

The eucharist involves the believer in the central event of the world's history. As participants in the eucharist, therefore, we prove inconsistent if we are not actively participating in this ongoing restoration of the world's situation and the human condition. . . . We are placed under judgement by the persistence of unjust relationships of all kinds in our society, the manifold divisions on account of human pride, material interest and power politics and, above all, the obstinacy of unjustifiable confessional oppositions within the body of Christ (E.20).

31.239

Such an understanding can have a powerful effect upon our education, life, and service and upon our connection of worship and work.

31.240

Finally, the text in its presentation of the richness of tradition and its openness to diversity as well serves as a model for the education of the ordained ministry and of the whole people of God in the meaning and power of the Lord's Supper.

31.241

4. The suggestions that the Presbyterian Church (U.S.A.) can make for the ongoing work of Faith and Order as it relates the material of this text . . . to its long-range research project . . .:

31.242

From a Reformed perspective there are several unresolved issues, and the commentary on the text points to most of them. Eucharistic theology in the past has tended to focus on such points of disagreement, and the much larger area of consensus has tended to be obscured. The reception of this document should be careful to avoid the opposite error, and the research and discussion of Faith and Order should seek to resolve the lingering differences.

31.243

Many very important questions of intercommunion and of the possibility of open communion as a means to intercommunion are not addressed in the document. The failure to deal with these questions will be seen by us as leading to a weakening of the mission of the church in the interest of protecting particular understandings of the eucharist. We recognize that behind these questions lie serious issues:

— the theological understanding of the sacrament and of the nature of ministry, and

— the relation of a proper understanding and validation of ministry to the appropriate celebration of the eucharist.

31.244

In that connection we wish to raise for consideration the importance of a worshipping congregation to complement the ordained ministers' roles in the administration of the sacrament. If, as the text suggests in E.29, "the minister of the eucharist is the ambassador who represents the divine initiative," the worshipping congregation represents the response of faith and obedience. Once again, as with baptism, there is the need to explore the complexity and fullness of the interrelationship of grace and faith. In "Baptism" the text seemed to us at times to stress faith and repentance at the expense of grace; in "Eucharist" the text seems to stress grace over the response of faith.

31.245

In our Reformed tradition the proclamation of the Word has been central to the worship of the Lord's Day. We acknowledge that we have often treated the sacraments too lightly and that we can learn from the text. At the same time we would wish to maintain the importance of the Word proclaimed along with the importance of the Word enacted in sacrament. Exploration of the relation of Word and sacrament seems to be called for beyond what has been dealt with in this text.

31.246

We would urge that the suggestions at the end of E.32 about the disposal of the elements be explored further, and that the implications of the eucharist for the ministry to the world and especially to the hungry and needy be kept in mind. There seems to be an emphasis upon the Table as the nourishment of the servants and apostles which could be even further developed, so that even as we anticipate the joyful feast of the Kingdom, we remember that we are the servants of the justice, peace, compassion, and reconciliation of the Kingdom here and now.

MINISTRY

31.247

1. The extent to which the Presbyterian Church (U.S.A.) can recognize in this text the faith of the church through the ages:

31.248

We can recognize the faith of the church concerning ministry in this text at many points, yet here more than in "Baptism" and in "Eucharist" we find the text at variance with our understanding of the faith of the church through the ages. It seems to us that often the understanding of the faith has been limited in such a way as to deny significant historical development and the communal experience of many Christians and particular churches.

31.249

We affirm with great joy the beginning of the exposition of ministry (M.1 – 5) with the calling of the whole people of God and the careful way in which ordained ministry is related to the ministry of all Christians. We also note that Baptism is a sign of gifts for ministry for all people and that the Eucharist is food for all missionaries.

31.250

We affirm also that ordained ministry has a special role in the preservation of apostolic tradition as the text defines it, that the orderly transmission of ordained ministry is important in the continuity of the church, and that the laying on of hands is the sign of such orderly transmission. We would want, however, to put an equal stress on the "free gift" (charism) character of the ministry of all believers and the importance of the recognition of particular gifts as qualification for ordination. (M.7)

31.251

We affirm the threefold pattern of ordained ministry understood functionally (M.19–25, 28–31), and we assent generally to the functions of ministry as described there. We have difficulty with the way in which the text seems, however, to fall back at many places to the definition of ministry more narrowly in sacramental or eucharistic terms, especially as it again and again refers to the local congregation as "the local eucharistic community," rather than the gathered community of the whole people of God. In so doing the text gives up its commitment to the ministry of the whole people of God at the beginning of this section and to ministry in the life and work of the world as in the section on the "Eucharist."

Furthermore, our tradition has demonstrated its conviction that ministry is the calling of the whole people of God by refusing to limit the office of presbyter to those who have received formal theological education and who perform the ministry of Word and sacrament. Our tradition has believed it important that the nurture and government of the church not be restricted to those who perform the ministry of Word and sacrament.

31.252

We have discovered that ordination to office in the church and to specific offices or functions of ministry may be understood to interpret the functions of presbyter and deacon more broadly. We further find that the three functions cannot be so easily divided as between the local and the wider area, for each of the functions may be and even should be exercised at each level of the life of the church.

31.253

We find that the categories personal, collegial, and communal are helpful in distinguishing patterns of the exercise of office in the church, but at points may create confusion. From the perspective of our particular understanding of the tradition these categories help to clarify the collegial nature of the exercise of the function of *episkopé*, as in our presbyteries and sessions. We are concerned that the definition of the personal exclusively as representing Christ omits the dimension of the ordained minister's representing the people of God. There is a strength in the category, communal, in its clear reference to the partnership of ordained ministry and the whole people of God. We believe that the categories should not be limited to a clerical understanding of ordained ministry.

31.254

We are in accord with the call of the text for deliberate efforts toward the mutual recognition of ordained ministries among the churches. Although we concur that the ordination of women is not an obstacle to our recognition of ordination from churches which do not ordain women, we are convinced that for biblical, historical, and practical reasons, the ordination of women is a faithful expression of the apostolic tradition. Not only is the understanding and practice of the past to guide us, but also the Holy Spirit, who is the one leading us to the future. We affirm that the Spirit has led churches, among them our own, to perceive the ordination of women as consistent with the gospel and, in the belief that God can do a new thing, to accept the ordination of women as a part of the tradition which is ongoing and developing.

31.255

We must affirm that we do not see the ordination of women as an issue which is expendable in the effort for unity of the church, for we have seen and heard that God is calling both men and women to ministry. We believe that the text errs and has caused harm to the community of faith when in M.50 it fails to challenge the churches in their refusal to consider candidates for ordination on the basis of gender as well as race, handicapping condition, and sociological group.

31.256

We have spoken at such length and with such qualifications about our recognition in this text of the faith of the church through the ages because we discern that the text itself is less consistent on ministry and because we find that in this text there is less recognition of the growth and change which the Spirit works in the tradition.

31.257

2. The consequences the Presbyterian Church (U.S.A.) can draw from this text for its relations and dialogues with other churches:

31.258

The statement on ministry will enhance the bilateral and multilateral conversations in which we engage at both denominational and local levels. The possibility of increased mutual recognition of ministry will affect the possibility of increased eucharistic fellowship.

31.259

Our own practice and provisions for the recognition and transfer of ministers from other denominations may require study and changes in our Constitution.

31.260

The study of the functional definitions of bishop, presbyter, and deacon and the effort to identify the ways in which the functions are located and exercised in our present system will be of help in understanding our own church and the churches with which we are joined in this ecumenical recognition. Such study will not be easy, for there are heavy emotional associations with such terms as bishop, priest, elder, and deacon, so that any study will involve not only intellectual endeavour but the struggle with loyalties and feelings. The text, however, with its bridge-building focus on likenesses and its helpful commentary on the differences is a positive inducement to conversation.

31.261

We must note honestly that in all such conversations we shall doubtless continue to seek to preserve the values of the collegial and communal understandings of ministry and thus to insure the participation of the people in all levels of governance, decision-making, and ministry in the life of the church. At the same time we are challenged to rethink our own understandings and practices of what we call "the parity of ministry," and to reevaluate our understanding and practice of *episkopé* and how that function might best be served.

31.262

3. The guidance the Presbyterian Church (U.S.A.) can take from this text for its worship, educational, ethical, and spiritual life and witness:

31.263

In our church we have ourselves been very unclear about the nature of ministry and of ordination. This text gives a basis for study and consideration which, because it represents both a different understanding of the tradition and a variety of traditions, can move our own discussion and attempts at statement to new levels.

31.264

One dimension which is both strange and suggestive is the treatment of the representative character of the ordained ministry in M.10–13. To be a representative of Jesus Christ is a dignifying reality, and the implications for the character and work of the ordained minister are of utmost importance. At the same time it is important to recognize as the commentary on M.13 notes that the ordained minister exercises the functions of ministry in a way that represents the ministry of all the people of God. We have stressed in recent years the humanness of the minister perhaps to the neglect of the representation of Christ which the ordained minister bears.

31.265

As we look afresh at the structure of the church in this particular time of reunion and reorganization of the Presbyterian Church (U.S.A.), we can be guided by the ways in which the text faces the issues of authority and of oversight. Our commitment to an understanding of the offices of presbyter and deacon not limited to the sacramental should lead us to seek new understandings and definitions of the functions and authority of ordained offices.

31.266

The implications of the ministry of the whole people of God are yet to be satisfactorily explored even in our tradition which prides itself on the affirmation of "the priesthood of all believers." The meaning of that concept seen in the light of the service which Jesus Christ calls the church to carry out in and for the world will become clearer as we engage in serious study of this document.

31.267

4. The suggestions the Presbyterian Church (U.S.A.) can make for the ongoing work of Faith and Order as it relates the material of this text . . . to its long-range research project . . .:

31.268

In the course of this response we have already raised major issues for consideration in the ongoing work of Faith and Order especially on this topic of ministry. We can therefore be briefer in this section.

31.269

A stronger orientation of the understanding of ministry from the perspective of the work of the whole people of God will lead to explorations which will be of help to the church. The ethical and missional implications of the apostolic ministry are crucial for our day and for the church's faithfulness to Scripture.

31.270

Further consideration of the offices of presbyter and deacon will be helpful. For more than 450 years some of the churches have been exploring different lines of interpretation of the offices of presbyter and deacon. The office of deacon especially was transformed in Geneva in the sixteenth century, and as heirs of John Calvin, we are constrained to agree with the document that it may need redefinition again today. The office of presbyter, too, needs to be examined to see whether it has more meaning than simply being a local counterpart of the bishop. Exploring the three offices first from the perspective of three distinct functions might move the whole discussion to a different level.

31.271

The text is helpful in relating authority in the church to the authority of Christ and in suggesting the three dimensions of authority: personal, collegial, and communal. Further exploring these dimensions and relating them to each of the offices of the church would be helpful.

31.272

While the discussion of authority is helpful, the concept of ministry as servanthood needs expansion and development. (M.15, 16) In baptism all are welcomed into the community and commissioned to serve the world. In the eucharist the community of faith is nurtured by God for the purpose of service in the world. (E.24–26) Recognizing that ministry which does not serve is not ministry at all, the church needs continually to emphasize the role of the people of God as servants in the world. Without such an understanding of ministry the focus on the authority of the ordained ministry (M.16) can be misleading.

31.273

The text recognizes the "free gift" (charism) character of ministry as well as its institutional/sacramental character. To explore the nature of the gifts for ministry and the implication of the richness and variety of gifts for the form and location of ministry would be a useful task. Apostolic continuity and proper ordination are necessary for the church, but without the gifts of the Spirit the ministry of the church will be rigid and lifeless. Likewise, the prophetic character of ministry which was briefly mentioned in the document

(M.33) needs to be developed particularly in relation to the priestly and official character of much of the text.

31.274

We have already stated that the ordination of women cannot be left as an issue for which there is no further discussion. We recognize that the consideration of this issue is painful for some of the churches, but its nonconsideration is equally painful to others. Mutual recognition of ministry cannot be fully achieved until all those ordained by any church are acceptable to all the other churches.

31.275

Finally, we would express the hope that the exploration of ministry should appeal not only to the biblical text, which is subject to different interpretations, and to the first four centuries of the life of the church, or even to the centuries since, but also should involve the commitment to discern what God is doing today and to take seriously what according to Scripture God has promised to do. (Cf. M.4.) The apostolate rests on the orderliness of being sent, on the authority of Jesus Christ the sender, and above all on the purpose and mission for which Christ sends the people of God in the power of the Holy Spirit. The church's understanding of ministry should be eschatological not only traditional. As we urge this perspective on Faith and Order, we acknowledge our need of such perspective in our own theological exploration of ministry.

Conclusion

31.276

We commend the text, we appreciate its significant congruence with our own tradition and our understanding of the tradition of the Church catholic, and we affirm its importance as an ecumenical statement which can bind us more closely to other branches of Christ's church as a basis for further worship and work together within the World Council of Churches and in our communities.

31.277

We urge the Faith and Order Commission to pursue its tasks of research "Towards the Common Expression of the Apostolic Faith Today" in the same spirit in which we have spoken directly about the next steps in the discussion of ministry. In particular we trust that there will be openness to the work of the Holy Spirit in the world today, understood as disciplined by the insights of Scripture and tradition, thus allowing for a balance between the values of continuity and institutional integrity and charismatic and prophetic insight, and honoring the eschatological nature of the faith which is rooted in the authority of the apostolic tradition.

Appendix A — The Process of Response
31.278

The response process for the Presbyterian Church (U.S.A.) was initially coordinated by the Advisory Committee on Ecumenical Relations and the Ecumenical Coordinating Team and was brought to completion through their successor body, the Coordinating Committee on Ecumenical Relations. Three selected congregations from each synod, several presbyteries, and the theological seminaries agreed to study the document and submit written responses by October 1984. Other congregations and presbyteries together with boards and agencies of the General Assembly were invited to study the document, using a study guide prepared for the church, and make response.

31.279

An extended response to the Baptism section was made by a Joint Task Force on Baptism through the Advisory Council on Discipleship and Worship and the Council on Theology and Culture. A similar response to the Eucharist section was made by the Committee on Worship of the Advisory Council on Discipleship and Worship. A somewhat briefer response to the Ministry section was made by the Vocation Agency and the Division of Partnership Services of the General Assembly Mission Board. A conference of representatives from the synods, seminaries, and other groups, held in March 1985, sharpened and extended understandings and suggestions from those papers through their own background in study and their consultation. In addition a small consultation of women examined the document from their particular perspective.

31.280

A three-person writing team was commissioned to prepare a response for the approval of the appropriate bodies and transmission to the 1985 General Assembly, using the various papers which had been submitted. The process, however, was extended in January 1985, and the writing team was expanded to include representation from the Advisory Council on Discipleship and Worship and the Council on Theology and Culture. That seven-person writing team together with two staff persons prepared this document, which is sent to the General Assembly from the Coordinating Committee on Ecumenical Relations by the General Assembly Mission Board and the Program Agency with the concurrence of the Advisory Council on Discipleship and Worship and the Council on Theology and Culture.

31.281

The writing team consisted of the following persons: Rev. Katherine Bottorff, pastor; Dr. Melva Costen, professor of worship; Rev. Nancy Ann DeVries, college chaplain; Rev. Dr. Francisco Garcia-Treto, professor of religion; Rev. Dr. C. Benton Kline, professor of theology; Rev. Lewis Lancaster, ecumenical staff (Atlanta); Rev. Cynthia Logan, associate pastor; Ms. Karen Summers, theological student; Rev. Dr. Margaret Thomas, ecumenical staff (New York).

PRESBYTERIAN CHURCH IN IRELAND

16. The Lima Report claims to "have already reached a remarkable degree of agreement" and a "significant theological convergence" which the Faith and Order department of the World Council of Churches "has discussed and formulated" (p. ix). This, if it is correct, is to be welcomed. The text and commentaries are to be understood in the following way: "the main text demonstrates the major areas of theological convergence; the added commentaries either indicate historical differences that have been overcome or identify disputed issues still in need of further research and reconciliation" (*Ibid*).

17. The Report is a subtly nuanced, carefully constructed one, designed to maximise agreements and to minimise differences. It is to be regarded as part of the ongoing ecumenical discussions on the nature of the unity of the Church and the place of baptism, eucharist and ministry within it. A genuine attempt is being made to set out a point of view which will embrace as many Churches as possible. This has only been partially successful.

18. We affirm with the report that the unity of the Church is God's will for his people and that continued efforts should be made to make that given unity a reality in life and doctrine.

19. The Committee on Doctrine has approached the Report as objectively as possible and has sought to find areas of agreement and acceptance. We are aware of the fact that a document which covers such a wide spectrum of different confessions can scarcely meet with the agreement of all and that what is offered here is convergence not consensus. We accept that the intention of the Report was to return "to the primary sources," namely, "The Tradition of the Gospel defined in Scripture transmitted by the Church through the power of the Holy Spirit" (ix). We believe, however, that this has not in fact been fully carried out. At the same time certain criteria of truth

---

• 353,000 members, 565 congregations, 390 parish ministers, 40 in specialized ministries. This response was accepted by the General Assembly in 1984.

could not be set aside in seeking to understand and assess the doctrinal significance of the Report, nor could one fail to query the ambiguity of many of the statements and the type of language often used. This tends to make Christian unity and Church fellowship depend upon agreeing sufficiently ambiguous consensus formulae, rather than frankly accepting differences which need not divide us in Christ.

20. We have, therefore, in the case of each section, set out briefly our areas of agreement and then proceeded to point out at greater length where in practical terms and in doctrine we found difficulties, problems and statements that were unacceptable to us.

BAPTISM

I. The doctrine of baptism

21. The doctrine of baptism as set out in this report has many commendable features. We affirm with the Report that baptism comes from Christ himself, is closely associated with his whole ministry, death and resurrection, is His will for His people and is to be continued to the end of the ages. We also affirm with the Report that many Scriptural passages refer directly to baptism and its meaning, that it is related to our union with Christ in his death and resurrection, the work of the Holy Spirit in conversion as well as pardon and cleansing and our membership of the Church. Further we affirm that it is related to faith and must be administered in the context of faith, that is both to it and with the expectation of it. The warning against "the practice of apparently indiscriminate baptism" (16, Comm. 21b) is clear and timely as is that against the "confusion between baptism and customs surrounding name-giving" (Comm. 21a). In this Report there is more evidence of Biblical and Reformed emphasis than in the other two.

22. Nonetheless the Report presents us with certain difficulties in understanding, particularly in relation to the meaning of baptism (2). While affirming that baptismal teaching in both Scripture and the worship of the Church is expressed in various images it goes on to make affirmations about baptism which are not sufficiently related to the total context of the New Testament revelation. In other words it does not adequately distinguish between the sign and the thing signified.

23. The Biblical context is that God acts in Christ for the salvation of man which is by grace through faith, justifying and sanctifying man. It is in and through Christ that all that is set out in the Report is true and valid. He brings us into union with himself in his dying and rising, converts, pardons, cleanses by the power of the Holy Spirit. He calls and enables us to live a life of faith, love, hope and obedience, conforming us to his will. As he unites us with himself so we are united with one another, our divisions are challenged and the goal of unity is set before us.

24. These are some of the main emphases in the Christian revelation affirmed in our tradition.

25. We see baptism as a sign and seal of this grace in which we stand and by which we are saved; it is also an affirmation of our own commitment to give ourselves to God in Christ and walk in his ways. (Westminster Confession of Faith, 28, 1). We also see the sacraments as implying "a spiritual relation, or sacramental union between the sign and the thing signified whence it comes to pass that the names and effects of the one are attributed to the other" (*Ibid.*, 27, 2). This means that by grace and the Spirit an indirect identity can be affirmed between the sign and the thing signified, between God's grace and baptism. Taken out of this context and relationship, baptism can assume the appearance of a rite that is automatically or mechanically effective *ex opere operato*. One must either assume that the Report makes this proviso stated in our confession or else query the meaning it gives to baptism. Since there are few signs of the former the following points must be made by way of critique of the Report.

26. It tends to make a too direct connection or identity between Christ's action and baptism. Baptism does not as such effectuate salvation but is a sign, seal (or confirmation) of it. But since Christ by the Spirit is active in the sacrament (a word the Report never uses) it is also a means of grace. There is thus established by Word and Spirit an indirect identity between grace and baptism so that one can speak of baptism in the more direct way the Report does. At one point (5), however, the Holy Spirit is indeed spoken of as "at work in the lives of people *before*, in and after their baptism" so that the priority of grace over baptism and their relationship is clearly stated.

27. Moreover, the Report speaks of baptism as "the sign of new life through Jesus Christ" (2) and as "a sign and seal of our common discipleship" (6). For us this subjective reference is not absent but is secondary to the meaning of baptism as "a sign and seal of the covenant of grace" (Westminster Confession, 28.1). The Report does, however, at one point (5) speak of baptism as a seal of the Holy Spirit. The statement in the same paragraph that "God bestows upon all baptised persons the anointing and promise of the Holy Spirit" is again not to be understood as automatically effective. The Holy Spirit is indeed promised in this sacrament "yet grace and salvation are not so inseparably annexed unto it, as that no person can be regenerated or saved without it, or that all that are baptised are undoubtedly regenerated" (*Ibid.*, 28, 5).

28. While most of the Scriptural passages (2) refer directly to baptism nearly all are taken from the Pauline writings and no mention is made of Acts and the early days of the Church. Moreover there are passages in the New Testament which speak of grace and faith but do not explicitly mention baptism at all. Further, Paul in 1 Corinthians 1 does not regard baptism as part of his missionary vocation but believes it is primarily to preach Christ and him crucified. Again it is difficult to see the relationship between

Eph. 5:14 and baptism unless, as some believe, it is taken from a Christian hymn related to baptism.

29. In the New Testament there are several forms of baptism mentioned — that of Christ himself by John in Jordan, the baptism of his death, that of the Holy Spirit and that of water baptism of believers and their households. All are inter-related, but this is not brought out in the Report. It sees water baptism and Spirit baptism as two sides of the same coin. But may it not be the case that the Spirit baptism (1 Cor. 12:13) does not refer to water at all?

30. Is there any evidence in the New Testament that Jesus was immersed in Jordan? The going down may suggest it but does not prove it. Again is it correct to make total immersion the almost exclusive form of baptism, however correct or expressive it may be? Are not sprinkling, representing cleansing with the blood of Christ, and pouring as the giving or outpouring of the Holy Spirit equally valid forms expressing other aspects of the truth of the Gospel?

31. The ecclesiastical and ethical implications of belief in one Lord, one faith, one baptism are clear. They indicate the unity of the Church in obedience to Christ and a new life expressing struggle, with victory over sin as well as a vocation to witness to the gospel and its relevance to the whole of life. But this is very directly tied to baptism in the Report as "baptismal unity" (6, 15) rather than unity in Christ which baptism signifies and the Spirit conveys. However, part 10 does speak more clearly of "baptised believers".

32. The Report is in line with the Westminster Larger Catechism which speaks of improving one's baptism (A 167) by going back repeatedly to Christ, in "life-long growth in Christ" (9 and Comm. 14, C). We would, however, like to have seen covenant theology as understood in the Reformed tradition included in the Report, particularly in relation to infant baptism.

II. Baptismal practice

33. We find §§11–13 express fairly the position of baptism of both infants and believers, the need for personal confession in the context of the believing community and growth in faith or into faith.

34. In §14 participation in Christ's death and the giving of the Spirit are both aspects of our faith. That baptism "effects both" can only be true as a work of the Spirit or as a means of confirming and receiving grace already given. Otherwise it is virtually identical with baptismal regeneration which we do not and cannot accept.

35. Prayer for and the expectation of the Spirit is what we believe and seek to practise, but no automatic identification of the Spirit and the rite of baptism can be envisaged or accepted.

36. Mutual recognition and renewal of baptismal practices as expressed in §§15 and 16 are both points with which we agree.

III. The celebration of baptism

37. Many of the features of these paragraphs we find acceptable, but we query the following:—

a) The value of chrismation together with the assumption (II above) that the Spirit comes (almost automatically) in baptism (19).

b) The statement that baptism gives us "a new identity as sons and daughters of God" (20) is true in the limited sense that those baptised are admitted into the visible Church and called to live as God's children. This sonship, however, comes by grace through faith in Christ and is not immediately identical with baptism, though related to it. Paragraph 21 needs a similar qualification added to it.

c) The question of the relationship between baptism and the Lord's Supper requires further elucidation (20). In our catechism (Westminster Shorter Catechism A92–95) baptism is a sacrament in the full meaning of the term and points to the beginning of the Christian life, whereas the Lord's Supper is the sacrament of the continuance and growth in that life.

EUCHARIST

38. The Lima Report on Eucharist has many features which can be commended to all Churches. It has the various elements which should be included in a doctrine of the Lord's Supper — thanksgiving, remembrance, communion and the hope of the coming again of the Lord to perfect his kingdom. The place given to memorial (5–13) as central (though not primary) indicates the abiding significance of this aspect. It has made an attempt to relate the sacrament to other aspects of Christian faith and life. In certain parts it has also the character of deeper theological penetration and insight, e.g. in its trinitarian structuring of the Lord's Supper (3–18) and the place of the Holy Spirit with the Father and the Son in the actual observance of the Supper (14). It is good also to see the Report emphasise that Christ's once for all sacrifice cannot be repeated (8) and that it is Christ who as the host calls and invites his people to his table (29).

39. Moreover one can agree not only with the central thrust of many passages but also with these and other areas of detailed exposition. Yet despite this the Report as a whole leaves a sense of dissatisfaction. The overall impression and interpretation is one with which we find it difficult to identify and this for the following reasons —

I. Meaning and language

40. The Report presents us with a largely unacceptable view of the Church; and such a view affects our whole concept of the Christian faith. The presupposition seems to be that Christianity expresses itself chiefly in ritual

celebration, is exercised by a specific form of ministry episcopally ordained, with the presumption of some form of sacrificial offering (Comm. 8).

41. It goes on from this general perspective to introduce much material which has a more Biblical and Reformed emphasis and with which we can more readily identify. However, the focus and centre of the Church is placed in the eucharist and the whole of Christian faith and life can be and is seen and interpreted from this central perspective. The Church is thus a eucharistic community, with a sacramental liturgy and life as its main feature. It is "the central act of the Church's worship" (1). This is consistent with a "Catholic" view of the Church but does not accord well with the view of the Churches of the Reformation based on the Biblical testimony. It is consistent too with the Report on Ministry, linked as it is to the bishop in episcopal succession who alone ordains ministers to preside at the celebration of the Eucharist.

42. This view is at variance with the New Testament teaching both on the place of the sacrament of the Lord's Supper and the nature of the Christian ministry. There the ministry is primarily related to the Word and, in this context, to the sacraments. The true Church is where the Word of God is preached and the sacraments properly administered. To see the sacrament of the Lord's Supper as the focal point and channel of the whole Christian faith and life is to give it an altogether greater place than is Biblically and theologically legitimate. It is to say too much and so too little.

A. Language

43. The Lord's Supper is consistently described as "Eucharist" — a term heavy with historical and doctrinal overtones. To us the "Lord's Supper" or "Communion" are more in keeping with our Reformed practice. And while "gift" (1, 2) is not incorrect, to speak of something coming from the Lord's institution is the more common and better term (see however 14).

44. Throughout the Report phrases are used to describe the Lord's Supper which are strongly biased in favour of centring on the idea of Eucharist as the all-inclusive central event of the Church, e.g. "eucharistic meal" (2, 13, 14) "eucharistic celebration" (14, 20, 23, 28, 32) "eucharistic event" (14) "eucharistic liturgy" (21, 27) and also "eucharistic congregation" (Comm. 19) [Compare the prevalence of the term "eucharistic community" in the Report on Ministry (21, 24, 27, 30)].

45. Moreover, it is somewhat too simple, if not misleading, to state that the various names of the Lord's Supper are to be set together (1) as if Divine Liturgy (Orthodox) and Mass (Roman Catholic and Anglo-Catholic) meant the same as Breaking of Bread, Holy Communion or the Lord's Supper. The doctrine behind each is very varied and in some opposed to the others. At several points in the Report the use of terms and phrases is obscure and ambiguous. "Eucharist includes both Word and Sacrament" (3, 12) where it seems to mean the whole service of worship. More often, however, it means the Eucharist itself and the lack of clarity in interpreting the two uses of the

term is apparent. There is also an ambiguity in the use of the term celebration; sometimes it simply refers to liturgical rites, at other times to the celebration of the mighty acts of God and particularly the recalling of the crucified and risen Lord. The problem of understanding what exactly is meant is a serious one throughout the Report and is more evident in this document on the Eucharist than in those on Baptism and Ministry. As in so much teaching on the Lord's Supper the Report gives inadequate reference to the resurrection (24 and 31) and fails to integrate this insight into its teaching.

B. The significance of the Lord's Supper

46. While it is true that the Lord's Supper is the sign and seal of the grace of God in the sacrifice of Christ for the sins of the world the Report goes on to make it all embracing. "The Eucharist embraces all aspects of life" (20). The totality of faith and life is channelled into this one sacrament and made to carry a weight it was scarcely intended to bear. The Christian revelation and many of its aspects is clearly set out here but when related, as it is, to the Eucharist it takes on a strange one-sidedness. This sacrament is one of the ways the faith is expressed but to make it the central way through which everything comes is not a Biblical approach. Several examples of this treatment are seen in the Report and may be referred to now.

47(a). The way in which the sacrament is related to the world generally calls for some comment. "The world" is said to be "present at every eucharist" (4, 23). It is present in bread and wine, thanksgiving for creation, in the person of the faithful. There is an element of truth in this; but here it is set at the forefront of the meaning of the sacrament and is a thought scarcely even adumbrated in the New Testiment or, if indicated, given second place. One more example may be given. The sentence which states that the eucharist "is a representative act of thanksgiving and offering on behalf of the whole world" (20) is unclear in meaning. To us it looks too much like the duplication of the once-for-all offering of Christ for the sins of the world and is at variance with the clear emphasis (8) that Christ's offering cannot be repeated or prolonged.

48(b). *Prayer.* Clearly one aspect of the Lord's Supper is prayer — the so-called Eucharist or thanksgiving. The Report goes on to state that "in the memorial of the eucharist, however, the Church offers its intercession in communion with Christ, our great High Priest. The anamnesis of Christ is the basis and source of all Christian prayer" (8, 9). To put this emphasis on anamnesis is to make too sweeping a statement. It is clearly meant to heighten the Lord's Supper as the centre of all Christian faith and worship.

49. The idea of Christ as High Priest and Intercessor linked to the eucharist highlights again the question of meaning and interpretation. On the one hand it could mean Christ's presence with the Father in the power and efficacy of his once-for-all sacrifice; in communion we are united with him by faith and receive the blessings of his death (cf. §54). On the other hand it

could mean a re-presentation of himself in his sacrifice to the Father and so a virtual offering of himself in the eucharist. Two such varied interpretations can scarcely be accommodated and represent an unacceptable variation in understanding.

49(c). *Unity and community.* The unity and community of the Church are seen as manifest in this sacrament. "It is in the eucharist that the community of God's people is fully manifested" (19). But is there not a full manifestation where two or three are gathered together in Christ's name and he is in the midst? It is he who makes the Church a community fully manifest and not the eucharist per se.

50. Christian unity also is too tied to this view. The Church becomes one people as it shares in the one meal of the Lord (26). One does not question the fact that this is one form of the manifestation of the unity of Christians. But they are one in Christ and form a community in and with him. This involves more than the sacrament, which is not centrally or exclusively the sacrament of unity. In fact what is said here about the eucharist might more readily be ascribed to the proclamation of the Gospel as a basis of unity.

51(d). *Witness and service.* The same is true of witness and service, of the Church's social and political concern for peace, reconciliation and justice. These are all aspects of the Church's message to and concern for the world. The Report speaks in fine terms of each of these areas but again relates this too exclusively and without proper Biblical support to the Lord's Supper.

II. The observance of the Lord's Supper

52. In a Church which has no fixed order of service for communion but where a certain structure is inevitable and necessary following Christ's example, we see the "eucharistic liturgy" (27) envisaged here as containing many of the essential elements in the observance of the Lord's Supper. However, we believe that a simpler form is better and follows more closely the words and example of Christ, both in his institution of the Supper and the later Biblical interpretation of it. We find here that the service envisaged would be more readily acceptable in the form of greater ritual and liturgy than we feel is necessary, though we do not disapprove of the various aspects of the service. We agree that increased frequency in the observance of the Lord's Supper may be beneficial and desirable.

53. We affirm that in the whole action of the sacrament Christ is really present to faith in accordance with his word of promise and by the power of the Holy Spirit. The nature of his presence is beyond our ability to explain, a reality greater than our practices at the Lord's Supper. Nonetheless not all views of the manner of his presence are equally valid and some are indeed injurious to the significance of the Lord's Supper.

54. We do not see Christ's presence (32) either in the elements themselves or tied to them, nor do we accept the presence afterwards necessitating consumption of all the elements or enabling further communion. Both

reservation of the elements and consumption of them imply that something happens to the bread and wine by way of change. This we see as coming very close to if not being identified with "Catholic" views of the eucharist and eucharistic theology where the change brought about makes a sacrament automatically effective. If we are asked to "respect the practice and piety of the others" (32) this can only be done if this is acceptable. But may not some of the practices and piety of others be regarded and in fact be both unbiblical and erroneous? Paragraph 32 simply confirms our fears that the Report presents us with a view of the Lord's Supper biased in a "Catholic" direction and as such contrary to what we believe. It is thus a continuing obstacle to rather than a manifestation of greater unity.

55. The Report does not give any consideration to sacramental discipline which is a prominent feature in some Churches. This operates both in admission of people to the table of the Lord on profession of faith and in dealing pastorally with those who misuse the sacraments either by infrequent attendance or by unworthy behaviour.

III. Scripture and tradition

56. This issue surfaces again in this section of the Report in its general emphasis, which relies heavily on what has been practised in many Churches for centuries but was challenged at the Reformation. It says more than the New Testament can legitimately be held to teach. In other words tradition is not subordinate to Scripture but tends in many cases to be the norm.

57. Should one test one's practice in administering the Lord's Supper by general agreement or should one not test it by the witness of Holy Scripture (28)? One cannot but agree with the conclusion reached about this Report by Professor Paolo Ricca of the Waldensian Church in Italy when he writes, "it remains to explain the discomfort which the Lima document on the Supper may provoke in the Protestant reader. It is not due to the little attention which the text ascribes to the Protestant theological tradition about the Supper, but rather to the general impression that the weight of ecclesiastical tradition prevails over the arguments of the evangelical tradition. Concerns about historical — liturgical — devotional *continuity* prevail over the demands of Biblical *authenticity*. The ecclesiastical situation prevails over exegesis!" (*Reformed World*, Volume 37, No. 37, 1983, p. 247). This is, in fact, a neat summary of the basic question mark that must be put to this whole Report, as indeed to that of the others on Baptism and the Ministry.

MINISTRY

I. General

58. There is much in this section that commands agreement, though opinions may differ in detail. For example, the setting of the ministry in the context of the doctrine of the Church (1–6); its relationship to the priesthood

of Christ, the Church and the individual (17); the nature of ordination (15–18); the emphasis throughout both on the unity of the Church and the variety of the gifts of the Spirit (including ministry and ordination) are all commendable features.

59. Nevertheless, within a general agreement, there are many unresolved differences which are explicitly mentioned. The Report on Ministry therefore (as on Baptism and the Eucharist) cannot be said to have that unanimity which has been so widely attributed to it.

60. There is considerable ambiguity in the Report in many passages where at least two meanings are possible. How far can such statements be accepted as a whole by the Churches and as pointers to unity when there is such underlying divergence?

61. There seem to be two different conceptions of the Church and ministry in the Report. On the one hand one finds views which are definitely "Reformed" and "Protestant", but side by side with these are those which are certainly much more "Catholic" in outlook. If one therefore takes the Report as a whole preference seems to be given to the Catholic as over against the Reformation traditions. The Reformation tradition of Word and sacrament, while clearly present in many places, is subordinated overall to a eucharistic conception of the Church and its ministry. This we find unacceptable. The predominance of the phrase and the repeated emphasis on "eucharistic community" points in this direction.

II. Scripture and tradition

62. The position of our Church is that the sole authority for faith and life is Holy Scripture and that all subsequent traditions within the Church are subject to this norm and criterion. While the Report gives considerable space to Biblical exposition, great emphasis is also put on an historical tradition or traditions and it is not always clear how they are related and which has the priority. Indeed it seems as if tradition has the primary place.

63. We agree with the Report that an ordained ministry is the will of God for his Church, that it existed in considerable variety in the New Testament, but that it identified bishop and presbyter in the earliest days. To go on, therefore, to give a second century threefold pattern of ministry, namely, bishop, presbyter and deacon, a priority over the witness of Scripture and to fail to acknowledge the justification of several Reformation Churches in returning to this Biblical pattern seems to us to set tradition — however long — over the authority of Holy Scripture (§§19, 21, 25). The same is true of §36 and the commentary on apostolic succession and §§41, 43 on ordination. While §§34 and 35 give an acceptable definition of Apostolic Tradition in one sense, in our opinion a clearer view of the priority of Scripture as the norm and judge of this tradition is necessary here also. If apostolic succession is "to be found in the Apostolic Tradition of the Church as a whole" a standard by

which true and false developments of this are to be judged is necessary. This the document fails to provide.

64. We question too whether the tradition of the threefold ministry that arose in the early centuries was due solely to the fact that "the Holy Spirit continued to lead the Church in life, mission and worship" (19). Were there not other features external to the Church which formed the earlier variety into a more general pattern, e.g. the threat of heresy, the cultural contexts and structures of the time, persecution and dangers? Is it not also true that later tradition went astray and cannot be said to be true to the essence of ministry? Is it not also true that at the Reformation and at other times in the history of Christianity the Church had to discard erroneous doctrines, false forms and structures in accordance with the Word of God? While this development is acknowledged it is never allowed to form a critique of the threefold ministry as such — a ministry not to be found in the New Testament. No Biblical evidence in support of the claims of a threefold ministry is given in any of the sections of exposition of the New Testament nor can there be.

III. The ordained ministry

65. We agree that the ordained ministry is to be understood in the context of the calling of the whole people of God (1–6), the priesthood of Christ, the priesthood of believers, and of the individual believer (17). It takes its authority from Christ himself as a form of service, as his life, ministry and death were. We do not, however, accept the word "priest" as a general term for a minister (Comm. 17). St. Paul in Romans 15:16 can scarcely be interpreted in this way. We note that throughout the Report the term priest is never explicitly used for the ordained ministry.

66. We question too the statement that "the ministry . . . . is constitutive for the life and witness of the Church" (8). The Church is constituted by the Word and sacraments and these are administered primarily by the ordained ministry. Only in this derivative and relative sense is the ministry constitutive of the Church.

67. We find §§9–13 set out in clear terms much of the teaching of the New Testament both on the place and nature of the twelve and the apostles and also the relationship of the ordained ministry to them and to the Church as a whole. While not questioning that forms of ministry have been and are subject to "complex historical developments" (Comm. 11) we find difficulty in accepting completely the negative implication of this statement, that one must avoid altogether attributing a particular form to the will and institution of Jesus Christ. Whereas we accept that history and cultural forms have influenced Church forms, nevertheless we affirm that some forms do conform more closely to the Biblical norm.

68. While §13 speaks clearly of the ordained minister's chief function as that of proclaiming the Word and administering the sacraments, §14 seems to contradict this order and priority by making "the eucharistic celebration"

central and prior. There is in fact a strong tendency and weakness in the whole Report to set the eucharist at the centre and subordinate the Word in most cases to this or give it only in this context.

69. Paragraph 18 on the ordination of women is not an entirely satisfactory one and it reveals no consensus on this. It tends, however, to state that on the one hand there is no Biblical reason against such ordination as held by some Churches, while on the other those Churches which retain non-ordination of women are said to base theirs on tradition. This does not seem to be a fair way of stating the differences since the latter would also claim Biblical support for their view (see Comm. 18).

A. The historic episcopate

70. The document sets out for consideration and acceptance a threefold form of ministry, the episcopate of bishops, presbyters and deacons (19). This is presented as the norm by which all other forms are to be evaluated and judged. Variations in this are attributable to particular crises in the Church and are to be regarded as of a temporary nature (19). While it is true that such a threefold form pertained for centuries, its development and maintenance cannot be regarded as necessarily a permanent feature of the Church's ministry, especially since it can find little foundation in the New Testament. Episcopé or oversight, as the Report admits (23), may be and is exercised effectively in many traditions without this threefold form. Moreover the name and role of bishop are also seen in Churches that do not make the threefold form essential or regard it as desirable. One could envisage a Church with a constitutional episcopacy, but question the role of the bishop as essential for the life and witness of the Church or as one of the main ways the unity of the Church is to be manifested. A threefold ministry can so easily degenerate into a three grade ministry.

71. Again, while the Churches that have a threefold ministry are asked to reform and renew this ministry, those that have not are required to accept this form of ministry into their system. No consideration is ever given that the reverse might in fact be necessary or desirable. Nor is any thought given to the synagogue pattern and practice as a guide to that of the New Testament and its ministry and Church. Further, the eldership as expressed in the Reformed Churches has been given no mention at all.

72. The Report clearly has a conception of the Church which tends to see it formed around the episcopate rather than vice versa. While there is no evidence that the old phrase "where the bishop is there is the Catholic Church" is accepted, nevertheless the bishop is the centre and focus as well as the sign of unity. Episcopé is clearly focused in the ministry and this again is centred in the bishop. Having already accepted the threefold ministry as the norm it is therefore natural to give the bishop a central and authoritative place. We question, however, whether the orderly transfer of minsterial authority (29) in the Church is not possible except through the bishop. We

also ask: is this not merely apostolic succession of bishops from the apostles by another name? Moreover, in past practice the bishop has not always been a sign of unity. In the Report no practical or doctrinal reasons are given why he is or should be so today. Is not Christ himself, as we know him through the Holy Scripture, both basis and focus of unity? The ministry, in whatever form, is his servant, as the Report in other places clearly indicates. It may and does form a focus of unity but does not require a threefold form to do so.

73. Since we do not accept the threefold form of ministry as necessary we cannot therefore accept what §29 says of the function of the bishop. As regards the statement in §24 "that the degree of the presbyter's participation in the episcopal ministry is still for many an unresolved question of far-reaching ecumenical importance" we wish to point out that, if there is but a twofold ministry with presbyter and bishop identical, this question scarcely arises or does so only in relation to their respective functions.

74. The variety of gifts in the Church and special charismatic leaders can be accepted as coming from the Spirit, as indeed is the ministry, but we question whether religious orders (32) are to be regarded as such gifts.

B. *Apostolic succession*

75. The Apostolic Tradition in the Church as described in §34 is largely acceptable, as is the idea and the commentary on the same section on Apostolic Tradition and Succession, being primarily in the apostolic word and witness. Unfortunately, while it is implied that the apostolic witness is given in Holy Scripture, this is not explicitly stated. Again we question in the next § (35) whether it is correct to say that "the primary manifestation of Apostolic Succession is to be found in the Apostolic Tradition of the Church as a whole". Is it not rather in the testimony of the prophets and apostles to God's revelation in Jesus Christ as we find it in Holy Scripture? And is not this the authority and norm by which the Church as a whole is to be judged? There seems to be considerable ambivalence as to how the succession of ministry is to be seen in the Report; it is clearly not to be regarded in the first instance as in succession to the totality of the Apostles' role. In §10 the Apostles are regarded as entrusted with "specific authority and responsibility" so that there is therefore "a difference between the apostles and the ordained ministers whose ministries are founded on theirs". Nevertheless, despite the fact that the ministry is not in direct succession to the apostles but only based on theirs, the bishop is to be regarded — if not absolutely essential — at least as the sign of apostolic continuity and unity in the Church, though not its complete guarantee (28). This seems to be virtually affirming apostolic succession in another form. Again the place and importance of orderly transmission of tradition and of ministry are both important, but one questions if the episcopate as understood in these paragraphs (especially 36) is permanently necessary and valid theologically.

76. While the Report recognises the validity, reality and function of other forms of ministry, at the same time it is tied to the historic episcopate and therefore to episcopal succession as a sign of the apostolicity of the whole Church. This we question, since the norm here set out is the superiority of episcopal orders with the historic episcopate recognised and required as the badge and form of true union.

C. Ordination

77. In §39 the Church is said to ordain some of its members to the ministry "to continue the mission of the apostles and to remain faithful to their teaching". But since (10) much of the mission of the apostles is once for all and unrepeatable how can the Church in its ordained ministry continue this work which is not to be continued? Some of the work of the apostles clearly is to be continued, namely, that of teaching and preaching, but is the mission to be seen alone in the episcopal succession to the apostles with their authority?

78. Again, in the commentary on §39, the bishop is now given the exclusive right of ordination and this seems to imply the older idea of apostolic succession of ministry. This we further query and cannot accept.

79. Finally, in §§41 and 43, we do not accept that ordination is to be given a sacramental status, to be regarded as a sacramental sign, in fact one of the sacraments of the Church.

D. Towards the mutual recognition of the ordained ministries

80. In §52 it is correct that the Churches in looking towards unity and mutual recognition must in particular study the nature of apostolic succession. But again, in §53 priority is really given to the Churches which have the episcopal succession of ministry and those that do not have it are required to accept it. The key sentence to which exception must be taken is that "the continuity with the Church of the apostles finds profound expression in the successive laying on of hands by bishops". Here indeed is the crunch issue, because here very explicitly what seems to be apostolic succession through bishops is a requirement for Church unity, even though it is called episcopal succession. This is something which we find unacceptable. Should, however, a basis of union be found different from the one envisaged here, the particular form in which the mutual recognition of Churches and their ministries should be carried out is a matter for the future. Meantime it is quite clear that the nature of episcopal ministry and unity envisaged here and the form of recognition which this final section puts before us is not acceptable to us as a Church.

Conclusion

81. In the light of our understanding of the relationship of Scripture to tradition and of the doctrine of ministry as set out in Holy Scripture the following conclusions can be made in relation to the Report.

1) It often gives a greater place to tradition than to the norm of Holy Scripture.

2) It does not accept the equal or greater validity of ministries which conform more closely to the New Testament pattern.

3) It requires the acceptance by all Churches of the "historic episcopate" as the badge and sign of Church unity.

ANSWERS

82. The Committee makes the following general response to the questions addressed to all the Churches on page x of the Preface to the Lima Report.

83.(I). The question assumes that there is an agreed "faith of the Church through the ages". This is true to a limited extent; there is agreement on certain fundamental doctrines like the Trinity, the deity and humanity of Christ, the Holy Spirit and the apostolic tradition embodied in Scripture. It is certainly not true that there was or is a common faith of the Church in our understanding of Baptism, Eucharist and Ministry, though we do recognise the place and need for all three.

84. The Doctrine Committee, as outlined in our Findings, affirms that the Lima Report points to many areas of agreement and convergence but at the same time sees other positions as unacceptable and indeed wrong. Our answer, therefore, can only be a very partial affirmative.

85.(II). The following considerations are suggested for future Inter-Church dialogue:

a) A clearer statement of what is the basis on which all such discussions are carried out. For us this means a more positive and definitive role for the Biblical revelation over against tradition but not divorced from it.

b) An attempt at greater clarity in the use of language and more definite understanding of what terms used are meant to convey. Ambiguity does not assist understanding.

c) A greater readiness to state doctrinal positions clearly even if (and possibly because) they do not always agree. Too many documents, like Lima, give the impression of agreement which, when looked at more closely, conceal considerable disagreement. We recognise that no conceptual terms of ours can ever adequately convey the unsearchable riches of Christ. At the same time we do not believe that statements which can have a variety of meanings help towards convergence in Faith and Order or lead to ultimate consensus and unity.

86.(III). The Report is a challenge at certain points to re-examine both doctrine and practice in the light of the faith of others and the actual measure of consensus arrived at despite the differences. The acceptance of two forms of Baptism, more frequent communion, the insight that communion has a trinitarian structure, are only a few of the areas that stimulate to new thought and action.

87. These and many other positive aspects of the Report we have already noted both in the introduction to each section and in the main content of our comments. However, we see in the Report not only possible lines of guidance but also warning against basing Faith and Order on what was done in the past rather than on what most nearly conforms to the spirit and letter of the biblical testimony.

88.(IV). Our general conclusion is that the basis and framework need to be seriously re-examined and the work of Inter-Church dialogue restated in a way that gives centrality to revelation as it is brought to us in Holy Scripture. To set the Biblical material in the framework of historical practice and continuity, as we feel Lima has done, is to fail to begin at the only possible point of entry, namely, where God has met and meets us continually in his Word. This Word is, of course, studied and interpreted in the context of the Church so that tradition is never absent. It must not, however, be given the priority.

89. Thus we feel that the unity of the Church on the Lima model is not a possible option for us. We, therefore, respectfully ask that these concerns be given serious consideration in all future discussions.

GENERAL CONCLUSIONS

90.(1) The Committee found much in all sections of the Report to commend and accept as consonant with Biblical and Reformed doctrine. Some of these points have been noted above, others are implied.

91.(2) The Report presents difficulties in comprehension on two fronts:

a) The language is in places obscure and unfamiliar.

b) The meaning of many passages is unclear and seems capable of at least two interpretations which may in fact be contradictory rather than complementary.

Such ambiguity does not help but hinders acceptance.

92.(3) Doctrinally the Report in its main thrust presents us with a model and conception of the Christian faith with which we find it difficult if not impossible to identify. Briefly, it gives priority to the "Catholic" over the "Protestant" view, to historical continuity and tradition over the witness of Scripture, to the sacraments over the Word, to a view of the Church centred more on rites than on proclamation and witness.

E. A. RUSSELL,
Convener

CUMBERLAND
PRESBYTERIAN CHURCH

To the General Assembly of the Cumberland Presbyterian Church in session in Odessa, Texas, 23–27 June 1986.

The Cumberland Presbyterian Church was asked to respond to the document Baptism, Eucharist, and Ministry that was prepared by the World Council of Churches. A task force of the Inter-Church Relations Committee and the Committee on Theological Studies was formed and made a response which was studied by each committee.

Response

This response to the study document, "Baptism, Eucharist, and Ministry" (BEM), published by the World Council of Churches, has been developed by the following process. The General Assembly of 1985 recommended that it be studied by Cumberland Presbyterian congregations with the proviso it be understood "as a study guide which does not conform in every respect with Cumberland Presbyterian theology" (Minutes, p. 221).

The World Alliance of Reformed Churches (WARC) had requested that the denominations belonging to the Alliance make response to the document. It did not seem practical to make a response based upon congregation studies because no adequate system exists to gather and refine such information from congregations. Therefore, the document was referred to the General Assembly committees on Inter-Church Relations and Theological Studies. The two committees appointed a task force to (1) request knowledgeable Cumberland Presbyterian theologians to write responses to the BEM document and (2) study the aforementioned responses and formulate a proposed response. The proposed response was submitted to the full membership of the two committees for critique and approval in principle. The result of this process is the proposed response which follows.

● 98,829 members, 831 churches, 761 clergy.

While it would be possible to discuss in detail most of the major statements in this remarkable document, it has seemed the better part of wisdom to deal with broad issues which the document as a whole raises. The organizing principle chosen for exploring these broad issues was that of starting where the Cumberland Presbyterian Church is prompted to: (1) affirm these statements of Christian faith and practice; (2) demur or hold reservations about them; and (3) be chastened and challenged by them. This has been done with each of the three major topics.

Baptism

1. Affirmation

The statements of BEM on this sacrament open up the richness of the sacrament by making some dimensions of the sacrament more vivid, emphasizing those dimensions which tend to be ignored or slighted in their attempt to rigorously defend a given doctrinal view of the sacrament. For example, the New Testament teaching of dying and rising with Christ in conversion is rarely heard in Presbyterian and Reformed proclamation of the Word or in teaching the meaning of baptism. By being willing to be open to other communions' interpretation of baptism, Presbyterian and Reformed churches may recover such a "lost" understanding of conversion without necessarily surrendering our sacramental position. Indeed, the deep meaning of the sacrament often is lost through a preoccupation with its mode of administration.

Two aspects of Baptism to which these statements in BEM call attention need affirmation and further development on our own communion: (1) Recognition that the modes of baptism may indeed be three in number — pouring, sprinkling, immersing — and that persons' previous baptism should be accepted as valid when they are received into our communion. This needs careful thought in our mission churches overseas as well as in the United States as persons are received into membership from other denominations. (2) Baptism should occur within the corporate community and not as a private rite. This needs special attention in our individualistic American culture.

2. Reservation

The BEM document does well in pointing out that each mode of baptism is better suited to symbolize a given aspect of the sacrament. It would, however, strengthen the document to point out those aspects of the sacrament which are better symbolized by pouring, just as the document does with immersion; e.g., pouring better symbolizes the outpouring of the Spirit. Also, it should be noted that every mode of baptism only partially expresses the rich diversity of meaning involved in baptism.

3. Chastening

The exploration of "believer's baptism" chastens us at the point of a valid but lax administration of the sacrament of baptism to children. "Believer's baptism" stresses not only the promise to the believer but also the expectation held of the believer. Too often baptism of infants is lacking in serious covenant-making and covenant-keeping and is an isolated event without the teaching preceding it, accompanying it, and following it. Expectation of both the parents and the child (as he/she matures) are too easily lost.

The BEM statements on baptism also challenge the church to think more rigorously about the consequences of baptism as it relates to admitting children to the Lord's Supper.

We are also challenged by the document's statement that baptism signifies a change in the whole life and has ethical consequences in all relationships of life, not merely of personal, individual salvation.

Eucharist

1. Affirmation

The sacramental nature of the eucharist is rightly elevated in the BEM document. The sacrament can be emptied of meaning by resistance to the doctrine of transubstantiation. The emphasis on thanksgiving and re-membering (anamnesis) as the two primary qualities of the eucharist is much needed. The joyfully grateful sign-act of re-presenting (making present again) the gift of our Lord is a pathway to renewal and unity at all levels and in all forms of the church's life.

2. Reservation

The document does not speak very strongly to the issue of "closed communion" whereby one communion excludes those from other communions from sharing the Lord's Supper. This avoids the critical tragedy that disunity is most visibly present at precisely the place where unity should be most visibly present; namely, at the Table of our Lord. Just as some communions' integrity is at stake when there is refusal to accept their administration of baptism, so is our integrity at stake when there is refusal to admit us to sharing in the eucharist.

The document should also emphasize more the relation of the proclamation of the Word to the celebration of the eucharist and the relation of this to the frequency with which this sacrament should be celebrated.

3. Chastening

We are chastened by how thoroughly the document explores the eucharistic liturgy. The richness of liturgy points to the richness of God's gift. Celebrations of the eucharist in the Free Church tradition often are marked by a paucity of liturgy and a consequent loss in richness and depth of meaning in the sacrament.

The statement on the "reservation" of the elements used in the eucharist is also chastening, inasmuch as the elements are often treated carelessly, especially after the eucharist has been celebrated. The sacred nature of this sacrament merits attention being given to the care given the elements both before and after their use.

Ministry

1. Affirmation

We affirm the document's statement that God's will is to call the whole of humanity as God's people and that the church exists both to proclaim and prefigure the Kingdom of God. All members of the church have a ministry by virtue of the diverse gifts God has given. Our tradition has also emphasized the "called" ministry; that is, that those seeking ordination as ministers have an experience of an "internal call," though this calling is verified by the wider church over a period of preparation and examination.

2. Reservation

The document seems to proceed on the assumption that there is general agreement on the biblical definitions of the offices of ministry as presented. It is our belief that there is no precise definition of these offices given in the New Testament and that the term "priest" is never used in describing the ministerial office of leader of a congregation. Although it is recognized that since all are called to belong to the priesthood of believers, "priest" may be an appropriate title for a leader. More attention needs to be given to the office of ministry. The movement toward unity would be strengthened by a more thorough exploration in this document of the Reformed interpretation of these offices.

Further, the document states that the ordination of women to ministry is not a "substantive hindrance for further efforts towards mutual recognition." We cannot agree, inasmuch as treatment of women, whether in ordination or any other act of the church, is a treatment of persons and therefore of the utmost substance in understanding Christian ministry.

3. Chastening

The emphasis on the apostolic tradition points to the fact that an understanding of the apostolic nature of the church can be lost in resisting the concept of apostolic succession. There is an apostolic succession of ministry entrusted to the church and this understanding enriches the church's life. This can and should be affirmed quite apart from the formal doctrine of apostolic succession.

Moreover, the understanding of the office of bishop chastens those who invest this office in a presbytery, when in fact, presbyteries often do not fulfill all the obligations of this office.

Recommendations:

Recommendation 1: That the proposed response of the task force on the Baptism, Eucharist and Ministry study be accepted in principle.

Recommendation 2: That the response be made available by the General Assembly to be utilized by particular congregations for study.

Recommendation 3: That the response be sent to the World Alliance of Reformed Churches, the World Council of Churches and the Faith Order Commission of the National Council of Churches.

Respectfully submitted

The Committee on Inter-Church Relations

The Committee on Theological Studies

ALL-UNION COUNCIL OF EVANGELICAL CHRISTIANS–BAPTISTS IN THE USSR

The WCC document "Baptism, Eucharist, Ministry" testifies in itself to the fact that it lacks the exhaustive theological coverage of the issues involved. We did not expect this since each dogmatic exposition of these issues is brought about by confessional upbringing and understanding of the Bible. Even in case of merger of related denominations, a new dogmatic teaching is elaborated, which would reflect the views of this church union.

The Evangelical Christians-Baptists in the Soviet Union have been living and working within a united multinational and multiconfessional fellowship for forty years. We would not assert that all the confessional differences in dogmatic understanding and church practice have been eliminated, for this would be just as impossible as erasing national and cultural differences among our believers. But we have found out that unity of witness to Christ is possible even in such a diversity. And this witness is united as long as we, as Christians, can contain each other.

We are convinced that spiritual unity in Christ is based on conscious receiving of him through faith as the personal Saviour and on revival from the word and the Holy Spirit. Such Christians have one Shepherd and constitute one fold (John 10:16). They are now branches of the vine and members of the body of Christ.

Our differences and confrontations began and continued in those cases when we tried by ourselves to take away branches that bore no fruit (John 15:2). This taking away was carried on in the history of Christianity both physically and spiritually and nobody was asking the wine-grower about it. These initiatives (or, rather, arrogance) of churches were the cause of disrespect and lack of recognition among Christians.

● 547,000 members, 5,545 parishes, 5,000 pastors.

Baptism, eucharist and ministry follow after the encounter of man with Jesus Christ as his Saviour. It seems to us that the proposed WCC document rather emphasizes another order of things: first comes the church, and then Christ. By their baptism Christians are brought to unity with Christ. Christ gives us fellowship with him in the eucharistic meal, in the act of consuming bread and wine. It is just the order the Evangelical Christians-Baptists have rejected since the very beginning of their history. We are convinced that first of all the personal encounter between man and Christ should take place, and then it must be followed by baptism, eucharist, and ministry.

Our understanding is based on the holy scripture (Acts 2:37–38; Matt. 28:19; Rom. 6:4–5; John 1:12–13). The years of experience of mutual work in the AUCECB and evergrowing ecumenical relations have convinced us that there is great diversity in spiritual experience.

We believe that the ecumenical fellowship of Christians does not require giving up confessional theological understanding and church practice of baptism, eucharist and ministry. We are also sure that the creation of "the visible unity of the Church" is not possible, nor is it necessary both formally and practically. What we do need is the good understanding of the fact that the presence of Jesus Christ and work of the Holy Spirit are not confined to external forms of baptism, eucharist or ministry. The discipline of each local church (and confessional community) requires a clear understanding and fulfilment of certain services in the name of Jesus Christ. Besides, the inner world of a man who witnesses to receiving the grace of God through outer ministry is of the utmost importance. We are convinced in this aspect that the grace of God can find its way to man only through the conscious faith in Jesus Christ.

That does not mean that we refuse to seek ecumenical ties on these issues as well. We believe that the ecumenical fellowship is possible not in the dogmatic field but rather in the human aspect, since we understand that ecumenical ties are like close relations among good neighbours and even relatives but are not ties typical of the inner life of a family.

We must extend hospitality to people who believe in another way, as Christian, for the sake of their witness to Christianity, without asking any questions about their views or their practice of baptism, eucharist, ministry. Of course, this does not exclude a dialogue on these issues.

The participation in the eucharist beyond one's confession depends on the inner convictions of a Christian.

When ecumenical contacts are consciously realized by us, they demand that we should recognize the ministry of certain persons in the context, understanding and respect that correspond to a given confession. We think that ecumenism attaches too much attention to the vestments of priests rather than their quality of ministry. It seems to us that the ministry can be defined only by a confessional church; for this reason we can only agree with it while carrying out ecumenical contacts.

We want to stress once again that we do not think that a discussion on the proposed dogmatic themes is necessary. The force and efficiency of the ecumenical movement depend on voluntary desires to have interconfessional contacts, which can be only short-term and have the character of Christian politeness as far as the issues of dogmatics or church practice are concerned. Therefore, using this possibility, we would like to remind you about more practical and long-term ecumenical contacts and tasks, including translations of the Bible, peace-making activities, aid to those who suffer, education in the spirit of religious toleration and respect among confessions, and dialogues among different confessions. If the Christians all over the world could unite their forces in these directions the ecumenical spirit would become the mighty witness to the love of God. We are called to it by the developments in the world, which announce the tragedy of humanity and stimulate eschatological hopes in Christians. The problems of humanity require a common Christian response and action.

We think this document of the WCC is valuable since it calls us to deepen once again our theological understanding of these issues studying the scriptures.

Riga   Janis Tervits
Good Friday, 1984   Bishop of the Fellowship
of Congregations

BAPTIST UNION OF SCOTLAND

I. Foreword

The Report "Baptism, Eucharist and Ministry" (BEM) is the fruit of a 50-year process of ecumenical study and conference, culminating in the World Council of Churches' Faith and Order Commission meeting at Lima, Peru, in 1982, in which Baptist theologians participated.

The Baptist Union of Scotland is not a member of the World Council of Churches but is a participating member of both the Scottish Council of Churches and the British Council of Churches. As a member of these two Councils our union has been invited to study this report and to formulate a response, and we feel it is right to do so.

This response is the work of the Inter-Church Relations and Doctrine Core Group of the Department of Mission of the Baptist Union of Scotland, and has been formulated after several meetings of the Core Group.

It has not been given formal approval by the Council or Assembly of the Baptist Union of Scotland, but is rather the response of a representative group of Scottish Baptists (lay and ministerial) to the BEM report.

The purpose in publishing this Scottish Baptist response is:
a) to draw the attention of Scottish Baptists to the BEM report which is recognizably a significant document in developing ecumenical relations;
b) to suggest some lines of response which might be of help to Scottish Baptists engaged in discussing BEM at their local interchurch level;
c) to communicate to the Scottish Churches' Council, the British Council of Churches, the World Council of Churches and other interested parties our response to BEM which, while not an officially approved statement, we nonetheless believe to be a typical reaction of Scottish Baptists to the report.

● 32,456 members, 599 congregations.

II. Response

a) The response that is requested (page x)

1. "The extent to which your church can recognize in this text the faith of the Church through the ages."

We find the phrase "the faith of the Church through the ages" difficult to understand and define in this context. Does it mean:
— the apostolic faith contained in the NT documents?
— the apostolic faith embodied in the historic creeds?
— the New Testament faith plus tradition?
— doctrine alone, or doctrine plus practice?

Does "faith" here mean simply the traditional body of doctrine derived from the Bible and basically accepted by the church through the ages? Our difficulties do not arise about the basic doctrines of God, Christ or the Holy Spirit. On these there would be broad agreement. Our difficulties arise over the doctrine of grace and the place of "faith-as-trust". How does the saving work of Christ in his death and resurrection become effective in the lives of individuals? This is bound up with the doctrine of the church. Is it the community of the baptized or the fellowship of believers? These difficulties appear in our response to each of the sections.

2. "The consequences your church can draw from this text for its relations and dialogues with other churches, particularly with those churches which also recognise the text as an expression of apostolic faith."

The document has brought sharply into focus the real issues in the search for unity, and will provide fresh impetus and relevance to dialogue on these issues.

3. "The guidance your church can take from this text for its worship, educational, ethical and spiritual life and witness."

Since we are not convinced that the document as a whole is an expression of apostolic faith and practice, we would find it difficult to use it for guidance in these areas.

Our appeal is to the scriptures themselves, illuminated and enriched by the labours and insights of biblical scholars of many generations and from many parts of the Christian church.

4. "The suggestions your church can make for the ongoing work of Faith and Order as it relates to the material of the text . . . to its long-range research project 'Towards the Common Expression of the Apostolic Faith Today'."

We would hope that the comments embodied in our response may be regarded as a significant contribution to this end.

b) Our reaction to the document as a whole

1. We recognize and respect the nature of this document. There must be something historic and far-reaching about any document that distils fifty

years of discussion of a wide range of theological viewpoints and traditions. We are therefore sensitive to the need to make a thoughtful response to BEM.

2. We welcome the approach the document takes inasmuch as it is not a belligerent exchange of ideas from fixed positions but more a common search for "the Tradition of the Gospel testified in Scripture transmitted in and by the Church through the power of the Holy Spirit" (page ix).

c) Our reservations with the document as a whole

1. We question the basic assumption that the goal of visible unity is either practicable or right.

Our own position has been clearly set out in our statement on "Christian Unity" and from which we quote here.

"*Our concept of unity.* Scottish Baptists are firm believers in the spiritual unity of all who belong to Christ regardless of denomination or background. Christ's prayer for the unity of His people is taken with the utmost seriousness by them and they have the strongest desire for fellowship with others who share their faith. They deplore any kind of exclusivism which denies the Christian name to other believers simply because they belong to a denomination or ecclesiastical organisation with whom, on certain issues, they may be at variance. They believe, however, that this spiritual unity exists already by virtue of the relationship of every Christian to His Lord although they also hold that the reality of this unity needs to be expressed in living fellowship and co-operative endeavour in the name of Christ. The New Testament picture of the Church as the Body of Christ suggests to Baptists a unity which depends not on the external structure of the Church but on the relationship of each Christian to Christ as the Head of his body. Where Christ is truly Lord spiritual unity exists. Where He is not truly Lord no amount of structural union can create spiritual unity.

"*Baptists and organic union.* Scottish Baptists believe that organic union is desirable only where it is the expression of spiritual unity between groups of Christians who have been previously divergent in their emphasis. It is pointless to establish a union of convenience which does not have as its basis a union of conviction on the fundamental doctrines of the Christian faith. Moreover, in any such organic union Baptists believe that the basis must always be voluntary and that there should be no discrimination against any whose consciences will not allow them to share in it. Further they believe that the local church must always be free to interpret and to obey Christ's will in the light of its understanding of Holy Scripture.

"Scottish Baptists do not believe that structural, organisational or ecclesiastical union are the necessary prerequisites of the spiritual unity of Christ's church but rather that spiritual unity must be the basis of any kind of structural union. Moreover, it is quite conceivable that a structural union may be achieved without arriving at any meaningful unity of heart and spirit. Thus, while not opposed to organic union where it is expressive of spiritual unity, Baptists are hesitant about organic union for the sake of promoting a merely external appearance of oneness which may in fact simply cover the inner tensions and divisions from view.

"The union between denominations. While Scottish Baptists have no criticisms to make of other denominations who decide to unite structurally they do not themselves have a strong conviction that the absence of such union is a major sin in the life of the Church. While we are most eager to share in the common tasks of Christian witness, evangelism and service there is no desire to be involved in artificial structural alterations which may lead to the abandonment of emphases which Baptists regard as being basic to their understanding of the New Testament faith or at the very least to its proper practice.

"Scottish Baptists, then, take seriously the concern of our Lord for the unity of His people and are as eager as any to manifest that unity. They do so in practical terms as they welcome believers of all backgrounds to share in the Lord's Supper and in their worship. The cause of Christian unity, however, depends on the spiritual oneness of those who are committed to Christ before the organisational oneness of Church structures. Unless this spiritual oneness is sought and achieved first, no structural unity can take its place."

2. We question the report's claim to convergence. Our impression is that two conflicting theologies have been put side-by-side on the assumption that to place them alongside one another was to marry them.

A fundamental incompatibility remains all through the document between a sacramentarian and an evangelical understanding of grace. We see neither consensus nor convergence but a continuing conflict between two theologies, that will not be dismissed by sleight of hand or smooth words.

3. We question the document's assumption that it reflects the common Christian tradition of the gospel testified in scripture.

Rather than simplifying, we find the report complicates and embellishes the biblical tradition in a way that confuses rather than clarifies issues. We note this particularly in the eucharist section where concepts are read into the eucharist that can by no stretch of the imagination be read into the apostles' understanding of the Lord's Supper.

4. We are disappointed at the way the document fails to grasp the sharpest nettles in interchurch dialogue. For instance, we feel that the ministry section tends to skate round the historic episcopate issue.

III. Baptism

a) Statements we welcome and recognize as true to the apostolic faith

1. We agree that "baptism upon personal profession of faith is the most clearly attested pattern in the New Testament documents" (§11). We are not convinced, however, that infant baptism cannot be excluded. According to our reading of the New Testament we believe it was.

2. We welcome the linking of baptism with faith (§8) and church membership (§6), though we do have difficulties with making faith corporate rather than personal, and prospective rather than immediate.

3. We rejoice in the rich theology of baptism expounded in the report. Paragraphs 1–11 we would largely accept — when applied to believers' baptism. The imposition of this impressive New Testament theology on an unaware infant we find very difficult.

4. We concur with the view that "Baptism into Christ" does constitute a call to unity (§6); whether baptism into water and baptism into Christ can be equated is part of our hesitancy.

5. We agree that no other rite need be incorporated between baptism and church membership (comm. 14b).

6. We welcome — and are challenged by — the emphasis on baptism as a call to a growing discipleship and not simply as a once-for-all event (§12).

b) Assumptions we cannot accept

1. The attributing to baptism per se of the automatic bestowal of the benefits described for instance in §2.

New Testament baptismal theology only fits New Testament baptismal practice where the candidate is at the point of conversion on profession of faith. To apply it to an infant is to claim too much for the infant and to give to baptism almost a magical quality. The question remains — if faith is necessary for the completion or wholeness of baptism where does that leave infant baptism in and of itself where such faith does not follow?

Equally if baptism is in and of itself the "open sesame" to the benefits of Christ how are we to account for the many whose baptism, as far as we can see, has had no influence on their later spiritual development?

And what are we to say about Quakers and Salvation Army believers? Are they not "in Christ" with us because they have not been baptized?

We cannot escape the conviction that too sacramentarian an understanding of baptism undermines, if not denies, the necessity of personal faith and tends to produce a Christianity that is institutional, impersonal, magical and lacking in evangelical thrust.

This is why we hold out for baptism as conversion/baptism in which the believer professes his or her faith and, buried and raised with Christ, consciously takes on the challenge of living out a New Testament style of discipleship.

We would say that if faith is necessary for the reception of salvation (as §8 claims) then it would be better to baptize those who confess that faith rather than baptize infants indiscriminately with the very real possibility that they may see baptism as dispensing with the necessity of faith (as, in our experience, many do).

2. We have difficulties over §6 where the report naively supposes that there is "one baptism" which forms the basis of the call to unity.

There are at least two baptismal theologies and practices each of which has very different presuppositions. Until these presuppositions are recognized and explored talk of "one baptism" is pointless.

(The practical implications of this for us are as follows. We have a church membership of professing believers. One of the bases of membership is personal testimony to faith in Christ as Lord. To ask us to admit to membership someone who has been baptized in infancy just because he has been baptized in infancy whether or not he has reached the point of personal faith would be to fly in the face of our conviction that personal faith is necessary for salvation and that the church should be a fellowship of believers only.)

3. We have very serious reservations about §13 where "re-baptism", as it is called, is decried.

We can understand why this is stated in the light of the ideal "once-for-allness" of baptism but we would be unhappy about any blanket refusal to allow any individual to be obedient to God's call as he or she understands it, even if that call means (as the report terms it) "re-baptism".

If, in the opinion of the enquirer, their infant baptism was a well-intended act on the part of their parents but devoid of biblical authorization and lacking in theological content should they be denied the right to be baptized according to the scriptures as they now read them?

Are they to be denied the right to act in loving obedience to their Lord as they see it and will his judgment fall more on them because they have been baptized twice than it would if they had not been baptized at all?

Our fear is that §13 has behind it something of a "closed shop" mentality. If infant baptism is right it has nothing to fear: If, in the view of a sincere believer, it is inadequate and believer's baptism is the biblical standard, why should it be denied to them?

4. Paragraph 16 leaves us with a certain uneasiness.

We are puzzled by the concept of infants needing to be placed under the protection of God's grace. We want to ask — protection from what?

And if infant baptism does give protection from whatever it may be where does this leave the millions of infants that are unbaptized?

We would feel that thanksgiving for the life of a child, acknowledgment of parental responsibility and commitment to God's care and guidance are fully embodied in a service of infant thanksgiving without importing the massive overtones of New Testament baptismal theology.

We also feel that this paragraph tends to misrepresent our problem about infant baptism. Our problem is not that it is indiscriminate (though that does compound the misunderstanding of baptism); our problem is with infant baptism as such — that we do not consider it biblical.

c) Areas for exploration

This report does pose certain challenges to us as Baptists and points out areas which we would benefit from exploring further.

1. We need to continue looking at the full implications of the New Testament theology of baptism. We have been in danger of letting our people treat baptism as a confessional device rather than an act of a much richer symbolic meaning (§§1–5).

2. We need to firm up our understanding of the link between baptism and church membership. There has been a tendency for many Baptists to divorce these and thus to rob baptism of part of its corporate significance (§6).

This return to sources, especially the biblical source, is one we readily share since as a matter of principle, as Baptists, we make scripture our authority in all matters pertaining to faith and practice.

3. We need to explore the lifelong implications of baptism and not to treat it as a one-off historical event in a believer's pilgrimage (§9).

4. We need to listen again to the arguments that would justify infant baptism on the basis of the biblical records; to decide quite definitely how we regard infant baptism — as a denial of the apostolic faith and practice, as an historical aberration, as an inadequate though justifiable alternative to believers' baptism, or what (§§11, 13–15)?

5. We need to explore the question of the relation between the Spirit and the sign of believers' baptism — an area in which all Baptists would not be agreed (§7).

IV. The eucharist

For our understanding of the meaning of the eucharist (or as we prefer to call it, the Lord's Supper) we depend only on the New Testament.

When our Lord instituted the Supper, his actions and his words were starkly simple. This is true both of the account in Paul's letter to the Corinthians and of the basic account in Mark's Gospel.

The essential words and actions were: "He took bread and gave thanks, broke it and gave it to the disciples, saying, 'Take, eat, this is my body.' In the same way he took the cup, gave thanks and gave it to the disciples and they all drank of it. And he said, 'This is my blood of the covenant, which is poured out for many.' (or, 'This is the new covenant in my blood')." Paul adds after both actions the words: "Do this in remembrance of me."

We understand the words and actions of Jesus as symbolic of his broken body and shed blood, pointing forward to that new covenant between God and man to be effected through his sacrificial death on the cross on the following day. That was the real covenant of which the actions of the Lord in the upper room were symbolic.

We do not therefore accept that the words "this is my body, this is my blood" can be taken literally as though there were a relation of identity. They could only be symbolic implying the disciples' share in the benefits of Christ's sacrificial offering of himself and their part in the new covenant and its people.

Just as the Passover was a "remembrance" of God's deliverance of Israel from slavery, so the Lord intended the continuing observance of his Supper to be a "remembrance" of him through whose broken body and shed blood salvation was wrought.

For the first disciples, the Last Supper looked forward to the cross and their sharing in the bread and wine symbolized their part in the benefits of Christ's sacrificial death. After the resurrection the Lord's Supper looked back as they joined to break bread and drink from the cup in remembrance and thanksgiving. The bread and wine are tokens of that remembrance. They are also symbols of the disciples' sharing in the life of the Risen Lord and in his body the Church (1 Cor. 10:16–17).

Therefore the Lord's Supper is more than a memorial feast. It is a joyful celebration of, and thanksgiving for, Christ's victory in a feast at which he is truly present as the host of his Table.

It becomes a focal point of blessing to the church and to individual worshippers as we remember him in his death and offer thanksgiving and worship in his Risen Presence.

The Lord's Supper also looks forward to the fulfilment in the "marriage supper of the Lamb", to the final consummation — "till he come".

Our understanding of the Lord's Supper is summed up in the eucharistic prayer of the Church of South India:

Amen, Thy death O Lord we commemorate,
Thy resurrection we confess and
Thy second coming we await.
Glory be to Thee, O Christ!

Whilst there are a number of statements in this section which we welcome and recognise as true to the faith of the New Testament, there is much more which we are unable to accept. Sometimes it may be a matter of interpretation; basically it comes down to the question of our differing doctrines of grace.

THE INSTITUTION OF THE EUCHARIST (§1)

We have much common ground in this paragraph, though we have reservations about the phrase "proclaim and enact" and the statement that "the eucharist is a sacramental meal which by visible signs communicates to us God's love in Jesus Christ".

THE MEANING OF THE EUCHARIST (§§2–26)

We question the statement: "Every Christian receives this gift of salvation through communion in the body and blood of Christ" (2). We do not find this true to the New Testament, where salvation is through faith in response to the gift of God's grace in Jesus Christ (Eph. 2:8–9).

We find no basis in the New Testament for the statement that "in accordance with Christ's promise, each baptized member of the body of Christ receives in the eucharist the assurance of the forgiveness of sins" (2).

We believe that the Lord's words, "this is my blood of the covenant which is poured out for many for the forgiveness of sins" refer to his death on the cross and not to the wine in the Supper. The new covenant itself was made on Good Friday.

A. *The eucharist as thanksgiving to the Father* (§§3–4)

Every celebration of the Lord's Supper is an occasion for praise and thanksgiving to God for the gift of his grace in Jesus Christ, as we remember his broken body and shed blood for the redemption of sinners.

We find difficulty in understanding such sentences as: "The Eucharist is the great sacrifice of praise by which the Church speaks on behalf of the whole creation. For the world which God has reconciled is present at every eucharist" (4).

That seems to be reading far too much into the New Testament understanding of the Lord's Supper. We would have to say that it lacks biblical basis.

B. *The eucharist as anamnesis or memorial of Christ* (§§5–13)

The references to anamnesis in the report seem to be concerned with expounding a liturgical term and justifying traditional liturgical practice, rather than the use of the word in the biblical sense. It may be true that the biblical concept of *anamnesis* means more than simple remembrance, but the massive weight it is called to bear in this report seems to us to be quite unbiblical. Surely the biblical concept of anamnesis in the Lord's Supper is fulfilled in simple remembrance of his death and in our rejoicing in the presence of our risen Lord.

C. *The eucharist as invocation of the Spirit* (§§14–18)

We question the need to invoke the Spirit. According to our reading of the New Testament he is ever present, indwelling the fellowship of the church and the hearts of believers. It is he who makes real to us the presence of the Risen Lord.

But we are puzzled by the sentence: "The Spirit makes the crucified and risen Christ present to us in the eucharistic meal, fulfilling the promise contained in the words of institution." Which promise? We do not accept that the words "this is my body" constitute Christ's promise to be present at his Table. We find much clearer his promise: "Where two or three are gathered in my name, there I am in the midst of them" (Matt. 18:20). Christ's presence is not limited to the eucharist. He is there wherever his people are worshipping and serving him.

D. *The eucharist as communion of the faithful* (§§19–21)

We question the statement that "The sharing of one bread and the common cup in a given place demonstrates *and effects* the oneness of the sharers with Christ and with their fellow-sharers in all times and places" (14).

We find no basis in the New Testament for this.

Certainly we believe that at the Lord's Table we share fellowship with him and with one another in him. This shared fellowship is symbolized in our sharing of bread and wine. We also believe that in and through our risen Lord we are in communion with Christians of every age.

But we do not accept that what takes place in the eucharist effects this. We see the Lord's Supper as focusing and symbolizing what is always true of our fellowship with Christ and his members.

We believe that far too much has been brought into the essentially simple celebration of the Lord's Supper. Much of what is claimed here for the eucharist is true of non-eucharistic worship, prayer, and daily commitment to Christ and his mission.

E. The eucharist as meal of the kingdom (§§22–26)

Here too, we have the impression that theological concepts have been superimposed on the New Testament understanding of the Lord's Supper.

We would question what is meant by the church as "eucharistic community" (26). Is this the same as "a fellowship of believers" or is it a radically different understanding of the church?

THE CELEBRATION OF THE EUCHARIST (§§27–33)

We welcome the emphasis on the frequent celebration of the Lord's Supper. In many of our churches the Lord's Supper is observed every Sunday as an additional service following a full worship service. Some of us regard it as the culmination of our worship or "the seal on the Word" (Calvin). Some of our churches may from time to time hold a "full communion", i.e. the whole service of worship is centred around the Lord's Table. These differences may make it difficult to identify all the elements in the order given in the report. However, in our total worship each Sunday we would identify most of these elements. Our understanding of *anamnesis* is in line with what has been said under B. The idea of *epiklesis* associated with the eucharist seems to us to stem from a sacramentarian doctrine of grace which we cannot accept.

GENERAL COMMENTS

1. The impression is gained from the report that the eucharist is almost exclusively the channel through which the blessings of Christ are to be received.

2. This section is heavily dependent on a sacramentarian theology of grace.

3. We find it surprising that in a document concerned with church unity nothing has been said about the vexed question of validity.

V. Ministry

A. Areas of general agreement

There are a number of emphases within the opening section, "The Calling of the Whole People of God" (1–6) with which we can unhesitatingly agree. We accept that belonging to the church "means living in communion with God through Jesus Christ in the Holy Spirit" (1) and that "the Holy Spirit bestows on the community diverse and complementary gifts. These are for the common good of the whole people and are manifested in acts of service within the community and to the world" (5).

The document sees the calling of the whole people of God as the starting point for its discussion on ministry. That is proper. It is the church which ordains those whom God raises up and this emphasis is made several times within the document. We warm to the assertion that it is Jesus Christ who is the true ordainer and who bestows the gift of ministry (39 and 44c) and that the redeemed community is involved (40). The ministry of individuals springs from the ministry of the whole body of the church. This emphasis is to be preferred to the view which sees the correctness of ordination as validating the church.

Neither would we wish to dissent from the general drift of the statements on ordination contained in §§15a and following. We welcome the insistence that ordination is not for its own sake, but for the sake of the community which it serves and seeks to upbuild, though some of us would hesitate over the assertion that "the basic reality of an ordained ministry was there from the beginning" (Comm. 11).

In the section on "The Forms of the Ordained Ministry" we accept the opening statement (19) that "the NT does not describe a single pattern of ministry which might serve as a blueprint or a continuing norm for all future ministry in the Church". We believe that simplicity of form and flexibility of response to the demands of the contemporary situation are always important factors in determining the shape of the ordained ministry.

B. Areas of disagreement or hesitation

Our disagreement begins when the document asserts the relationship between the apostles and the ordained ministry of the church. "There is a difference between the apostles and the ordained ministers whose ministries are founded on theirs" (10) only serves as an introduction to an assumption of something akin to apostolic succession. The authority of the ordained ministry and its function as a focus for unity are based on this succession which is assumed in the document, not proved. For example, the document insists that the apostles had a unique role, yet they passed on part of their function of providing "a focus for unity" (8) to the ordained ministry which has existed "from very early times" (8). We, accordingly, dissent from the assumption (e.g. in Comm. 14) that it is appropriate, since the eucharist is the focus of unity, "that the ordained minister preside". We ask "appropriate in what sense and to whom?"

We have welcomed the statement (§19) saying that the NT does not describe a single pattern of ministry. We are, therefore, surprised when the document goes on to accept, without much question, the threefold ministry of bishop, presbyter and deacon. Its ground, or authority, lies in the statement: "Historically, it is true to say, the threefold ministry became the generally accepted pattern in the Church in the early centuries and is still retained today by many churches" (§22). So much, in the document, proceeds to be built on the assertion (§22) " . . . nevertheless the threefold ministry . . . may serve today as an expression of the unity we seek and also as a means of achieving it". Too much, in this area of the document, seems to depend on assertion and assumption and, consequently, we find its statements on the nature of the ordained ministry today to be inconsistent with the statements it has earlier made on the nature of ordination, statements which we find generally acceptable.

This basic inconsistency in the document is again evidenced in §34 which concludes with a striking and acceptable statement on the meaning of apostolic tradition. This statement is spoiled immediately by a paragraph (35) on the orderly transmission of the ordained ministry being a powerful expression of the continuity of the church throughout history.

We see no biblical justification in asserting (§17) that ordained ministers "may appropriately be called priests".

In our judgment the section on ministry is the least satisfactory of the three sections in the document. The fact that it is also the longest strengthens our disquiet at the dominance of clerical issues within the church.

C. *Areas meriting further discussion*

Obviously there would be value in continuing study on the nature of ordination. Even if it is accepted that God calls and bestows the gift of ministry, is the role of the church simply that of recognizing and accepting? Is anything bestowed on the person ordained? What is the nature of ordained authority and can it be exercised, if it is God's gift, without the ceremony of ordination? Can the person ordained be said to possess, in any sense, a priestly function?

Again, it will not do to devote only a single sentence to the ordination of women. This topic requires considerable discussion especially as it possesses considerable divisive qualities in the current church scene.

Paragraph 31 on the role of the deacon seems to reflect confusion. Some of the points made there on his role could equally well be made of the laity. Wherein lies the difference? Is there a place for the diaconate in the threefold ministry? What is the origin of the diaconate? To some of us its origin lies in the ministry of Jesus. To others it finds its basis in Acts 6.

We are not clear on the function of our own superintendent who has been appointed and welcomed as a pastor pastorum without much theological thought being given to his authority and role. The document's assertions on the role of a bishop are incentives to that study on our part.

Appendix: The practice of baptism, eucharist and ministry in Scottish Baptist churches

Baptism

Because of the independency of Baptist churchmanship there are no hard and fast regulations relating to baptismal practice. There is a minister's manual (published by the Baptist Union of Great Britain and Ireland in 1960) which many follow, but not slavishly. All that can be described is general practice — to which there will be exceptions.

It is unusual for candidates to be baptized before their early teens (though some have been baptized at 10–11 years of age). Because church membership is normally (though not inevitably) linked with baptism it is thought prudent to delay baptism until the candidate is mature enough to take on a church membership responsibilities.

The request for baptism is normally left to the candidate's own initiative though such requests frequently arise from a public appeal at the close of a baptismal service.

It is exceptional for candidates not to undergo a course of instruction (lasting 6–8 weeks) before baptism and church membership. The course of instruction will cover such topics as personal faith, the biblical basis for baptism, the meaning of baptism, baptist history and principles and church membership. Interested enquirers are usually invited to join in such a course without any obligation to go forward to baptism.

Applications for baptism are approved in many instances by the minister alone though if the baptism is to lead directly into church membership the applicant is then interviewed by two church members who present a recommendation for acceptance to a church meeting.

The baptisms take place on Sundays in the context of a public service and normally follow the sermon. Lady candidates are dressed in robes and men candidates in washable trousers and shirts (robes are no longer so common for men). The minister usually wears waders and a robe though younger ministers are now tending to favour a similar form of dress to the male candidates.

In many churches, prior to their baptism, candidates are expected to give some confession of faith in a testimony or a text of Scripture. Once in the water the minister usually puts a final question to the candidate regarding his or her personal faith.

The minister immerses the candidate in the name of the Father, Son and Holy Spirit, by lowering him or her backwards into the water. The candidate then usually leaves the baptismal pool after a brief pause for private prayer. In some instances, though rarely at present, a minister may lay his hands on the candidate and offer a public prayer.

Soon after baptism, sometimes at the same service, the candidates are welcomed into church membership in the early part of a communion service.

Eucharist

The eucharist, or the Lord's Supper, as it is more familiarly known in our churches, has held a central position in worship and in the shaping of the pattern of Christian obedience. The sharing of the bread and wine of communion has been considered one of the greatest privileges of believers, and in accordance with the word of institution it has been a frequent celebration. In many churches the service is held weekly, on the Sunday morning, and in others fortnightly or monthly. Until the turn of the century it was held in the afternoon, and was pre-eminently the members' service, where matters of discipline and fellowship business could be announced and discussed. More recently the communion has been held at the end of the other service, and this has unfortunately led to its being devalued and treated as an extra service by some. Yet for most of our people it remains a precious meeting place with the Lord, and an indispensable act of love and obedience.

Liturgically the key word has been simplicity, and the atmosphere of the upper room, and of the meeting of friends has been sought. The words of Jesus are our warrant, and his action in prayer of thanksgiving is imitated by the deacons of the church. The minister normally presides, but any designated believer, authorized by the church, may on occasion be called on to lead the service. Bread is generally, but not always, diced, and the unfermented wine is served in individual cups. There is often a fellowship offering, originally a love gift of the membership for the poor of the congregation.

In several churches the eucharist has been taken into the whole service, and in others a quarterly or monthly celebration is "integrated". This would seem to be a move back to an authentic Baptist tradition.

Ministry

A personal sense of God's call to ministry is normally the first stage in the process that climaxes in ordination and induction.

An early discussion usually takes place with the superintendent of the Baptist Union when advice is given on further reading and any necessary preparatory steps. (The superintendent of the Baptist Union is a senior minister appointed full-time by the Union to be responsible for the pastoral care of ministers, churches and applicants for ministry.)

The next step is a meeting with the Joint Ministerial Board, a board that comprises members of the College Board of Studies and the Ministerial Recognition Committee of the Baptist Union of Scotland.

Before meeting with the Board in a two-day series of interviews, the candidate will have completed an application form, undergone a medical examination and preached a "trial" sermon. His church and two other referees will also be required to support his application.

During the Joint Ministerial Board interviews, the candidate will be questioned concerning his Christian commitment and sense of call, his educational record and abilities, his personal beliefs and relationships, and his understanding of Baptist doctrine and practice.

To become an approved candidate for the ministry a substantial majority of the Board must be supportive of the application.

Given the approval of the Joint Ministerial Board the candidate will be set a course of studies normally at a Baptist College and incorporating both academic and pastoral instruction.

Provided the course of study is satisfactory the candidate's name will be submitted (after interview) by the superintendent to vacant churches where it is thought appropriate.

Given a satisfactory call from a vacant church (not less than 2/3rds of the voting members) the candidate will then be ordained and inducted to his first charge.

It is increasingly common for students to be ordained in their home church prior to induction though traditionally Baptists used to regard ordination as taking place in the act of induction when a man's pastoral service began.

Whether or not the two acts are kept together it is customary for ordinations and inductions to be representative occasions with members present and sharing in the service from the Baptist Union of Scotland and the area association as well as the local church. At the laying on of hands during the ordination these representatives participate in recognition of the out-working of this ordination and induction in the wider denominational framework.

In addition to questions being put to the minister-elect regarding his faith, sincerity of purpose and acceptance of responsibilities, the congregation are also asked to acknowledge their role in accepting the candidate as their pastor.

In terms of authority the minister will not be seen as having power over his congregation other than the personal and moral authority deriving from his own integrity and spiritual leadership. He will normally act in fellowship with his deacons (and elders in some cases) in proposing church policies and always in recognition of the fact that in a Baptist church the congregation itself in its business meetings has the final power of decision.

While the congregation will look on the minister as having a special role in the light of his giftedness, call and training, this will not carry sacerdotal overtones. He will normally lead the worship, pastor the congregation and conduct the sacraments—but not exclusively. Because the ministry of the church is seen as the calling of the whole people of God, not just of a priestly caste, it will not be seen as unacceptable for a layman to undertake any or all of these "ministerial" functions. In some cases the church may even have as minister a lay-pastor.

The movement of ministers from one church to another takes place by invitation of a local church calling a man to pastoral office, the man himself sharing the conviction that the move is also God's purpose for him. Should a minister seriously lapse morally, theologically or in the fulfilment of his ministerial vows, it is within his congregation's powers to ask for his resignation. Such events are fortunately rare.

The Baptist Union keeps a list of accredited ministers on which are the names of men whose suitability for ministry and standard of training have denominational approval. An approved candidate's name appears on the list as a probationer when he is first inducted and he remains in this category for his first three years while completing a course of probationary studies. After interview by the Ministerial Recognition Committee, provided his studies are completed and the report of his ministry satisfactory, his name is transferred to the full list. While a Baptist church may choose to call a man whose name is not on the accredited list (a quite rare occurrence) it is a rule that only accredited ministers can serve grant-aided churches. A man may only qualify to participate in the superannuation fund whose name is on the above list.

While the question of women in the ministry is under discussion at the present time in the Baptist Union of Scotland, it has not been the Union's policy hitherto to recognize the ministry of women in full-time pastoral leadership.

BAPTIST UNION OF DENMARK

Introduction

Having received the document of convergence on "Baptism, Eucharist and Ministry" we want to convey to the Faith and Order Commission our gratitude and the delight which has been expressed in the Danish Baptist Union in many ways and on different levels.

As a member church of the WCC we are ready to contribute to the dialogue about the church's present understanding of sacraments and ministry (even if this terminology is not used by us the factual contents are familiar to us). We also invite the Commission to let this response from us be part of the basis of work of the Commission on the farsighted study project: "Towards the Common Expression of the Apostolic Faith Today".

Though we understand it to be outside the framework of the Lima text to set forward an elaborated *ecclesiology* as the background for the evaluation of baptism, eucharist and ministry, we are glad to notice that the idea of the general priesthood is a basic element in the ecclesiology of the document. This appears clearly in the central places of the document where ideas such as the church as the people of God, the message of Jesus on the kingdom, and the manifold gifts of the Holy Spirit are underlined. This is seen especially in the section on ministry (§§1–6, 17 and 23), but also in the sections on baptism (§§8–10) and the eucharist (§§24–26). We appreciate that this ecclesiological understanding inherent in the text is thought of in dynamic mission categories, with the *imitatio Christo*-concept clearly underlined with reference to the individual in the fellowship. In our tradition this understanding of the church has always been the framework and basis for the view on baptism, eucharist as well as ministry.

We regret that we have not been able to find a similar equality between the text and our tradition concerning *the understanding of unity*. The essence of the understanding of unity set forth in the document is the idea that unity

---

• 6,400 members, 44 congregations, 39 pastors.

finds its complete expression only through the common sharing in the eucharist by the people of God (Eucharist, §19), and that this goal is attained only through the ordained ministry of the church, the priesthood (Ministry §§14 and 22). In our tradition unity has never been founded primarily on baptism, eucharist or ministry, but on faith in Christ and on the fellowship of the Holy Spirit. A mutual recognition of baptism, eucharist and ministry(es) is not a condition of unity, but a joyful recognition of it. Baptism *may* be a sign of and a means to unity (Baptism §15) just as the eucharist *may* reveal and create unity (Eucharist §19). Yet in themselves these acts are not the foundation of unity. We are convinced, however, that the continued study by the churches of the document *may* cause the unity given through faith in the death and resurrection of Christ to become an external reality — even with regard to the understanding of baptism, eucharist and ministry.

Against this background we feel able to answer the questions of the Faith and Order Commission thus:

— We recognize in the document "the faith of the Church throughout the ages" though we find this expression more a description of the creative power of the ecclesiastical tradition than the norm of confession which alone can be found in the canonical scriptures.

— We receive the document as an enriching and on several points correcting perspective for our own Christian tradition.

— We ask the Faith and Order Commission to work continually on these questions just as we ourselves, when requested, will give our share in such a process. The following commentaries are to be seen as our first contribution to this work.

Baptism

Throughout the later decades our view on baptism has become more comprehensive than was earlier the case. In the chapters of the text on the institution of baptism (§1), the meaning of baptism (§§2–7) and the inner relation between faith and baptism (§§8–10) we thus find the theology on baptism which we today try to expound in the preaching and teaching of our churches.

It is a special pleasure for us to notice the richness of images by which the importance of baptism is presented and evaluated. We recognize (at the beginning of §8) one of the classical formulations by Baptists describing the mutual relation between faith and baptism. Finally we notice that the teaching of our tradition is expressed in the saying of the text concerning "a life-long growth into Christ", "a continuing struggle" and "a continuing experience of grace" (§9), and the statement on "the ethical implications of baptism" (§10).

To us already these paragraphs (§§6 and 7) give rise to two problems which are expounded later on. (We shall deal with them in more detail below.) Both of these problems arise out of the application of the expounded theology on baptism (§§1–10) on the two different modes of baptism (§§11–13) as "equivalent alternatives" (§12, comm.):

a) In §6 the text speaks of "our *common* baptism" as "a basic bond of unity". However, already in the commentary to §6 the problems regarding the *practice* of baptism are foreseen (§§11–16) when the concern is about "reconquering the unity of baptism" — a theme which is also hinted at at the end of §6 which talks about "the one baptism" which all ought to understand as "a call to the churches to overcome their divisions . . ." (see point 1 below).

b) Paragraph 7 states that "baptism initiates the reality of the new life". This raises for us — with reference to the above-mentioned lack of clarity in §6 — the question whether this may prove tenable when baptism later on is viewed under both modes (see point 2 below).

The chapter on baptismal practice (§§11–16) makes us comment on three aspects of the offered text:

1. As Baptists we appreciate the statement of the text that "baptism upon personal profession of faith is the most clearly attested pattern in the New Testament documents" (§11). Although "the possibility that infant baptism was also practised in the apostolic age cannot be excluded" (§11), serious problems arise still for many Baptists when the document applies the indeed excellent theology on baptism (§§1–10) equally to both modes of baptism, and calls them "equivalent alternatives". To our minds there are still *theological* difficulties involved in maintaining that the church has one baptism in two different forms that are on the same level. Underlining this difficulty we frankly admit that the greatest challenge to us is precisely here. However, the treatment of the problem by the document is not convincing to us.

2. Seen in this perspective we consequently have problems with §13 which says that "baptism is an unrepeatable act". We agree in principle as we too see baptism as primarily a "gift of God" (§8). However, problems arise when "the human response to that gift" (§8) is totally missing. We find ourselves in a cultural and ecclesiastical situation where the Evangelical Lutheran Church as a folk church practises infant baptism "often in an apparently indiscriminate way" (§21, Comm. b), so that this act of baptism cannot be conceived of as a genuine "sign of new life through Jesus Christ" (§2), nor leads the baptized person into "the reality of the new life given in the midst of the present world" (§7). On this background we find good reason to ask: On which grounds ought it to be regarded as a mistake to baptize a person who comes to the Baptist church from an entirely secular background and here becomes a personal Christian by being confronted with the preaching of the gospel, and as a consequence of this hears the call to receive the gift of salvation through believers' baptism — even if the person concerned has been baptized as an infant for merely conventional reasons? On the other hand, we

are happy to know that God uses those churches who baptize believers as well
as those baptizing infants as signs of the kingdom in this world (§7). Where a
positive consequence of a baptismal act is clearly seen we find a growing will
expressed among Danish Baptists also to overcome the problem of re-
baptism.

3. The emphasis on baptism as an act of worship is essential to us (§§12
and 23). We regard it furthermore as an important dimension to insist on the
proleptic character of baptism — the experience of baptism as a "new ethical
orientation under the guidance of the Holy Spirit" (§4). It is essential to us to
underline the doubleness of viewing baptism as a gift of God to the individual
receiving this gift in faith as well as viewing the baptized person as a
gift of God to the church. Carried out in a proper way baptism is thus to be
seen as an addition of "new life" to the one baptized as well as to the
church.

Eucharist

We are glad to let our view of the eucharist be challenged by the theology of
the text. This applies both to the description of the connections which
constitute the biblical background for the institution of Jesus at the eucharist
(§1), as well as the description of the perspectives in which the eucharist is
described (§§2–26). We meet in both parts a theology and a proclamation
which may enrich the celebration of the eucharist in our tradition immensely.
Many of the views brought forward are felt as new and challenging at the
same time as they are in accordance with the biblical witness about the
eucharist.

We want, however, to point to three problematic themes for us in the stated
text on the eucharist — three aspects of the theology and practice of the
eucharist which ought to be more thoroughly scrutinized in the continuing
dialogue.

1. The first difficulty is that the eucharistic act is described by a series of
concepts which are simply seen as synonyms (§1) and, as we see them, they are
not precisely defined. While some of these concepts are regarded as the
eucharistic act being one detail of the worship service (e.g. "the breaking of
bread"), others point at the eucharistic service as a total worship service (e.g.
"the mass"). In connection with this ambiguous language we find it necessary
to ask whether a worship service of the church not including the eucharist
("the breaking of bread") is a true and whole church service according to the
document (e.g. Matt. 18:20). The same question arises with even greater force
when it is said of the eucharist that "its celebration continues as the *central* act
of the Church's worship" (§1), and when it is pointed out later on that
"Christ's mode of presence in the eucharist is unique" (§13). In the spirit of
the Lima terminology we want to assess that — in our tradition — it is the
word, Christ, who is *the* sacrament, and that the elements of the worship

service are to be subordinated to this. The primary and central act among these is the preaching of the gospel.

2. The text on the eucharist contains furthermore a series of sayings on the connection between baptism and eucharist. In this context some remarks are given on children's participation in the eucharist. It is thus taken for granted (§2) that the promise of Christ in the eucharist is limited to those who are baptized (". . . each baptized member of the body of Christ receives in the eucharist . . ."). This is a saying which resumes the thoughts from the chapter on baptism (§14, Comm. b), and which is carried on in the chapter on the eucharist (§19, Comm.). Here it is described as a matter of discussion, but in the text itself it is not commented on. In our tradition, where we have emphasized the role of faith more than the text seems apt to do, it is possible to invite all believers — whether baptized or not — to the table of our Lord. In this way the problem about communion across confessional limits has a preliminary solution when we invite all Christians who confess Jesus Christ as their Lord to the Lord's Table. In our tradition the hints of the text give rise to a further question concerning the participation of unbaptized children from Christian homes. It is to us questionable whether the New Testament makes it possible to claim that any Christian was baptized although it has been the normal practice. Furthermore it is questionable whether the character of the eucharist as communion (§19) has not naturally included (unbaptized) children of Christian parents.

3. Taking about the relation between the ordained ministry and the presiding at the table the text reflects a position foreign to us. Having regarded the local church as an authentic manifestation of the one universal church, we have always seen it as the privilege of the local church to be free to celebrate the eucharist with a servant properly called from the midst of the church as presiding officer. Most frequently the eucharist is conducted by a minister who has received ordination in our denomination, but we have in principle no theological hesitations to communion conducted by lay members who are called as described above. Another aspect of this complex of problems will appear in our commentary to the chapter on ministry.

Ministry

Danish Baptists are glad to be able to endorse the confession of the text to God who "calls the whole of humanity to become God's people", to "Christ's victory over the powers of evil and death" as the basis of the church, and to the Holy Spirit by whose "liberating and renewing power" the church lives (§§1–3). And we feel ourselves completely in accordance with the assertion of the text concerning the calling of the church:

— that it is "called to proclaim and prefigure the Kingdom of God . . . by announcing the Gospel to the world, and by its very existence as the body of Christ";

— that this calling comprises "all members of the Church (who are) called to confess their faith and to give account of their hope"; and
— that the gifts of the Holy Spirit are given to the "Church", because "all members are called to discover, with the help of the community, the gifts they have received, and to use them for the building up of the Church and for the service of the world to which the Church is sent" (§§4–6).

In spite of our fundamental adherence to these thoughts who comprise the calling of God's people in its totality — that is, the ordained as well as those not ordained — we find ourselves faced with an essential weakness of the text as it does not deal with and unfold the concept of ministry "in its broadest sense" (§7b) to a larger degree.

The following commentaries are mainly to be viewed in the light of this criticism.

1. The tradition of the Baptist church is congregational, and this tradition decides our understanding of the "ministry in its broadest sense" as well as "the ordained ministry". It is the whole church, the body of Christ, which is rendering the royal and priestly ministry of Christ. On this background we cannot easily see "the ordained ministry" as "constitutive for the life and witness of the Church" (§8) on a higher level than other gifts given by the Holy Spirit to the church to equip it for witness and service. And we are not able to conceive of any ministry — ordained or not — as a "focus of its unity", that is, the unity of the church (§8). We find this focus alone in Christ. In the background of our tradition we find that there is a need of a far more thoroughgoing discussion of what it means, that "any member of the body may share in proclaiming and teaching the Word of God, and may contribute to the sacramental life of that body" (§13, Comm.).

We think first and foremost of the celebration of the eucharist. Because "it is Christ who invites to the meal and who presides at it" (§14), we cannot exclude any member of the body of Christ from fulfilling this function "in a representative way" (§13, Comm.). Even if it is common practice that it is an ordained minister who presides at the table because the church has confirmed its choice of her/him through its act of ordination, this does not exclude the church from choosing one who is not ordained for this ministry. We are aware that this practice raises two questions by the Baptist Church itself:

a) How is it guaranteed that this function proves to be representative, and does not become casual?

b) What consequenses does this practice have for our understanding of ordination?

When this is said we can adhere to the understanding of the text about the necessity of the ordained ministry as expressed in §12, and its functions as expressed in §13.

2. In principle we as Baptists in Denmark have no aversion to the ordination of women for ministry. Theoretically we have full equality on this point even if this equality has found expression only in later years. It is,

however, remarkable to us that the text gives so little consideration to the ordination of women. Furthermore the document reveals a strange ambiguity. The question of the service of women in the church is placed in the very centre of the Christian faith, that is in Christology. To this it can be added that the text finds reasons in scriptures for the equality of women and men in service of the church (§18). On the background of this exceedingly central position of the theme of theology we must regard the conclusion of the document concerning the practice of the churches and its recommendations to the churches as something of an anti-climax (§18).

3. As has been said earlier we find the unity of the church in Christ, and we consider it the task of the church to discover and realize that unity given by faith in Jesus Christ through the guidance of the Holy Spirit. We acknowledge in this connection the need of a ministry of *episkopé* which serves "the continuity and unity in the Church" (§29) as well as of a "pastoral ministry" which serves the "local eucharistic community" (§30), and the need of "a ministry of love within the community" (§31). We hesitate, however, at the "threefold ministry" with bishop, presbyter and deacon as "an expression of the unity we seek and also as a means for achieving it" (§22). It ought to be so, even with regard to the ordained ministries, that the church still seeks "relevant forms of witness and service in each situation" (§4). Furthermore we notice that the text itself declares that the "threefold pattern stands in need of reform" (§24).

4. We welcome that the question of the apostolic succession of ministry is conceived in the text in the light of the continuity of the whole church with the apostles and their preaching. In this connection we understand the apostolicity of the church as its continual faithfulness to the prevailing signs of the apostolic church (§34).

5. The ordination, accompanied by the laying on of hands and prayer for the gifts of the Holy Spirit, is regarded by us as "an act of the whole community" (§41) in the radical sense that even church members, who are not ordained, take part in the laying on of hands together with ordained ministers representing sister churches and the denomination and "by intention, the Church universal" (§42). This understanding is also expressed in our practice of ordination. It always takes place at a eucharistic service in *the local* church where the ministry shall be carried out in the days ahead. We may add that we conceive of the ordination in a similar way as the document (§§42–44) as to the believing invocation of the church for the equipment of the minister to undertake a service in the church as "the servant of the servants".

Concluding remark

A Danish writer talks in an aphorism about "stumbling in one's own horizon". This experience has often been made by the churches — also by us belonging to the Danish Baptist Union. We have received the Lima document as a help to avoid this concerning "Baptist, Eucharist and Ministry". And we will continually endeavour that this document is received within our denomination on as many levels as possible.

November 1985

Jens Christensen
Peter Grarup
Bent Hylleberg

COVENANTED BAPTIST CHURCHES IN WALES

The following is a summary of the main recommendations of the Committee of the Covenanted Baptist Churches in Wales arising from a recent comprehensive study of matters of faith and practice in the context of the Covenant.

It is based primarily upon the World Council of Churches' recent report on doctrine but also takes into account several reports of the Commission of the Covenanted Churches in Wales, including "Principles of Visible Unity".

Our response is addressed to the Commission and our proposals are to be seen as part of our covenanted commitment. Copies are, however, being sent to other bodies concerned with the unity of Christ's church.

The background to our recommendations, providing the context in which they should be received and understood, is contained in the fuller document "The Response of the Covenanted Baptist Churches in Wales to 'Baptism, Eucharist and Ministry' and Other Reports".

There we have tried to explain at some length our readiness to reconsider cherished Baptist principles in the light of the Covenant but our genuine difficulties in so doing. We hope in this way to encourage our fellow covenanters to consider afresh particular points in their own several traditions. At the same time we hope that mutual trust will encourage us to explore together possible ways to grow closer to each other in the unity we seek in Christ and to which we have all committed ourselves in the spirit of the covenant.

The theme of the recommendations

The core of our recommendations is that there should be *a norm which allows for variation in controlled experiment*. We believe that this can show that broad agreement has been reached on a number of important matters

---

● 2,000 members, 13 congregations, 13 pastors.

but that we have mutual trust in exploring areas where subservience to too fast a rule would stifle the freedom of the Holy Spirit to guide us together into a fuller understanding of the truth.

Baptism

1. We accept that *the norm* should be that baptism is seen as unrepeatable. We also undertake for the future — whatever may have been the practice in the past in "open-membership" churches — only to receive as new members (as distinct from those transferring from other churches) those who are baptized. By the same token, we wish to stress that there should be no "reconfirmation" of those who, already full members of one of the Covenanted churches, may apply to join another in the Covenant. To us *mutual recognition of membership is explicit.*

2. We invite further study as to practical ways in which a proper doctrine of Christian conscience can be shown to be compatible with the corporate discipline of the constitution of the Christian fellowship, so that the norm of "no re-baptism" allows for the baptism of a believer where a corporate judgment of the circumstances deems this to be right and proper. To support such study we undertake, and invite others to undertake, not to practise baptism indiscriminately, and to have particular regard for the consciences of those whose views concerning baptism are at variance to one's own.

Eucharist

1. We suggest that we take a closer look together at the principle of a presidency authorized by the church, to include all such safeguards that are necessary to ensure that the celebration of communion is properly conducted, notwithstanding the need also to examine other matters under the heading of ministry.

2. We invite a further examination of the reasons behind the current agreement in "The Holy Communion" (Green Book) that "the service should be presided over by an ordained minister of one of the Covenanted Churches. At the point of Thanksgiving and Communion such presidency should be shared by ordained ministers representing the several denominations present." Is this latter point an unnecessarily ultra-cautious safeguard in the context of the Covenant, as if to imply that without the specific involvement of ordained ministers of *all* denominations present the service is defective?

Ministry

1. We accept that the historical succession (though not of necessity the "apostolic" succession) of ordained ministry is for the good of the church. We will work towards greater clarity in the meaning and practice of ordination, observing that as a norm an ordained minister should preside at the eucharist, provided that under certain circumstances, to be worked out together, lay persons may be authorized by the church to preside.

2. We recommend that further discussion take place on "the three-tier concept" of ministry, taking full account of the points raised in recent reports ("Baptism, Eucharist and Ministry", "Principles of Visible Unity", "Report of the Anglican/Reformed International Commission 1984", etc). We believe that more consideration should be given to the role of elders, lay preachers/pastors/readers, a lay diaconate and the ordination of women. In particular, we feel that we should try to evolve a scheme of authorized ministry that is particularly suited to the unique needs of the mission of the church within Wales in the foreseeable future.

Conclusion

Our concluding contribution to this discussion, as an initial response to current questions relating to baptism, eucharist and ministry, underlines the two themes that have run through all the sections discussed in more detail in our full report.

1. We invite our fellow Christians within the Covenant to act with us in faith concerning the future and to be prepared *to experiment* in mutual trust and integrity to discover together new experiences of the grace of God. We appeal to others as we urge upon ourselves to look forward to where God is leading us, approaching our task "with openness to the Spirit" as we have already pledged ourselves to do in vows made solemnly to God, declaring that "we believe that God will guide his Church into ways to truth and peace, correcting, strengthening, and renewing it in accordance with the mind of Christ".

2. Because we recognize that our proneness to fallibility needs a steadying, controlling hand, we commend to those responsible for drawing up tentative agreements the concept of *the norm* which, whilst allowing for flexibility, makes clear those things which history has demonstrated to be of abiding benefit to ongoing generations of the people of God, thus providing a check against excessive zeal that may offend the conscience of others.

Above all, we continue in our pledge to work and pray for that unity which is Christ's will for us.

October 1984   The Committee

AMERICAN BAPTIST
CHURCHES IN THE USA

Preamble*

The American Baptist Churches in the USA is a covenanted fellowship of churches, united by a common confession of Jesus Christ as Lord and Saviour according to the scriptures, and committed to nurture, mission and service. This fellowship is rooted in the gospel freedom of each American Baptist congregation to follow Christ, the living word, as Christ is made known to each through the scriptures. The Bible is the sole rule of faith and practice, the Holy Spirit the guide and interpreter, and the local congregation of believers the fundamental community of confession for members of churches affiliated with the American Baptist Churches in the USA. American Baptists freely covenant together to seek the mind of Christ, and thus to seek correction and counsel of each other; to manifest the love of Christ, and thus to unite for mission and evangelism; and to share the fellowship of Christ, and thus to uphold and support each other.

The leaders and representative bodies of the American Baptist Churches in the USA speak for American Baptists and to American Baptists, subject always to the discernment and consent of each of the congregations. As members of the General Board of the American Baptist Churches in the USA, we respond to the document "Baptism, Eucharist and Ministry" (BEM) in this spirit. We are grateful for the opportunity to express the faith as it is commonly understood among us and to affirm our oneness in Christ with other Christians; yet we are mindful that we may not and do not seek to bind the heart or conscience of any among us. Our response has no authority to commit our churches: its authority consists in the extent to which it speaks authentically for them and is received and affirmed by them.

- 1,616,992 members, 5,814 congregations USA, 8,618 congregations overseas, 6,780 pastors (USA), 12,493 church workers overseas.
- * Key biblical texts: John 17, Ephesians 4, Acts 2 and 1 Corinthians 12.

We are grateful for the long labours of the Faith and Order Commission of the World Council of Churches (WCC) over the church-dividing issues of baptism, eucharist and ministry. We give thanks to God for the "Baptism, Eucharist and Ministry" document — for the cooperation and dialogue among Christians that made it possible, for the extensive biblical study and the insights which are represented in it, for the way in which many historical confusions and divisions among Christians are addressed in it. We commit ourselves to encourage the study of BEM among our churches and to support the long-standing American Baptist commitment to Christian unity. We further affirm that study of the document may be an occasion of growth and reformation for us as Baptists. We learn how our own tradition may be enhanced by the insights of other Christians. We better understand our own convictions by an appreciation of the contrasts with other traditions which remain. Discussion of BEM among us can play an important role in our own dialogue concerning the observance or practice of baptism and the Lord's Supper, and the conduct of ministry in our churches.

As American Baptists, we share a vision of Christian unity, not Christian uniformity. We find a personal confession of faith in Jesus Christ as Lord and Saviour to be sufficient basis for our life together. We also experience discipleship — the practice of evangelism, the struggle for justice, the bearing of each other's burdens — as an essential key to our oneness in Christ. Thus a rich and faithful pluralism is affirmed by both the unity that we experience as American Baptists and the unity among all Christians which we recognize as given in Christ and for which we long. In our communion we find represented a pluralism not only of races and cultures, but also of various Christian traditions and various forms of Christian confession — through united, yoked, and dually aligned congregations. We confess that we do not experience the full unity of Christ, and our diversity often divides and separates us from each other. We accept, however, the riches of our pluralism as a gift from God. We look forward with hope to a wider Christian unity which would multiply these riches and maintain the freedom of the Spirit's witness to Christ.

We would suggest that the ongoing work of Faith and Order in the WCC give special attention to the character of legitimate diversity. Even further, though it is understandable that in dealing with baptism, eucharist and ministry there is a tendency to stress the maintenance of structure and form, attention must be given as well to the transforming mission of the church, to the witness of the scriptures not only as the legitimizer of the church's structure but also as judge and prophet to the church.

We find that to make an authentic response to BEM we must at least partially reformulate some of the questions that have been posed to us. For instance, Baptists do not generally address BEM with the question of whether they recognize therein "the faith of the Church through the ages". Baptists more readily ask if the faith they find expressed in BEM is agreeable to the scriptures, than whether it has been held "everywhere, at all times, by all". What we express in this paper as the shared convictions of American Baptists represents our understanding of the scriptural witness. Also, Baptists tend to regard baptism, eucharist and ministry (ordination) each as rites which necessarily follow on a prior and inward response to divine initiative or grace. The responses to the three sections of the document which follow reflect this and other concerns that Baptists share.

Baptism

We wish to commend the affirmation in BEM that believer's baptism is the clear pattern of the New Testament, as well as the plain statements on the necessary relation between baptism and personal commitment and the significance of immersion (§§11,12 and 18). We are grateful for the many ways in which this section gives evidence that the broader Christian church has attended seriously to the believer's church understanding of baptism, and to the dangers of indiscriminate baptism. And accordingly, we acknowledge that the emphasis of other churches on the initiative and action of God, or on the community of faith as the most appropriate context for the administration of baptism *is* important for us so as to avoid an excessive and unbiblical individualization or privatization of our understanding of baptism.

Some Baptists among us accept only believer's baptism as fully valid and thus as a basis for church membership. Others view infant baptism and a later personal confession of faith as a sufficient basis for church membership. Thus, our own family already encompasses some who have adopted a view similar to that expressed in the document (§15), while still affirming believer's baptism and immersion as the full and biblical expression of baptism. Most American Baptists would agree with the document that the presentation/ dedication of infants and their reception into the care and community of the church are of great importance.

American Baptists, however, would have continuing difficulty with some aspects of the section on the practice of baptism. This is particularly true of §13, in which it is stated that any practice "which might be interpreted as 'rebaptism' must be avoided". American Baptists certainly wish to avoid unnecessary scandal or offence to their Christian sisters and brothers of other traditions. Though sometimes persecuted as "rebaptizers", Baptists have never so understood themselves. Yet American Baptists have been—and largely still are—unwilling to commit themselves to deny the ordinance of baptism to those who may in all sincerity seek it in accordance with the biblical practice of combining personal confession of faith with the experience of baptism.

We greet with pleasure the exposition of the meaning of baptism in BEM, noting the rich variety of biblical images and sources which are used as the basis for interpretation. We commend this section particularly to American Baptists for their study and consideration, as a way of deepening our own appreciation of the nature and meaning of baptism as the "sign of new life through Jesus Christ" (§2). One reservation that many Baptists would express about this section concerns §4, which seems to come very close to implying that an ethical cleansing of the person baptized is effected by the baptism itself. As indicated above, Baptists stress that salvation and grace come through Christ and not through any ordinance or observance in itself.

Eucharist

"The Lord's Supper" is the most common designation among us for what BEM and most Christians call the "eucharist". We recognize the biblical validity of understanding this meal in terms of thanksgiving. At its institution Jesus gave thanks, broke the bread and poured the wine. Nevertheless Baptists have preferred this title, stressing that the table is not the church's table, but the Lord's Table, and also stressing Jesus's words: "Do this in remembrance of me". We believe that this is also completely consistent with the centrality which BEM gives to *anamnesis* (remembrance or memorial) in understanding this celebration.

We are grateful for the rich exposition of the meanings of the Lord's Supper which are given in BEM. *Anamnesis* or "memorial" has been a central aspect of Baptist understanding of the Supper, and we affirm the central place it has in the document. We acknowledge that BEM offers us the opportunity to deepen our understanding of this "memorial", to escape from a very "thin" notion of "remembrance", and to appreciate anew the way in which this commemoration draws us into deeper communion with God and is the occasion for Christ to be truly present.

Other challenging meanings of the Supper are set forth in the document under the headings "thanksgiving", "invocation of the Spirit", "communion of the faithful", and "meal of the kingdom". We immediately perceive some of these as illuminating for our faith, while we consider the remainder to be items for our later study. We particularly appreciate the manner in which the section on "the eucharist as thanksgiving to the Father" deals with many of the long-standing and painful divisions among Christians over the idea of "sacrifice" in connection with the Lord's Supper. Again, as Baptists, we stress the sole sufficiency of Christ's sacrifice, and we affirm the manner in which this section lifts up the Supper as a "proclamation and celebration of the work of God" (§3).

Most Baptists would have reservations about the suggestion that Christians receive "the gift of salvation" through communion (§2), or that the eucharist "transforms Christians into the image of Christ" (§26). One of the reasons that Baptists have tended to avoid the terminology of "sacrament" is that they have wished to avoid any suggestion that rites in themselves convey grace, while at the same time affirming that they may be occasions and means of grace (though not of salvation). Thus, a "sacrament" does not transform us, but the grace of God does.

We affirm the understanding of the Lord's Supper as an occasion for the fellowship of the whole people of God. We also affirm the understanding of the Lord's Supper as a sign of God's rule, an eschatological sign, which nourishes the church for its mission journey. We recognize the pain and the scandal that at such a table we should be divided from each other by race, culture, language, and class as well as by our various traditions. Acknowledging our own sin in this matter, we believe that this concern should be part of the continuing exploration of the Supper's meaning.

As American Baptists, we find our celebration of the Lord's Supper usually to be open. The invitation to the table most often is extended to all who are believers in Christ, though this is not the universal practice among us. In our relation to other Christian churches, we find that this table, which for most of us is the easiest thing to open to other Christians, is for many in other traditions the hardest to open to us. We respect the convictions of other traditions, but welcome the BEM document as a significant movement towards reconciliation and fuller fellowship.

The treatment of the celebration of the Lord's Supper in BEM offers much out of Christian traditions other than our own which may be of significant value for Baptists as well. We affirm the positive statement on liturgical diversity (§28) since among us there is no settled or normative form for the celebration of the Lord's Supper. The scriptural words of institution would be common to us all; indeed many of the elements outlined in the document (§27) would be found in our services. Study of BEM may encourage our congregations to enrich their celebrations. We stress both a simplicity in our observance and an avoidance of extensive or standardized forms that would "routinize" the celebration. Although many Baptists would be sympathetic to the statement that the Lord's Supper should be celebrated frequently (§30), most would not be ready to affirm that this must mean weekly (§31). We recognize, however, that we need to retain a sense of the Supper as a crucial part of our worship. Many of our churches identify the service of prayer, testimony and confession of sin as preparation for the Sunday service of communion. Others are liable to the peril of making the Supper appear to be either an "add on" or marginal part of the church's life.

Ministry

We affirm the point of departure in BEM for the discussion of ministry: the calling of the whole people of God. Numbering ourselves among those Christian traditions which have wished to realize the priesthood of all believers, we are grateful for the acknowledgment that all of the people of God are called to ministry. The document puts such emphasis upon the ministry of the ordained, however, that the ministry of the laity (both in unordained church ministries and in secular vocations) is nearly obscured.

As Baptists, we affirm that some are called by God to the gospel or pastoral ministry. This call to individuals, from God, "to equip the saints for the work of the ministry", is recognized and affirmed by the church and the person is set apart by ordination for this ministry. Yet we further believe that the church is never without gifts that God provides for its life, and that there is no function which is exclusively reserved to the ordained clergy, in the sense that lay persons at the call of the church could not perform these ministries as the church has need. This does not mean that the ordained ministry is peripheral or without authority, but only that the ordained ministry is called into the service of the church.

In the document we do not find sufficient recognition of the importance of the call to ministry. Baptists see a dynamic between God's calling and gifting of ministers for the life of the church and the church's discerning of this call and recognizing it. A similar dynamic exists between God's call of all believers into a "ministry of reconciliation" whose concrete form they must discern with the help of the church. To this ministry we are all ordained.

Among American Baptists, women are being called in increasing numbers to all of the church's ministries. Their calls from God are recognized by churches, their gifts for ministry are confirmed by the fruits of their service. We cannot claim that full equality for women is a reality in our denominational life. Nevertheless, we are experiencing the full ministry of women (i.e. at every level) as a matter of recognizing God's liberty, and our mutuality and equality in Christ, and not as something that is optional or indifferent for the church as a whole or for its ministry. The whole of our life in Christ is impoverished when women's gifts are denied or marginalized as they are in BEM's treatment of women's ordination.

We appreciate the discussion of the threefold ministry in BEM, particularly the acknowledgment that the Bible provides no single blueprint for ministry (§19) and that the apostolic faith and the "episcopal" ministry have been preserved in churches like our own which have no historic episcopate or apostolic succession (§37). We are equally appreciative of the understanding of apostolic tradition which is expressed here (§34).

In regard to the recognition of ministries, it is rare among American Baptists to find anyone barred from our pulpits because of denominational affiliation, the character of ordination or lack of ordination. Likewise, our attitude towards another tradition's celebration of the Lord's Supper or practice of baptism does not turn upon the character of the officiant's ecclesiastical status. Where there are difficulties in these matters, as also for instance in the acceptance of those ordained in other traditions into our own ministry, they are related to issues other than the form and understanding of ministry discussed in BEM.

Closing statement of commitment and celebration

We affirm our readiness to cooperate with and to recognize as our Christian sisters and brothers all who confess Jesus Christ as Lord and Saviour according to the scriptures. As we respond voluntarily to the one

Christ, we find ourselves knit together with other believers in worship, discipleship and service. We celebrate the unity we now share and long for it to become more nearly complete and whole.

We give thanks for the occasion of reflection on "Baptism, Eucharist and Ministry" and commit ourselves to continue this process of reflection and reception. We express our appreciation for the process pertaining to BEM, one in which various traditions, cultures and contexts are heard and valued.

We will seek to learn from the document. We will explore ways in which the document can serve as an instrument of dialogue with other churches involved in the same process, and lead to new levels of unity and agreement among us. We affirm our continuing search to understand our own witness within the context of the whole Christian family — to listen, to speak, and to grow ever closer to the fullness and the unity of oneness in Christ.

June 1985   General Board

CHRISTIAN CHURCH
(DISCIPLES OF CHRIST) IN CANADA

The document "Baptism, Eucharist, and Ministry" presents to us a wide-ranging statement of the faith of the church. The Christian Church (Disciples of Christ) in Canada has followed a process of study and discussion in relation to the questions asked of us by the Faith and Order Commission of the World Council of Churches, within the introduction to the document. We wish to commend the Faith and Order Commission for bringing these issues to us. The discussions we have had have led us to respond positively to the tone and intent of the document. Though we accept this document as an expression of the faith of the ages, we find it continues to challenge us in a number of areas. In that light, we offer the following comments about the content of the document for future consideration by the World Council of Churches and the churches involved in their further discussion.

Baptism

Comments

This is perhaps the best ecumenical statement that has been produced in portraying a very full meaning to the act.

We appreciate the emphasis placed by the document upon the practice of believer's baptism, and the implications of the symbolism of immersion, upon the meaning of baptism.

The text assumes that all practices of baptism equally convey all the meanings of baptism, as outlined. We might allow that infant baptism portrays some meanings (e.g. II.5 and 7), but we wonder how it can convey others (e.g., II.3 and 4)?

We do not consciously practise or promote re-baptism, but recognize that other traditions regard us as having rebaptized their members on certain occasions. This may cause us to be more careful in our pastoral counselling of

---

• 4,000 members, 30 parishes, 23 pastors.

persons transferring membership to our congregations, but since we hold individual conscience and the free expression of faith to be above the prescriptions of church discipline, we cannot forbid it. We do it only for pastoral reasons, and not just to satisfy any membership requirements. (Each of our congregations determines its own membership policies; in recent years, there have been an increasing number practising open or inclusive membership with immersion not a requirement when transferring from another denomination. This is now the policy of over half our congregations.)

Challenges

The baptism section confronts us in the area which some would call indiscriminate baptism. We also find ourselves called to do more work on the nurture of those newly baptized. Some of us are further challenged to be more understanding of the baptismal practices of other churches recognizing this document. Further, we recognize the possibility that changes in our liturgies of baptism, and the increased use of other symbols, may enrich our celebration of baptism.

Eucharist

Comments

We are excited by the preference given to at least weekly celebration of the eucharist (though we call it communion, or the Lord's Supper).

We have not been a liturgical church in the sense of the fuller ritual recommended in the text. We believe that a very simple liturgy, based on one or two of the models in the New Testament, (1 Corinthians or one of the synoptics) is sufficient for most services. We have been known to use longer (in terms of the BEM text: fuller) liturgies on occasion, to enrich our worship.

We welcome the implications of unity around the eucharist. It is an expression of God's will for the world and solidarity with all for whom Christ died. Unity at the table has always been our position and our practice. We also appreciate the ethical connections made in the text.

Although the text says that Christ's presidency at the table is signified by an ordained minister in most churches, we would say that it could equally be signified by a lay person. The thought that the person presiding should signify the wider church (and not just that particular worshipping community) is one we might consider further. Could not this be signified by having both lay persons and ordained ministers assisting one another in the prayers at the table and announcing the words of institution?

Challenges

The section of the document on eucharist calls on us to do more explanation of the theological significance of the eucharist, especially since it is historically the central part of our worship. The format and suggested makeup of a eucharistic celebration challenge us to a more expanded and deliberate celebration. We might consider inclusion of liturgy which is not historically part of Disciple tradition, such as the assurance of pardon, the exchange of the sign of peace, and other similar liturgical practices. The connection of the celebration of the eucharist with issues of our witness provides us with opportunities for increased education about the eucharist.

Ministry

Comments

As represented in our practice of laity presiding at the eucharist (normally an elected or "ordained" elder), we feel the text does not develop fully the ministry of the laity and what implications this truth has for the ministry of the church.

Though its omission in the document may be understandable, because of the position of many large communions, we wholeheartedly endorse and encourage the equal role of women as ordained ministers in the church. We see this as an issue of the reconciling message of the gospel. The paragraph commentary for §17 suggests that the priest is the representative, not only of Christ, but also of the whole community. The question then becomes "how can the whole community be adequately represented by only half of humankind?"

We see no current formulation of the office of bishop as being adequate, and therefore suggest further consideration and study of the episcope and the office of bishop.

We uphold the need for mutual recognition of ministry, as recommended in the text.

Challenges

The ministry section provides the most challenge to our tradition of congregational autonomy. The issues of authority need to be discussed, especially in relation to the ministry, but also in their connection to baptism and eucharist. The threefold expression of ordained ministry also challenges us to consider our historical tendencies in comparison to the other parts of Christ's church. We within our church need to do further examination and clarification of the meaning of ordination and the *role* of the ordained minister, within our particular structure. The mention of apostolic succession calls upon us to consider how we might feel it to be exhibited within our part of the church.

Conclusion

We find within the text a fair representation of the faith of the apostolic church, yet we see further theological work necessary, particularly in the sections on baptism and ministry. The process of reception by the Christian

Church (Disciples of Christ) in Canada will involve first a further process of study to see what "Baptism, Eucharist, and Ministry" actually says. This will need to be followed by an educational process about where our tradition agrees and disagrees with BEM. Only after those processes would it be possible to envision us making any changes to further convergence within the church.

Original response by
Board of Directors 8–10 November 1985

Revised response by
All-Canada Committee
3 March 1986

UNION OF WELSH INDEPENDENTS

Preamble

As a communion of churches, each of which bears responsibility to the Lord Jesus Christ for its life and faith, the Congregationalists of Wales have no central body empowered to define a common standard of faith and practice. Fellowship between the individual churches is expressed through the medium of the Union of Welsh Independents. It is also the body which promotes common action. This response is the product of a working party, appointed by the assembly of the Union. The assembly has also endorsed the response. It will however be appreciated that the response, owing to the nature of our denominational structure, has sought to represent the views typically held by our congregations although individuals amongst us would exercise their legitimate liberty to dissent in detail from some of the points enunciated in the response. But we believe that the main thrust of our conclusions would meet with general approval in our churches.

Preface

It seems to us that the concept of "visible unity" is now being extended to include uniformity of practice. That restricts the discussion because the implication is that "visible unity" is inconsistent with variety. There is an ambivalence on pp. viii – ix where it is suggested on the one hand that unity leads to consensus on the matters discussed in the document, while on the other hand it is contended that consensus leads to visible unity. In any case, the preface in encouraging discussion makes it clear that the aim of the discussion is the promotion of "visible unity". In other words, the conclusion of the discussion has been stated before it has begun. We felt that if this was to be a truly ecumenical contribution, then we should seek to define our reaction to the Lima document as honestly as we could, and draw whatever conclusions our study imposed upon us.

- 60,000 members, 680 congregations, 18 associations, 160 pastors.

Baptism

We are happy to say that there is much in this section with which we find ourselves in agreement. On the general question of the proper recipients of baptism, we acknowledge both believers' baptism and the baptism of infants. We agree with §§3, 5, 8, 9, 10, 13, 16, 17, 18, 21, 22, 23.

We feel that the section in general is deficient in two respects.

a) We hold that God's word, as it is read and preached, takes precedence over the sacraments. The word of God is essential to salvation because it is through the preaching of it that faith is elicited (Rom. 10:8, 14). The document, insofar as it does not emphasize the primacy of the word, gives the impression that the administration of the sacraments is itself a means of salvation. It seems to suggest, for example, that the sacrament of baptism contains a special grace in addition to that received through the word. If it is the intention of the document to convey that impression, then we must express our dissent.

b) Although §1 mentions the New Covenant the remainder of the section makes no mention of the covenant of grace. This creates a real difficulty for us since our understanding of the practice of infant baptism is rooted in a covenant theology. As our *Service Book* (Llyfr Gwasanaeth) puts it, baptism "is a sign and seal of the Covenant of the blessed God's covenant of grace, which brings us into union with Christ and his people". For us this covenant was reaffirmed in the days of Abraham (Gen. 17:1–8) and finally sealed by Jesus Christ with his blood and so it became the New Covenant. It seems to us that the failure to make an adequate appreciation of the significance of the covenant of grace has led to serious weaknesses in §§11 and 12, as we shall explain.

Thus, we would accept §1, if the opening sentence read: "The basis of Christian baptism is the covenant of grace, as it was renewed in the ministry of . . ."

Paragraph 2: It is not sufficient to say that baptism is a "sign". It is also a "seal". Before we say that baptism symbolizes something about our spiritual life, we need to say that it a "seal" which God has affixed to believers to indicate to whom they belong. He seals us with the Holy Spirit to preserve us until the day of our redemption (2 Cor. 1:22; Eph. 1:13; 4:30).

Paragraph 4 is true of believers' baptism but it is not applicable as it stands to infant baptism. But what is remarkable about the paragraph is that it makes no mention of the word of God. Baptism cannot do two things named here apart from God's word — and that ought to be made clear.

Paragraph 6: The first part is acceptable, but the last two sentences are ambiguous. What is meant by saying, "when baptismal unity is realized in one holy, catholic, apostolic Church, a genuine Christian witness can be made to the healing and reconciling love of God"? There are two points: (a) Is it meant that consensus on the doctrine of baptism must lead to a particular, centralized form of church government? If so, the point should be argued rather than asserted. (b) There is no historical evidence that consensus on the doctrine of baptism has of itself led to the union of churches.

And what are the grounds for believing that "baptismal unity" will promote witness "to the healing and reconciling love of God"? Historically, it was precisely the belief that they possessed the true baptism, that enabled powerful churches to claim rights of compulsion over dissenting groups, even when those groups administered baptism in the same way and in the same words.

Paragraph 7: This is insufficient because it divorces baptism from the word.

Paragraph 11: Accepted, but with the information that we do not acknowledge godparents since their responsibilities are borne by the Christian congregation.

Paragraph 12: There seems to be a misunderstanding at this point. It has to do with the part played by faith in the baptism of infants. In the case of those outside the covenant of grace, i.e. unbelievers, baptism is conditional upon repentance and belief in Jesus Christ. In their case personal faith is essential. But infants are not baptised upon the basis of their personal faith. The supposition that they are leads to either (a) the teaching that parents or godparents exercise a surrogate on behalf of infants, or (b) the teaching mentioned in this paragraph that, in the case of infants, "the personal response will be offered at a later moment in life". But both possibilities involve divorcing the recipient's personal faith from the confessing of baptism. As we understand it, the relation between faith and baptism, in the case of infants, is different. They are *not* baptized on the basis of personal faith. The Christian faith of the parents is relevant not because they exercise it on behalf of their infants but because it secures for them the blessings of the covenant of grace. The child's personal faith does not enter into it any more than his name is a personal choice. Our *Service Book* says: "The blessings of the Gospel are not only for us who believe, but also to our children." The biblical basis for this assertion are clear and numerous as Deut. 5:2–3; Psalms 90:16; 102:28; 103:17–18; Isaiah 44:2–4; 59:21; 65:23; Heb. 11:9. And the remarks of Paul on the status of children whose mothers alone are Christians (1 Cor. 7: 13–14).

The apostle shows how the blessings of the covenant of grace are an influence for good upon the unbelieving husband, but especially upon the children, who are deemed holy, even though the father is an unbeliever. So we conclude that the role of baptism in the case of children is to set God's seal upon them as heirs of the promises. It is God's will that is signified by baptism. The children of course cannot inherit salvation and baptism does not show that they are saved. They inherit the *promises* about justification, forgiveness, salvation through faith in Jesus Christ and eternal life. They have been placed in the providence of God, in the situation which will be most advantageous to make that personal commitment of Christ, which is the exercise of personal faith.

A peculiar admonition in Commentary 14 says: "Those churches which baptize children but refuse them a share in the eucharist . . . may wish to ponder whether they have fully appreciated and accepted the consequences of baptism." The above exposition will show that it is precisely on the basis of our understanding of infant baptism that we do not admit them to the eucharist. It is on the basis of an attempt to apply the doctrine of adult baptism to infants without a fuller consideration of scripture principles that the question suggested in the Commentary is posed.

Paragraphs 14 and 19: The Holy Spirit is at work before baptism, in baptism and after baptism. As to additional rites Congregationalists would prefer to make their use a matter of Christian liberty, not to be governed by any general rule.

Eucharist

Our churches and ministers are not bound to a prescribed liturgical form in celebrating holy communion, although typical orders of service are to be found in our *Service Book*. In practice, therefore, there are some variations in the forms of liturgy adopted by our ministers, ranging from the use of the *Book of Common Order* to a bare re-enactment of the rite described in 1 Corinthians. These variations are tolerated as valid expression of Christian freedom and it would be considered an ungenerous development if it were argued that because we find it possible to appreciate a specific rite, we should be prepared to accept it as the only acceptable rite, or as the only valid rite. We are not happy about the search for uniformity in detail.

Because we hold this view, there is much in the section on the eucharist that we can applaud, and there is much also to which we would not make objection, if others find such elements spiritually helpful.

Even so, we take the classical Protestant view that the practice of our Lord at the Last Supper is definitive. And we believe that we should look critically at any accretions, no matter how suggestive or beautiful they may be, which derive from the later tradition of the church. Again, as regards the meaning of the eucharist, we are agreed that the theology of the NT and especially its teaching about the redemptive work of Christ should be respected.

We are able to welcome in the section the emphasis on communion as an act of thanksgiving and as the feast of the Christian community. No less welcome is the prominence given to the whole work of Christ in his incarnation, his crucifixion, his resurrection and his glorification. On the negative side, we approve of the omission of such terms as "transubstantiation", although the text continues to use a word like *epiklesis* which is a transcription of the Greek word.

In general, it is our feeling that the section shows a strong tendency to allow the conviction of the "Catholic" traditions to influence the analysis, without a sufficiently critical appraisal of their scriptural validity.

I. THE INSTITUTION OF THE EUCHARIST

1. We are in warm agreement with this summary but would make a minor change in the opening words of the second paragraph, thus: "proclaim and enact the nearness of the kingdom *and express its fellowship* . . . In his last meal, *this* fellowship . . ."

II. THE MEANING OF THE EUCHARIST

2. The second sentence ought to be made to read thus: "Every Christian receives this gift of Salvation through communion *by faith* in the body and blood of Christ."

A. The eucharist as thanksgiving to the Father

We accept this section.

B. The eucharist as anamnesis or memorial of Christ

While we subscribe to the assertions in §§5,6 and 7, we feel that the concept of *anamnesis* has been unduly extended. This is seen in the contrast between §8 and the commentary upon it. We welcome the emphasis in §8 on the once-for-all nature of our Lord's work for the salvation of the world. We would only wish to add, after the reference to Heb. 7:25, the sentence: "Here we have an insight into the priesthood and mission of the whole family of believers."

In the Commentary on §8, however, it is suggested "the Eucharist as intercession" can justify thinking of it as a "propitiatory sacrifice". The next sentence seems to suggest (although it is not made explicit) that Christ's sacrifice is a unique, unrepeatable "expiation", while the eucharist (as intercession) may be thought of as a repeatable propitiatory sacrifice. We agree heartily that justice cannot be done to the eucharist without speaking of it in its connection with Christ's atoning sacrifice on the cross. And one cannot do that without a doctrine that emphasizes that our Lord satisfied the demands of the Father's love and righteousness. In other words there was in Christ's unique and unrepeatable sacrifice an element of propitiation as well as of expiation. We cannot therefore ascribe the latter element to the work of Christ on the cross and understand the former element as an alternative way of saying "intercession".

As regards Christ's unique and finished sacrifice, we cannot supplement it or re-enact it by means of the eucharist. The eucharist represents (but does not re-present!) that one unique sacrifice on Calvary. As Hebrews empha-sizes, Christ entered the heavenly tabernacle, bearing the blood of his own sacrifice. There he intercedes for us. It is the intercession that continues, not the sacrifice (Heb. 10). It is the blessed consequences of that one offering that are effective through his intercession. So the believers exercise their joint priesthood as they unite their own intercession with those of the great High

Priest who presented his one sufficient sacrifice at his ascension and for ever intercedes on the basis of that sacrifice.

For this reason, after careful consideration, we find ourselves unable to speak of the eucharist as a "propitiatory sacrifice". It can only be spoken of as a "sacrifice of praise" and that is a metaphor.

We accept §§9, 10, 11. And §12 also, except that the inclusion of the word "properly" seems to suggest that the eucharist can dispense with the "proclamation of the Word". This prompts us to observe that the whole section on the eucharist should have a stronger and more explicit emphasis on the crucial role of the preaching of the word in association with the sacrament. To us it is an essential accompaniment, not a disposable addition.

The Commentary on §13 raises a fundamental question about the enterprise of which the Lima document is a part. The reference is to the difference between belief in a real corporeal presence and a real spiritual presence of Christ in the eucharist. The Commentary ends with this sentence: "The decision remains for the churches whether this difference can be accommodated within the convergence formulated in the text itself." Are we engaged, after all, in an attempt to manipulate words in order to persuade ourselves that we have come to a common mind? Is it a convergence of *words* that we seek, rather than a convergence of thought?

That these questions are pertinent ones is shown by attending to the wording of §13. It says: "the eucharistic meal is the sacrament of the body and blood of Christ, the sacrament of his real presence". It is a studiously ambiguous sentence. Its subject is "the eucharistic meal". That focuses our attention on the elements, the bread and the wine. They are sacramental symbols of the body and blood of Christ. In that sense we agree fully with the document. But what precisely is the significance of the added words: "the sacrament of his real presence"? Do they mean that the bread which we eat and the wine which we drink *contain* the blood and flesh of the Son of Man? Is the formula intended to permit the possibility of belief in transubstantiation? If so, we could not subscribe to it. Or is it meant to say that the bread and wine are sacraments of the real *spiritual* presence of Christ? If so, then it conveys our convictions. Apparently the solution is to be found in the accompanying Commentary, namely, that the words are carefully chosen to allow both possibilities. And that is disquieting.

Then, again, there is ambiguity in the sentence: "But Christ's mode of presence in the eucharist is unique." Does it mean that Christ's presence there is *different* from his presence in the preached word, or in baptism, or at the right hand of God? Or does it mean that the eucharistic presence is *superior* to the others?

In lines 10–11, we read "what Christ declared is true, and this truth is fulfilled every time the eucharist is celebrated". There is a strong suggestion here that the ritual is effective *ex opere operato*. True, that conclusion must be qualified by what is said about the necessity for faith. Nothing however is said about the influence of the Holy Spirit.

As we understand it, bread and wine symbolize the spiritual nourishment we receive from Christ's redemptive work. The document, we feel, is misleading in that it speaks of Christ's presence as a presence "in" the eucharist. The body of Christ is now in heaven and what occurs in the eucharist, when the Holy Spirit enlightens the minds and touches the hearts of worshippers, is that they are elevated spiritually to the "heavenly places" to be with Christ, to feed spiritually on his life, his sacrifice, his resurrection and ascension. So the final sentence in §13 is, to our way of thinking, misleading insofar as it suggests that if people do not discern the body and blood of Christ "in the eucharist" (i.e. in the bread and wine on the communion table or altar), it is due to lack of faith. If this construction of the sentence is correct, then it is hard on those whose belief is that Christ's body is glorified in heaven and is not ubiquitously present wherever the bread and wine are laid out for that rite of the eucharist.

C. *The eucharist as invocation of the Spirit*

There is tension between the text of §14 and commentary. We accept the text of §14 as we understand it, but if it is meant to do what the Commentary suggests, we have reservations. Says the Commentary: "The invocation of the Spirit was made both on the community and on the elements of bread and wine. Recovery of such an understanding . . ." The shadow of transubstantiation clouds the analysis. In fact §15 expresses our view succinctly. It is the repetition of Jesus' words at the institution of the Lord's Supper that confirms a sacramental status upon the elements. The Holy Spirit graciously enables the worshippers to discern the body and blood of Christ — the spiritual reality of which the elements are symbols. That is why we feel unhappy about applying the *epiklesis* to the elements. So "recovery of such an understanding. . ." would mean a fundamental change in our position. If "consecration" is understood as the emergence of the presence of Christ in the elements when certain words are enunciated, then we cannot accept the concept of "special moment of consecration".

But with the above qualification, we accept the text of §§14,15,16,17,18.

D. *The eucharist as communion of the faithful*

In general, this section fails to maintain the balance between various aspects of Christian life with the result that the eucharist is accorded an all-embracing significance.

19. "It is in the eucharist that the community of God's people is fully manifested." Presumably, this is an expression of an ideal. Historically, the eucharist has been a major hindrance to Christian unity — a fact which has made the present discussion necessary. In any case, the assertion that in it "the community of God's people is fully manifested", needs justification. Does not

Jesus again and again affirm that the fellowship of the kingdom is most clearly manifested in love of neighbour, forgiving enemies, service of the poor and the distressed?

"Eucharistic celebrations always have to do with the whole Church, and the whole Church is involved in each local celebration." If this statement is intended to assert that at communion a congregation intercedes for the Christian churches throughout the whole world, then it states a valuable truth. But what is the force of the word "involved" in the second clause? Is it a reference to spiritual involvement in the sense that each communion is a local manifestation of the *koinonia* of the whole company of saints?

20. This is a very disturbing paragraph. It opens with an astonishing assertion: "The eucharist embraces all aspects of life." There is nothing in the New Testament to justify it. It could be that it wishes to say that the eucharist has symbolic significance for all aspects of life, or that a full eucharistic liturgy has implications for all aspects of life. But "embracing" is very different from "symbolizing" or "implying".

The root of our difficulty is to be found in the sentence, "Through the eucharist the all-renewing grace of God penetrates and restores human personality and dignity."

Although §12 emphasizes the importance of the preaching of the word in connection with the eucharist, the subsequent analysis makes confusing reading for those of us who still observe the classical distinction between the liturgy of the word and the liturgy of the upper room. Presumably, when we come across the word "eucharist" in the text, we are to understand it as including both liturgies. But the consequence is that insufficient distinctive emphasis is given to the role of the word of God as the channel of grace. So the impression is given in the sentence now under discussion that the elements, together with the accompanying ritual, are displacing the spiritual substance. It is through Jesus Christ ("full of grace and truth"), and by the unction of the Holy Spirit, nurturing our faith in the word of God, that the "all-renewing grace of God" is mediated to us. The eucharist is the seal on God's promise of mercy towards us, it is a sign that directs us to the Saviour, by nourishing our faith. Without faith, without the spiritual feeding upon Christ, grace does not penetrate our personality, whether we partake of communion or not. Unless this is made clear, we are fostering a mechanical conception of the efficacy of the sacrament and depersonalizing grace.

All this needs to be kept in mind in pondering the statement: "All kinds of injustice, racism, superstition and lack of freedom are radically challenged when we share in the body and blood of Christ." Is this a statement about what ought to be or a statement about the actual consequences of participating in the eucharist? Does the fact that the political leaders of South Africa are diligent attenders at holy communion modify their racism? Does attendance at the eucharist diminish the appetite for violence amongst Protestants and Catholics in Ulster? Ought we not to be a little more realistic in acknowledging that one of the historical consequences of an emphasis on a formal sacramentarianism is to deaden the sense of responsibility for removing social and political injustice?

"The eucharist involves the believer in the central event of the world's history." But it is the Holy Spirit who bridges the temporal gap between the worshipper today and the event on Calvary. And the Spirit performs the same miracle through the word — through the Bible and the sermon.

Again, it seems that in redrafting the document, careful critical attention should be paid to the use of the word "eucharist" as an inclusive term, comprehending the preaching of the word, the unction of the Holy Spirit, the exercise of faith, the manifestation of love and the partaking of the elements. Granted that the need for brevity in a document of this kind leads to the use of a liturgical or theological shorthand, it is hardly conducive to clarity of thought.

20. It would be charitable to omit the final clause. It conveys a veiled suggestion that all "confessional oppositions" are obstinate and unjustifiable.

E. The eucharist as meal of the kingdom
    We accept §§22–26.

III. THE CELEBRATION OF THE EUCHARIST

27. After the words, "the breaking of the bread", add "the pouring of the wine". And before "final act of praise", add "the offertory for the needy". In the reference to "the invocation of the Holy Spirit", we would omit the words, "and the elements of bread and wine". At the end of the list, we would add: "Since these elements are of diverse importance, a closer study of the Gospels and Epistles would enable us to see which are of primary importance."

28. We welcome the disclaimer in the last sentence and in consequence in the Commentary (28) we would change the last clause to read: ". . . Instituted by Jesus, and which features represent those areas in which the Lord wished his people to exercise their Christian freedom."

29. Since reference is made to Christ as prophet and priest, it is appropriate (and, in our view, important) to include the third of his offices, by adding the words, "the King who rules the people of God".

30, 31. Christians should celebrate the eucharist regularly, but not necessarily frequently.

32. As has been explained, we do not hold the position that Christ's presence is in the elements. Consequently, there is no question of reserving the elements. And since the elements have their sacramental function only for the duration of the eucharistic service, we do not feel it necessary to make the mode of their disposal a matter of scruple.

One point, however, needs to be explained with regard to taking communion to the sick, whether at home or in hospital. We see communion as essentially a congregational act, only to be celebrated in the presence of the assembled church. In principle, therefore private communion is excluded and many Congregationalists would object strongly to being offered private communion at a time of sickness. In other words, our tradition takes very seriously the points made in §19. But, as with other aspects of celebration, private communion is tolerated as an exercise of Christian freedom, but with the proviso that the minister should be accompanied by representatives of the congregation.

33. Accepted.

Ministry

I. THE CALLING OF THE WHOLE PEOPLE OF GOD

It is appropriate that the discussion of the ministry should begin with consideration of the calling of the whole people of God, because the doctrine of the church should precede the doctrine of the ministry. But we are disappointed that the section does not succeed in being consistent with this fundamental principle.

1. Accept.

2. In the third line, "calls" would be more appropriate than "invites".

3. Change the last sentence to read: "It is the Spirit who keeps the Church in the truth . . ." The sentence, as it is in the text, leaves the impression that the church is always infallible and never deviates from the truth.

4. Accept.

5. Primacy should be given to preaching (1 Cor. 1:17; Rom. 10:17) amongst the gifts listed.

6. Accept.

II. THE CHURCH AND THE ORDAINED MINISTRY

7. Accept.

A. *The ordained ministry*

8. Delete the words "and thereby provide, within a multiplicity of gifts, a focus of its unity". The principle enunciated in the previous sentence must be insisted upon: Christ, not the minister, is the focus of unity. This paragraph is already deviating from the principle proclaimed in §1. The impression is given that ministers come to the church as if it were from outside. (At the present juncture, there is a significant psychological point here. It is only a small step to the position that individual congregations are not responsible in any way for nurturing the gifts of those amongst its members who are likely to make good ministers.)

9. "The Church has never been without persons holding specific authority and responsibility." True, as long as we are careful — very careful! — to observe our Lord's admonition in Matt. 20:25–8. In the church authority is

grounded in service. But the tendency in the following paragraphs is to move away from this principle to a position where the ordained ministry is elevated into an independent institution over against the congregation. In fact, the discussion from now on concentrates in a remarkable way on the ordained ministry, without seeking to explore the significance of the various ministries to be found in the whole congregation.

10. Instead of "renewed Israel", read "new Israel".

11. Alter to read, "ordained ministers are representatives of Jesus Christ to the community *of believers*. . . As leaders and teachers they call *this* community. . ."

12. Instead of "ordained and lay", read "ordained and unordained". This paragraph reveals an unreadiness to emphasize the responsibility of the congregation for ministry. "Their [i.e. ministers] presence reminds the community of the divine initiative. . . " and in §42 the same idea is repeated. "The otherness of God's initiative of which the ordained ministry is the sign. . . " One consequence of this emphasis is obvious in §8 where it is said that ordained ministers are "constitutive for the life and witness of the Church. . ." That is, the principle that the church, under God, constitutes the ministry, has now been transformed into the opposite.

14. "It is especially in the eucharistic celebration that the ordained ministry is the visible focus of the deep and all-embracing communion between Christ and the members of his body. . ." We find this assertion quite unacceptable and far removed from anything we find in the New Testament. Two points may be made. (1) It is not at all clear on what grounds the sacramental role of the bread and wine in communion is transferred to the minister. (2) Here we have the commencement of the attempt, developed later in the document, to assign a portentous theological significance to the presiding person in the eucharist — a significance not hinted at in the New Testament, nor indeed in the earliest Christian literature of the second century. We seek to respect the early Christian tradition by observing the principle that an unordained person may celebrate communion at the invitation of the congregation, although the regular practice in our churches is for an ordained minister to officiate.

B. Ordained ministry and authority

15. Accept.
16. Accept.

C. Ordained ministry and priesthood

17. The attempt to justify calling a minister a "priest" despite what is said in Commentary (17) is unacceptable to us. It seems to us that an old ecclesiastical tradition is here clouding biblical truth. It is misleading to quote "living sacrifice" (Rom.12:1) to justify calling a minister a priest. Romans 12:1 does not use the words in a liturgical context. Rather the context is

Christian moral behaviour in the world. We feel obliged to reject the meaning given to the word "priest" in BEM, namely, an order of officers in the church. We acknowledge the unique priesthood of Jesus Christ and we acknowledge the priesthood of all believers. We cannot see that any other meaning can be given to the word "priesthood" in the church.

D. The ministry of men and women in the church

18. We do not believe that quoting Galatians 3:28 settles the argument about the place of women in the church. Even at the beginning of the present century many of our churches restricted voting to male members and prior to World War I, not a single woman was ordained. Today, however, practice has changed. Women vote in our churches and we ordain women into the ministry.

III. THE FORMS OF THE ORDAINED MINISTRY

A. Bishops, presbyters and deacons

Paragraphs 19 to 25 may be taken together. It is with regret that we must express our feeling that the reasoning is quite unsatisfactory and we feel that the attitude to non-episcopal churches is ungenerous and hardly befitting an ecumenical document.

In §19 it is asserted that there is no fixed pattern of church order in the New Testament (a point, by the way, which some of us would be disposed to challenge!) and in §22 it is said that the Holy Spirit has led churches from time to time to adopt various patterns of ministry. And then, in §22, the statement is made that the threefold ministry of bishop, presbyter and deacon "may serve today as an expression of the unity we seek and also as a means for achieving it". Here theological argument is abandoned and there is no attempt to discuss the biblical evidence. The only reason given here for commending the threefold ministry is that it could promote the unity of the church. Of course it could — provided everyone accepts it! But on what theological grounds should they accept it? The whole argument needs critical revision. In §19 it is said that the Holy Spirit guided the church in the early period to adopt the threefold ministry; in §22 it is asserted that the Spirit has led the church to adopt a variety of patterns.

Surely, very careful reasoning is necessary to explain why those who followed the guidance of the Spirit in rejecting episcopacy should now join those who, under the guidance of the same Spirit, adopted it? The answer actually given is the demand for unity, or rather the need to symbolize unity. In discussing *episkopé* insufficient emphasis is put on New Testament conceptions of the work and there is a distinct tendency to explain in the light of ideas that emerged much later. Nor is the point made in BEM that there is no New Testament evidence for distinguishing between "bishop" and "presbyter".

B. Guiding principles for the exercise of the ordained ministry in the church

26, 27. The attempt is made to interpret the three modes ("personal, collegial, communal") in terms of the threefold ministry. The search for convergence would have been better served if some recognition had been given to the way in which they can be equally fruitful in the life of churches that have rejected the pattern of threefold ministry.

C. Functions of bishops, presbyters and deacons

29, 31. Here we have a very idealistic description of the three orders. Again, it is regrettable that no attempt has been made to acknowledge that what is here claimed for the threefold ministry can be found in churches that have embraced a different type of order. It is worth remarking too that other types of ministry in the congregation have dropped completely out of the picture.

Yet we appreciate what is said in §31 about the work of deacons. We have every reason to be grateful for the immense contribution they have made to the life of our churches.

D. Variety of charisms

32, 33. Many times the church has enjoyed renewal, thanks to the work and testimony of those who stand outside the ranks of the threefold ministry.

IV. SUCCESSION IN THE APOSTOLIC TRADITION

A. Apostolic tradition in the church

34. In §34 and the Commentary upon it, there is no mention of the scriptures. As we understand it, the "apostolic tradition" is precisely the contents of the New Testament. We suggest, therefore, that in the Commentary 34 "in the New Testament" should be added to the sentence that ends, "the words and acts of Jesus transmitted by the apostles".

The point is that the "tradition" embodied in the New Testament is merged with a later and wider tradition. That is why it is possible to say: "Within this apostolic tradition is an apostolic succession of the ministry which serves the continuity of the Church. . ." So the threefold ministry is seen as an integral part of the "apostolic tradition". Our difficulty is that there is no foundation in the New Testament itself for such an assertion. And the whole argument puts intense strain on the healthy emphasis at the beginning of the section on the ministry of the whole people of God.

B. Succession of the apostolic ministry

35. "Where churches see little importance in orderly transmission. . ." It would be interesting to know which churches those are.

36. We feel that an improper emphasis is placed here both on the office of bishop and on the succession of bishops as one way ("together with the transmission of the Gospel and the life of the community") of expressing the

apostolic tradition of the church was expressed. Commentary 36 needs correction. It says: *"Clement is primarily interested in the means whereby the historical continuity of Christ's presence is ensured. . ."* Not so! His interest is purely practical; he wishes to ensure that presbyter-bishops who are regularly elected are not ejected by irregular means. And what of the reference to "the *historical* continuity of Christ's presence"? Are we to understand that the glorious and gracious presence of Our Lord is secured by a valid succession of bishops? And what exactly is meant by the adjective "historical"?

Ignatius is misunderstood, too. Ignatius took no interest in an "apostolic succession". In fact, in Ignatius it is not the bishop who is compared with the apostles but the presbyters. Ignatius compares the bishop with God the Father, and the deacons with Christ. What is the meaning of the statement, "the Christian community assembled around the bishop in the midst of presbyters and deacons as the *actual* manifestation in the Spirit of the apostolic community"? As it stands it is a very obscure statement.

37. Nothing is said about *how* church officers are appointed and this is an important point.

There is some special pleading in this paragraph. The text admits "that the reality and function of the episcopal ministry have been preserved in many of these (*sc.* non-episcopal) churches". So what need is there for bishops. The argument is moving in a circle. It is contended that bishops are necessary to discharge certain functions. Then it is admitted that these functions are otherwise discharged in non-episcopal churches. So, it is triumphantly concluded, bishops are indispensable. Obviously, a *non sequitur*!

38. The lame logic continues in this paragraph. It is argued that the episcopal succession is a "sign, though not a guarantee, of the continuity and unity of the Church". Why is a sign which is not a guarantee necessary? Of what is a heretical bishop a sign?

The last sentence should be deleted. The argument, apart from its logical weaknesses, is quite non-ecumenical in its bias against non-episcopal churches. To ask them outright to accept episcopacy on the basis of such flimsy reasoning as is presented in §§35–8 is to untie the knot by cutting it. Ought not a word be addressed to the episcopal churches to consider more critically their own intransigence on this topic?

V. ORDINATION

A. *The meaning of ordination*

39, 40. We can accept these statements, but with the observation that it would be helpful if there were some reference to "setting apart". For us, it is helpful because ordination is to be understood in the context of the ministry of the whole people of God, where some are "set apart" by the others to discharge particular offices, rather than elevated into a different order of Christians.

As for the Commentary on 39, it continues the mission to make us all into episcopalians! We have not admitted that the bishop is "the sign of the apostolic succession", and so we do not have bishops. And since we have no bishops, we cannot have episcopal ordination. It is a great injustice to the whole discussion to suggest that the condition upon which Christians can unite together is that they agree, contrary to every conviction we possess regarding the meaning and status of the New Testament, that bishops (in the Church of England or Church in Wales or Orthodox church understanding of the word) and bishops alone, should ordain.

B. *The act of ordination*

41. "A long and early Christian tradition places ordination in the context of worship and especially of the eucharist." Of course, where virtually every act of public worship included a eucharist, then ordination would be accompanied by holy communion. But what theological implications follow?

Paragraphs 41 and 43 seek to lead us along the road which would lead us to the conclusion that ordination is a sacrament. The laying-on of hands is described as a "sacramental sign" (41), and even more explicitly in (43) it is said, ". . . the Church ordains in confidence that God . . . enters sacramentally into contingent, historical forms . . ." We cannot approve this view because it endangers the emphasis on the value of every form of ministry in the congregation. And more specifically, Paul seems to utter a very serious warning against so elevating some ministries as to denigrate others. "And those members of the body, which we think to be less honourable, upon these we bestow more abundant honour . . ." (1 Cor. 12:20–23).

44. There is a clause in this paragraph which we find quite extraordinary as an indication of the role of the whole people of God in the act of ordination. "By receiving the new minister in the act of ordination the congregation acknowledges the minister's gifts and commits itself to be open towards these gifts." To us, it is a strange idea that the only function of the congregation in an ordination ceremony is to "receive" a minister and "acknowledge" his gifts. Obviously, this description presupposes that the minister is appointed by some person or body outside the congregation. To us, it is the congregation through the medium of the person invited by it to preside, that ordains. And that is done by means of a covenant between congregation and minister, that includes much more than receiving the minister and being open to his gifts.

As for the "collegial" relationship, for us that is fraternal fellowship of a personal nature since we have no institution that gives formal expression to this collegiality.

C. *The conditions for ordination*
We accept §§45–50.

VI. TOWARDS THE MUTUAL RECOGNITION OF THE ORDAINED MINISTRIES

51. Accept.

52. "Apostolic succession is of particular importance." We have to confess again that for us a historic apostolic succession is a subsidiary matter. Faithfulness to apostolic truth is the essential thing.

If §49 were taken seriously, there would be no need for §§51–3.

53. And now the non-episcopal churches get their marching orders! "Those churches are asked to realize that the continuity with the Church of the Apostles finds profound expression in the successive laying on of hands by bishops. . ." They "are asked"—not "invited to consider". And they are asked "to realize", i.e. to shake themselves out of their present ignorance and face the real fact. And the fact they are to realize is bare assertion.

It is all a most regrettable demand in an ecumenical document.

54. We accept.

55. We accept.

* * *

We were asked to answer four questions.

1. Since the "faith of the Church through the centuries" contains so many diverse elements, only to a very limited extent does BEM express it.

2. That there is need for much more, and much franker discussions, especially as regards the doctrine of ministry.

3. We found the study of the document most instructive not least because it compelled us to examine our own faith and practice more critically.

4. It is a matter of some uneasiness that we are attempting to find agreement in words rather than in substances. At some points (e.g. with regard to episcopacy) the position of BEM is that one side must yield completely to the other. Ought Faith and Order not to be examining a little more frankly the theology of Christian freedom? Are there not areas and doctrines where unanimity is attainable at the present time?

March 1986

MORAVIAN CHURCH IN GREAT BRITAIN AND IRELAND

We are grateful for all the work that has been done over the past half century resulting in the publication of BEM and for the stimulus it has given to discussion on central questions of the Christian faith. Our prayer is that this common study may help the different branches of the Christian Church to a deeper understanding of the varied expressions of the faith that have arisen out of our common commitment to the one Lord Jesus Christ and to a closer fellowship with him and with one another.

The Moravian Church and statements on doctrine and theology

Recognizing the Bible as the ultimate source and rule of faith, doctrine and life and believing that the mystery of Jesus Christ cannot be comprehended completely by any human statement, the Moravian Church has always allowed great freedom in matters of doctrine. The historic creeds and statements of the church have been accepted, not as binding on believers, but as of value in helping Christians to formulate their thought and as "the thankful acclaim of the Body of Christ".

It is out of this tradition that we come to the study of BEM. Since there are no detailed statements of Moravian thought on baptism, eucharist or ministry, dealing with this document has helped us in clarifying some of our own thinking. For that, we are grateful. *We recognize in the document an expression of the historic Christian faith without in any way regarding the document as definitive. Indeed to our way of thinking, no such definitive statement would be possible.*

Baptism

The statement on baptism is, in broad terms, in accordance with Moravian belief and practice.

• 4,050 members, 40 congregations, 29 pastors.

The emphasis on baptism as related to life-long growth into Christ and not only to momentary experience (9) we welcome as an important insight. We are also thankful for the recognition that baptism should always take place in the setting of the Christian community, since at every baptism the congregation reaffirms its faith and pledges itself to provide the necessary environment for the nurture of the baptized (12). We would certainly accept the emphasis on the ethical implications of baptism (4). However, there would be reservations if some of the wording here implies baptismal regeneration.

With us, infant baptism is the normal practice. With many other churches at the present time, we are particularly concerned to emphasize the importance of faith and commitment on the part of those who bring the child to be baptized and of the congregation who receive the child. Faith must be not just a future possibility for the child being baptized but a present reality among those who accept responsibility for the baptism, whether parents or sponsors or congregation (11, 12, 16).

Perhaps the text could speak more fully of the importance of confirmation for those who practise infant baptism, with its opportunity for the confirmands to make public affirmation of their faith and commitment to Christ. We believe that infant baptism, followed by confirmation at an age of discretion, is an adequate equivalent to believers' baptism.

We would not, however, restrict the gift of the Spirit to the time of confirmation, nor indeed to the act of baptism, for God's grace is not limited by ritual, even sacramental ritual (14). *Perhaps the most persistent general question from reading BEM is: does it allow enough space for God's freedom of action outside the sacraments and rites of the Christian church?*

Where a person is baptized as an adult (because baptism has not taken place earlier in life) there seems to us no theological reason why the person should be confirmed. The normal practice in the Moravian church has been for confirmation or adult baptism to be the point of admission to the holy communion. There is at present considerable discussion about the admission of baptized children to communion (14b).

Eucharist

Moravian emphasis, especially in relation to the Lord's Supper, has been on simplicity both in theology and in worship. The heart of the matter for us has been in Christ's words at the Supper: "This is my body. . . this is my blood. . . ." It has not been our practice to try to interpret too rigidly the meaning and implication of these words. Much of the language of this section, therefore, would be, outside the boundaries of our usual discussion. It is helpful for us to study these statements, however, not as definitive but as guides to a deeper understanding.

We do not find anything in BEM which directly contradicts our understanding of the Lord's Supper but make the following comments.

We find the use of the name "Eucharist" as the principal name for this sacrament rather surprising since it already assumes the centrality of one feature of the rite. Whilst we acknowledge that celebration and thanksgiving are important aspects, these are our response to what Christ has done for us in his life, death and resurrection. The heart of the sacrament is God's gift to us in Christ. We love because he first loved us. Normally we would speak of "the Holy Communion" but suggest that "the Lord's Supper" might be the best name to use in such a document as this, being more objective, all embracing and less tendentious than "Eucharist".

It is our practice that the Lord's Table should be open to members of all Christian churches.

We find the insights in §20 concerning the all-embracing nature of the Lord's Supper helpful and challenging. But does not the congregation's ability to share in ministries of reconciliation and renewal and restoration depend on their first having received forgiveness? It seems to us that this aspect of the Lord's Supper is not given much weight in the text, being mentioned explicitly only in §2.

We recognize the elements listed in 27 as those included in the historic liturgy of the church but we are glad to note the text's recognition that these are found "in varying sequence and of diverse importance".The essence of the Lord's Supper for us is somewhat simpler than is suggested here and we could recognize as a valid celebration a form that did not include all these elements, as long as there was a sharing of bread and wine, a recital of the words of institution according to the New Testament tradition and a remembrance of the life, death and resurrection of the Lord.

We find §29 particularly helpful and in accord with our own thinking.

Although we recognize the centrality of the Lord's Supper to Christian worship we do not think that this necessitates a weekly celebration (31).

Ministry

This section outlines a concept of ministry which is generally in accord with our own history and understanding though the following paragraphs will try to indicate some of the ways in which our understanding differs from that of other historic episcopal churches.

We have a threefold ordained ministry coming to us from the earliest days of the Unitas Fratrum (1467) though we do not hold any mechanical view of apostolic succession.

The *bishop* ordains (at the request of the church, usually represented by the Provincial Elders' Conference) and gives spiritual leadership to the church but does not have administrative authority by virtue of his office. He is pastor to pastors.

Because of theological and historical difficulties connected with the word "priest" we use "presbyter". *Presbyter* and *deacon* are both ministers of word and sacraments and may exercise pastoral oversight in a local congregation.

There is no difference in function between the two orders in the Moravian Church. The consecration of a deacon to the presbyterate after some years of service is confirmation and sign of approval of his ministry by the church.

While this is the pattern Moravians have accepted for their own ministry, they do not believe that episcopacy is of the essence of the church nor that episcopal ordination is essential for a valid ministry. They have no difficulty therefore in working in the closest union with churches whose understanding of ministry is different from theirs. We welcome the commentary on §11.

We accept women into the ordained ministry.

We regard the whole people of God as involved in ministry and, again, welcome the commentary on §13.

* * *

We hope that the answers to the questions asked by the Faith and Order Commission have been implied in the material already given but in conclusion we try to summarize and give more specific answers to questions 2, 3 and 4.

The consequences your church can draw from this text for its relations and dialogue with other churches, particularly with those churches which also recognize the text as an expression of the apostolic faith.

Our church has always sought to have friendly and cooperative relations with other churches and to be open to other understandings of ministry and other forms of worship wherever there is a recognition that Jesus Christ is Saviour and Lord. We are thankful for the theological undergirding that this report gives to that endeavour.

Studying BEM has reminded us that although for us it has always been more important to work out the meaning of the gospel in service than in detailed and precise theological statements, for others correct doctrine is central. If, therefore, dialogue is to advance, we have to prepare ourselves more adequately to take part in discussions of this nature. This may mean that we have to try and work out more formal declarations of doctrine than has previously been our practice.

The guidance your church can draw from this text for its worship, educational, ethical and spiritual life and witness.

We do not see any immediate application of the text in these various areas of our church life but it will remain a seminal document which will continue to influence thought and action. Especially as we work on revising the church's liturgy, the text's position will have to be considered.

We note also the statement in §20 of the section on eucharist indicating the ethical demands, personal and social, that come to us when we share the bread and wine at the Lord's Supper. This we found deeply challenging.

The suggestions your church can make for the ongoing work of faith and order as it relates the material of this text to its long range research project.

As we have already said, the BEM text will remain a seminal document and will continue to stimulate discussion among the churches. Perhaps certain churches, finding much common ground in the text, may be encouraged to develop a closer working relationship.

It is clear that on certain issues, there is a need for clarification and further discussion with a view to attaining greater agreement, e.g. ordination of women.

GENERAL MENNONITE
SOCIETY (NETHERLANDS)

Introduction

In this reaction we wish to begin by stating that we believe the unity of the church to be founded in and to be dependent on the work of the God and Father of Jesus Christ. It is he who, according to the scriptures, is engaged in liberating humankind from its rebellion against him and from the division and dissent resulting from this rebellion against him by gathering people into his congregation which is to be a symbol of reconciliation, liberation and hope in this sinfully divided world. We consider this to be the reason why the churches cannot and may not resign themselves and accept the division existing within their own church and among each other, but must consider themselves to be a uniting church, a church engaged in a continuous struggle to resist through the power of God's Spirit all forces that bring with them and sustain division and strife.

This approach to the division in churches within their own sphere and among each other also defines the status of this reaction. It has been formulated by two members of the teaching staff of the Mennonite Seminary as the result of discussions within the Commission for Spiritual Affairs of the General Mennonite Society (ADS) of the Netherlands and of reactions asked for and received from within the Mennonite Brotherhood. The reaction should therefore be considered in the first place to be an important contribution to the discussion in the Brotherhood aimed at a mutual understanding of the themes presented by Faith and Order. It does not pretend to put into words this kind of a mutual understanding as yet. Nevertheless the ADS considers it to be sufficiently representative to be offered to the World Council in reply to a request sent to its member churches asking for a reaction to the statements presented by Faith and Order.

When we state that the churches must consider themselves a uniting church engaged in a ceaseless struggle to resist through the power of God's Spirit all

---

● 39,000 members.

forces that carry with them and sustain division, it is our conviction that in this struggle a definite priority will have to be given to questions of peace and justice. We have noted that it is these questions that oppress the minds of a large number of members of the Brotherhood. Simultaneously, the questions centring around baptism, eucharist and ministry appear to attract little attention. Rather, it is found that active Christians of different churches celebrate the Lord's Supper together as a matter of course without worrying about denominational obstacles. They are obviously not waiting for a consensus on the eucharist.

This causes one to wonder how it is that the Lima topics could stir people's hearts to such a degree that in the past they have led to schisms, whereas today people barely get excited over them. Could this be related to the possibility that at the time questions connected with baptism, eucharist and ministry had socio-political.implications which today they more or less seem to have lost? Especially in questions centring around infant baptism and believer baptism we feel this to be so. In the sixteenth century the rejection of infant baptism drove a wedge into the dominant social order of the period. As a result the reaction of the rulers in that order was of a piece.

We would like to offer the following commentary on the three statements.

The baptismal statement

1. To begin with it prompts us to make ourselves clear on the nature of baptism. According to our convictions it expresses and records that from then on the person baptized belongs to the congregation and is accounted a "new creation". As such the person knows himself or herself to be accepted by the other members of the congregation, and to be held accountable by them.

The transition to the new existence as a member of the congregation to our mind, however, is not a result of the actual baptism. Along with Menno Simons and Karl Barth we hold that it is uniquely the baptism by the Holy Spirit which will operate this transition and that baptism must be seen to be a human act of confession in which the person receiving baptism and the congregation together express the social signification of the turn God has caused this person's life to take. This human act of confession insofar as the person receiving baptism is concerned must be seen to be his or her first act of obedience at the outset of a new existence as a member of the congregation.

When the statement on baptism declares that baptism *is* incorporation into Christ, that it *is* entry into the New Covenant between God and God's people and that it *is* a gift of God (§1) we reserve to ourselves the freedom to interpret these and similar expressions in the sense described above. With this reservation we are able to agree with a great many of the positions taken in this statement.

For example we are happy to accept: "Baptism is participation in Christ's death and resurrection (Rom. 6:3–5, Col. 2:12); a washing away of sin (1 Cor.

6:11); a new birth (John 3:5); an enlightenment by Christ (Eph. 5:14); a reclothing in Christ (Gal. 3:27); a renewal by the Spirit (Titus 3:5); the experience of salvation from the flood (1 Pet. 3:20–21); an exodus from bondage (1 Cor. 10:1–2) and a liberation into a new humanity in which barriers of division whether of sex or race or social status are transcended (Gal. 3:27–28, 1 Cor. 12:13). The images are many but the reality is one." (§2)

We would like to underline what is said in §6 on the importance of baptism to the unity of the church: "Our common baptism, which unites us to Christ in faith, is thus a basic bond of unity. We are one people and are called to confess and serve one Lord in each place and in all the world. The union with Christ which we share through baptism has important implications for Christian unity. 'There is . . . one baptism, one God and Father of us all . . . ' (Eph. 4:4–6). When baptismal unity is realized in one holy, catholic, apostolic Church, a genuine Christian witness can be made to the healing and reconciling love of God. Therefore, our one baptism into Christ constitutes a call to the churches to overcome their divisions and visibly manifest their fellowship."

We wish to direct the attention to the pronouncement found in §7: "Baptism initiates the reality of the new life given in the midst of the present world," and to the comment in §9: "The life of the Christian is necessarily one of continuing struggle yet also of continuing experience of grace. In this new relationship the baptized live for the sake of Christ, of his Church and of the world which He loves, while they wait in hope for the manifestation of God's new creation and for the time when God will be all in all (Rom. 8:18–24; 1 Cor. 15:22–28; 49–57)."

We naturally agree with the statement contained in §12 on baptism as a personal confession of faith in the setting of the assembled congregation.

When §16 calls on those practising believer baptism to express more visibly the fact that children are placed under the protection of God's grace, one might point to the custom of "thanksgiving for a birth" or "dedication of the child" in which parents who themselves are members of the congregation thank God during public worship for the birth of their child, dedicate it to him and pray for his guidance in the raising of the child, so that at a certain moment it will make its own commitment to the congregation.

2. To consider oneself and to act as a uniting church excludes the churches' supporting any sectarian absolutism of their own traditions. The Mennonites who practise believer baptism because this is considered to be the only baptismal practice on a biblical foundation and who consequently reject infant baptism are forced to admit that the church as a whole is also divided on this point. For the sake of the unity of the church and for the sake of the quality of its community we consider this to be an unacceptable situation, which obliges us to continue discussing the question of the right baptismal practice, hoping and trusting that together we will be guided by the Spirit towards the truth in this matter as well.

3. Bearing in mind this position we must add that in our opinion the statement in question has a distinct tendency to play down the existing differences by accepting both baptismal practices side by side (§12). To our way of thinking this is only possible when infant baptism is the accepted practice. According to the statement (§11), too, the words of the New Testament clearly speak of baptism based on personal confession of faith so much so that it will be impossible for the adherents of infant baptism not to make room for believer baptism. On the other hand, those who consider believer baptism to be the only legitimate baptismal practice on a biblical foundation cannot be expected to see such a diversity of baptismal service as anything but an unsatisfactory and temporary compromise. We are therefore unable to agree with this tendency in the report on baptism, and we consider it to be a serious lack of recognition of what is at stake in the struggle about the right baptismal practice and what this involves for the quality of the community of the congregation and for the authenticity of the position it holds in the world. At the same time we are forced to admit that the practice of believer baptism in itself is not a guarantee for such quality and authenticity.

The statement on the eucharist

We began our reaction to the statement on baptism with a pronouncement on the nature of baptismal practice; similarly we shall first state our position on the Lord's Supper. Mennonite tradition sometimes refers to the celebration of this meal as "keeping oneness". It should therefore be regarded in the light of the work of God, who is liberating mankind from its rebellion against him and from the mutual opposition and strife which is the result of this rebellion, by joining people together in the new community of the congregation.

"Baptized into union with him, you have all put on Christ as a garment." Paul writes to the Galatians (3:27ff.): "There is no such thing as Jew and Greek, slave and freeman, male and female; for you are all one person in Christ Jesus." Three fundamental oppositions that were characteristic for the world he lived in, viz. between Jew and Greek, between slaves and the free, between male and female, had been designated to be eliminated by Jesus Christ according to the apostle. As a result concrete steps had been made possible and thus should be taken towards their elimination, to begin with within the congregation itself. This implies that the congregation forms the specific part of the world that by virtue of God's conciliating and liberating work does not have to resign itself to being divided, but may consider itself empowered to resist division with all its strength and to distinguish itself from the world as a community of peace, a peace church. That it has been called and empowered to do this is expressed in its celebration of the Lord's Supper. This celebration should therefore be seen — no different from the celebration of baptism — as an act of confession. This is contained in the designation "keeping oneness". "Oneness" presupposes the willingness of the members of the congregation not to resign themselves to entrenched social contrasts and to the unruliness of the heart, but to overcome all obstacles and thus to confirm Jesus Christ as the Conqueror, the King of Peace, based on the belief that we are allowed to live thanks to his victory and that we are empowered by the Spirit to uphold the Messianic practice of peace-makers. Consequently every celebration of the Lord's Supper puts pressure on the congregation to distinguish itself in the right way from the world as a city on a mountain. So wherever this does not happen, the question imposes itself whether Christ is present at that particular celebration.

The foregoing leads to the conclusion that the new community of the congregation does not materialize by the celebration of the Lord's Supper, but that such a celebration presupposes the new community founded by God. On the other hand each celebration of this meal — if it is a true celebration — will benefit the quality of the community of the congregation. And if it is in fact a true celebration will depend on whether the participants know themselves to be part of God's conciliating and liberating work to such a degree that they are prepared, in their capacity of living members of this new community, to fight all divisionary and reactionary forces together with their sisters and brothers. This preparedness is presupposed in the total baptismal happening. However, the members of the congregation have to uphold this preparedness among each other continuously. This is the true function of pastoral care.

Clearly this non-sacramental interpretation of baptism and the Lord's Supper raises a number of questions on some of the formulations of this statement as well. When for instance §2 states: "In the eucharistic meal, in the eating and drinking of the bread and wine, Christ grants communion with himself. God himself acts, giving life to the body of Christ and renewing each member", we reserve to ourselves the right to interpret this kind of pronouncement in the light of the foregoing.

When we put forth this view of the Mennonite interpretation of the Lord's Supper as a reaction to the statement, we do so in a spirit of readiness to test our own communion practice against it. An essential part of this practice is in fact its open character. This means that everyone is invited who wants to share with us the community of the Lord. This open practice does justice to our conviction that only those can join in the Lord's Supper who heartily wish to do so. However, it pays little heed to the particular nature of the community of the congregation and consequently to the necessary willingness of the members of the congregation to take on the responsibility for each other and to accept a challenge to the way in which they put their faith into practice. That this willingness to do so is seriously lacking in our present congregational activity points to a type of individualism that is not limited to Mennonite churches but may be considered characteristic for our Western society. It signifies a diminution of the particular nature of the community of the congregation which also has serious consequences for the celebration of the Lord's Supper, especially insofar as it is meant as a celebration and enforcement of the existing community. We feel that it is of decisive importance to regain the true community of the congregation for all of our churches in the Western hemisphere and consider this to be at the heart of our ecumenical problem. If we should recover this real community we feel that intercommunion shall no longer be a problem. This is confirmed in all those places at the base where members of different churches know themselves to be united into a true community in a shared service for the Lord and consequently have no reservations about this kind of communion celebrated and enforced around the Lord's Supper.

Finally we would like to add that we have been very much interested to learn about the various aspects of the Lord's Supper that are highlighted in this statement. We wondered if that great variety of aspects could each in turn be given its due by a more frequent celebration than is usual in our churches.

The statement on the ministry

The Mennonite tradition makes it possible to agree with the description of the calling of the *whole* people of God, called by God, founded in Christ, and living through Jesus Christ in the Holy Spirit, to proclaim the kingdom of God and to embody this even if in a provisional way. We should add, however, that for the Christian church to call itself "God's people" it needs to consider itself to be "grafted and having come to share the same root and sap as the olive" (Rom. 11:17–18), i.e. God's people Israel.

In particular the emphasis on the fact that this ministry must be carried out in varying political, social and cultural circumstances with its attendant pluriformity is to be welcomed, as well as the accent on the gift of the Holy Spirit to the entire community. It cannot be denied that in the Christian church there have always been people who were given a specific authority and a particular responsibility for proclaiming the gospel and for service; on the other hand it is inadmissable that the unity of the church should be supposed to depend on ordained ministers in an apostolic succession. After all, the unity of the church is constituted by the proclamation of Christ; it is founded in him and sealed by baptism and communion. God's unilateral initiative does not necessarily require an ordained ministry but is linked to the proclamation that in principle is a task of each member of the congregation. In accordance with New Testament witness the royal and prophetic priesthood of all who have been baptized should be stressed, in which no difference need be made between man and woman.

The historic and contextual character of the development of the ministry does not allow the exclusive choice of the threefold pattern of bishop and presbyter and deacon, the office of bishop being the centre of unity within the entire community. Rather, this is the result of a post-Constantinian development and a reflection of the secular, c.q. Roman structure of government. The emphasis on the ordained ministry being the guarantee of the truth of the proclamation and of the unity of the church does not do justice to its prophetic and charismatic character.

The continuity of the apostolic tradition, insofar as it implies the organic unity with the apostolic proclamation, is considered to have a critical function in relation to the apostolic succession of the ministry according to Mennonite ideas and does not have to coincide with this ministry. In Mennonite tradition the fact that members of the congregation are called by the congregation to carry a particular responsibility for the proclamation and service is not given expression by ordination along the lines of the succession of the ministry, but by confirmation with the laying on of hands and the invocation of the Holy Spirit according to New Testament custom.

Especially in connection with the controversial issue of the apostolic succession of the ministry, religious communities in the Mennonite tradition have their questions on the identification, too lightly undertaken, of the apostolic succession of the proclamation of the gospel and the apostolic succession of the ministry as is done in §52 in the words: "the ministry of Word and sacrament in continuity with apostolic times". Preferably the emphasis should be put on the truth and the authenticity of the witness of the entire congregation in their proclamation and their life (together with a pluriform and functional concept of "the ministry",) along the lines of §33, instead of on the uniformity of the ordained ministry as a guarantee for the unity of the Christian church.

The four questions put before us by the Commission

1. To what extent can your church recognize in this text the faith of the church through the ages?

In this question we are bothered by the expression "the faith of the Church through the ages". This expression obscures the fact that for instance in the matter of baptism there is a centuries-old opposition between believer baptism and infant baptism with its far-reaching ecclesiological implications. The same can be said on the subject of the Lord's Supper and of the ministry. Consequently we cannot answer the above question.

2. What are the consequences your church can draw from this text for its relations and dialogues with other churches, particularly with those churches which also recognize the text as an expression of the apostolic faith?

We should like to begin by noting that "the apostolic faith" is not anywhere described or fixed as such. In the Bible, too, we are confronted with interpretations of the word of God, defined by different contexts. It has continued far too long that churches in the Western hemisphere felt they could impose their understanding of the word of God as the "apostolic faith" on the rest of the world without realizing the degree to which this understanding had been determined by its context. In any case, one consequence of this text is the need for the Netherlands General Mennonite Society (ADS) to keep introducing the discussion concerning the right baptismal practice within the concept of the uniting church. At the same time we realize that in our days there may be more important angles from which to promote the quality of the community of the uniting church. We would like to mention in particular the ecclesiological concept of the "church of the poor". We consider the struggle for the quality of the community of the congregation both within each church and between different churches to be an essential precondition for a fruitful discussion of themes such as are introduced in these statements.

3. In how far can your church take guidance from this text for its worship, educational, ethical and spiritual life and witness?

The language of this text is no different from this reaction in that it is too much influenced by the language used by schooled theologians for the text to be used in the life of the community in its various aspects. However, we are prepared to stimulate the use by our churches of the text of the report in their discussions on the style of worship, on education and on the practice of the life of the community and of faith.

4. What suggestions can your church make for the ongoing work of Faith and Order as it relates the material of this text on baptism, eucharist and ministry to its long-range research project "Towards the Common Expression of the Apostolic Faith Today"?

It is our conviction that in the common expression of the apostolic faith today a statement on baptism should be included, indicating that it marks an act of transition, of crossing a frontier, because baptism gets men and women, living in a world torn by division and strife, involved in the conciliating and liberating work of God, aimed at renewing this world.

QUAKERS OF NETHERLANDS

Report presented to the Council of Churches in the Netherlands by the Dutch Yearly Meeting of Friends (Quakers) — February 1985.

To develop a clear understanding of the attitude of Quakers with regard to the sacraments, it is useful to take the history of Quakers into account. The first Quakers did not unite on a new interpretation of the sacraments or of being a church in the ecclesiastic sense but on the existential experience of faith and the witness of God's covenant with people, the recognition of his renewing spirit in Jesus Christ.

Amongst other Christians Quakers wish modestly to seek their way without the outward certainties of dogmas and sacraments. Since institutions, rituals, forms of exclusiveness and power structures in the established churches became impediments to personal experience of faith, Quakers chose a modest and communal waiting upon God in silence, without an order of service, without a minister or official, without congregational hymns, without formal prayers and without outward sacraments.

The basis of the community of the faithful does not lie with sacraments as institutions of salvation or symbols but with the deep desire for and the experience of this community, the concealed association with God (Psalms). For Quakers this becomes fully expressed in the silent meeting for worship where the spontaneously spoken word, the (Bible) reading, witness and prayer are an expression of that desire, that hope and that experiential faith. Inseparable therefrom is participating actively in the world and the awareness of our responsibilities towards our fellow human beings and creation. After

---

● 150 members.

all, the word of God does not only refer to personal inner renewal, but also to a new earth. The signs of peace and justice are signs of salvation that cannot be reduced to sacramental-ritual forms. They only get substance in the world and in our living together as fellow human beings. This is not to imply that the community of the faithful is an action group in the limited sense of the word, but to express that faith and practice do not stand side by side as holy and profane. Life as a whole is an assignment subject to salvation and grace. Assignment and grace form a unity that can be experienced in the silent association with God. They move us to act.

Quakers have not assigned the concept "sacral" a place in their tradition. When we say that Quakers know the sacraments of baptism and eucharist in their inward significance, this refers to the direct experience of renewal and community as a spiritual event. They did not only get to know this from the letter of the gospel, but experienced this in their personal life and in the community (congregation) as a living testimony. Without denying the value of the different outward symbols as these are inseparable from their faith to many Christians, Quakers abstain in their meeting for worship from ritual symbols that may precede or even confine the experience of faith itself.

In Quaker meeting for worship and daily life *baptism* by the Holy Spirit may become a reality which will make us experience that there is one Lord, one faith, one baptism transcending theological debates on the one correct interpretation of the sacrament.

Where the *eucharist* is concerned, Quaker tradition similarly seeks earnestly for the existential significance underlying ritual and outward forms. After the last supper Jesus had with his disciples the breaking and sharing of bread together may always be seen to hold the perspective of the reaffirmation of God's relationship with humanity (covenant) and the restoration of human relationships with our fellowmen (communion). Thus a table at which people sit to eat their daily bread becomes the table of the Lord when they break and share bread in remembrance of him. Quakers have broken with the ecclesiastical tradition to reduce the "table of the Lord" to a ritual and sacral exclusiveness and/or the obligation of periodical participation. Without this ritual a Quaker meeting for worship also knows the experience of the inward light and of communion, that is communion in God's spirit with its promise of peace and justice. Even then this communion is not reserved to such places or instances as the table and the meeting. On the contrary, Quakers hold that (daily) life as a whole should be steeped in this experience of communion with God and fellow human beings. We are well aware though of the need not to take this conviction too lightly or too superficially.

Meeting in silence, Quakers get to know the earnestness and austerity of a sincere desire for an inspiring association with God that joins worship and life, faith and practice. Concerning the *ministry*, we hereby quote from a Quaker document published in 1944:

Quakers have wanted every step and stage of salvation and worship to be a living process. They are afraid of phrases which are supposed to have some sacred efficacy. They are anxious not to have officials who belong in a special class and are assumed to have peculiar powers that others lack.[1]

---

[1] Rufus Jones, quoted by Gerald Hibbert in "Friends and the Sacraments".

CANADIAN YEARLY MEETING OF THE RELIGIOUS SOCIETY OF FRIENDS

In our process of receiving and responding to "Baptism, Eucharist and Ministry", Friends have found much of the form, language and content to be foreign to us. Therefore, we are unable to reply within the categories suggested by the Commission, and are responding to the underlying spirit rather than the specific questions. We were, however, able to meet the request to "enable the widest possible involvement of the whole people of God at all levels of church life in the spiritual process of receiving this text". Friends appointed at Canadian Yearly Meeting 1984 circulated copies of "Baptism, Eucharist and Ministry" and resource material to all Monthly Meeting and worship groups, inviting considered and prayerful responses from Meetings and individuals. These responses were collated and presented to Canadian Yearly Meeting sessions to produce the following statement:

The Religious Society of Friends is rooted in the Christian tradition. Friends also believe that we share a common spiritual life with other religious faiths and our membership contains those who call themselves Christian and those who do not.

We reaffirm the words of the Quaker statement made at the Faith and Order Conference at Lausanne (1927), where way was opened for the Society of Friends to join the World Council of Churches, when it came into being:

> . . . We do not in any way belittle the importance of the problems we have been working upon, but we believe that the "unity of Christians never did, or ever will or can, stand in uniformity of thought or opinion, but in Christian love" (Thomas Story, 1737). And we believe that a corporate practice of the presence of God, a corporate knowledge of Christ in our midst, a common experience of the work of the living Spirit, constitute the supremely real sacrament of a Holy Communion.

Our experience leads us to emphasize the fact that to become a member of the community of Christ's people requires not an outward rite but an inner

---

• 1,146 members, 29 parishes.

transformation and commitment; and to continue to affirm that we are called to ministry, women and men alike, within the silent, expectant, meeting for worship, where we respond to the guidance of the Spirit as we wait upon the Lord.

In the light of these affirmations, we must report that a sense of exclusion from the current draft of "Baptism, Eucharist and Ministry" weighs heavily on Friends. This comes from its emphasis on the sacramental experience and hierarchical ordering of the church.

We can recognize, with the Salvation Army representative who spoke on a panel addressing "Baptism, Eucharist and Ministry" at our last Yearly Meeting, that "there are certain sacramental observances, which, though not practised by us, are a means of grace to the believer who desires to share in the spiritual reality of which the sacrament is a symbol". We would go further and affirm:

> The unity of Christians is not something that needs to be created; it is already here, and needs only to be recognized and acted upon. All those who love our Lord Jesus Christ, and in whose lives his character is being manifested, know this inner unity, whatever diversities there may be in the formulas by which they express themselves, or in the practices by which they seek to cherish his life in their souls (London Yearly Meeting 1917, revised 1937).

While we value the search of the Faith and Order Commission for a deeper unity, and the devoted work of many individuals on the document, we have reservations about the type of unity implicit in this "Baptism, Eucharist and Ministry" statement. We see differences, in theological expression as well as in practice, as a source of growth and an opportunity to enrich our own spiritual experience. We would prefer to celebrate a continuing diversity, within which we can all move freely as the Spirit leads. For us, unity is to be found, and will continue to grow, in worshipping and working together, and through sharing our individual spiritual journeys.

Studying and discussing "Baptism, Eucharist and Ministry" has led us to a valuable re-examination of our beliefs and practices in the light of this document, and confirmed our belief that the way forward lies through experiences such as the one contained in one Friend's response to "Baptism, Eucharist and Ministry".

> I met an Episcopalian layman in Wisconsin . . . (and) I was struck by the depth of his totally unselfish devotion to finding a way to be helpful. As we drove toward the migrants' camp he spoke about what motivated him. He described with a simple intensity the feelings he experienced at the moment of the elevation of the host. I responded in my own fumbling way with a description of those rare moments in meeting for worship in which I felt searched by the Inner Light. Then we were silent for a long while, because there was no more to be said. That was communion, a mystical unity of persons where souls embrace.

We, in the Canadian Yearly Meeting, do not always live up to our ecumenical vision and we are not always mindful of the excerpt from our *Advices and Queries* which asks: "Are you loyal to the truth; and do you keep your mind open to new light from whatever quarter it may arise?" Nevertheless, we affirm the London Yearly Meeting (1916) statement that: "True unity may be found under great apparent differences. This unity is spiritual, it expresses itself in many ways, and we need divine insight that we may recognize its working. We need forbearance, sympathy, and love, in order that, while remaining loyal to the truth as it has come to us, we may move forward with others to a larger and richer experience and expression of the will of God".

The general response to the draft has been "alleluia" and "amen". We are deeply moved by the searching that has gone on about our own spirituality as well as about our relationship to other churches. Friends have wrestled with this matter over a number of years in special interest groups, threshing meetings, Monthly Meetings and in Yearly Meeting.

We approve this minute as amended with deep gratitude to those Friends who have spent so long developing and drafting it.